TERRORISM
ACCOUNTABILITY, REMEDIES, AND REFORM

A Report of the IBA Task Force on Terrorism

TERRORISM AND INTERNATIONAL LAW: ACCOUNTABILITY, REMEDIES, AND REFORM

A Report of the IBA Task Force on Terrorism

Elizabeth Stubbins Bates

Edited by
IBA Task Force

Justice Richard Goldstone
HHJ Eugene Cotran
Gijs de Vries
Julia A Hall
Juan E Méndez
Javaid Rehman

OXFORD
UNIVERSITY PRESS

OXFORD

UNIVERSITY PRESS

Great Clarendon Street, Oxford OX2 6DP

Oxford University Press is a department of the University of Oxford.
It furthers the University's objective of excellence in research, scholarship,
and education by publishing worldwide in

Oxford New York

Auckland Cape Town Dar es Salaam Hong Kong Karachi
Kuala Lumpur Madrid Melbourne Mexico City Nairobi
New Delhi Shanghai Taipei Toronto

With offices in

Argentina Austria Brazil Chile Czech Republic France Greece
Guatemala Hungary Italy Japan Poland Portugal Singapore
South Korea Switzerland Thailand Turkey Ukraine Vietnam

Oxford is a registered trade mark of Oxford University Press
in the UK and in certain other countries

Published in the United States
by Oxford University Press Inc., New York

British Library Cataloguing-in-Publication Data

Data available

Library of Congress Cataloging-in-Publication Data

Data available

Typeset by Glyph International, Bangalore, India
Printed in Great Britain
on acid-free paper by
CPI Group (UK) Ltd, Croydon, CR0 4YY

1006737323
ISBN 978–0–19–958918–0

3 5 7 9 10 8 6 4

PREFACE

It was in response to the terrorist attacks of 11 September 2001 that the International Bar Association (IBA) established its first Task Force on International Terrorism. Its report, which was published in 2003, suggested that the seismic events of 11 September had set governments, international law-makers, and non-governmental organizations on a long journey to tackle the many complex legal challenges inherent in responding to this new form of global terrorism. At the core of this journey lay the task of combating terrorism without jeopardizing the protection of basic rights and freedoms.

Today the threat of terrorism remains as potent as ever, arguably more so. Large-scale attacks have taken place in major cities around the world, including London, Madrid, and Mumbai, and several other attempts have been foiled. In attempting to strike the balance between maintaining national security and preserving fundamental rights, the practices and policies of governments in response to this threat have often been controversial. The rhetoric of the Bush administration's 'war on terror' has stood in sharp contrast to the belief that terrorist threats are the proper purview of policing, rather than military intervention. The invasion of Iraq, Guantánamo Bay, extraordinary rendition, the increase of police and surveillance powers, restrictions on free speech and association, have all generated strong and vocal public opinion. Some have even questioned whether contemporary international law is equipped to meet the challenges of modern terrorism. Governments and law-makers have been confronted with complex legal questions, such as: Do state's human rights obligations apply extra-territorially? Does the use of force in counter-terrorism constitute armed conflict, meaning that international humanitarian law should apply, and if so what is its relationship with international human rights law? To what extent are states obliged to provide remedies for victims of terrorist attacks and victims of violations which occur in the course of counter-terrorism operations?

Given the considerable developments in international law and state practice since the publication of the first Task Force report, it became clear that a fresh and updated analysis of the legal issues and challenges was needed. The IBA therefore convened a new Task Force to provide expert analysis of international law and how it continues to regulate states' counter-terrorism policies, and to provide a global overview of developments in state practice, including but not restricted to the US-led 'war on terror'.

It was important for the IBA to attract a range of expertise to the Task Force, in order to reflect the multidisciplinary nature of these complex challenges. The IBA's Human Rights Institute was fortunate enough to have as its outgoing Co-Chair Justice Richard Goldstone, who had also acted as Co-Chair of the IBA's previous Task Force on Terrorism in 2003. Justice Goldstone kindly accepted the invitation to Chair the current Task Force, which he has done with the same intellectual rigour and fair-mindedness that has characterized his long and distinguished career.

His Honour Professor Judge Eugene Cotran, visiting professor and Chairman of the Centre of Middle Eastern and Islamic law at the School of Oriental and African Studies, London, is a distinguished jurist and recognized as a prominent scholar of the Arab region. Ms Julia A Hall is Amnesty International's expert on counter-terrorism in Europe and has authored several reports documenting the transfer of alleged terrorism and national security suspects. She brought with her a wealth of experience from the field and has added a valuable practitioner's viewpoint to the Task Force. Professor Juan E Méndez, Co-Chair of the IBA's Human Rights Institute, is one of the world's leading human rights lawyers. He is a former President of the Inter-American Commission on Human Rights and of the International Center for Transitional Justice and his scholarship in the field of international law and knowledge of the Americas has proved indispensible. Professor Javaid Rehman is an internationally recognized legal scholar and an expert on Islamic law, international human rights law, and international terrorism, in particular relating to Afghanistan and Pakistan. Professor Rehman brought with him critical insight into the challenges affecting this troubled region. Mr Gijs de Vries was the EU's Counter-Terrorism Coordinator between 2004–07, and has provided an important policy-maker's perspective to the Task Force's consideration of the multi-faceted issues in this complex area.

Elizabeth Stubbins Bates, formerly David Davies of Llandinam Research Fellow and currently Visiting Fellow at the London School of Economics and Political Science, was commissioned to write the Report. With its intention of providing expert analysis of such a broad range of legal issues and global coverage of examples of state practice, the Report was ambitious in its aims and scope. However, from the very inception of the project Elizabeth demonstrated her outstanding technical expertise and skilful understanding of the key debates in counter-terrorism and international law in formulating the structure of the Report and consistently producing drafts of exceptional quality.

Two plenary meetings of the Task Force were convened, both at the IBA Headquarters in London. During the first, held in July 2009, the Task Force considered and agreed the structure, aims, and scope of this ambitious work. Throughout 2009 and 2010, draft chapters were then authored by Elizabeth with typical diligence and academic precision and offered to the Task Force, who critically analysed the issues at stake, providing input and detailed comments according to the members' vast range of expertise and experience, which were then incorporated into the text. The Task Force oversaw and supported the author by offering its guidance on research and latest developments. The Task Force held its second and final plenary meeting in May 2010, towards the end of the drafting process, approving final drafts of the Report and its Conclusions and Recommendations.

The IBA's view is that combating terrorism requires insight from a variety of different, potentially contradictory perspectives, with the ultimate aim of reaching consensus on as many issues as possible. This was reflected in the multilateral approach of the Task Force which strives to present the range of opinion of its members whilst remaining scholarly and rigorous. Whilst the Task Force members are not acting representatively for their respective organizations or institutions, this Report has been shaped by the convergence of rich and diverse viewpoints.

The Report itself is intended to appeal to the broad range of actors working in this multi-faceted area, and to reflect the diversity of academics and practitioners in the IBA membership. It is sufficiently discursive and cognisant of theoretical debates to appeal to academics and policy-makers, yet set out clearly and concisely enough, and with a broad range of examples and case studies, to appeal to practitioners, particularly those who are not experts in the field. The chapters on international human rights law and international humanitarian law offer a clear framework of analysis and updates on how each of these branches of international law continue to regulate states' counter-terrorism policies. The Report analyses the key current issues in counter-terrorism, including the extra-territorial application of international human rights law; the interoperability of international human rights law and international humanitarian law; reform in counter-terrorism; and victims' rights to a remedy and reparations. We also hope that significant value lies in its updated analysis of case law and examples of state practice drawn from a truly global selection of jurisdictions, ranging from Colombia to the Philippines.

The Report does not include detailed analysis of the international law on the use of force, international refugee law, extradition, mutual legal assistance, or the private law consequences of counter-terrorism. The exclusion of the international law on the use of force is a significant choice, as the Report aims to articulate clearly when international humanitarian law does and does not apply to the regulation of terrorism and counter-terrorism operations, and to avoid the inference (from politics rather than law) that terrorism and counter-terrorism operations always take place through the lens of 'war'.

Lastly, the Task Force aims to contribute and add value to the current debates surrounding counter-terrorism and international law through providing authoritative conclusions and recommendations for states, inter-governmental and non-governmental institutions, the judiciary, and policy-makers to consider how to strike the balance between ensuring respect for fundamental rights whilst protecting the global public from terrorist violence. In formulating its recommendations, the following themes seemed to capture the essence of the issues at stake:

- States must place international law at the centre of their counter-terrorism efforts, engaging fully with the ratification, implementation, and enforcement of IHL and IHRL treaties.

- States should train their armed forces personnel, law enforcement officials, and intelligence officials in applicable IHL and IHRL, as a means of preventing violations of IHL and IHRL.

- In addition to complying with the monitoring mechanisms which exist at the international and regional levels, states should monitor their own enforcement of IHL and IHRL by ensuring compatibility between their treaty obligations and conditions in practice.

- The prevention of future violations may be encouraged by a full implementation of states' obligations to investigate and prosecute violations of IHL and IHRL: and by states' obligations to ensure a remedy and reparation both for victims of terrorist attacks and for victims of violations of international law committed in counter-terrorism operations.

The Task Force wishes to thank the IBA Foundation Inc for its generosity in funding this important project. The Task Force acknowledges the generosity of the London School of Economics and Political Science Department of International Relations, the David Davies of Llandinam Research Fellowship, and the Dinam Charity in allowing Elizabeth Stubbins Bates to work on this exciting project and for funding her work from 2008 to 2009. The LSE Department of Law, where Elizabeth Stubbins Bates was a Visiting Fellow in 2009–10, also facilitated work on the book. The Task Force is also extremely grateful to the European Human Rights Advocacy Centre/Memorial (EHRAC) for its expert advice regarding Russian counter-terrorism legislation.

The work of the Task Force would not have been possible without the support of IBA staff. Alex Wilks, as the Senior Programme Lawyer assigned to the Task Force, managed the different aspects of this complex project from its inception and deserves credit for the broad project design. Lucy Winder, as IBA Senior Content Editor, provided invaluable editorial expertise and assistance throughout the process. Thanks must also go to Mahmuda Ali and Aurora Garcia, who dealt with the considerable administrative requirements of the project, as well as Nicole Pellicena for her help with the IBA's marketing strategy.

The Task Force should also like to thank the following IBA Human Rights Institute interns for their tremendous assistance in compiling research materials for the report and assisting with the Task Force meetings: Edwina Brown, Jo Buckley, Peter Hamm, Catharine Hubner, Zoe Jacob, Shyam Kapila, Tarini Mehta, Peter Morcos,

John Nee, Lindsay Oak, Tricia Patel, Vijaya Poopalasingam, Joy Reddy, Melissa Ritchie, Katie Rivkind, Matthew Sands, Mattais Schain, and Daniel Thompson.

Finally, both the Task Force and the IBA would like to thank Roxanne Selby and Fiona Sinclair at Oxford University Press for their unwavering support and patience throughout the project.

The law and facts were last updated on 30 May 2010.

IBA Task Force on Terrorism, International Bar Association

CONTENTS

BIOGRAPHIES OF TASK FORCE AND AUTHOR

Justice Richard Goldstone (Chair)

Justice Goldstone, previously a South African Constitutional Court judge, former Chief Prosecutor of the United Nations International Criminal Tribunal for Rwanda and the former Yugoslavia, is also a past IBA Human Rights Institute Co-Chair. Justice Goldstone has been involved in human rights interventions and missions in almost all parts of the world. Justice Goldstone served as National President of the National Institute of Crime Prevention and the Rehabilitation of Offenders (NICRO) and Chairperson of the Bradlow Foundation, a charitable educational trust. He founded and for some years chaired the board of the Human Rights Institute of South Africa (HURISA). He was a member of the International Group of Advisers of the International Committee of the Red Cross and a member of the committee appointed by the Secretary-General of the United Nations to investigate allegations regarding the Iraq Oil for Food Programme. In 2009 Justice Goldstone led an independent fact-finding mission created by the UN Human Rights Council to investigate international human rights and humanitarian law violations related to the Gaza War. The mission's findings that Israel and Hamas had both committed serious violations of the laws of war led to a major international controversy. Justice Goldstone has been a visiting Professor at New York University, Fordham, Harvard, and Georgetown law schools.

Professor Judge Eugene Cotran

Judge Cotran joined the School of Oriental and African Studies (SOAS) in 1960 as a Research Officer and lecturer in African law. He continues to work with the institution, sits as an International Arbitrator, and is a legal consultant to the Qatar Financial Centre (QFC) Civil and Commercial Court and its Judiciary. Judge Cotran was appointed a High Court Judge in Kenya in 1977, and later a Circuit Judge in the UK in 1992. He has acted as a Chairman or member in various Middle Eastern Arbitrations, the International Criminal Court of Arbitration, the Immigration Appeal Tribunal, the London Court of International Arbitration, and the Centre of Islamic and Middle Eastern Law. He is also Secretary of the Pan African Council and Vice-Chairman of Medical Aid for Palestinians. Judge Cotran has published a number of works on African and Middle Eastern law, immigration law, and international law. He is the General Editor of Butterworths

Immigration Law Service and is on the Editorial Board of various Commonwealth and Middle Eastern journals.

Mr Gijs de Vries

Mr Vries is currently a member of the Board of the Netherlands Court of Audit. He was Deputy Interior Minister of the Netherlands between 1998 and 2002, and was the European Union's Counter-Terrorism Coordinator from March 2004 to March 2007. Since September 2008, he has served as chairman of the European Security Research and Innovation Forum (ESRIF). Mr Vries was also Chairman of the EU Integration Programme, Center for European Policy Studies, Co-founder of the European Council on Foreign Relations, and Member of the Advisory Council of the Center on Global Counter-Terrorism Cooperation.

Ms Julia A Hall

Ms Hall is a human rights lawyer and a counter-terrorism and human rights expert at Amnesty International's London-based secretariat. She has conducted extensive research and advocacy in a number of areas, including the prohibition against torture and unlawful ('extraordinary') rendition. Ms Hall previously served as senior legal counsel for the Terrorism and Counter-Terrorism Program at Human Rights Watch, where she worked from 1996–2009. She has authored numerous reports, articles, and amicus briefs on a range of counter-terrorism topics, conducted sustained advocacy at the United Nations, the Council of Europe, and the European Union, and served as an expert on individual cases before the European Court of Human Rights. In July 2008, she monitored the military commission of Salim Hamdan, Osama bin Laden's former driver, at Guantánamo Bay.

Professor Juan E Méndez

Professor Méndez, currently a Co-Chair of the IBA's Human Rights Institute, served as the United Nations Secretary-General's Special Adviser on the Prevention of Genocide from July 2004 to May 2007. He worked with Human Rights Watch for 15 years, where he served as general counsel. From 1996–99, Professor Méndez served as the executive director of the Inter-American Institute of Human Rights in Costa Rica and became president of the Inter-American Commission on Human Rights of the Organization of American States in 2002. Professor Mendez also served as President of the International Center for Transitional Justice, before being appointed Special Adviser on Crime Prevention at the International Criminal Court, Office of the Prosecutor. Professor Mendez has taught international human rights law at Georgetown Law School, the University of Notre Dame School of Law, and at the Johns Hopkins School of Advanced International Studies (SAIS). He also teaches regularly at the Oxford Master's Programme in International Human Rights Law.

Professor Javaid Rehman

Professor Rehman is a Professor of Law and Head of the Brunel Law School at Brunel University in West London. He has extensive experience as an advocate and as a human rights lawyer. He has taught international law at the Universities of Hull, Leeds, and Ulster, and has been a visiting professor at various institutions in the US, Japan, Pakistan, and France. Professor Rehman is a member of the International Law Association (ILA) and is Co-Rapporteur of the ILA Committee on Islamic Law and International Law. He has acted as a consultant on human rights law, minority rights, and terrorism for the European Commission, the United Nations, the World Bank, Northern Ireland Human Rights Commission, the Government of Pakistan, and Minority Rights Group. He regularly advises on the development of higher education in both the UK and South Asia.

Ms Elizabeth Stubbins Bates (author)

Elizabeth Stubbins Bates is based at the London School of Economics and Political Science (LSE). She has researched and taught in international law and is part of the inaugural teaching team for LSE's pioneering undergraduate course, LSE100. In 2008–09, Ms Stubbins Bates was the David Davies of Llandinam Research Fellow at the LSE Department of International Relations, working on international humanitarian law, international human rights law, and counter-terrorism. Before coming to LSE, Ms Stubbins Bates was a consultant to the Program on Humanitarian Policy and Conflict Research at Harvard University (HPCR) and to the Coalition to Stop the Use of Child Soldiers; a Legal Adviser at Amnesty International; and an American Society of International Law (ASIL) Arthur C Helton Fellow. Ms Stubbins Bates is a member of the ASIL and of the British Institute of International and Comparative Law. She works in English and French, and speaks some Russian.

TABLE OF CASES

NATIONAL CASES

United States

INTERNATIONAL CASES

European Union (EU)

Human Rights Committee

Inter-American Commission on Human Rights

Inter-American Court of Human Rights

International Court of Justice

International Criminal Tribunal for the former Yugoslavia

Permanent Court of International Justice

Special Court for Sierra Leone

TABLE OF NATIONAL LEGISLATION

TABLE OF INTERNATIONAL TREATIES
AND CONVENTIONS

1

INTRODUCTION: TERRORISM IN INTERNATIONAL LAW

Defining terrorism in international law

No agreed definition of terrorism in international law

International law obliges states to prevent and repress terrorism but fails authorita- **1.01**
tively to define the concept of terrorism itself. The duty to prevent and repress
terrorism is found in a patchwork of 15 subject-specific multilateral conventions or
protocols,[1] seven regional treaties,[2] and a range of UN Security Council and General

---

[1] Convention on Offences and Certain Other Acts Committed on Board Aircraft 1963;
Convention for the Suppression of Unlawful Seizure of Aircraft 1970; Convention for the
Suppression of Unlawful Acts against the Safety of Civil Aviation 1971, and its Protocol 1988;
Convention on the Prevention and Punishment of Crimes against Internationally Protected
Persons 1973; International Convention against the Taking of Hostages 1979; Convention on the
Physical Protection of Nuclear Material 1980, as amended 2005; Convention for the Suppression of
Unlawful Acts against the Safety of Maritime Navigation 1988, and its Protocol 2005; Protocol for
the Suppression of Unlawful Acts against the Safety of Fixed Platforms Located on the Continental
Shelf 1988; Convention on the Marking of Plastic Explosives for the Purpose of Detection 1991;
International Convention for the Suppression of Terrorist Bombings 1997; International Convention
for the Suppression of the Financing of Terrorism 1999; International Convention for the Suppression
of Acts of Nuclear Terrorism 2005.

[2] Organisation of American States (OAS) Convention to Prevent and Punish Acts of Terrorism
Taking the Form of Crimes against Persons and Related Extortion that are of International Significance
1971; European Convention on the Prevention of Terrorism 2005; South Asian Association for
Regional Cooperation (SAARC) Regional Convention on the Suppression of Terrorism 1987; Arab
Convention on the Suppression of Terrorism 1998; Treaty on Cooperation among States Members
of the Commonwealth of Independent States in Combating Terrorism 1999; Convention of the
Organisation of the Islamic Conference on Combating International Terrorism 1999; Organisation
of African Unity (OAU) Convention on the Prevention and Combating of Terrorism 1999.

Assembly resolutions.[3] These proscribe specific acts of terrorism and impose duties on states to criminalize and investigate those acts, to prosecute or extradite suspected perpetrators,[4] and to freeze the assets of suspected terrorists.[5] States implementing these obligations must do so in full compliance with international humanitarian law (IHL), where it applies,[6] international human rights law (IHRL), and international refugee law (IRL).[7] However, none of the multilateral or regional instruments has yielded a single, universally accepted definition of terrorism. Negotiations for a Draft Comprehensive Convention on Terrorism (Draft Convention) have reached a point of 'inertia'.[8] Three lasting points of disagreement can be summarized as follows:

- first, whether the Draft Convention should adopt an armed conflict or law enforcement approach to counter-terrorism;[9]
- second, whether a definition of terrorism should include or exclude 'state terrorism',[10] and whether it should include or exclude the acts of state armed forces;[11] and
- third, whether armed resistance to an occupying regime or to colonial or alien domination should be included or excluded from the Draft Convention's definition of terrorism.[12]

The following paragraphs examine two of the many available definitions of terrorism and terrorist acts, with reference to these three controversies, and the stalled

---

[3] UN Security Council Resolutions 1267 (1999), 1269 (1999), 1333 (2000), 1368 (2001), 1373 (2001), 1390 (2002), 1452 (2002), 1455 (2003), 1526 (2004), 1535 (2004), 1540 (2004), 1566 (2004), 1617 (2005), 1624 (2005), 1730 (2006), 1735 (2006), 1787 (2007), 1805 (2008), 1822 (2008), 1904 (2009); UN General Assembly Declaration on Measures to Eliminate International Terrorism 1994; Declaration to Supplement the 1994 Declaration on Measures to Eliminate International Terrorism 1996; UN World Summit Outcome Document 2005, General Assembly Resolution 60/1, 2005.

[4] Convention for the Suppression of Unlawful Seizure of Aircraft 1970, Art 7; Convention for the Suppression of Unlawful Acts against the Safety of Civil Aviation 1971, Art 7; Convention on the Prevention and Punishment of Crimes against Internationally Protected Persons 1973, Art 3(2); International Convention against the Taking of Hostages 1979, Art 5(2); International Convention for the Suppression of Terrorist Bombings 1997, Art 7(2); International Convention for the Suppression of the Financing of Terrorism 1997, Art 7(4); International Convention for the Suppression of Acts of Nuclear Terrorism 2005, Art 9(4).

[5] International Convention for the Suppression of the Financing of Terrorism 1999; UN Security Council Resolutions 1267 (1999), 1373 (2001), 1526 (2004), 1566 (2004), 1617 (2005), 1735 (2006), 1822 (2008), 1904 (2009).

[6] See paras 2.02 and 2.22–2.32.

[7] UN Global Counter-Terrorism Strategy, annexed to General Assembly Resolution 60/288, 8 September 2006, para 3; UN General Assembly Resolution 60/158, 16 December 2005; UN Security Council Resolution 1624 (2005), Preamble, para 2.

[8] Report of the Ad Hoc Committee established by General Assembly Resolution 51/210 of 17 December 1996, 13th session, 29 June–13 July 2009, Annex II, para 4.

[9] Ibid, Annex II, para 5(a), (c), and (e).

[10] Ibid, Annex I, paras 1 and 6.

[11] Ibid, Annex I, para 6.

[12] Ibid, Annex I, para 6.

efforts to agree a Draft Comprehensive Convention on Terrorism.[13] This section ends by emphasizing two principles which should be made explicit in any future international law definition of terrorism. The next section ('The scope of states' obligations to counter terrorism') charts the scope of states' duty to prevent and repress terrorism: a duty which must be carried out in accordance with existing IHL, IHRL, and IRL. Finally, the last section sets the structure for Chapters 2–7.

Terrorism and armed conflict

Treaty definitions

Both the International Convention for the Suppression of the Financing of Terrorism (Terrorism Financing Convention) and the International Convention for the Suppression of Terrorist Bombings (Terrorist Bombings Convention) offer definitions which may form part of a defined and comprehensive international crime of terrorism.[14] The definition in the Terrorism Financing Convention includes offences under other subject-specific terrorism treaties,[15] and also proscribes:

1.02

> Any other act intended to cause death or serious bodily injury to a civilian, or to any other person not taking an active part in hostilities in a situation of armed conflict, when the purpose of such act, by its nature or context, is to intimidate a population, or to compel a government or an international organisation to do or abstain from doing any act.[16]

In contrast, Article 1 of the Terrorist Bombings Convention refers neither to armed conflict nor to civilians or non-combatants, and Article 19(2) explicitly excludes '[t]he activities of armed forces during an armed conflict, as those terms are understood under international humanitarian law' from the scope of the Convention, noting that such activities are governed by IHL.[17] The Terrorist Bombings Convention is silent as to whether the activities of non-state armed groups in a non-international armed conflict[18] may or may not be regulated by the Convention. A person would be guilty of an offence under the Terrorist Bombings Convention if he or she:

> . . . unlawfully and intentionally delivers, places, discharges or detonates an explosive or other lethal device in, into or against a place of public use, a State or government facility, a public transportation system or an infrastructure facility.[19]

---

[13] A comprehensive analysis of definitions of terrorism can be found in Ben Saul, *Defining Terrorism in International Law* (OUP, 2006).

[14] International Convention for the Suppression of Terrorist Bombings 1997, Arts 1–3; International Convention for the Suppression of the Financing of Terrorism 1999, Art 2 (1)(a)–(b).

[15] Terrorism Financing Convention, Art 2(1)(a).

[16] Ibid, Art 2(1)(b).

[17] Terrorist Bombings Convention, Art 19(2).

[18] See para 2.08.

[19] Terrorist Bombings Convention, Art 2(1).

In order to constitute a crime under the Terrorist Bombings Convention, these acts must be accompanied by an 'intent to cause death or serious bodily injury'[20] or 'to cause extensive destruction of such a place, facility or system, where such destruction results in or is likely to result in major economic loss'.[21]

1.03 These two definitions, selected from the many available in the multilateral and regional terrorism conventions,[22] show divergent approaches as to whether terrorism should be seen, at least in part, through the lens of armed conflict. Despite these differences, both Conventions are grounded in individual criminal responsibility: there is no reference to states' obligations to prevent and repress terrorist attacks being a 'war' in itself, or to terrorists being fighters. These obligations to criminalize specific terrorist offences, and to prosecute or extradite suspected offenders, reflect similar provisions in other multilateral terrorism treaties.[23] States' duties to prevent and repress terrorism must be carried out through domestic criminal law, extradition, and mutual legal assistance. Chapters 4 and 6 of this volume analyse some of these issues, and paragraphs 3.134–3.155 of Chapter 3 explore the right to fair trial in the prosecution of terrorism offences.

The need for clarity and accuracy in the use of IHL terminology

1.04 The definition of terrorism in the report of the UN High-Level Panel on Threats, Challenges and Change (UN High-Level Panel) shows that the concept of 'civilians' as victims of terrorism has crept into the concept of terrorism, whether the terrorist attacks occur in peace or war.[24] The proposed definition in the UN High-Level Panel report builds on the existing multilateral conventions on terrorism, the Terrorism Financing Convention, and UN Security Council Resolution 1566 (2004),[25] but it ultimately conflates the use of the term 'terrorism' in the Four Geneva Conventions and their First and Second Additional Protocols with acts of terrorism more broadly.[26] The UN High-Level Panel's approach is different from that in the Terrorist Bombings Convention, which expressly excludes bombings

---

[20] Ibid, Art 2(1)(a).

[21] Ibid, Art 2(1)(b).

[22] In addition to the conventions in nn 1 and 2, see European Union, Council Framework Decision 2002/475/JHA of 13 June 2002 on combating terrorism, as amended by Framework Decision 2008/919/JHA.

[23] See n 4, Convention for the Suppression of Unlawful Seizure of Aircraft 1970, Art 7; Convention for the Suppression of Unlawful Acts against the Safety of Civil Aviation 1971, Art 7; Convention on the Prevention and Punishment of Crimes against Internationally Protected Persons 1973, Art 3(2); International Convention against the Taking of Hostages 1979, Art 5(2); International Convention for the Suppression of Terrorist Bombings 1997, Art 7(2); International Convention for the Suppression of the Financing of Terrorism 1997, Art 7(4); International Convention for the Suppression of Acts of Nuclear Terrorism 2005, Art 9(4).

[24] UN High-Level Panel on Threats, Challenges and Change, 'A More Secure World: Our Shared Responsibility', UN Doc A/59/565, 2 December 2004, para 164(a) and (d).

[25] Ibid, para 164(b)–(c).

[26] Ibid, para 164(a) and (d).

by state armed forces during armed conflict.[27] The UN High-Level Panel's definition arguably conflates the language of IHL ('civilians') and the broader phenomenon of terrorism in peace or war. There are six legal and policy reasons why this definition shows a questionable approach which should not be transposed into an eventual Comprehensive Convention on Terrorism.

First, as paragraphs 2.01–2.05 of Chapter 2 will explain, IHL only applies in armed **1.05** conflict (whether international or non-international) or belligerent occupation.[28] As the existence of armed conflicts and belligerent occupation is objectively determined,[29] it should neither be assumed that terrorist violence necessarily triggers the applicability of IHL, nor that counter-terrorist operations which use force are necessarily an armed conflict.[30]

Second, although some armed conflicts have been fought with a counter-terrorist **1.06** aim,[31] it is important to separate out the 'component hostilities', to borrow an expression from Marco Sassòli, where IHL applies,[32] from broader policies to prevent and repress terrorism. Using the term 'war' to cover all policies in counter-terrorism, as the US did under George W Bush's 'global war on terror',[33] conflates the situations to which IHL applies and those in which it does not.[34] In particular, the use of criminal justice mechanisms to prevent and repress terrorism in peacetime is not a 'war'. The questioning, prosecution, and extradition of terrorism suspects must all accord with IHRL, as Chapter 3 will explain. Inaccurate references to 'war' in the criminal justice context do not make IHRL any less binding.

Third, as paragraphs 2.22–2.32 of Chapter 2 explain, IHL's prohibitions on 'ter- **1.07** rorism' and 'acts or threat of violence the primary purpose of which is to spread terror among the civilian population' are distinct from the popular or media conception of terrorism in peacetime.[35] IHL's use of the term 'terrorism' is a particular,

---

[27] Terrorist Bombings Convention, Art 19(2).

[28] See paras 2.01-2.05.

[29] Four Geneva Conventions of 12 August 1949, Common Article 2, para 1 (for international armed conflicts and situations of belligerent occupation); Additional Protocol II to the Four Geneva Conventions of 12 August 1949 (Additional Protocol II), Art 1 (for non-international armed conflicts where Additional Protocol II is ratified).

[30] See para 2.03.

[31] See para 2.03.

[32] Marco Sassòli, 'Terrorism and War' (2006) 4 *Journal of International Criminal Justice* 959–981.

[33] President George W Bush, Address to the US Congress, 20 September 2001; *Washington Post*, '"Global War on Terror" is Given New Name', 25 March 2009.

[34] International Law Association (ILA) Committee on the Use of Force, Initial Report on the Meaning of Armed Conflict in International Law, 2008, analysed in Mary Ellen O'Connell, 'Defining Armed Conflict' (2009) 13 *Journal of Conflict & Security Law* 393–400; Marco Sassòli, 'Terrorism and War' (2006) 4 *Journal of International Criminal Justice* 959–981; Gabor Rona, 'International Law under Fire: Interesting Times for International Humanitarian Law: Challenges from the "War on Terror"' (2003) 27 *Fletcher Forum of World Affairs* 55–70 at 60.

[35] Fourth Geneva Convention, Art 33; Additional Protocol I, Art 51(2); Additional Protocol II, Arts 4(2)(d) and 13(2).

context-specific meaning of the term, referring to violations of the principle of distinction between combatants and civilians, which includes a prohibition on targeting civilians and civilian objects.[36] The passage quoted in paragraph 1.02 above from Article 1(b) of the Terrorism Financing Convention draws on this concept, but that latter convention is both narrower and broader than IHL's specific meaning of 'terrorism'.

- 'Terrorism' in IHL is prohibited whether it is perpetrated by state armed forces or non-state armed groups. It does not require acts 'intended to cause death or serious bodily injury' as in the Terrorism Financing Convention, but would include any deliberate targeting of civilians. In this sense, the Terrorism Financing Convention is narrower than IHL's concept of 'terrorism'.
- In conflicts regulated by either Additional Protocol I or Additional Protocol II to the Four Geneva Conventions, IHL's specific meaning of 'terrorism' requires a 'primary purpose' of 'spread[ing]' terror among the civilian population'.[37] Moreover, Additional Protocols I and II proscribe both acts and threats of violence which have this primary purpose. An aim to 'compel a government or international organisation to do or abstain from doing any act', as in Article 1(b) of the Terrorism Financing Convention, would not be regarded as 'terrorism' in IHL's specific sense, whereas Article 1(b) of the Terrorism Financing Convention does not include threats; it includes only acts. These subtle differences between IHL and the use of armed conflict terminology in the Terrorism Financing Convention further highlight the importance of clear and accurate references to IHL in international instruments on terrorism.

1.08 Fourth, a related reason for clarity and accuracy in the use of terms from IHL has been highlighted by Emanuela-Chiara Gillard, namely the risk that 'acts that are not unlawful under IHL' might be included in the list of crimes which states must either prosecute or extradite under the subject-specific terrorism conventions.[38] This could create an inconsistency between IHL and terrorism treaties where there is an armed conflict, potentially undermining the implementation of IHL.[39] To avoid this, Gillard proposes either 'careful . . . drafting' or a 'safeguard clause' so that the Draft Comprehensive Convention would exclude acts unlawful under IHL from its definitions of terrorist crimes.[40]

---

[36] Additional Protocol I to the Four Geneva Conventions, Art 48; Jean Marie Henckaerts and Louise Doswald-Beck, *Customary International Humanitarian Law, Volume 1: Rules* (International Committee of the Red Cross and Cambridge University Press, 2005), Rule 1.

[37] Additional Protocol I, Art 51(2); Additional Protocol II, Art 13(2).

[38] Emanuela-Chiara Gillard, 'The Complementary Nature of Human Rights Law, International Humanitarian Law and Refugee Law', in *Terrorism and International Law: Challenges and Responses* (International Institute for Humanitarian Law et al, 2002), pp 50–56 at p 54.

[39] Ibid.

[40] Ibid.

Fifth, the victims of terrorist attacks committed in peacetime, where IHL does not **1.09** apply, are 'victims' of those attacks, who have a right to remedy and reparation in accordance with international standards (see Chapter 5). In contrast to the definition of terrorism in the UN High-Level Panel report quoted above,[41] they do not gain a status as 'civilians' as a result of being attacked. Nor would those responsible for terrorist attacks become 'combatants'.

Finally, the UN High-Level Panel's inclusion of the language of IHL departs from **1.10** the criminal justice model of the multilateral and regional conventions on terrorism. The UN General Assembly has recognized the criminal nature of terrorist attacks, when it '[u]nequivocally condemn[ed], *as criminal*, all acts, methods and practices of terrorism wherever and by whomever committed'.[42] International conventions on specific terrorist acts and regional conventions on terrorism mandate states to criminalize various terrorist acts,[43] and to investigate those crimes, prosecuting or extraditing those suspected of involvement,[44] all in full accordance with existing international law.[45] The language used in international documents should reflect that of criminal justice processes and not a selective use of terminology from IHL.

Sources which relate terrorism and jus ad bellum

However, there are additional, binding sources which relate terrorism and war **1.11** explicitly. They do so not by using the language of IHL, by stating that terrorism is 'war' or that its victims are 'civilians', but instead by invoking the international law on the use of force or *jus ad bellum*. *Jus ad bellum* should be distinguished from IHL, which is also known as the law of armed conflict or *jus in bello*. *Jus ad bellum*, which is outside the scope of this book, begins with the prohibition on the unilateral use of force in Article 2(4) of the UN Charter and is tempered by an 'inherent right of self-defence' as defined in Article 51, and the permissible use of force under a Chapter VII resolution of the Security Council.[46] IHL or *jus in bello*, which is considered in Chapter 2, regulates the means and methods of warfare, and provides protections for prisoners of war, civilians, and other non-combatants once an armed conflict is under way.[47]

A number of UN Security Council Resolutions passed in response to terrorist **1.12** attacks have characterized such attacks as threats to international peace and security.

---

[41] UN High-Level Panel on Threats, Challenges and Change, 'A More Secure World: Our Shared Responsibility', UN Doc A/59/565, 2 December 2004, para 164(d).

[42] UN General Assembly Resolution 40/61, 9 December 1985, para 1 (emphasis added).

[43] See nn 1 and 2.

[44] See n 4.

[45] See paras 1.01, 1.17–1.18, 1.26, 6.03–6.04.

[46] UN Charter, Art 39.

[47] See para 2.01.

These resolutions invoke Article 39 (Chapter VII) of the UN Charter. [48] Security Council action taken under Chapter VII may authorize the use of force. UN Security Council Resolution 1368, passed immediately after the terrorist attacks on the US on 11 September 2001, expressly recognizes the inherent right to self-defence (Article 51, UN Charter) in its Preamble.[49] UN Security Council Resolution 1373 considers 'any act of international terrorism' to be a threat to international peace and security.[50] This indicates that terrorist attacks may constitute an 'armed attack' under Article 51 of the UN Charter to which the inherent right of self-defence may be considered. Although any use of force directly pursuant to and explicitly authorized by a Chapter VII resolution would be lawful under *jus ad bellum*, there are shortcomings to an approach which relates states' counter-terrorism obligations to the international law on the use of force:

- Given the lack of an internationally agreed definition of terrorism, it is unclear which terrorist acts would constitute a threat to international peace and security, and which should be investigated or prosecuted in domestic criminal courts. *Jus ad bellum* offers no guidance on the legal definition of terrorism.
- Other UN Security Council Resolutions on terrorism reflect the multilateral conventions on terrorism in requiring UN member states to criminalize specific terrorist offences,[51] or to impose assets-freezes on those 'listed' as being suspected of involvement in financing terrorism.[52] Although the Security Council has acted under Chapter VII of the UN Charter in passing these resolutions, this does not amount to a statement that armed force may be used as a means of preventing the financing of terrorism. States' obligations to prevent and repress terrorism are implemented through criminalization, investigation, prosecution, extradition, and mutual legal assistance. *Jus ad bellum* is irrelevant to these obligations.

State terrorism and state sponsors of terrorism[53]

1.13   The definitions in the Terrorist Bombings Convention and in the Terrorism Financing Convention give no indication that their conceptions of terrorist attacks include attacks committed, planned, or financed by state actors: definitions of crimes in both Conventions use the concepts and terminology of individual criminal responsibility ('Any person commits an offence within the meaning of this Convention...').[54]

---

[48] UN Security Council Resolution 1368, 12 September 2001; UN Security Council Resolution 1373, 28 September 2001.
[49] UN Security Council Resolution 1368, 12 September 2001, Preamble, para 3.
[50] UN Security Council Resolution 1373, 28 September 2001, Preamble, para 3.
[51] Ibid, paras 1(b) and 2(e); UN Security Council Resolution 1540, 28 April 2004, para 3(d).
[52] UN Security Council Resolutions 1267 (1999), 1373 (2001), 1390 (2002), 1526 (2004), 1566 (2004), 1617 (2005), 1735 (2006), 1822 (2008), 1904 (2009).
[53] Gilbert Gillaume, 'Terrorism and International Law' (2004) 53 Int'l & Comp L Quarterly 537–548; Ben Saul, *Defining Terrorism in International Law* (OUP, 2006), p 2.
[54] Terrorist Bombings Convention, Art 2(1); Terrorism Financing Convention, Art 2(1).

Both Conventions include 'State or government facilit[ies]' in the list of potential targets of terrorist attacks.[55] The absence of state terrorism and state sponsorship of terrorism from these two multilateral conventions is reflects the ongoing disagreements among states as to whether state terrorism should be included in the definition of terrorism in the Draft Comprehensive Convention.[56] The UN High-Level Panel report also specifically excluded state terrorism from its recommended definition of terrorism in 2004.[57]

However, if terrorist attacks can be attributed to states under the non-binding **1.14** International Law Commission Articles on the responsibility of states for internationally unlawful acts (ILC Articles on State responsibility),[58] or if money to fund terrorist groups can be traced to state sources, then the existence of state terrorism or state-sponsored terrorism might be said to have been established. This is a far cry from the simple assertion of lists of 'State sponsors of terrorism', where the inclusion or exclusion of specific countries from the list might reflect a combination of factual evidence and subsequent diplomatic leverage.[59] The evidence for each state's involvement in terrorism needs to be established separately, and with attention to regional, institutional, and political interactions between armed groups and the states alleged to be so involved.[60]

Chapter 6 briefly notes scholarship on improving governance in failing and failed **1.15** states,[61] and suggests measures to prevent state terrorism and state sponsorship of terrorism, with reference to US state practice[62] and the proviso that any targeted sanctions comply in full with economic, social, and cultural rights.[63] Paragraph 6.09 of Chapter 6 also address the arguments of Israeli scholar Tal Becker, who recommends a change to the traditional international law on the responsibility of states for internationally unlawful acts so as to provide for state responsibility, where factual causation, legal causation, and policy reasons indicate that a state has

---

[55] Terrorist Bombings Convention, Art 2(1); Terrorism Financing Convention, Art 7(2)(b).

[56] See para 1.01.

[57] UN High-Level Panel.

[58] ILC Articles on the Responsibility of States for Internationally Unlawful Acts 2001, adopted by UN General Assembly Resolution 56/83, 12 December 2001.

[59] Terence Roehrig, 'North Korea and the US State Sponsors of Terrorism List' (2009) 24 *Pacific Focus* 85–106.

[60] Katerina Dalacoura, 'Middle East Studies and Terrorism Studies: Establishing Links via a Critical Approach', in Richard Jackson, Marie Breen Smyth, and Jeroen Gunning, *Critical Terrorism Studies: A New Research Agenda* (Routledge, 2009), pp 124–138, at p 130.

[61] Robert I Rotberg, 'Failed States in a World of Terror' (2002) 81 *Foreign Affairs* 127; Chester A Crocker, 'Engaging Failed States' (2003) 82 *Foreign Affairs* 32; Mai Yamani, 'Yemeni Detainees and Jihadis: Guantanamo Repatriation and Saudi Arabia', Chatham House, 16 April 2009; Fawaz A Gerges, 'A Broken Middle East: A Wasted Decade of War on Terror', Inaugural Lecture, London School of Economics and Political Science, 10 February 2010.

[62] US Department of State, Country Reports on Terrorism 2008, Chapter 3, 'State Sponsors of Terrorism'.

[63] See paras 6.07–6.08.

encouraged or acquiesced in the development of terrorist groups.[64] If an internationally accepted definition of terrorism is to be reached, it should require states to prevent and repress terrorist violence by state and non-state actors alike; and should include measures to prevent state terrorism and the state sponsorship of terrorism. Currently, only 'terrorism' in IHL's particular sense prohibits such acts by state armed forces.[65]

Terrorism and self-determination

1.16   The Arab Convention on the Suppression of Terrorism 1998 and the Convention of the Organisation of the Islamic Conference (OIC) on Combating Terrorism 1999 both exclude armed resistance to an occupying regime from their definitions of terrorism.[66] Both Conventions echo the international law right to self-determination,[67] but the Arab Convention on the Suppression of Terrorism only excludes acts of armed resistance against occupation or colonialism if that resistance is not applied against an Arab state.[68] This partiality is both regrettable and unacceptable. Both the UN High-Level Panel report and the Secretary-General's report *In Larger Freedom: Towards Development, Security and Human Rights for All* reject the right to resist occupation through armed violence. The reports concur that self-determination cannot justify the 'targeting and killing of civilians'.[69] To do so would be a violation of IHL and a war crime. While the latter two sources are non-binding, and the former Conventions are binding only on their states parties (members of the Arab League and of the OIC which have ratified each treaty), the contrast between these sources helps to explain the impasse in negotiations for a Draft Comprehensive Convention on Terrorism.[70] In the Working Group established to negotiate a Draft Comprehensive Convention on Terrorism, the Arab Group, the OIC, Malaysia, and Iran were among the states to insist upon the exclusion of violence in self-determination from an international definition of terrorism.[71]

---

[64] Tal Becker, *Terrorism and the State: Rethinking the Rules of State Responsibility* (Hart Publishing, 2006).

[65] See para 1.07 and paras 2.22–2.32.

[66] Arab Convention on the Suppression of Terrorism 1998, Art 2(a); Convention of the Organisation of the Islamic Conference on Combating International Terrorism 1999, Art 2(a).

[67] Arab Convention on the Suppression of Terrorism 1998, Preamble, para 4, Art 2(a); Convention of the Organisation of the Islamic Conference on Combating International Terrorism 1999, Preamble, para 8, Art 2(a).

[68] Arab Convention on the Suppression of Terrorism 1998, Art 2(a).

[69] UN High-Level Report, p 53; *In Larger Freedom: Towards Development, Security and Human Rights for All*, Report of the Secretary-General, A/59/2005, 21 March 2005, para 91; see also Report of the United Nations Fact-Finding Mission on the Gaza Conflict, UN Doc A/HRC/12/48, 15 September 2009, paras 269, 308, 1639.

[70] See para 1.01.

[71] Report of the Ad Hoc Committee established by General Assembly Resolution 51/210 of 17 December 1996, Fifth Session 12–23 February 2001, A/56/37, paras 12–13.

Article 18 of the current Draft Comprehensive Convention on Terrorism specifically excludes armed conflicts, including those fought with the aim of self-determination, from the Draft Comprehensive Convention's definition of terrorism in Article 2.[72]

Two guiding principles for a future definition of terrorism

As there is no internationally accepted definition of terrorism, this book does not **1.17** suggest or invoke any particular definition. When the terms 'terrorist attack', 'terrorism suspect', 'terrorist group', or 'counter-terrorism operations' are used, it is not suggested that these are legal terms of art in international law. Nonetheless, if states agree an internationally accepted definition of terrorism, they should be guided by the following two principles:

- When states implement their obligations under multilateral or regional conventions to prevent and repress terrorism, or when they act pursuant to General Assembly and Security Council Resolutions aimed at combating terrorism, states must act in accordance with their obligations under IHL, IHRL, and IRL.[73] A brief note on IRL can be found at paragraphs 1.27–1.28 below. Compliance with IHL, IHRL, and IRL in states' action to combat terrorism is not a mere political nicety: it is obligatory and embedded in the framework of intergovernmental efforts to combat terrorism. For this reason, any Draft Comprehensive Convention on Terrorism should reiterate this core obligation, requiring states to comply with existing international law when they act to combat terrorism.
- References to 'war' or to 'civilians' in the context of states' obligations to prevent and repress terrorism should not be included in the Draft Comprehensive Convention on Terrorism, unless they relate to international or non-international armed conflicts.[74] In that case, IHL should be the *lex specialis*, trumping the effect of any agreed Comprehensive Convention if there are any conflicts in their co-applicability. If the impasse in negotiations for a Draft Comprehensive Convention is overcome, the text must exclude any misguided or inaccurate references to IHL terminology, such as those in the UN High-Level Panel report.

---

[72] Arvinder Sambei, Anton du Plessis, and Martin Polaine, *Counter-Terrorism Law and Practice: An International Handbook* (OUP, 2009), p 8.

[73] UN Global Counter-Terrorism Strategy, annexed to General Assembly Resolution 60/288, 8 September 2006, para 3; UN General Assembly Resolution 60/158, 16 December 2005; UN Security Council Resolution 1624 (2005), Preamble, para 2.

[74] International Law Association (ILA) Committee on the Use of Force, Initial Report on the Meaning of Armed Conflict in International Law, 2008, analysed in Mary Ellen O'Connell, 'Defining Armed Conflict' (2009) 13 J of Conflict & Security Law 393–400; Marco Sassòli, 'Terrorism and War' (2006) 4 J of Int'l Crim Justice 959–981; Gabor Rona, 'International Law under Fire: Interesting Times for International Humanitarian Law: Challenges from the "War on Terror"' (2003) 27 *Fletcher Forum of World Affairs* 55–70 at 60.

Any such inaccuracies could have unfortunate consequences in domestic courts that are called upon to adjudicate cases involving IHL.[75] The obligations in existing treaties to prevent and repress terrorism are anchored in the criminal justice process, fair trials, and the rule of law.[76] Article 18 of the current Draft Comprehensive Convention on Terrorism specifically excludes armed conflicts from its definition of terrorism in Article 2.[77] This approach should be welcomed.

The scope of states' obligations to counter terrorism

Criminal justice mechanisms

1.18 The subject-specific conventions on terrorist crimes require their states parties to criminalize specific acts, and to prosecute or extradite suspected offenders.[78] States are obliged to prevent and repress aircraft hijackings,[79] hostage-taking by terrorist groups,[80] attacks against the safety of sea vessels,[81] and the proliferation of nuclear weapons to terrorist groups.[82] States parties to these treaties must prosecute or extradite terrorism suspects,[83] denying them safe haven,[84] and exercising jurisdiction on the basis of territory or nationality. The crimes defined in these subject-specific treaties must not be considered political offences: a class of crimes for

---

[75] David Weissbrodt and Nathaniel H Nesbitt, 'The Role of the United States Supreme Court in Interpreting and Developing Humanitarian Law', *Minnesota Law Review* (forthcoming). *Minnesota Legal Studies Research Paper No. 10-31* (available on SSRN, draft dated 25 May 2010).

[76] Convention for the Suppression of Unlawful Seizure of Aircraft 1970, Art 7; Convention for the Suppression of Unlawful Acts against the Safety of Civil Aviation 1971, Art 7; Convention on the Prevention and Punishment of Crimes against Internationally Protected Persons 1973, Art 3(2); International Convention against the Taking of Hostages 1979, Art 5(2); International Convention for the Suppression of Terrorist Bombings 1997, Art 7(2); International Convention for the Suppression of the Financing of Terrorism 1997, Art 7(4); International Convention for the Suppression of Acts of Nuclear Terrorism 2005, Art 9(4).

[77] Arvinder Sambei, Anton du Plessis, and Martin Polaine, *Counter-Terrorism Law and Practice: An International Handbook* (OUP, 2009), p 8.

[78] See nn 1 and 2.

[79] Convention on Offences and Certain Other Acts Committed on Board Aircraft 1963; Convention for the Suppression of Unlawful Seizure of Aircraft 1970; Convention for the Suppression of Unlawful Acts against the Safety of Civil Aviation 1971, and its Protocol 1988.

[80] International Convention against the Taking of Hostages 1979.

[81] Convention for the Suppression of Unlawful Acts against the Safety of Maritime Navigation 1988, and its Protocol 2005.

[82] Convention on the Physical Protection of Nuclear Material 1980, as amended 2005; International Convention for the Suppression of Acts of Nuclear Terrorism 2005.

[83] See n 4; International Convention for the Suppression of Terrorist Bombings 1997; International Convention for the Suppression of Acts of Nuclear Terrorism 2005.

[84] UN Security Council Resolution 1373, 28 September 2001, para 2(c).

which suspects cannot be extradited.[85] As noted in paragraphs 1.01 and 1.17 above, all these obligations must be exercised in accordance with existing international law: compliance with IHL, IHRL, and IRL is embedded in the documents which regulate states' duties in counter-terrorism.[86]

This framework of obligations on individual states and the emphasis on criminal **1.19** justice mechanisms reflect the lack of an international court with jurisdiction to prosecute a defined crime of terrorism.[87] As Chapter 4 argues, the precedents for prosecution of 'terrorism' and 'spread[ing] terror among the civilian population' in the jurisprudence and indictments of international criminal tribunals do not create jurisdiction in international criminal law for the prosecution of terrorist attacks. Instead, they reflect IHL's specific meaning of 'terrorism',[88] which is dependent upon the context of an armed conflict, and refers to intentional acts which violate the principle of distinction between combatants and civilians.[89] In the absence of an internationally accepted definition of a crime of terrorism in international criminal law, and in the absence of this crime from the jurisdiction of the International Criminal Court,[90] only domestic courts or ad hoc tribunals with a specific mandate to prosecute terrorist offences can prosecute crimes of terrorism.[91]

UN Security Council Resolution 1624 prohibits all acts of terrorism, regardless of **1.20** their stated motivation, and calls on states to '[p]rohibit by law incitement to commit a terrorist act or acts'.[92] The Council of Europe Convention on the Prevention of Terrorism, which entered into force in 2007, obliges its states parties to criminalize 'public provocation to commit a terrorist offence'.[93] Chapter 3 considers the nexus between the obligation to criminalize terrorism offences and state practice in domestic criminal law. On the obligation to criminalize incitement to terrorist acts, Chapter 3 notes the tension between the strict necessity and proportionality tests in the IHRL freedom of expression and states' obligations

---

[85] Convention for the Suppression of Unlawful Seizure of Aircraft 1970, Art 7; Convention for the Suppression of Unlawful Acts against the Safety of Civil Aviation 1971, Art 7; Convention on the Prevention and Punishment of Crimes against Internationally Protected Persons 1973, Art 3(2); International Convention against the Taking of Hostages 1979, Art 5(2); International Convention for the Suppression of Terrorist Bombings 1997, Art 11; International Convention for the Suppression of the Financing of Terrorism 1997, Art 14; International Convention for the Suppression of Acts of Nuclear Terrorism 2005, Art 15.

[86] UN Global Counter-Terrorism Strategy, annexed to General Assembly Resolution 60/288, 8 September 2006, para 3; UN General Assembly Resolution 60/158, 16 December 2005; UN Security Council Resolution 1624 (2005), Preamble, para 2.

[87] See paras 4.05–4.06.

[88] See paras 2.22–2.32.

[89] Ibid.

[90] See para 4.05.

[91] Statute of the Special Tribunal for Lebanon. UN Security Council Resolution 1757 (2007); UN Doc S/RES/1757.

[92] UN Security Council Resolution 1624 (2005), para 1(a).

[93] Council of Europe Convention for the Prevention of Terrorism, Art 5(2).

under Security Council Resolutions and regional conventions.[94] Chapter 3 also explores the right to a fair trial in terrorism cases, noting over-breadth in some states' definition of terrorist offences, which in some instances criminalize the peaceful exercise of rights under the International Covenant on Civil and Political Rights (ICCPR).[95]

Sanctions and assets-freezing

1.21 Under the Terrorism Financing Convention, and UN Security Council Resolutions 1267 and 1373 (as subsequently amended),[96] states must cooperate to prevent the financing of terrorism. The procedure under Resolution 1267 and 1390 differs from that under Resolution 1373 and subsequent Resolutions. The former procedure established a Security Council Al-Qaeda and Taliban Sanctions Committee, and requires member states to freeze the assets of, and impose travel restrictions and an arms embargo on, entities or individuals named by that Committee as having participated, financed, or supported terrorist acts.[97] There is no right of appeal against such a finding by the Al-Qaeda and Taliban Sanctions Committee. The procedure under Resolution 1373 is a broader obligation on member states to prevent the financing of terrorism: there is no need for individuals or entities to have been listed by the Al-Qaeda and Taliban Sanctions Committee in order for states to take measures to freeze their assets.[98]

1.22 The processes mandated by these and subsequent Resolutions do not permit a formal appeal on the merits;[99] the UN Sanctions Committee remains a political, not a judicial body; and there is no duty to give reasons for a 'listing' decision.[100] Both the UN Human Rights Committee and the European Court of Justice of the European Communities have noted the erosion of the right to a fair hearing in the context of terrorism 'listing' and the freezing of assets pursuant to UN Security Council Resolution 1267 (1999).[101] Chapter 3 analyses intergovernmental

---

[94] See paras 3.160–3.164.

[95] See paras 3.08 and 3.169.

[96] International Convention for the Suppression of the Financing of Terrorism 1999; UN Security Council Resolutions 1267 (1999), 1373 (2001), 1526 (2004), 1566 (2004), 1617 (2005), 1730 (2006), 1822 (2008), 1904 (2009).

[97] UN Security Council Resolutions 1267 (1999), 1390 (2002).

[98] UN Security Council Resolution 1373, 12 September 2001; United Nations Office of Drugs and Crime, *Digest of Terrorism Cases,* May 2010, paras 4–5.

[99] UN Security Council Resolution 1730 (2006)—focal point delisting mechanism; UN Security Council Resolution 1904, 17 December 2009.

[100] UN Security Council Resolution 1267 (1999).

[101] Human Rights Committee, *Nabil Sayadi & Patricia Vinck v Belgium,* Communication No 1472/2006, CCPR/C/94/D/1472/2006, Views, 22 October 2008; European Court of Justice and Court of First Instance of the European Communities, Joined Cases C-402/05P and C-415/05P *Kadi and Al Barakaat International Foundation v Council of the European Union and Commission of the European Communities,* 3 September 2008, *Organisation des Modjahedines du peuple d'Iran v Council* [2006] ECR II-4665 ('*OMPI 1*'), T-256/07 23 ('*OMPI 2*') October 2008.

practice on terrorist 'listing' against the right to a fair hearing by a competent, independent, and impartial tribunal established by law, and notes that even the reforms in UN Security Council Resolutions 1730 and 1904 passed in response to extensive litigation still fail to provide court-based review on the merits of the decision to 'list' an individual and freeze his or her assets.[102] Any administrative or judicial decision to place an individual on a terrorist 'list' must be capable of challenge on the merits before a competent, independent, and impartial court. The most recent introduction in UN Security Council Resolution 1904 of an Office of the Ombudsperson to review 'listing' decisions fails to amount to merits-based, independent, and impartial judicial review, as Chapters 3 and 6 will show.[103]

Intergovernmental reporting obligations

States must report regularly to the UN Counter-Terrorism Committee (CTC) **1.23** established by UN Security Council Resolution 1373; and may receive technical assistance from the UN CTC Executive Directorate, established by UN Security Council Resolution 1535.[104] That same resolution provided for a human rights expert to sit on the CTC Executive Directorate, and liaise with the Office of the High Commissioner for Human Rights (OHCHR).[105] In 2008, Resolution 1805 established a working group within the CTC Executive Directorate, to consider the human rights concerns which arise from Resolutions 1373 and 1625.[106] Chapter 6 argues that this piecemeal, gradual inclusion of human rights monitoring at the UN CTC should be expanded; and that states should ensure that their reports to the UN CTC take full account of their counter-terrorism policies' compliance with IHL and IHRL.[107] Without a thorough 'mainstreaming' of human rights concerns in the CTC, the material collected from states on their counter-terrorism policies will be patchy. There is a risk of two parallel tracks of communication in the UN system about human rights and counter-terrorism, with a scant approach to IHRL in the UN counter-terrorism machinery, which contrasts with the assessments of states' human rights records in the output of UN treaty bodies and special procedures of the UN Human Rights Council.

As Chapter 6 argues, states should submit reports to UN treaty bodies; allow visits **1.24** or extend an open invitation to the special procedures of the UN Human Rights Council; and implement in full not only treaty obligations but also the judgments or views of regional courts and UN treaty bodies where the latter have found

---

[102] See paras 3.150–3.151 and 3.155.; para 6.41 and 7.18.

[103] UN Security Council Resolution 1904, 17 December 2009; See para 3.150 and para 6.13.

[104] UN Security Council Resolution 1373 (2001); UN Security Council Resolution 1535 (2004).

[105] UN Security Council Resolution 1535 (2004).

[106] UN Security Council Resolution 1805 (2008).

[107] See paras 6.02 and 6.04.

violations of IHRL by that state.[108] This recommendation would address IHRL violations of any type in any context. The prevalence of violations of IHRL in the counter-terrorism context makes this recommendation highly relevant.

Preventing the proliferation of weapons to terrorist groups

1.25 Under UN Security Council Resolution 1540, states are obliged to prevent non-state terrorist groups from accessing weapons of mass destruction.[109] The UN Global Counter-Terrorism Strategy addresses this duty in some detail. It emphasizes inter-state, regional, and international cooperation in preventing the proliferation of 'small arms and light weapons, conventional ammunition and explosives, and nuclear, chemical, biological or radiological weapons and materials';[110] and calls on the International Atomic Energy Agency (IAEA) and the Organisation for the Prohibition of Chemical Weapons to build states' capacities to prevent terrorist groups from having access to nuclear and chemical weapons.[111] Chapter 6 endorses this approach, and notes that preventing the proliferation of weapons to terrorist groups, whether they are state or non-state, can be carried out without risking violations of IHL, IHRL, or IRL. Measures to prevent the proliferation of weapons should be accompanied by the investigation, prosecution, or extradition as appropriate of those suspected of involvement in the illegal trade in these arms. If successful, the negotiations of an Arms Trade Treaty at the UN in 2012 should address not only the proliferation of small arms in general, but should also address the specific issue of preventing the proliferation of such arms to terrorist groups.

Countering terrorism in accordance with international law

1.26 As noted in the first of the two principles noted in paragraph 1.17 above, in the UN Global Counter-Terrorism Strategy (the Strategy),[112] and a number of UN Security Council and General Assembly Resolutions,[113] states' obligations to counter terrorism must be carried out in accordance with states' existing obligations in IHL, IHRL, and IRL, even where terrorist acts are deemed threats to international peace and security.[114] IHRL and IRL remain applicable regardless of the existence of a

---

[108] See paras 3.94 and 6.04.

[109] UN Security Council Resolution 1540 (2004).

[110] UN Global Counter-Terrorism Strategy, II, Measures to prevent and combat terrorism, para 13.

[111] Ibid, III, Measures to build states' capacity to prevent and combat terrorism and to strengthen the role of the United Nations system in this regard, para 9.

[112] UN Global Counter-Terrorism Strategy, annexed to General Assembly Resolution 60/288, 8 September 2006, para 3.

[113] UN General Assembly Resolution 60/158, 16 December 2005; UN Security Council Resolution 1624 (2005), Preamble, para 2.

[114] International Convention for the Suppression of the Financing of Terrorism 1999; UN Security Council Resolutions 1267 (1999), 1373 (2001), 1526 (2004), 1566 (2004), 1617 (2005), 1735 (2006), 1822 (2008), 1904 (2009).

terrorist threat, while IHL applies in armed conflict or belligerent occupation. Counter-terrorism operations must be conducted with full respect for these branches of international law, regardless of whether the terrorism in question is state or non-state, or whether it is carried out with self-determination as an aim.

International refugee law (IRL)

A brief note is required on IRL, which is outside the scope of this book.[115] The UN **1.27** Global Counter-Terrorism Strategy recognizes that full compliance with IRL also entails taking 'appropriate measures to ensure that the asylum-seeker has not engaged in terrorist activities'.[116] This reflects existing IRL.

- First, Article 1(F) of the 1951 Convention on the Status of Refugees (Refugee Convention) provides that the Convention as a whole does not apply 'to any person with respect to whom there are serious reasons for considering that': (a) he or she has committed 'a crime against peace, a war crime or crime against humanity';[117] (b) 'a serious non-political crime outside the country of refuge';[118] or (c) 'has been guilty of acts contrary to the purposes and principles of the United Nations'.[119] Where a state considers that an individual has been involved in terrorist crimes which would satisfy any of the headings in Article 1(F)(a)–(c), that individual may be excluded from refugee protection while he or she is seeking asylum, or refugee status may be cancelled or revoked if there is subsequent evidence that he or she has committed any of the crimes in Article 1(F)(a)–(c).[120] The asylum seeker does not need to have been convicted of any of the crimes in Article 1(F)(a)–(c) in order to be excluded from refugee protection.[121]
- Second, those already granted refugee status may lose protection under Article 33 of the Refugee Convention. The *non-refoulement* obligation in that Article does not apply where a refugee is considered a threat to national security, or where he or she has been convicted of a particularly serious crime.[122] This means that an individual in one of those categories may be sent back to a state where 'his life or freedom would be threatened on account of his race, religion, nationality, membership of a particular social group or political opinion'.[123]

---

[115] Colin Harvey, 'And Fairness For All? Asylum, National Security and the Rule of Law' in Victor V Ramraj, Michael Hor, and Kent Roach (eds), *Global Anti-Terrorism Law and Policy* (Cambridge University Press, 2005), pp 152–179.

[116] UN Global Counter-Terrorism Strategy, II, Measures to prevent and combat terrorism, para 7.

[117] Refugee Convention, Art 1(F)(a).

[118] Ibid, Art 1(F)(b).

[119] Ibid, Art 1(F)(c).

[120] UN High Commissioner for Refugees (UNHCR), 'Guidelines on International Protection: Application of the Exclusion Clauses: Article 1F of the 1951 Convention relating to the Status of Refugees', para 6.

[121] Ibid, para 35.

[122] Refugee Convention, Art 33(2).

[123] Ibid, Art 33(1).

- Third, states parties to the Refugee Convention can only expel a refugee who is lawfully in their territory on grounds of 'national security or public order'.[124] Article 32(2) of the Refugee Convention provides that such expulsion 'shall be only in pursuance of a decision reached in accordance with due process of law'.[125] Moreover, prior to an expulsion, 'the refugee shall be allowed to submit evidence to clear himself, and to appeal to or be represented for the purpose by competent authority or a person or persons specially designated by the competent authority'.[126] This does not necessarily require that the refugee have access to counsel of his or her own choice. Pending expulsion under Article 32, refugees shall be allowed a 'reasonable period within which to seek legal admission to another country', during which time, states may impose 'such internal measures as they deem necessary'.[127]

1.28 These IRL provisions do not remove individuals from the continuing subsidiary protection of IHRL, which is explained in detail in Chapter 3. The *non-refoulement* obligation in Article 3 of the Convention against Torture remains absolute, and is not 'balanced' by competing national security concerns.[128] An individual subjected to exclusion from refugee protection under Article 1(F) or to *refoulement* under Article 33(2) of the Refugee Convention would retain subsidiary protection from Article 3 of the Convention against Torture if there 'are substantial grounds for believing that he would be in danger of being subjected to torture'.[129] The Committee against Torture's General Comment No 2 offers an authoritative interpretation of the Convention against Torture, and notes that 'articles 3 to 15 are likewise obligatory as applied to both torture and ill-treatment'.[130] This indicates that the Convention against Torture's *non-refoulement* protection should also apply where there are substantial grounds for believing that an individual would be in danger of being subjected to cruel, inhuman, or degrading treatment or punishment, given that 'the definitional threshold between ill-treatment and torture is often not clear'.[131]

Structure

1.29 This chapter has noted the lack of an internationally accepted definition of terrorism in international law, and has sketched the scope of states' duties to prevent and repress terrorism while complying with IHL, IHRL, and IRL. Chapter 2 defines

---

[124] Ibid, Art 32(1).
[125] Ibid, Art 32(2).
[126] Ibid.
[127] Ibid, Art 32(3).
[128] European Court of Human Rights, *Saadi v Italy* (2008) 24 BHRC 123.
[129] Convention against Torture, Art 3(1).
[130] Committee against Torture, General Comment No 2, para 6.
[131] Ibid, para 3.

and explains IHL for non-specialists, clarifying when terrorist attacks and forcible action in counter-terrorism are and are not regulated by IHL, and also clarifying the difference between IHL and the international law on the use of force (*jus ad bellum*), which is beyond the scope of this book. A terrorist attack does not create a situation of war, nor does the use of force in counter-terrorism automatically create an armed conflict to which IHL applies. Although IHL has a context-specific meaning of 'terrorism' and 'acts or threat of violence the primary purpose of which is to spread terror among the civilian population',[132] this meaning relates to IHL's principle of distinction between combatants and civilians, and to civilians' immunity from attack: it should be distinguished from the popular or media conceptions of terrorism, and from the many definitions of terrorism offences in domestic criminal legislation. In addition to analysing a number of conflicts designated as 'terrorist' or 'counter-terrorist' in terms of applicable IHL, Chapter 2 considers a number of controversies in IHL and counter-terrorism, including drone attacks and 'targeted killings', the co-applicability of IHL and IHRL, and IHL's position on the use of certain weapons.

Chapter 3 clarifies the continued application of international human rights law to states' counter-terrorism laws and policies, with reference to global examples of legislation and state practice in Algeria, China, Indonesia, Israel, Jordan, Pakistan, Peru, the Russian Federation, Spain, Sri Lanka, Swaziland, the UK, the US, Uzbekistan, and Yemen. The chapter shows the worldwide reach of violations of civil, political, economic, social, and cultural rights in the name of counter-terrorism, with reference to findings from intergovernmental and non-governmental organizations, and analysis of legislation in translation.   **1.30**

Chapter 4 notes the dual imperative of ensuring individual criminal responsibility for terrorist attacks and for serious violations of IHL and IHRL committed in counter-terrorism. As there is no defined crime of terrorism within the Rome Statute of the International Criminal Court (ICC), terrorism suspects should be tried in domestic civilian courts in fair trials, or extradited, subject to the IHRL prohibition on *refoulement*. War crimes and crimes against humanity committed in counter-terrorism should be tried in domestic courts, pursuant to any ground of jurisdiction, or referred to the ICC if a state is unable or unwilling to conduct a genuine investigation. Chapter 4 also examines the range of criminal investigations, the one successful criminal prosecution, civil cases, national and international inquiries into violations of IHL and IHRL committed in counter-terrorism, and notes the pervasive impunity which remains.   **1.31**

Victims' rights to a remedy and reparation are closely linked to the obligation to investigate and prosecute serious violations of international law. Chapter 5 analyses   **1.32**

---

[132] Fourth Geneva Convention, Art 33; Additional Protocol I, Art 51(2); Additional Protocol II, Art 4(2)(d) and Art 13(2).

the development of remedies and reparations for violations of IHL and IHRL, in ICL and the non-binding Basic Principles and Guidelines on the Right to a Remedy and Reparation for Victims of Gross Violations of International Humanitarian Law and Serious Violations of International Human Rights Law (Basic Principles and Guidelines),[133] and then applies this analysis to victims of terrorism and violations of international law in states' counter-terrorism operations. It notes that states have largely failed to implement the international law and standards on victims' rights to a remedy and reparations, and that states should instead make judicial remedies available to victims of terrorism and victims of violations in counter-terrorism. States should also encourage victims' participation in public inquiries, criminal cases, and civil suits. In line with recent jurisprudence of the Court of Appeal of England and Wales,[134] Chapter 5 urges states to reform state secrets doctrines so that they are not used to forestall accountability for violations of IHRL.

1.33 Chapter 6 is forward-looking and prescriptive. It analyses broad and specific mechanisms for the prevention of terrorist attacks; and argues for a range of measures to prevent violations of IHL and IHRL in counter-terrorism. Chapter 6 lays the foundations for the book's Recommendations of the IBA Task Force on Terrorism, in Chapter 7, 'Conclusion and Recommendations'.

---

[133] UN Basic Principles and Guidelines on the Right to a Remedy and Reparation for Victims of Gross Violations of International Human Rights Law and Serious Violations of International Humanitarian Law (Basic Principles and Guidelines), adopted by UN General Assembly Resolution 60/147, A/Res/60/147, 16 December 2005.

[134] *Al-Rawi and Others v Security Service and Others* [2010] EWCA Civ 482.

2

COUNTER-TERRORISM IN
INTERNATIONAL HUMANITARIAN LAW

What is international humanitarian law and when does it apply?

What is IHL?

International humanitarian law (IHL), also known as the law of armed conflict, or **2.01** *jus in bello*, applies to regulate the conduct of hostilities and to provide for the protection of civilians and other non-combatants in international armed conflict, belligerent occupation, and non-international armed conflict. It does not apply outside these situations. IHL treaty law provides extensive guarantees for wounded, sick, and shipwrecked combatants,[1] and for prisoners of war in international armed conflicts;[2] and a range of provisions for protected persons in international armed conflicts and belligerent occupation.[3] Its provisions in non-international armed conflicts[4] are less extensive than those in international armed conflicts, but at a minimum, the former prohibit a range of acts against persons taking no active part in the hostilities, and provide that the wounded and sick be collected and cared for.[5] All these terms are defined below.[6]

---

[1] First and Second Geneva Conventions of 12 August 1949.
[2] Third Geneva Convention of 12 August 1949 (Third Geneva Convention).
[3] Fourth Geneva Convention of 12 August 1949 (Fourth Geneva Convention).
[4] Four Geneva Conventions, Common Article 3, and where ratified, Additional Protocol II to the Four Geneva Conventions.
[5] Four Geneva Conventions, Common Article 3.
[6] See paras 2.06–2.08.

When does IHL apply?

2.02   The term 'armed conflict' is not defined in IHL treaty law, but there is a definition in case law. The Appeals Chamber of the International Criminal Tribunal for the former Yugoslavia (ICTY) in the *Tadić* case defined 'armed conflict' as a 'resort to armed force between States or protracted armed violence between governmental authorities and organised armed groups or between such groups within a state'.[7] The existence of an armed conflict is determined objectively,[8] so a state's choice to term hostilities 'terrorist' or 'counter-terrorist' has no bearing on whether IHL applies. In particular, IHL can still apply even if one state involved in an international armed conflict does not recognize a state of war;[9] and it still applies to objective armed conflicts even if war is not declared.[10]

2.03   A terrorist attack does not necessarily create an armed conflict. Nor is the use of force in counter-terrorism automatically an armed conflict. Therefore, it should neither be assumed that all terrorist violence triggers the applicability of IHL, nor that all counter-terrorist operations which use force are regulated by IHL (see paragraph 2.04 below). Where politicians or the media refer to a 'global war on terror', this can be misleading where the term 'war' is used to underline the political importance of countering terrorism, rather than to refer to specific international or non-international armed conflicts.[11] The US-led 'global war on terror' of 2001–09[12] should be distinguished from its 'component' hostilities (to borrow an expression from Marco Sassòli which refers to objective armed conflicts fought in the course of the broader counter-terrorism policy) in Afghanistan and Iraq,[13] and from any other armed conflict waged with a counter-terrorist aim. The use of criminal justice mechanisms to prevent and repress terrorism is not a 'war' to which IHL applies. As Chapter 1 has shown, this obligation derives from a network of subject-specific

---

[7] International Criminal Tribunal for the former Yugoslavia (ICTY), *Prosecutor v Tadić*, Case No IT-94-1-A, Appeals Chamber, Decision on the Defence Motion for Interlocutory Appeal on Jurisdiction, 2 October 1995, para 70.

[8] Four Geneva Conventions, Common Article 2, para 1 (for international armed conflicts and situations of belligerent occupation); Additional Protocol II to the Four Geneva Conventions (Additional Protocol II), Art1 (for non-international armed conflicts where Additional Protocol II is ratified).

[9] Four Geneva Conventions, Common Article 2, para 1.

[10] Ibid.

[11] International Law Association (ILA) Committee on the Use of Force, Initial Report on the Meaning of Armed Conflict in International Law, 2008, analysed in Mary Ellen O'Connell, 'Defining Armed Conflict' (2009) 13 *Journal of Conflict & Security Law* 393–400; Marco Sassòli, 'Terrorism and War' (2006) 4 *Journal of International Criminal Justice* 959–981; Gabor Rona, 'International Law under Fire: Interesting Times for International Humanitarian Law: Challenges from the "War on Terror"' (2003) 27 *Fletcher Forum of World Affairs* 55–70 at 60.

[12] President George W Bush, Address to US Congress, 21 September 2001; Washington Post, 'Global War on Terror is Given New Name', 25 March 2009.

[13] Marco Sassòli, 'Terrorism and War' (2006) 4 *J of Int'l Crim Justice* 959–981; Marko Milanovic, 'Lessons for Human Rights and Humanitarian Law in the War on Terror: Comparing *Hamdan* and the Israeli *Targeted Killings* Case' (2007) 89 *International Review of the Red Cross* 373–393 at 376.

multilateral conventions against terrorism, and a range of UN Security Council Resolutions. IHL does not regulate counter-terrorism which takes place outside armed conflict (whether international or non-international) or belligerent occupation.

International human rights law (IHRL), which is considered in depth in the next **2.04** chapter, regulates states' policies, laws, and actions in counter-terrorism in peace and war:[14] the use of force by law enforcement officials outside an armed conflict or belligerent occupation does not engage IHL, and is instead regulated by IHRL.[15] Similarly, IHRL and not IHL governs the *ad hoc* use of force by armed forces personnel outside an armed conflict or belligerent occupation. For this reason, 'targeted killings' of terrorism suspects outside armed conflict are prima facie extrajudicial executions: arbitrary deprivations of life under IHRL.[16]

Importantly, IHL regulates the conduct of hostilities *during* armed conflicts. IHL **2.05** is sometimes referred to as *jus in bello*, which is distinct from the international law on the use of force or *jus ad bellum*, in Article 2(4) and Article 51 of the UN Charter, which provide for the prohibition on the unilateral use of force and for the inherent right of self-defence against an armed attack. *Jus ad bellum* and *jus in bello* are two separate branches of international law. This chapter's case studies and broader discussion are concerned with *jus in bello*, and not *jus ad bellum*, which is beyond the scope of this book.[17] As a result, the text does not consider 'the inherent right to individual or collective self-defence' under Article 51 of the UN Charter, or Security Council Resolutions passed under Chapter VII of the UN Charter, which can authorize forcible or non-forcible measures to address a threat to international peace and security.

Definitions

The Four Geneva Conventions of 12 August 1949, and Protocol Additional to the **2.06** Four Geneva Conventions of 12 August 1949 and relating to the protection of victims of international armed conflicts of 8 June 1977 (Additional Protocol I) are the core of IHL treaty law applicable to international armed conflicts.

- Common Article 2, paragraph 1 of the Four Geneva Conventions of 12 August 1949 states that the law on international armed conflicts only applies to conflicts between 'two or more of the High Contracting Parties' (states parties) to the Geneva Conventions. As non-state armed groups cannot be High Contracting Parties, the IHL on international armed conflicts can only bind them if the armed

---

[14] See paras 2.38–2.40.
[15] See paras 3.28–3.35; 3.40–3.45.
[16] Report of the UN Special Rapporteur on Extrajudicial, Summary and Arbitrary Executions, Mission to the USA, A/HRC/11/2/Add.5, 28 May 2009.
[17] See paras 1.11–1.12 and 1.29.

group is integral to, or subject to the overall control of a state which has ratified the Four Geneva Conventions. This is reflected in the case law of the ICTY.[18] It makes no difference to the objective applicability of IHL if armed groups are considered 'terrorist' by one or more states.

• Common Article 2, paragraph 1 continues by stating that the Four Geneva Conventions apply to 'all cases of declared war or of any other armed conflict which may arise between two or more of the High Contracting Parties, even if the state of war is not recognised by them'.[19] It is significant that IHL applies to the objective fact of an international armed conflict, and that the characterization of a conflict by one or more of the parties as a declared war, a liberation struggle, a police operation, or a counter-terrorism operation has no impact on the applicability of IHL. It makes no difference to the objective applicability of IHL if states declare that IHL does not apply to a particular conflict, or if they declare that a new type of conflict exists to which IHL applies only in part or not at all.[20]

• Article 1, paragraph 4 of Additional Protocol I adds a further category of international armed conflict: 'armed conflicts in which peoples are fighting against colonial domination and alien occupation and against racist régimes in the exercise of their right to self-determination . . . ' In all other circumstances where a state armed force fights an armed group, this would be a non-international armed conflict. Conflicts fought between a state which has not ratified Additional Protocol I and a non-state armed group which may claim that it is 'fighting against colonial domination and alien occupation and against racist regimes' would not be an international armed conflict as a matter of treaty law, as the applicability of Additional Protocol I is dependent upon its ratification by a state. The UK is among the states which has entered a reservation to Article 1, paragraph 4 of Additional Protocol I, noting that: ' . . . (d) It is the understanding of the United Kingdom that the term "armed conflict" of itself and in its context denotes a situation of a kind which is not constituted by the commission of ordinary crimes including acts of terrorism whether concerted or in isolation.'[21]

• The *Tadić* case before the Appeals Chamber of the ICTY defines international armed conflict as follows: 'It is indisputable that an armed conflict is international if it takes place between two or more States. In addition, in case of an internal armed conflict breaking out on the territory of a State, it may become international (or, depending upon the circumstances, be international in character alongside an internal armed conflict) *if (i) another State intervenes in that*

---

[18] ICTY, *Prosecutor v Tadić*, Case No IT-94-1-A, Appeals Chamber, 15 July 1999, paras 137–145.

[19] Four Geneva Conventions, Common Article 2(1).

[20] See paras 2.33–2.35.

[21] Additional Protocol I, United Kingdom Reservation Text.

conflict through its troops, or alternatively if (ii) some of the participants in the internal armed conflict act on behalf of that other State.'[22]

- The IHL applicable to international armed conflicts provides for the protection of wounded, sick, or shipwrecked combatants on land and at sea in the First and Second Geneva Conventions of 12 August 1949; makes detailed prescriptions for the treatment of captured combatants who are detained as prisoners of war (POWs) in the Third Geneva Convention of 12 August 1949; and requires guarantees for protected persons (individuals who are in the hands of a party to the conflict, and of which they are not nationals)[23] in the Fourth Geneva Convention of 12 August 1949. Additional Protocol I (where ratified) enlarges and further specifies the protections available to civilians and other non-combatants in international armed conflicts.

The IHL of belligerent occupation is found in the Regulations concerning the Laws **2.07** and Customs of War on Land, annexed to the Hague Convention (IV) respecting the Laws and Customs of War on Land (Hague Regulations), and the Fourth Geneva Convention Relative to the Protection of Civilian Persons in Time of War (Fourth Geneva Convention).

- Belligerent occupation occurs when one state's army has actual control over some or all of the territory of a hostile state, as per Article 42 of the Regulations concerning the Laws and Customs of War on Land, annexed to the Hague Convention (IV) respecting the Laws and Customs of War on Land (Hague Regulations).[24] Territory is occupied 'when it is actually placed under the authority of the hostile army. The occupation extends only to the territory where such authority has been established and can be exercised'.[25] The occupying power must 'take all the measures in his power to restore, and ensure, as far as possible, public order and safety, while respecting, unless absolutely prevented, the laws in force in the country'.[26] Under the Fourth Geneva Convention, *protected persons* are 'entitled, in all circumstances, to respect for their persons, their honour, their family rights, their religious convictions and practices, and their manners and customs. They shall at all times be humanely treated . . . '[27] The Fourth Geneva Convention also imposes a range of humanitarian obligations on the occupying power,[28] subject to restrictions based on 'imperative reasons of security'.[29] Internment and

---

[22] ICTY, *Prosecutor v Tadić*, Case No IT-94-1-A, Appeals Chamber, 15 July 1999, para 84 (emphasis added).

[23] Fourth Geneva Convention, Art 4.

[24] Regulations concerning the Laws and Customs of War on Land, annexed to the Hague Convention (IV) respecting the Laws and Customs of War on Land (Hague Regulations), 18 October 1907, Art 42 .

[25] Hague Regulations, Art 42.

[26] Hague Regulations, Art 43.

[27] Fourth Geneva Convention, Art 27.

[28] Fourth Geneva Convention, Arts 59–62.

[29] Fourth Geneva Convention, Art 62.

assigned residence of protected persons are the most stringent methods of control available to the occupying power.[30]

- The IHL of belligerent occupation will apply to terrorism and counter-terrorism only where the armed force of one state has control over some or all of the territory of *another* state. Belligerent occupation does not occur as a result of the occupation of some or all of a state's own territory by its army in the context of a traditional non-international armed conflict which occurs within one state's boundaries.

2.08 Non-international armed conflicts are the residual category, which cover all armed conflicts which are not international armed conflicts:

- Non-international armed conflicts can be between one or more states and one or more armed groups, or between multiple armed groups generally within the territory of one state, but also where such conflicts cross state boundaries.
  - Non-international armed conflicts therefore encompass traditional *intrastate* non-international armed conflicts, and newer *transnational* or *internationalized* armed conflicts.[31] The expansion of non-international armed conflict to include these newer types of conflict contrasts with the wording in Common Article 3 of the Four Geneva Conventions that such conflicts occur 'in the territory of *one* of the High Contracting Parties' (emphasis added), yet Common Article 3 still applies to these conflicts. Terms such as 'internationalized' or 'transnational' armed conflict are not found in IHL treaties.
  - Despite recent calls for the distinction between international and non-international armed conflicts to be abandoned,[32] to reflect the erosion of this distinction in case law,[33] and in the International Committee of the Red Cross' Study on Customary International Humanitarian Law,[34] armed hostilities between armed forces and non-state armed groups remain non-international armed conflicts, even when they cross state boundaries, or involve multiple state armed forces fighting against non-state armed groups. This is because of the definition of international armed conflicts in Common Article 2, paragraph 1, 'armed conflict which may arise between two or more of the High Contracting Parties', ie between two or more states.

---

[30] Fourth Geneva Convention, Arts 41 and 78.

[31] James Stewart, 'Towards a Single Definition of Armed Conflict in International Humanitarian Law: A Critique of Internationalized Armed Conflict' (2003) 85 *Int'l Rev of the Red Cross* 313–350.

[32] Ibid; Emily Crawford, 'Unequal Before the Law: The case for the Elimination of the Distinction Between International and Non-International Armed Conflict (2007) 20 *Leiden Journal of International Law* 441–465.

[33] ICTY, *Prosecutor v Tadić*, Case No IT-94-1-A, Appeals Chamber, 15 July 1999.

[34] Jean Marie Henckaerts and Louise Doswald-Beck, *Customary International Humanitarian Law, Volume 1: Rules* (International Committee of the Red Cross, Cambridge University Press, 2005) (Henckaerts & Doswald-Beck).

- Following the jurisprudence of the ICTY in the *Tadić* case,[35] it is possible for an international armed conflict and a non-international armed conflict to coexist in the same territory or territories, where two or more states are in an international armed conflict, and where one or more of those states is fighting one or more armed groups.
- The IHL relating to non-international armed conflicts binds non-state armed groups as well as state armed forces, although only states can ratify treaties. Common Article 3 binds 'each party to the conflict'.
- Non-international armed conflicts can be subdivided into those which are regulated only by Common Article 3 of the Four Geneva Conventions of 12 August 1949, and, those which are regulated by both Common Article 3 and the Protocol Additional to the Four Geneva Conventions and Relating to the Protection of Victims of Non-International Armed Conflicts of 8 June 1977 (Additional Protocol II). Common Article 3 requires minimal protections for non-combatants and for the wounded and sick; whereas Additional Protocol II gives much more detail on the protection of civilians. Traditional, intra-state non-international armed conflicts take place where domestic law and international human rights law are assumed to apply, with the possibility for derogation, despite the fact of an armed conflict. This explains what would otherwise appear to be a lacuna in the law. Given that Additional Protocol II is not universally ratified, and the protections for those *hors de combat* in Common Article 3 are minimal requirements only, the prevalence of non-international armed conflicts is a significant concern for the protection of civilians. This concern extends to non-international armed conflicts fought between one or more armed groups which are deemed 'terrorist' and armed forces fighting with the aim of counter-terrorism.
- As noted above, Common Article 3 to the Four Geneva Conventions binds 'each party to the conflict': this means that both armed forces and armed groups are bound by Common Article 3, with no additional prerequisites before non-state armed groups are bound. Under Article 1(1) of Additional Protocol II, however, non-state armed groups are only bound if they control territory within the non-international armed conflict, and if they are subject to 'responsible command' and 'exercise such control over a part of its territory as to enable them to carry out sustained and concerted military operations and to implement this Protocol'.
- Article 1(2) of Additional Protocol II sets a threshold between 'isolated and sporadic' violence short of an armed conflict (where Additional Protocol II does not apply) and non-international armed conflict (where Additional Protocol II does apply if ratified by the state in question). Therefore, IHL regulates neither 'isolated and sporadic' terrorist violence nor the 'isolated and sporadic' use of force in counter-terrorism, whether this force is used by law enforcement officials or a state army. However, this definition of non-international armed conflict is

---

[35] ICTY, *Prosecutor v Tadić*, Case No IT-94-1-A, Appeals Chamber, 15 July 1999, paras 73, 84.

negative and incomplete: it defines only the threshold below which Additional Protocol II does not apply, and does not give positive indicators for violence which is more than 'isolated and sporadic'. Common Article 3 does not include this limitation, but nonetheless requires 'an armed conflict not of an international character':[36] not occasional skirmishes.

2.09   Civilians are defined negatively and cumulatively in Article 50 of Additional Protocol I: 'A civilian is any person who does not belong to one of the categories of persons referred to in Article 4(A)(1), (2), (3) and (6) of the Third Geneva Convention and in Article 43 [of Additional Protocol I].' These provisions indicate *inter alia* that a civilian is anyone who is not a member of armed forces, militia, volunteer corps,[37] a member of regular armed forces 'who profess allegiance to a government or an authority not recognised by the Detaining Power',[38] or part of a *levée en masse*, when inhabitants of a non-occupied territory spontaneously take up arms to resist invading forces.[39] Combatants are defined in Article 43, paragraph 2 of Additional Protocol I as '[m]embers of the armed forces of a Party to a conflict (other than medical personnel and chaplains . . .)'.

In treaty law, these definitions apply to international armed conflict only. An explicit combatant/civilian distinction is not found in the treaty law applicable to non-international armed conflicts, but the word 'civilian' can be read into the broader concept of '[p]ersons taking no active part in the hostilities' who must always be treated humanely, under Common Article 3, paragraph 1. The International Committee of the Red Cross (ICRC) Study on Customary International Humanitarian Law,[40] and the codification of war crimes in international and non-international armed conflicts offer strong evidence for the applicability of the principle of distinction to non-international armed conflicts, even though the expressions 'combatant' and 'civilian' are not found in Common Article 3 or Additional Protocol II.[41]

2.10   Combatants in international armed conflict have a combatant's privilege: they can kill and be killed.[42] Civilians enjoy immunity from attack: they cannot kill or be killed.[43] Armed forces 'shall at all times distinguish between the civilian population and combatants and between civilian objects and military objectives . . . direct[ing] their operations only against military objectives'.[44] This is known as the principle of distinction between combatants and civilians, which also gives rise to a prohibition

---

[36] Four Geneva Conventions, Common Article 3.
[37] Third Geneva Convention, Art 4(A)(1)–(2).
[38] Ibid, Art 4(A)(3).
[39] Ibid, Art 4(A)(6).
[40] Henckaerts & Doswald-Beck, supra, Rule 1.
[41] Rome Statute of the International Criminal Court 1998, Art 8(2)(e)(i).
[42] Additional Protocol I, Art 43(2).
[43] Additional Protocol I, Art 51.
[44] Additional Protocol I, Art 48.

on indiscriminate attacks, as defined by Article 51(4) of Additional Protocol I; and a duty to take precautions in attack, to avoid excessive civilian casualties on land,[45] on sea, or in the air.

Only if a civilian takes a direct part in hostilities can he or she be targeted, and then **2.11** only for 'such time as' he or she does so.[46] The direct participation of civilians in hostilities does occur in international and non-international armed conflicts alike, including those labelled 'terrorist' or 'counter-terrorist' by the parties to the conflict. The controversy of the direct participation of civilians in these conflicts will be considered in paragraphs 2.41–2.45, with reference to the ICRC's new Interpretive Guidance on the issue,[47] and accompanying academic debate.[48]

Proportionality in IHL has a different meaning from that in IHRL, as the section **2.12** on targeted killings in armed conflict will explain. The principle of proportionality is codified in Article 51(5)(b) of Additional Protocol I to the Four Geneva Conventions, and in Protocol II and Amended Protocol II to the UN Convention on Prohibitions or Restrictions on the Use of Certain Conventional Weapons which may be Deemed to be Excessively Injurious or to Have Indiscriminate Effects (CCW) 1980. The principle of proportionality requires that armed forces calculate the 'direct and concrete military advantage' of a planned attack as against the 'incidental loss of civilian life, injury to civilians, damage to civilian objects, or a combination thereof'.[49] If this 'incidental loss' is deemed 'excessive in relation to' the military advantage, an attack would be disproportionate in IHL.[50] This principle is also found in Rule 41 of the ICRC Study on Customary International Humanitarian Law, where it is believed to have crystallized into a norm of customary IHL which applies to international and non-international armed conflicts alike.[51]

States must 'respect and ensure respect'[52] for the Four Geneva Conventions 'in all **2.13** circumstances'; they must enact penal legislation to criminalize certain grave breaches,[53] search for suspected perpetrators, and prosecute them or extradite them for trial in another concerned state.[54] Grave breaches in international armed conflicts include but are not limited to: 'wilful killing, torture and inhuman treatment',

---

[45] Additional Protocol I, Arts 49(3) and 57(4).
[46] Additional Protocol I, Art 51(3).
[47] ICRC, *Interpretive Guidance on the Notion of Direct Participation in Hostilities under International Humanitarian Law*, June 2009.
[48] Nils Melzer, *Targeted Killing in International Law* (OUP, 2008); Michael Schmitt, 'The Interpretive Guidance on the Notion of Direct Participation in Hostilities: A Critical Analysis' (2010) 1 *Harvard National Security Journal* 5–44.
[49] Additional Protocol I, Art 51(5)(b).
[50] Ibid.
[51] Henckaerts & Doswald-Beck, supra, Rule 41, pp 46–50.
[52] Four Geneva Conventions, Common Article 1.
[53] First Geneva Convention, Art 49; Second Geneva Convention, Art 50; Third Geneva Convention, Art 129; Fourth Geneva Convention, Art 146; Additional Protocol I, Art 85.
[54] Ibid.

hostage-taking, and 'unlawful deportation or transfer [and] unlawful confinement' of protected persons.[55] Article 85 of Additional Protocol I extends this list still further. Violations of IHL which are short of grave breaches can be the subject of enquiries, at the request of any party to the conflict: '[o]nce a violation has been established, the Parties to the conflict shall put an end to it and shall repress it with the least possible delay.'[56]

In short, compliance with IHL is obligatory, and violations of IHL must be repressed and suspected perpetrators held to account. As IHL applies in full to objective armed conflicts, and is neutral as to the political aims of the parties to a conflict, these obligations are binding, regardless of whether a conflict is fought with a counter-terrorist aim.

Sources

2.14 The Four Geneva Conventions of 12 August 2009 are universally ratified, so that their provisions apply to all international armed conflicts and belligerent occupations. The two Additional Protocols to the Four Geneva Conventions are less widely ratified than the Four Geneva Conventions themselves, meaning that the obligations in Additional Protocol I (regulating international armed conflicts) and in Additional Protocol II (regulating non-international armed conflicts) only apply where a conflict involves a state or states which have ratified them.[57] Where the state or states in question have not ratified either or both Additional Protocols, the principles therein are binding on armed forces and groups only where they are considered to be customary international humanitarian law (CIHL). Apart from the 161 Rules identified in the ICRC Study on Customary International Humanitarian Law, certain Articles in the Additional Protocols are deemed to be customary international law. The best example is Article 75 of Additional Protocol I, which sets out fundamental guarantees such as the prohibition of torture and due process rights for those persons in the power of a party to the conflict.

2.15 CIHL is formed of widespread and consistent state practice and *opinio juris sive necessitates* (abbreviated to *opinio juris*), or the belief that a certain practice is binding as a matter of law. International Court of Justice (ICJ) case law has held that customary IHL is binding on a state even if it has not ratified a particular treaty, as long as it is not a 'persistent objector' to the customary international law norm in question.[58] There can be no 'persistent objection' to *jus cogens* (peremptory) norms.

---

[55] First Geneva Convention, Art 50; Second Geneva Convention, Art 51; Third Geneva Convention, Art 130; Fourth Geneva Convention, Art 147; Additional Protocol I, Arts 11, 85(3)–(4).

[56] Fourth Geneva Convention, Art 149.

[57] See paras 6.18–6.19.

[58] *Asylum Case (Colombia v Peru)*, ICJ Reports 1950, para 277; and *Fisheries Case (United Kingdom v Norway)*, ICJ Reports 1951, para 131.

However, there are vivid controversies as to the appropriate methodology to select in finding evidence of state practice and *opinio juris*.[59]

In 2005, the ICRC published a wide-ranging study of state practice, military man-   **2.16** uals, and international organization practice from which it deduced 161 Rules of customary IHL.[60] Some states, including the UK, criticized the methodology of the ICRC Study on Customary International Humanitarian Law and expressed reservations as to its findings, arguing that the practice of specially affected states was insufficiently uniform to amount to customary international law; and that the ICRC's inclusion of its own practice represented *lex ferenda*, or what the law ought to be, rather than established state practice.[61] The ICRC Study on Customary International Humanitarian Law lists the practice of armed opposition groups as 'Other practice' in its Volume ii, in recognition that the practice and *opinio juris* which forms customary international law should be that of states, and not non-state actors.[62] This approach to customary IHL contrasts with the IHL treaty law on non-international armed conflicts, which bind state armed forces and non-state armed groups, subject to the requirements in Common Article 3 and Additional Protocol II (where ratified).

Although they are not a formal source of law, the ICRC's Commentaries on the   **2.17** Four Geneva Conventions and their Additional Protocols are considered authoritative interpretations of treaty IHL, and offer useful insights into the drafting history for each of the Four Geneva Conventions and their Additional Protocols. The ICRC is responsible for the promotion of IHL rules both publicly and via confidential outreach activities with states and some armed groups. The ICRC also visits detainees through its network of detention delegates. Common Article 3 specifies the duties of the ICRC in relation to non-international armed conflicts.[63]

Additional treaties regulate the means and methods of warfare in international   **2.18** armed conflicts, including but not limited to the Hague Rules of Aerial Warfare 1923; the Geneva Protocol for the Prohibition of the Use in War of Asphyxiating, Poisonous or Other Gases, and of Bacteriological Methods of Warfare 1925; the Hague Convention for the Protection of Cultural Property in the Event of Armed Conflict 1954, its Regulations, First and Second Protocols (the Second Protocol applies equally to international and non-international armed conflicts); the UN Convention on Prohibitions or Restrictions on the Use of Certain Conventional Weapons which may be Deemed to be Excessively Injurious or to Have

---

[59] Elizabeth Wilmshurst and Susan Breau (eds), *Perspectives on the ICRC Study on Customary International Humanitarian Law* (Cambridge University Press, 2005).

[60] Henckaerts & Doswald-Beck, supra.

[61] Colin Warbrick (ed), 'United Kingdom Materials on International Law' (2005) 76 *British Yearbook of International Law* 683–970 at 694–695.

[62] Henckaerts & Doswald-Beck, supra, p xxxvi.

[63] Four Geneva Conventions, Common Article 3, para 2.

Indiscriminate Effects 1980 (Article 1 of which was amended in December 2001 to extend the Convention's application to non-international armed conflicts), and its Protocols; and the Ottawa Convention on the Prohibition of the Use, Stockpiling, Production and Transfer of Anti-Personnel Mines and on their Destruction 1997. These treaties bolster the principles of distinction and proportionality, the prohibition on indiscriminate attacks, and the duty to take precautions in attack which were defined above. While the Four Geneva Conventions are universally ratified, fewer states have ratified the Additional Protocols, and even fewer have ratified treaties on the means and methods of warfare (see paragraphs 6.18–6.20).

Structure, methodology, and thesis

2.19 Paragraphs 2.01–2.18 have defined and explained IHL for non-specialists, clarifying when terrorist attacks and forcible action in counter-terrorism are and are not covered by IHL. Paragraphs 2.22–2.32 analyse IHL's specific use of the terms 'terrorism'[64] and 'acts or threat of violence the primary purpose of which is to spread terror among the civilian population'[65] to note the differences between this IHL sense of the term and the media, political, or domestic criminal law meanings of the word 'terrorism'. Current controversies in IHL and counter-terrorism are examined critically in paragraphs 2.33–2.67, and paragraphs 2.68–2.116 consider a global range of conflicts which have been labelled 'terrorist' or 'counter-terrorist', to analyse these conflicts against applicable IHL.[66]

2.20 Case studies apply the following methodology. The background for the discussion of these conflicts draws on UN and ICRC sources, with supporting references from state positions, non-governmental organization (NGO) reports, and news reports. The IHL analysis is done afresh, without relying on the conclusions from these sources. The approach is to consider applicable IHL law and analyse reports of violations in terms of that IHL. There is no attempt to address exhaustively every conflict in the world which states have termed 'terrorist' or 'counter-terrorist'. As Chapter 1 demonstrates the lack of an internationally accepted definition of terrorism, the inclusion of a case study here does not amount to a determination that the conflict is or was 'terrorist' or 'counter-terrorist' as a matter of law.

2.21 While IHL treaty law lacks comprehensiveness in its regulation of non-international armed conflicts,[67] all of IHL is obligatory. The political motives of an armed group do not excuse or justify violations of IHL committed by that group. Similarly, citing a motive of 'counter-terrorism' does not erase or mitigate any violations of

---

[64] Fourth Geneva Convention, Art 33; Additional Protocol II, Art 4(2)(d).
[65] Additional Protocol I, Art 51(2); Additional Protocol II, Art 13(2).
[66] See para 2.05.
[67] See para 2.01.

IHL committed by a state. This chapter reveals not only inaccuracies in states' conceptions of IHL,[68] but also global examples of violations of IHL in conflicts fought with a counter-terrorist aim. These violations have been committed by both state armed forces and armed groups and encompass grave breaches of the Four Geneva Conventions.[69] The political motives of an armed group do not excuse or justify violations of IHL committed by that group. Similarly, citing a motive of 'counter-terrorism' does not erase or mitigate any violations of IHL committed by a state. Chapters 4–6 emphasize the need for accountability for IHL violations,[70] victims' right to reparation under international standards,[71] and measures to prevent future violations of IHL in conflicts fought with a counter-terrorist aim.[72] Chapter 7 includes a set of recommendations intended to prevent violations of IHL in counter-terrorism operations.

'Terrorism' in IHL: a particular context and meaning

'Terrorism' and the principle of distinction

The introduction to IHL above is followed by a specific analysis of IHL treaty provisions which prohibit 'terrorism'[73] and 'acts or threat of violence the primary purpose of which is to spread terror among the civilian population'.[74] The analysis below suggests that IHL has a context-dependent, particular meaning of the term 'terrorism', which relates to the principle of distinction between combatants and civilians, and to civilians' immunity from attack.[75] The use of quotation marks around the word 'terrorism' throughout this book simply indicates the IHL-specific meaning of terrorism and not the broader concept in politics, media, or other branches of international law. The use of quotation marks to identify this IHL-specific meaning of terrorism does not imply questioning of the reality of terrorism, or of its severity. **2.22**

IHL contains several provisions which proscribe 'terrorism',[76] '[a]cts or threats of violence the primary purpose of which is to spread terror among the civilian population',[77] or 'acts of terrorism'.[78] A close reading of the treaty provisions which refer to 'terrorism' suggest that IHL's use of the term 'terrorism' is distinct from its **2.23**

---

[68] See paras 2.33–2.37 and 2.46–2.54.
[69] See para 2.13.
[70] See paras 4.25–4.27, 4.35–4.36, and 4.40.
[71] See paras 5.12–5.24 and 5.38–5.53.
[72] See paras 6.18–6.27.
[73] Fourth Geneva Convention, Art 33; Additional Protocol II, Art 4(2)(d).
[74] Additional Protocol I, Art 51(2); Additional Protocol II, Art 13(2).
[75] Additional Protocol I, Arts 48, 51(2); Henckaerts & Doswald-Beck, supra, Rule 1.
[76] Fourth Geneva Convention, Art 33.
[77] Additional Protocol I, Art 51(2); Additional Protocol II, Art 13(2).
[78] Additional Protocol II, Art 4(2)(d).

common usage in politics or the media, and distinct also from the varied definitions of terrorist crimes in the subject-specific conventions on terrorism discussed in Chapter 1. The IHL sense of 'terrorism' is not premised on non-state actors using explosives, hijacking aircraft, or financing groups that do so. As IHL only applies in international armed conflict, belligerent occupation, or non-international armed conflict, it follows that 'terrorism' in the IHL sense is restricted to these situations. Moreover, the analysis below demonstrates a linkage between the IHL sense of 'terrorism' and IHL's principle of distinction between combatants and civilians. 'Terrorism' in IHL may be one shorthand for such a violation, and cannot be committed if combatants are the target of a particular attack. The IHL-specific meaning of 'terrorism' also diverges from the list of offences in US law which relate to engaging in hostilities against the US or its Coalition partners.[79]

'Terrorism' and the duty to respect and ensure IHL

2.24 In the IHL of international armed conflicts, 'terrorism' is not listed explicitly as a grave breach in any of the relevant provisions of the Four Geneva Conventions,[80] so at first sight, it does not trigger an obligation for states to legislate to criminalize 'terrorism' as it is defined in IHL, to search for suspected offenders and bring them to justice in their own courts, or to extradite them for trial if the requesting state makes out a prima facie case.[81] All these obligations would apply to grave breaches of the Four Geneva Conventions or of Additional Protocol I.[82] However, all High Contracting Parties to the Four Geneva Conventions are required to 'respect and ensure respect' for the Conventions 'in all circumstances',[83] any violation can trigger an 'enquiry', and parties must cooperate to end the violation in question.[84] This procedure should apply to 'terrorism' in the IHL sense.

'Terrorism' in the Fourth Geneva Convention

2.25 Article 33 of the Fourth Geneva Convention prohibits '[c]ollective penalties and likewise all measures of intimidation or of terrorism' and appears in the part of the Convention which applies equally to international armed conflict and belligerent occupation. The ICRC Commentary on this Article refers to historic conflicts in which belligerents 'hoped to prevent hostile acts' by imposing collective penalties

---

[79] Military Commissions Act of 2009, HR 2647-386, §948a, 950t, especially (24)–(25).
[80] First Geneva Convention, Art 50; Second Geneva Convention, Art 51; Third Geneva Convention, Art 130; Fourth Geneva Convention, Art 147; Additional Protocol I, Arts 11, 85.
[81] Ibid.
[82] First Geneva Convention, Art 49; Second Geneva Convention, Art 50; Third Geneva Convention, Art 129; Fourth Geneva Convention, Art 146.
[83] Four Geneva Conventions, Common Article 1.
[84] Fourth Geneva Convention, Art 149.

or otherwise terrorizing the civilian population.[85] Such strategies had the opposite effect, 'strengthen[ing] the spirit of resistance'.[86] As collective penalties 'strike at guilty and innocent alike' and 'are opposed to all principles based on humanity and justice',[87] Article 33's prohibition on collective punishment is accompanied by the prohibition of 'all measures of intimidation or terrorism with regard to protected persons, wherever they may be'.[88] Although the ICRC Commentary equates collective punishment, terrorism, and intimidation by their indiscriminate and unjust nature, it does not define 'terrorism'. The victims of collective punishment, intimidation, and terrorism are all the objects of practices and policies which undermine civilian immunity from attack.

'[S]pread[ing] terror'– Additional Protocol I

Additional Protocol I is also applicable to international armed conflicts where the **2.26** belligerent states have ratified it. Article 51(2) prohibits '[a]cts or threat of violence the primary purpose of which is to spread terror among the civilian population', in a paragraph which explicitly recalls civilian population's and individual civilians' immunity from attack. The text shows that both acts and threats of violence are prohibited if their 'primary purpose' is to terrorize a civilian population. This is more explicit than the largely undefined prohibition on 'terrorism' in the Fourth Geneva Convention. The ICRC Commentary on this Article recalls the diplomatic history of Additional Protocol I, and clearly distinguishes between brutality against combatants and the deliberate infliction of 'terror' against civilians.[89] The ICRC Commentary provides evidence that in the IHL applicable to international armed conflict, 'terrorism' does not include attacks on armed forces where the aim is to make soldiers surrender:

> This provision is intended to prohibit acts of violence the primary purpose of which is to spread terror among the civilian population without offering substantial military advantage. It is interesting to note that threats of such acts are also prohibited. This calls to mind some of the proclamations made in the past threatening the annihilation of civilian populations.[90]

The reference to 'substantial military advantage' links the prohibition on 'spread[ing] terror among the civilian population' to the principle of proportionality defined in paragraph 2.12 above, in addition to the emphasis on the principle of distinction identified in paragraph 2.10 above.

---

[85] ICRC Commentary, Fourth Geneva Convention, Art 33.
[86] Ibid.
[87] Ibid.
[88] Ibid.
[89] ICRC Commentary, Additional Protocol I, Art 51(2).
[90] Ibid.

'[A]cts of terrorism' and 'spread[ing] terror' in non-international armed conflicts regulated by Additional Protocol II

2.27   Where Additional Protocol II is ratified, and where a particular conflict satisfies the stringent threshold of applicability contained in Article 1 of Additional Protocol II, Additional Protocol II applies alongside Common Article 3 to regulate conduct in non-international armed conflicts. Article 4(2)(d) of Additional Protocol II prohibits 'acts of terrorism' in non-international armed conflicts. Article 13(2) uses the same language as Article 51(2) of Additional Protocol I.

2.28   The ICRC Commentary to Article 4(2)(d) of Additional Protocol II suggests that the distinction between combatants and civilians does exist implicitly in the IHL of non-international armed conflict, at least at the level of general principles. This supports the general trend in the ICRC Study on Customary International Humanitarian Law and in some ICTY case law that reads principles of IHL relating to international armed conflict into the IHL on non-international armed conflict.[91] There is no explicit 'combatancy privilege' for armed groups in non-international armed conflicts: although fighters may be killed, there is no assumption that they fight lawfully. Attacks by armed groups on armed forces (rather than non-combatants) in non-international armed conflicts are in fact permitted by IHL, although they may be criminal acts under domestic law. Thus the bombing of a barracks or a convoy of tanks by an armed group may be lawful in IHL despite this being called 'terrorism' in the media, by politicians, or in domestic criminal law.

Case studies: 'terrorism' in the IHL sense

2.29   The concepts of 'terrorism' and 'spread[ing] terror among the civilian population' have been raised in the context of the war between Israel and Hezbollah in Lebanon in 2006. Amnesty International suggested that the Israeli Defence Force's (IDF) practice of dropping leaflets to warn civilians of imminent air strikes may have amounted to 'spread[ing] terror among the civilian population' rather than to a precaution taken to avoid civilian casualties.[92] On a first reading, this contention fails to convince, largely because of the absence of evidence of a 'primary purpose' to 'spread terror among the civilian population'. Instead, dropping leaflets could be a precaution to avoid civilian casualties. However, this precaution is meaningful only if the civilians are able to escape the combat zone. Where civilians are concentrated in densely populated areas which are bombarded from the air, and where these civilians cannot escape, the dropping of leaflets may be inadequate in practice to prevent civilian casualties, and therefore does not discharge the obligation to take

---

[91] Henckaerts & Doswald-Beck, supra; *Prosecutor v Tadić*, 2 October 1995, supra.
[92] Amnesty International USA, 'Israel/Lebanon: Israel and Hizbollah Must Spare Civilians: Obligations under International Humanitarian Law of the Parties to the Conflict in Israel and Lebanon', 25 July 2006 (AI Index: MDE 15/070/2006).

precautions to prevent harm to civilians.[93] In addition, while a failure to take precautions to avoid civilian casualties prior to attack is a violation of IHL, it is distinct from 'spread[ing] terror among a civilian population'.

Belligerents' choice of weapons may be evidence of a 'primary purpose' to spread **2.30** terror among a civilian population. The Fact-Finding Mission established by the UN Human Rights Council to investigate violations of IHRL and IHL during Operation Cast Lead, the conflict between Israel and Hamas in the Gaza Strip from 27 December 2008 to 18 January 2009,[94] considered that an IDF strike with fléchette shells on a condolence tent was 'not only an attack intended to kill but also to spread terror among the civilian population, given the nature of the weapon used'.[95] The Fact-Finding Mission also reasoned that the purpose of Hamas rocket and mortar strikes on Israeli communities was to 'spread terror amongst the Israeli civilian population, in violation of international law'.[96] This conclusion was based on the lack of precision in Hamas' weaponry.[97] This balanced conclusion, in which evidence of violations of the prohibition on 'spread[ing] terror among a civilian population' was discussed in relation to both Israel and Hamas, illustrates the position in treaty law that IHL's specific concept of 'terrorism' prohibits violation of the principle of distinction by both armed forces and armed groups.

Summary

The analysis above shows that 'terrorism' in IHL is closely linked to violations of the **2.31** principle of distinction between combatants and civilians. The ICRC Commentary to Article 33 of the Fourth Geneva Convention and Article 51(2) of Additional Protocol I indicates that 'terrorism' was prohibited because it had been carried out by state armies in an inter-state conflict. In non-international armed conflict, 'acts of terrorism' are prohibited whether the acts involved are committed by armed forces or armed groups, as the IHL relating to non-international armed conflicts binds both. Both Additional Protocols prohibit both 'threat[s]' and acts of violence which have the 'primary purpose' of terrorizing a civilian population.

'Terrorism' in IHL therefore includes violence by state actors, and may encompass **2.32** the deliberate targeting of civilians by a state army in a nominally 'counter-terrorist' operation. IHL's specific use of the term 'terrorism' differs from the nebulous idea of terrorism in politics and in media discourse. The IHL meaning of 'terrorism' is

---

[93] Henckaerts & Doswald-Beck, supra, Rules 23–24.
[94] Report of the United Nations Fact-Finding Mission on the Gaza Conflict, UN Doc A/HRC/12/48, 15 September 2009 (Fact-Finding Mission on the Gaza Conflict), endorsed by General Assembly Resolution A/Res/64/10, 5 November 2009 and Human Rights Council Resolution A/HRC/Res/S-12/1, 16 October 2009.
[95] Fact-Finding Mission on the Gaza Conflict, para 880.
[96] Fact-Finding Mission on the Gaza Conflict, para 108.
[97] Ibid.

unrelated to any political ideology. '[T]errorism' or 'spread[ing] terror among a civilian population' is equally prohibited whether the attacks in question are committed by state armed forces in international or non-international armed conflict, or by non-state armed groups in non-international armed conflict.

Current controversies in IHL and counter-terrorism

A 'war on terror' to which IHL did not apply?

2.33 There has been extensive criticism of the Bush administration's use of the privileges of war in conjunction with a denial of the obligations of IHL.[98] A 2001 joint resolution of the House of Representatives and the Senate, the Authorization for the Use of Military Force (AUMF) gives the US President quasi-limitless powers as Commander in Chief to 'use all necessary and appropriate force against those nations, organizations, or persons *he determines* planned, authorized, committed, or aided the terrorist attacks that occurred on September 11, 2001, or harboured such organizations or persons'.[99] There is no reference in the AUMF to IHL, whether the law of international armed conflict or that of non-international armed conflict; and no explicit curb on Presidential discretion from international law. Nor is there any explicit geographical limit: under the AUMF, Presidential discretion to use force extends to 'nations' in the plural.

2.34 Statements by Bush administration officials that IHL did not apply to the 'war on terror' are not only politically important: they may also constitute a violation of the obligation to 'respect and ensure respect' for IHL 'in all circumstances'.[100] Such statements carry a risk that other states will consider international law optional rather than binding, and that violations may increase as a result.[101] One indicative example among many is the Memorandum regarding the President's Power as Commander in Chief to Transfer Captured Terrorists to the Control and Custody of Foreign Nations, 13 March 2002,[102] which states that the provisions in the Four Geneva Conventions on the transfer of terrorism suspects from Afghanistan to

---

[98] For two examples among many, see Marco Sassòli, 'Terrorism and War' (2006) 4 *J of Int'l Crim Justice* 959–981; Mary Ellen O'Connell, 'Crying War', in Thomas J Biersteker, Peter J Spiro, Chandra Lekha Sriram, and Veronica Raffo (eds), *International Law and International Relations: Bridging Theory and Practice* (Routledge, 2007), pp 93–110.

[99] Authorization for the Use of Military Force (AUMF) of 18 September 2001, Public Law 107-40 [SJ RES.23], s 2(a) (emphasis added).

[100] Four Geneva Conventions, Common Article 1.

[101] Emanuela-Chiara Gillard, 'The Complementary Nature of Human Rights Law, International Humanitarian Law and Refugee Law', in *Terrorism and International Law: Challenges and Responses* (International Institute for Humanitarian Law et al, 2002), pp 50–56.

[102] US Department of Justice: Office of Legal Counsel, Memorandum: Re: The President's Power as Commander in Chief to Transfer Captured Terrorists to the Control and Custody of Foreign Nations, 13 March 2002.

Guantánamo Bay and elsewhere do not apply because Al-Qaeda is not a state and because President Bush had determined that Taliban detainees were not prisoners of war. While it is self-evident that Al-Qaeda is not a state, this Memorandum, and the policy which flowed from it are troubling for a number of reasons:

- First, the conflict in Afghanistan was at least initially an international armed conflict, between the US and its allies on one side against the Taliban as the de facto government of Afghanistan (see paragraphs 2.68–2.72 below). This triggers the application of the Four Geneva Conventions in full, including the grave breaches provisions which prohibit the 'unlawful deportation or transfer' of protected persons from the location of the conflict.[103] High Contracting Parties to the Fourth Geneva Convention must criminalize grave breaches and must prosecute or extradite those suspected of perpetrating them. These obligations are unequivocal and cannot be dissolved by a Memorandum.
- Second, the use of Presidential discretion in place of a presumption of prisoner of war status is troubling. Under the Third Geneva Convention, which applies to international armed conflicts, a detainee's status as a prisoner of war is presumed, and he or she receives the guarantees applicable to prisoners of war, unless he or she is found by a 'competent tribunal'[104] not to satisfy the criteria for prisoners of war in Article 4 of the Third Geneva Convention.

Although the Convention against Torture and Other Inhuman or Degrading Treatment or Punishment is discussed (simply to assert that it does not apply extraterritorially),[105] there is no discussion in the Memorandum of whether the conflict in Afghanistan in 2002 was an international or a non-international armed conflict, nor of the geographical scope of the 'war on terror'. IHL obligations are absent, possibly ignored.

In *Hamdan v Rumsfeld*,[106] the US Government had attempted to argue before the **2.35**
Supreme Court that there was a gap between international armed conflicts on the one hand, and non-international armed conflicts on the other, and that the 'global war on terror' fell into that gap, so that it was unregulated and uncontrolled by IHL. The US Supreme Court characterized the 'global war on terror' as (at least) a non-international armed conflict, or a conflict which 'does not involve a clash between nations'. As the US has not ratified Additional Protocol II, Common Article 3 therefore applied to detainees held at Guantánamo Bay, and President Bush's initial military commissions fell short of that standard. For the first time in US constitutional law, the IHL of non-international armed conflicts was used as a source of binding precedent. The judgment is correct in its analysis of Common Article 3's

---

[103] Fourth Geneva Convention, Art 147.
[104] Third Geneva Convention, Art 5.
[105] US Department of Justice, Office of Legal Counsel, Memorandum, 13 March 2002 supra, para 3.
[106] *Hamdan v Rumsfeld*, 126 S Ct 2749, 548 US 557 (2006).

creation of a default category of conflicts 'not of an international [ie inter-state] character'.[107] Paragraphs 3.113–3.116 and 3.121–3.123 of Chapter 3 consider US policy and case law on the detention of terrorism suspects.

Conflating international and non-international armed conflicts

2.36 While the terminology of the 'global war on terror' has reportedly changed under President Obama,[108] there is a continued emphasis on invoking the privileges of war in the context of a 'self-defence' authority to detain terrorism suspects,[109] and in the US' policy of 'targeted killings'.[110] However, the US executive branch now insists on analogizing from the IHL of *international* armed conflict in its counter-terrorism policies, despite fighting non-state armed groups in Afghanistan and Iraq. In a speech to the American Society of International Law (ASIL) Annual Meeting in March 2010, the Legal Adviser to the US State Department Harold Koh relied on the AUMF to ground the Obama Administration's detention policy, although he acknowledged that this should be *'informed by the laws of war'*.[111]

> Those laws of war were designed primarily for traditional armed conflicts among states, not conflicts against a diffuse, difficult-to-identify terrorist enemy, therefore construing what is 'necessary and appropriate' under the AUMF requires some 'translation,' or analogizing principles from the laws of war governing traditional *international* conflicts.[112]

2.37 The difficulty with this analysis is that objectively, the US is engaged in a non-international armed conflict with armed groups in Afghanistan and Iraq (it is not fighting the Afghan state or Iraqi armed forces, so Common Article 2, paragraph 1 of the Four Geneva Conventions is not engaged), and elsewhere, the US is not engaged in an armed conflict at all. In Pakistan's Swat Valley, there was sustained armed violence between militant groups and the Pakistan army in April–June 2009, and the ICRC terms the ongoing situation 'military operations' and 'armed violence',[113] but the US is not involved in an armed conflict in Pakistan. Drone attacks and 'targeted killings' outside armed conflict will be considered below. It is suggested that Harold Koh's invocation of the IHL of international armed conflict is an attempt to enlarge the powers available to the US in its counter-terrorism methods, in effect continuing the impression created by the AUMF of borderless global

---

[107] Ibid.

[108] *Washington Post*, 'Global War on Terror is Given New Name', 25 March 2009.

[109] US Deputy Assistant Attorney-General, Response to Petition on Rehearing en Banc, *Al-Bihani v Obama et al* No 09-5051, 13 May 2010, pp 7–8 (citing *Hamdi v Rumsfeld* plurality to argue that the AUMF gave authority to detain terrorism suspects until the end of hostilities).

[110] Harold Hongju Koh, Legal Adviser, US Department of State, 'The Obama Administration and International Law', ASIL Annual Meeting, 25 March 2010.

[111] Ibid, 1b. Legal Authority to Detain (emphasis in US Department of State transcript).

[112] Ibid.

[113] ICRC, 'Pakistan: Protection of Civilians a Priority as Violence Grows', 23 October 2009.

war against a 'diffuse' enemy. While the norms regulating international and non-international armed conflicts have converged to some extent through case law and the ICRC's articulation of customary IHL,[114] this does not turn a non-international armed conflict into an international armed conflict. In particular, the authority to detain is absent from non-international armed conflict.[115] It is only under the Third Geneva Convention, applicable in international armed conflicts, that prisoners of war may be detained until the close of hostilities[116] and under the Fourth Geneva Convention that protected persons may be subjected to internment or assigned residence, as the most stringent methods of control possible in international armed conflicts[117] and belligerent occupation[118]—'for imperative reasons of security'.[119]

The co-applicability of IHL and IHRL

IHL should not be confused with IHRL, which will be considered in detail in the next chapter. The two branches of law have separate origins, aims, and rules. Although there is a growing consensus that where IHL applies, IHRL will also apply,[120] the idea of co-applicability is contested by some states,[121] and there are few practical guidelines on the interaction between the two branches of law.[122] ICJ case law provides scant guidance for the interoperability of these two branches of international law,[123] leaving detailed recommendations for the co-applicability of these

2.38

---

[114] ICTY, *Prosecutor v Tadić*, supra, 15 July 1999, paras 73, 84; Henckaerts & Doswald-Beck, supra.

[115] Marco Sassòli and Laura M Olson, 'The Relationship between International Humanitarian and Human Rights Law Where it Matters: Admissible Killing and Internment of Fighters in Non-International Armed Conflicts' (2008) 90 *Int'l Rev of the Red Cross* 599–627.

[116] Third Geneva Convention, Art 118.

[117] Fourth Geneva Convention, Art 37.

[118] Fourth Geneva Convention, Art 78.

[119] Ibid.

[120] International Court of Justice (ICJ), *Legality of the Threat or Use of Nuclear Weapons,* Advisory Opinion, ICJ Reports 1996, p 226, para 25; *Legal Consequences of the Construction of a Wall in the Occupied Palestinian Territory*, Advisory Opinion, 9 July 2004, paras 101–106.

[121] Committee against Torture, Concluding Observations on the second report of the United States of America, CAT/C/USA/CO/2, 25 July 2006, para 14; Human Rights Committee, Concluding Observations on the initial report of Israel, CCPR/C/79/Add.93, 18 August 1998, para 10; Concluding Observations on the second periodic report of Israel, CCPR/CO/78/ISR, 21 August 2003, para 11.

[122] Jelena Pejic, 'Procedural Principles and Safeguards for Internment/Administrative Detention in Armed Conflict and Other Situations of Violence' (2005) 87 *Int'l Rev of the Red Cross* 375–391, now adopted by the ICRC in: International Committee of the Red Cross, 'International Humanitarian Law and the Challenges of Contemporary Armed Conflicts', Document prepared by the International Committee of the Red Cross for the 30th International Conference of the Red Cross and Red Crescent, Geneva, Switzerland, 26–30 November 2007, 30IC/07/8.4, Annex I.

[123] ICJ, *Legality of the Threat or Use of Nuclear Weapons*, Advisory Opinion, ICJ Reports 1996; ICJ, *Legal Consequences of the Construction of a Wall in the Occupied Palestinian Territory*, Advisory Opinion, 9 July 2004, ICJ, *Case Concerning Armed Activities on the Territory of the Congo (Congo v Uganda)*, 19 December 2005.

two branches of law to the case law of individual jurisdictions,[124] and to academic debate.[125] In particular, the ICJ *Nuclear Weapons* Advisory Opinion indicated that IHL should apply as *lex specialis* where IHL and IHRL co-apply, but failed to dissect that concept or its practical application.[126] The ICJ Advisory Opinion on the *Construction of a Wall in the Occupied Palestinian Territory* indicated merely that some matters might be regulated by IHL alone, others by IHRL, and still others by both areas of law.[127] The paucity of regulation to protect civilians, and to provide a lawful basis for detention in the IHL of non-international armed conflicts, is one particular area where IHRL might fill a gap in IHL,[128] but without careful and publicized standard-setting, this gap-filling is 'analogizing' only. The development of non-binding guidelines to regulate detention in multi-state military operations has been the subject of an ongoing intergovernmental process sponsored by the Danish Ministry of Foreign Affairs,[129] the results of which are still awaited.

2.39 There are important differences between the two branches of law which make simple co-applicability difficult.

- First, in international armed conflict, the combatancy privilege permits one combatant to kill another. As noted in the definitions section above, the principle of proportionality allows a limited number of civilian casualties, although civilians must never be deliberately targeted. These two points present conflicts with the IHRL on the right to life and its proportionality test, as Chapter 3 will explain.

- Second, in contrast to IHRL, where certain rights can be derogated from, or temporarily suspended, in time of 'war or public emergency threatening the life of the nation',[130] IHL is non-derogable in its entirety: under Common Article 1, 'High Contracting Parties undertake to respect and to ensure respect [for the Geneva Conventions] in all circumstances'. Where there is an international

---

[124] *Public Committee against Torture in Israel et al v Government of Israel et al*, Supreme Court of Israel sitting as the High Court of Justice, HCJ 769/02, 13 December 2006.

[125] Hans-Joachim Heintze, 'On the Relationship between Human Rights Law Protection and International Humanitarian Law' (2004) 86 *Int'l Rev of the Red Cross* 789–814; Noam Lubell, 'Parallel Application of International Humanitarian Law and International Human Rights Law: An Examination of the Debate' (2007) 40(2) *Israel Law Review* 648–660.

[126] ICJ, *Legality of the Threat or Use of Nuclear Weapons,* Advisory Opinion, ICJ Reports 1996; Nancie Prud'Homme, '*Lex Specialis*: Oversimplifying a More Complex and Multifaceted Relationship?' (2007) 40(2) *Israel L Rev* 355–395.

[127] Advisory Opinion, ICJ Reports 1996, para 26; *Legal Consequences of the Construction of a Wall in the Occupied Palestinian Territory*, Advisory Opinion, 9 July 2004, paras 101–106.

[128] Orna Ben-Naftali and Yuval Shany, 'Living in Denial: The Application of Human Rights in the Occupied Territories' (2003–04) 37 *Israel L Rev* 17–118.

[129] Ministry of Foreign Affairs of Denmark, Legal Department, 'The Copenhagen Process on the Handling of Detainees in International Military Operations' 1 Annex, December 2007.

[130] International Covenant on Civil and Political Rights (ICCPR), Art 4; American Convention on Human Rights, Art 27; European Convention for the Protection of Human Rights and Fundamental Freedoms (ECHR), Art 15.

armed conflict, belligerent occupation, or non-international armed conflict, the relevant provisions of IHL apply. States cannot invoke the imperative of countering terrorism to excuse violations of IHL.

- Third, while in international armed conflicts it is permitted to detain prisoners of war, and subject to 'imperative reasons of security' to intern or to assign the residence of protected persons—in both instances, until the end of hostilities,[131] prolonged administrative detention without the right to challenge the lawfulness of detention is prima facie a violation of the right to liberty and security of the person in IHRL.

These differences between the two branches of law must be considered in any **2.40** standard-setting exercise which aims to apply IHL and IHRL together. It is suggested that the co-applicability of IHL and IHRL has greatest relevance to the detention of terrorism suspects in counter-terrorism operations. IHL should be *lex specialis* as regards targeting decisions in counter-terrorism operations which take place in armed conflict, while where there is no armed conflict and IHL does not apply, the IHRL on the right to life and accompanying standards regulates all use of force in counter-terrorism.

Direct participation in hostilities

The problem of civilians who take a direct part in hostilities has considerable rele- **2.41** vance for IHL and counter-terrorism operations. It is suggested that this problem is more acute in non-international armed conflicts than in international armed conflicts, and that is exactly where IHL treaty law falls short. Only Additional Protocol II (Article 13(3)) and not Common Article 3 offer guidance on the lawfulness or otherwise of targeting civilians who take a direct part in hostilities.

Where the IHL of international armed conflicts applies, and where Additional **2.42** Protocol I has been ratified by the states in question, Article 51(3) of Additional Protocol I provides an exception to the general prohibition on targeting civilians so that a civilian who takes a direct part in hostilities may be targeted for the duration of his or her participation: 'Civilians shall enjoy the protection afforded by this Section, unless and for such time as they take a direct part in hostilities.'[132] It should be emphasized that this provision allows for the *targeting* of civilians who take a direct part in hostilities, and is separate from the issue of capturing and prosecuting civilians who take up arms. The ICRC Study on Customary IHL reproduces this provision in Rule 6.[133]

The text of Article 51(3) offers little clarity on (a) the behaviours that may **2.43** constitute direct participation in hostilities and (b) the temporal scope of 'for such

---

[131] Third Geneva Convention, Art 117; Fourth Geneva Convention, Arts 37, 78.
[132] Additional Protocol I, Art 51(3).
[133] Henckaerts & Doswald-Beck, supra, Rule 6.

time as', although the ICRC Commentary to Article 51(3) offers some limited help:

> It seems that the word 'hostilities' covers not only the time that the civilian actually makes use of a weapon, but also for example the time that he is carrying it, as well as situations in which he undertakes hostile acts without using a weapon.[134]

The vagueness of this guidance is a concern: 'hostile acts' are defined as those 'intended to cause actual harm to the personnel and equipment of the armed forces'.[135] There is no detail on how these 'hostile acts' can be perpetrated 'without using a weapon', nor on how a target can be reliably identified (eg from the air if no weapon is visible) while he or she is directly participating in this manner. The civilian regains protection 'once he ceases to participate', although he can be subsequently captured and tried.[136]

2.44 There is no provision equivalent to Article 51(3) of Additional Protocol I or Article 13(3) of Additional Protocol II in non-international armed conflicts regulated by Common Article 3. In an attempt to clarify the uncertainties and apparent gaps in treaty law, the ICRC issued a non-binding *Interpretive Guidance on the Notion of Direct Participation in Hostilities under International Humanitarian Law* (ICRC Interpretive Guidance), extending its analysis to international and non-international armed conflicts.[137] In international armed conflicts, the ICRC Interpretive Guidance reproduces the definition of civilians in Article 50 of Additional Protocol I. In non-international armed conflicts, however, the ICRC Interpretive Guidance suggests a tripartite division between members of armed groups (who can be targeted and killed), civilians who take a direct part in hostilities (who can be targeted and killed for the duration of their direct participation), and civilians who do not take a direct part in hostilities (who must not be targeted or killed). This approach roughly transposes Article 51(3) of Additional Protocol I by analogy to non-international armed conflicts, but the ICRC Interpretive Guidance applies an odd additional condition to membership of armed groups (rather than state armed forces) in non-international armed conflicts: members of armed groups must have a 'continuous combat function'.[138] The ICRC Interpretive Guidance then transposes the criteria for direct participation in hostilities from Article 51(3) into its non-binding statements on non-international armed conflict.

2.45 The ICRC Interpretive Guidance is a controversial document. As Michael Schmitt notes, several of the expert participants requested that their names be deleted from

---

[134] ICRC Commentary, supra, Art 51(3), pp 618–619.
[135] Ibid, p 619.
[136] Ibid.
[137] ICRC, *Interpretive Guidance on the Notion of Direct Participation in Hostilities under International Humanitarian Law*, June 2009.
[138] Ibid, II.

the final document, and eventually all the participants' names were excluded from the publication.[139] Schmitt believes that the document 'skews the balance towards humanity' and away from military necessity:[140] the two values which are in tension in IHL's principle of proportionality. An alternative criticism could be that the Interpretive Guidance purports to create a third category of personnel in conflict: members of armed forces or armed groups (including the novel 'non-State armed force'), civilians who take a direct part in hostilities, and civilians who do not take a direct part in hostilities. However, the ICRC Interpretive Guidance does succeed in increasing the specificity of the ICRC's existing definition of 'hostile acts'. In the non-binding Interpretive Guidance, such acts now require a cumulative three-part test, which is quoted below. The specificity of this test is to be welcomed because it should require precision in intelligence-gathering prior to targeting a civilian who is allegedly directly participating in hostilities:

1. The act must be likely to adversely affect the military operations or military capacity of a party to an armed conflict or, alternatively, to inflict death, injury, or destruction on persons or objects protected against direct attack (threshold of harm), and
2. there must be a direct causal link between the act and the harm likely to result either from that act, or from a coordinated military operation of which that act constitutes an integral part (direct causation), and
3. the act must be specifically designed to directly cause the required threshold of harm in support of a party to the conflict and to the detriment of another (belligerent nexus).[141]

Targeted killings and drone attacks in IHL

Targeted killings and drone attacks by unmanned aerial vehicles (UAVs) have **2.46** occurred both during and outside armed conflicts: in the latter case as isolated strikes to supplement counter-terrorist operations in peacetime. For example, CIA Predator and Reaper drone attacks on individual suspected terrorists and terrorist cells have been carried out by US forces or agents in Yemen,[142] and in the border areas between Afghanistan and Pakistan,[143] where a combination of US military forces and CIA agents (who are not combatants) have carried out targeted killings of suspected terrorists.[144] Human Rights Watch reported failed assassination

---

[139] Michael N Schmitt, 'The Interpretive Guidance on the Notion of Direct Participation in Hostilities: A Critical Analysis' (2010) 1 *Harvard National Security Journal* 5–44 at 6.

[140] Ibid.

[141] ICRC Interpretive Guidance, supra, V.

[142] Jane's Defence Business News, 'Yemen Drone Strike: Just the Start?', 8 November 2002.

[143] Jane Mayer, 'The Predator War: What are the Risks of the CIA's Covert Drone Program?', *The New Yorker*, 26 October 2009.

[144] Mary Ellen O'Connell, 'Unlawful Killing with Combat Drones: A Case Study of Pakistan, 2004–2009', in Simon Bronitt (ed), *Shooting to Kill: The Law Governing Lethal Force in Context* (November 2009 draft available on SSRN); Notre Dame Legal Studies Paper No 09-43.

attempts on Saddam Hussein and 'Chemical Ali' in Iraq in 2003.[145] In 2008, Turkey began cross-border drone attacks into northern Iraq.[146] Drone aircraft were reportedly used by Israel in Gaza during Operation Cast Lead,[147] while targeted killings from ground forces have been a mainstay of the IDF counter-terrorism policy in the West Bank for some years.[148]

2.47　Targeted killings fall to be analysed under IHL when they take place in armed conflict, whereas they are prima facie violations of the right to life in IHRL where they take place outside armed conflict.[149] Where targeted killings take place in armed conflict, there have been repeated instances of many civilians dying in a single targeted strike.[150] US forces have also admitted to intelligence errors in the selection of targets.[151] These instances raise serious concerns relating to the IHL principles of distinction and proportionality, and each such instance should be investigated, with prosecutions or reform of means and methods of warfare following where the targeting or weapons system is inadequate. Chapter 3 argues that targeted killings outside armed conflict should be prohibited as extrajudicial killings: where IHL does not apply, there is no right to kill suspected militants, only to arrest and prosecute.[152]

Is there an armed conflict?

2.48　As a preliminary matter, it is important to clarify whether IHL applies in each example where targeted killings and drone attacks have taken place. If there is no international armed conflict, belligerent occupation, or non-international armed conflict in the case in question, then IHL cannot apply, recalling the arguments in paragraphs 2.02–2.05 above. Where IHL does not apply, the 'targeted killings' or drone attacks must be analysed under the IHRL prohibition on the arbitrary deprivation of life.[153] As the chapter on IHRL will show, the right not to be arbitrarily deprived of one's life is non-derogable, so states cannot extricate themselves from this obligation in time of war or public emergency threatening the life of

---

[145] Human Rights Watch, 'Off Target: The Conduct of the War and Civilian Casualties in Iraq', December 2003.

[146] *The Economist*, 'The Kurds: Turkey Invades Northern Iraq', 28 February 2008.

[147] Human Rights Watch, 'Precisely Wrong: Gaza Civilians Killed by Israeli Drone-Launched Missiles', 30 June 2009.

[148] *Public Committee against Torture in Israel et al v Government of Israel et al* (The Targeted Killings Case), Supreme Court of Israel sitting as the High Court of Justice, HCJ 769/02, 13 December 2006.

[149] See paras 3.40–3.45.

[150] International Security Assistance Force (ISAF) Afghanistan, 'Gardez Investigation Concludes', 4 April 2010; ISAF, 'US Releases Uruzgan Investigation Findings', 28 May 2010.

[151] ISAF Afghanistan, 'Update to Escalation of Force Incident in Khost', 18 April 2010.

[152] See paras 3.29–3.30, 6.32.

[153] Christian Tomuschat, 'Human Rights and International Humanitarian Law' (2010) 21 *European Journal of International Law* 15–23.

the nation.[154] Nor is there a specific limitation on the right to life on the grounds of national security. The non-binding Basic Principles and Guidelines on the Use of Force and Firearms by Law Enforcement Officials should also inform states' counter-terrorism responses.[155]

IHL applied to the international armed conflict in Iraq at the time of the assassination attempts on Saddam Hussein and 'Chemical Ali'. Targeted killings in the non-international armed conflicts in Afghanistan, and between Israel and Hamas are governed by IHL. However, there was no armed conflict in Yemen in 2002, at the time of the US' first drone attack there, which killed a suspect in the October 2000 bombing of the *USS Cole*.[156] That was the first use of force by the US outside Afghanistan since 11 September 2001. It is barely plausible to suggest that this targeted strike be seen as the start of a non-international armed conflict in Yemen, unless we accept the notion of a borderless, global 'war on terror' as defined by the US Congress in the AUMF. The current non-international armed conflict in Yemen between state armed forces and Shia militias began in 2004, and both Common Article 3 and Additional Protocol II apply since then. Before the armed conflict, IHL did not apply. **2.49**

US drone attacks in the border areas between Afghanistan and Pakistan require different analyses. There is an ongoing non-international armed conflict in Afghanistan, so Common Article 3 and customary IHL apply, binding US armed forces. If civilians are killed in Afghanistan as a result of 'targeted killing' attacks by the US military in Afghanistan, there must be an investigation into whether these attacks have violated the customary IHL principles of distinction or proportionality.[157] However, there is an important distinction here: CIA operatives are not members of the US armed forces and do not satisfy the definition of 'combatant' in IHL. When CIA operatives remotely launch drone attacks therefore, they are not combatants, and are not bound by IHL. CIA operatives should be held accountable under domestic criminal law. There is a blurring of the notion of combatancy and a gap in accountability in US practice when CIA operatives carry out quasi-military functions.[158] **2.50**

In 2009, the ICRC noted the 'armed violence' between Pakistan's armed forces and the Taliban in Pakistan.[159] This may have reached the level of a non-international **2.51**

---

[154] See paras 3.17–3.21 and 3.29.

[155] See paras 3.34–3.35.

[156] Jane's Defence Business News, 'Yemen Drone Strike: Just the Start?', 8 November 2002.

[157] Human Rights Council, 14th session, 'Report of the Special Rapporteur on extrajudicial, summary or arbitrary executions, Philip Alston', A/HRC/14/24/Add.6, 28 May 2010; ISAF Afghanistan, 'US Releases Uruzgan Investigation Findings', 28 May 2010.

[158] For a general discussion on CIA operatives and drone attacks, see Mary Ellen O'Connell, 'Unlawful Killing with Combat Drones' (November 2009), supra.

[159] ICRC, 'Pakistan: Protection of Civilians a Priority as Violence Grows', 23 October 2009, supra.

armed conflict in the Swat Valley from April to July 2009,[160] but the US is not involved in any non-international armed conflict in Pakistan. In September 2008, Pakistan objected to the US' use of force from Afghanistan into Pakistan, and threatened to close down supply routes along the border in protest.[161] This suggests that the US is not assisting Pakistan in any such armed conflict. As a result, IHL is not applicable to US 'targeted killings' of terrorism suspects in Pakistan. These killings must be investigated under IHRL only:[162] as potential violations of the right to life and extrajudicial killings.[163]

Current US policy on targeted killings

2.52 At the 2010 meeting of the American Society of International Law, US Department of State Legal Adviser Harold Koh addressed arguments against the lawfulness of remote drone attacks by reiterating the importance of the principles of distinction and proportionality, and by echoing the US' right to self-defence:[164] a principle from *jus ad bellum* rather than *jus in bello*. There was no attempt to differentiate between international and non-international armed conflicts; or between counter-terrorism operations outside armed conflict where IHL does not apply.[165] Harold Koh referred briefly to the ICRC Interpretive Guidance only in relation to detention authority[166] (which was not covered by the ICRC Interpretive Guidance)[167] and not to direct participation in hostilities providing a legal basis for targeted killings.

Targeted killings and the principle of proportionality

2.53 The notion of targeting civilians who take a direct part in hostilities is one dimension of the legal regulation of assassination attacks by drones where IHL applies. Another dimension is the IHL concept of proportionality. The Supreme Court of Israel has reasoned that a combination of proportionality tests in IHL and IHRL should apply to regulate the targeting decisions when the IDF kills terrorism suspects in the West Bank.[168] In the 'Targeted Killings' case, the Supreme Court of

---

[160] Geneva Academy of International Humanitarian Law and Human Rights (ADH) Rule of Law in Armed Conflicts Project (RULAC)—Pakistan.

[161] Sean D Murphy, 'The International Legality of US Military Cross-Border Operations from Afghanistan into Pakistan' (2009) 84 *Int'l Legal Studies* (US Naval War College, forthcoming).

[162] Tomuschat, 'Human Rights and International Humanitarian Law' (2010), supra.

[163] See paras 3.40–3.45.

[164] Harold Hongju Koh, 'The Obama Administration and International Law', supra, B Use of Force.

[165] Ibid.

[166] Ibid, b Legal Authority to Detain.

[167] Michael Schmitt, 'The Interpretive Guidance on the Notion of Direct Participation in Hostilities: A Critical Analysis' at 49, supra.

[168] *Public Committee against Torture in Israel et al v Government of Israel et al*, supra; HPCR Policy Brief 'On Legal Aspects of 'Targeted Killings': Review of the judgement of the Israeli Supreme Court, May 2007.

Israel imposed a number of procedural and substantive hurdles on this IDF policy, quoting proportionality not only in its IHL sense of a balance between the military advantage of an attack and the risk of harm to civilians, but also in its IHRL sense of minimizing harm to human rights, in this case, civilians' right to life.[169] The court's approach should be commended for its emphasis on maximizing the protection of civilians and accountability for a policy which risks civilian casualties. However, as a general principle, it is important not to conflate proportionality in IHL and proportionality in IHRL.

In IHL, the principles of distinction and precaution in attack require armed forces **2.54** and groups not to target civilians and to minimize civilian casualties, but the principle of proportionality requires an explicit balancing of two qualitatively different notions: military advantage and the risk to civilians. Proportionality in IHRL, however, requires that any restriction on a right in service of a competing aim (such as national security) should infringe that right to the minimum extent possible, as Chapter 3 will show. This comparison does not make targeted killings lawful in IHRL: as Chapter 3 demonstrates, they are extrajudicial killings in IHRL, and prima facie violations of the right to life.

Accountability and reform

Where drone attacks which take place in armed conflict have killed a number of **2.55** civilians for each alleged militant targeted,[170] there should be an independent investigation into the targeting decision. If there is evidence that an attack involved the deliberate targeting of civilians, those suspected of involvement should be prosecuted for war crimes. If there is evidence that the principle of proportionality has been breached, the armed force should reform its means and methods of warfare, and improve intelligence-gathering and precautions in attack. If the use of the unmanned drones flying at high altitudes is found to increase the risk of disproportionate civilian casualties, this practice must be urgently reformed.

Chapter 6 and the recommendations in Chapter 7 urge states to prohibit targeted **2.56** killings outside armed conflict, where IHL cannot apply; and to implement IHL in full where combatants are targeted in armed conflicts fought with a counter-terrorist aim. Where there is evidence of violations of IHL in a targeted killing, there must be a prompt, independent, and impartial investigation, with prosecutions following if there is evidence of a violation. Victims of serious violations of IHL have a right to reparation, as Chapter 5 demonstrates.

---

[169] *Public Committee against Torture in Israel et al v Government of Israel et al*, supra.

[170] David Kilcullen and Andrew MacDonald Exum, 'Death from Above, Outrage Down Below', *New York Times*, 17 March 2009, cited in Mary Ellen O'Connell, 'Unlawful Killing with Combat Drones: A Case Study of Pakistan, 2004–2009' (November 2009; draft available on SSRN) supra.

Weapons used in counter-terrorism operations

2.57 Paragraph 2.18 above briefly listed a number of treaties on the means and methods of warfare. These treaties bolster the principles of distinction and proportionality, the prohibition on indiscriminate attacks, and the duty to take precautions in attack. Paragraph 6.20 notes the low rates of ratification of treaties on specific weaponry, particularly the Convention on Cluster Munitions and the Convention on Prohibitions or Restrictions on Certain Conventional Weapons which may be Deemed to be Excessively Injurious or to Have Indiscriminate Effects (CCW Convention) and its Protocols. These Conventions apply in international and non-international armed conflicts. Chapter 6 urges states to ratify these treaties, but even where they have not ratified them, armed forces and armed groups must abide by the customary IHL principles of distinction and proportionality, and must avoid using weapons which cause unnecessary suffering.[171] Rules 70 and 71 of the ICRC Study on Customary IHL prohibit weapons of a nature to cause superfluous injury and unnecessary suffering, and weapons that are by nature indiscriminate.[172] Where Additional Protocol I applies, Article 36 obliges states to ensure that any new weapon, means, or method of warfare does not violate existing IHL.

Cluster munitions

2.58 The US admitted to the use of cluster munitions in Operation Enduring Freedom—the international armed conflict phase in Afghanistan. These weapons leave unexploded bomblets over a wide area, resulting in a lasting risk of civilian casualties both during and long after conflict. Only in the extreme theoretical situation where cluster munitions were to be used on combatants only, with all unexploded ordinance cleared post-conflict, would the use of cluster munitions respect the principle of distinction between combatants and civilians. The US has not yet ratified the Convention on Cluster Munitions, which is now in force as regards its states parties, following the last required ratification in early 2010.[173] According to Human Rights Watch, US armed forces used 10,782 cluster munitions and UK armed forces used 2,170 cluster munitions (both air- and ground-launched) in Iraq, risking indiscriminate attacks on civilians.[174]

Depleted uranium

2.59 In Iraq in 2003, it was reported that US armed forces used depleted uranium.[175] Long-term health effects on the Iraqi population have been documented, and

---

[171] Hague Regulations, supra, Art 23; ICJ, *Nuclear Weapons* Advisory Opinion, supra, paras 77–78.

[172] Henckaerts & Doswald-Beck, supra.

[173] Convention on Cluster Munitions.

[174] Human Rights Watch, 'Off Target: The Conduct of the War and Civilian Casualties in Iraq', December 2003, supra.

[175] Duncan Graham-Rowe (with Rob Edwards), 'Depleted Uranium Casts Shadow over Peace in Iraq', *New Scientist*, 15 April 2003.

alleged to have been caused by depleted uranium,[176] but this is not yet admitted by all parties concerned. Depleted uranium is thought to cause mutations to DNA and to be carcinogenic,[177] but the World Health Organisation (WHO) has not found conclusive evidence of the health risks of depleted uranium.[178] Jason Beckett's analysis of all the applicable evidence suggests two trends in discussions on the health risks of depleted uranium: first, a tendency towards acceptance of anecdotal evidence, and second, the WHO's unquestioning citation of evidence from the RAND Corporation, which 'insist[s] . . . that all results so far are inconclusive'.[179]

Anecdotal evidence from alleged victims, witnesses, or experts in the field should **2.60** trigger further investigation: not a simple denial that that evidence has value. As there is no treaty prohibition yet on the use of depleted uranium, it is necessary to assess the available evidence to see whether depleted uranium causes unnecessary suffering, in violation of Rule 70 of the ICRC Study on Customary IHL. Where civilians are thought to have been harmed by depleted uranium, there should be an investigation into the inherent harms of the weapons used, and into whether the weapons were used in breach of the IHL principles of distinction and proportionality. The deliberate targeting of civilians, or indiscriminate use of depleted uranium in civilian areas, would always violate customary IHL, regardless of the state of the scientific evidence.

Incendiary and thermobaric weapons

The US initially denied, and then admitted, the use of white phosphorus munitions **2.61** in 'shake and bake' operations in Iraq in 2004.[180] NGO sources have collected evidence of white phosphorus use by Israel in Lebanon in 2006[181] and in the Gaza Strip in 2008–09.[182] The latter evidence was corroborated by the Fact-Finding Mission on Operation Cast Lead,[183] and Israel subsequently admitted to targeting errors in white phosphorus attacks which killed civilians.[184] White phosphorus

---

[176] Ibid.

[177] Ibid.

[178] World Health Organisation (WHO), 'Health Effects of Depleted Uranium', A/54/19/Add.1, 26 April 2001, web resource cited in Jason Beckett, 'Interim Legality: A Mistaken Assumption? An Analysis of Depleted Uranium Munitions under Contemporary International Humanitarian Law' (2004) 3 *Chinese Journal of International Law* 43–86, footnote 16.

[179] Jason Beckett, ibid.

[180] International Humanitarian Law Research Initiative, Program on Humanitarian Policy and Conflict Research at Harvard University (HPCR), 'IHL Primer #5—White Phosphorus Munitions'; Agence France Presse, 'US defends use of white phosphorus against Iraq insurgents', 16 November 2005.

[181] Amnesty International USA, 'Israel/Lebanon: Israel and Hizbullah Must Spare Civilians: Obligations under International Humanitarian Law of the Parties to the Conflict in Israel and Lebanon', 15 July 2006, supra, 93.

[182] Human Rights Watch, 'Rain of Fire: Israel's Unlawful Use of White Phosphorus in Gaza', 25 March 2009, III.

[183] Fact-Finding Mission on the Gaza Conflict, supra, para 1721.

[184] The State of Israel, 'Gaza Operation Investigations: An Update', January 2010, para 99.

ignites immediately on contact with oxygen, leaves remnants for months or years after conflict, and burns victims from skin to bone.[185]

2.62   Protocol III to the CCW Convention, which the US has recently ratified,[186] and which Israel has not yet ratified, does not ban white phosphorus outright, unless its use can be deemed to be 'primarily designed to set fire to objects or to cause burn injury to persons'.[187] As Protocol III permits 'munitions which may have incidental incendiary effects, such as illuminants, tracers, smoke or signalling systems', the use of white phosphorus as a smokescreen for troops, or against lawful military targets, is currently permitted by IHL.[188] However, customary IHL prohibits its use against civilians and other non-combatants.[189] The customary IHL principle of distinction between combatants and civilians, and the prohibition on indiscriminate attacks require states not to use indiscriminate weapons in civilian areas.[190] When used in civilian areas, white phosphorus munitions give rise to smouldering fragments, which ignite over a wide area.[191] This characteristic makes it impossible to target combatants with accuracy if white phosphorus is used in a civilian area. In these circumstances, white phosphorus is an indiscriminate weapon.

2.63   Chapter 6 indicates that the lack of an explicit treaty provision on the use of white phosphorus munitions should be reconsidered, and recommends that states parties to Protocol III amend the text at a conference of states parties to include a specific prohibition on the use of white phosphorus.[192] A review of state practice in the ICRC Study on Customary IHL indicates that several states expressed a wish to ban certain incendiary weapons outright when the CCW Convention was being negotiated in 1978.[193] However, these selective *travaux préparatoires* are insufficient to ground the widespread and consistent state practice and *opinio juris* required for the formation of a customary IHL rule prohibiting all incendiary weapons containing phosphorus in all circumstances. It remains prohibited in customary IHL to use white phosphorus munitions in violation of the principles of distinction and proportionality, and the prohibition on indiscriminate attacks. The deep burns caused by white phosphorus munitions add weight to the argument that white phosphorus

---

[185] International Humanitarian Law Research Initiative, Program on Humanitarian Policy and Conflict Research at Harvard University, 'IHL Primer #5—White Phosphorus Munitions', July 2009.

[186] US Department of State, 'US Joins Four Law of War Treaties', 23 January 2009; see para 6.21.

[187] Protocol on Prohibitions or Restrictions on the Use of Incendiary Weapons (CCW Convention, Protocol III), Art 1, para 1.

[188] Inter-American Commission of Human Rights, *Juan Carlos Abella v Argentina*, Report No 55/97, Case 11.137, 18 November 1997, para 187.

[189] Ibid.

[190] Henckaerts & Doswald-Beck, supra, Rules 23–24.

[191] Human Rights Watch, 'Rain of Fire: Israel's Unlawful Use of White Phosphorus in Gaza', 25 March 2009, III.

[192] See para 6.20.

[193] Henckaerts & Doswald-Beck, supra, Vol II, p 1923, para 31 (Iraq), para 33 (Japan—re yellow phosphorus); p 1924, para 37 (Madagascar—re napalm and phosphorus).

munitions should be banned explicitly in treaty law, to implement Rule 70 of the ICRC Study on Customary IHL as regards white phosphorus munitions.

Amnesty International gathered evidence that the thermobaric weapons known as **2.64** vacuum bombs were used in the war between Israel and Hezbollah in 2006.[194] According to Amnesty International researchers, vacuum bombs 'introduce . . . an aerosol cloud of volatile gases in the target area, which is then ignited to create a fireball that sucks air out of the atmosphere and produces lethal effects, such as severe burns and lung collapse, to individuals in the target area'.[195] As noted above, Israel is not a party to Protocol III. If it were, then vacuum bombs might be included in Protocol III's definition of incendiary weapons: 'any weapon or munition which is primarily designed to set fire to objects or to cause burn injury to persons through the action of flame, heat or combination thereof'. Even though Israel is not bound by Protocol III as a matter of treaty law, it remains bound by the principles of distinction and proportionality, and the prohibition on indiscriminate attacks. Any use of these weapons which breaches these principles must be independently investigated, and those suspected of involvement should be prosecuted.

Indiscriminate use of weapons

In the international armed conflict phase in Afghanistan, scholars noted the dis- **2.65** connect between technological progress which permitted the use of so-called 'smart bombs' or Joint Direct Attack Munition (JDAM), which use sensor technology to guide air strikes, and the number of civilians killed.[196] Despite the availability of precision weapons in Iraq, NGOs reported flawed targeting decisions. Human Rights Watch criticized the use of GPS technology prior to launching air strikes, as GPS technology has a margin of error ranging up to 100m away from an intended target. In Human Rights Watch's words, this practice 'turned a precision weapon into a potentially indiscriminate weapon'.[197]

The section on IHL's specific meaning of 'terrorism' above noted the Fact-Finding **2.66** Mission's conclusion that both Israel and Hamas used weapons indiscriminately, 'to spread terror' among the civilian population.[198] Hamas' rockets and mortar shells 'cannot be aimed with sufficient precision . . . at military targets'.[199] These are indiscriminate weapons, used in violation of the principle of distinction when they are specifically directed at civilian areas.

---

[194] Amnesty International USA, 'Israel/Lebanon: Israel and Hizbullah Must Spare Civilians: Obligations under International Humanitarian Law', 15 July 2006, supra, 93.

[195] Ibid.

[196] David D Jividen, '*Jus in bello* in the 21st Century: Reaping the Benefits and Facing the Challenges of Modern Weaponry and Military Strategy' (2004) 7 *Yearbook of International Humanitarian Law* 113–152 at 130.

[197] Human Rights Watch, 'Off Target', supra.

[198] See para 2.30.

[199] Fact-Finding Mission on the Gaza Conflict, supra, para 1747.

Synthesis

2.67 Both armed groups and state armed forces are equally bound by the IHL of non-international armed conflict. As noted in paragraphs 2.03–2.21 above, the aims of a 'terrorist' group and the 'counter-terrorist' aims of a particular operation do not affect the applicability and binding force of IHL. Even where particular treaties on the means and methods of warfare lack specificity or are ratified by few states, the Four Geneva Conventions and, where ratified, Additional Protocol I continue to regulate weapons use in international armed conflicts; and Common Article 3 and, where ratified, Additional Protocol II regulate weapons use in non-international armed conflicts.

Case studies and analysis

Counter-terrorism in international armed conflicts

Afghanistan

2.68 **Classification of the conflict** This case study adopts the following initial premise as to the classification of the conflict in Afghanistan, and then examines counter-arguments to this initial position. There was a non-international armed conflict between the Northern Alliance and the Taliban prior to the bombing by a US-led Coalition which began on 7 October 2001.[200] That non-international armed conflict continued, while an international armed conflict applied from that date between the state armed forces in the US-led Coalition, and the Taliban, as de facto representatives of Afghanistan, until the temporary defeat of the Taliban and the establishment of a transitional government, supported by the US-led Coalition on 19 June 2002.[201] The transitional government was not a party to any conflict. After 19 June 2002, therefore, the conflict in Afghanistan arguably became a non-international armed conflict with all parties bound by Common Article 3 and customary IHL with those states in the NATO International Security Assistance Force (ISAF) which had ratified Additional Protocol II also bound by its provisions.

2.69 This presents a three-part analysis of: (i) a non-international armed conflict; to which was added (ii) an international armed conflict and the applicability of the IHL of belligerent occupation; which was followed by (iii) another non-international armed conflict.[202] There are four main counter-arguments to this three-part analysis:

- First, the classification of the conflict in Afghanistan as an international armed conflict from 7 October 2001 to 19 June 2002 is controversial, as the Taliban had not signed and ratified the Four Geneva Conventions.

---

[200] International Security Assistance Force (ISAF), Timeline (web resource).
[201] Ibid.
[202] US Naval College War Workshop, 'The War in Afghanistan: A Legal Analysis' in Michael N Schmitt (ed), *International Law Studies*, Vol 85 (2009) (US Naval War College Press).

- Second, as the Taliban were recognized only as the de facto representatives of Afghanistan in October 2001, the arguments in favour of applying the IHL of international armed conflict from 7 October 2001 to 19 June 2002 seem to rest on an assumption grounded in popular conceptions of war rather than IHL, namely that when troops of one state are sent abroad to fight, this should be considered an international armed conflict.[203]

- Third, the classification of the conflict from 19 June 2002 onwards as a non-international armed conflict might be said to be problematic as a matter of policy because of Common Article 3's minimalist protection of civilians, and its lack of enforcement power. Violations of Common Article 3 are not grave breaches. Non-international armed conflicts regulated by Common Article 3 alone do not have a list of grave breaches which states are obliged to criminalize through legislation, while searching for and trying, or extraditing, those suspected of being responsible. This contrasts with the grave breaches provisions in the IHL of international armed conflict.

- Fourth, some commentators have suggested that the phase of the conflict from 19 June 2002 onwards was an 'internationalized' armed conflict, because of the involvement of multiple state armies and several non-state armed groups.[204]

However, as the analysis in paragraph 2.08 shows, the term 'internationalized' is **2.70** not known to IHL treaty law.[205] Common Article 3 shows that non-international armed conflicts are a residual category which covers all conflicts other than international armed conflicts governed by the Four Geneva Conventions. This residual category logically includes non-international armed conflicts which cross state boundaries (so-called 'transnational' armed conflicts), non-international armed conflicts within the boundaries of one-state (traditional or intra-state non-international armed conflicts), and non-international armed conflicts where several states' armed forces fight one or more armed groups (so-called 'internationalized' armed conflicts).[206]

Evidence of grave breaches   Studies indicate that civilian casualties in the interna- **2.71** tional armed conflict phase were caused primarily by the air strikes in the US' Operation Enduring Freedom, though estimates of civilian casualties vary from 3,000 to 20,000.[207] These variations can be explained by differences in methodology and whether the statistics counted indirect casualties, from malnutrition, injuries

---

[203] John Cerone, 'Status of Detainees in International Armed Conflict, and their Protection in the Course of Criminal Proceedings', ASIL *Insight*, January 2002, note 1.

[204] Sylvain Vité, 'Typology of Armed Conflicts in International Humanitarian Law: Legal Concepts and Actual Situations' (2009) 91 *Int'l Rev of the Red Cross* 69–94 at 93.

[205] See para 2.08.

[206] Ibid.

[207] IRIN Asia, 'Afghanistan: UNAMA Raps New Report by Rights Watchdog', 22 January 2009; Human Rights Watch, 'Troops in Contact', 8 September 2008.

in battle, or illness left untreated as a result of ongoing hostilities.[208] While high numbers of civilian casualties in and of themselves do not prove violations of the principles of distinction and proportionality, and the prohibition on indiscriminate attacks, they do engage the responsibility of the attacking force to investigate any incident where civilians are killed and injured, and to prosecute those alleged to be responsible where there is evidence that civilians have been targeted. In international armed conflict, the deliberate targeting of civilians is a grave breach which states must criminalize in penal legislation and where offenders must be prosecuted or extradited.[209] Wilful killing is also unequivocally prohibited by Common Article 3, so the same result is prohibited in the non-international armed conflicts which, according to the premise above, coexisted with and then postdated the international armed conflict from 7 October 2001 to 19 June 2002.

2.72 '[T]orture and inhuman treatment' are also grave breaches of the Geneva Conventions, and must be prohibited by penal legislation, investigated, and the suspected perpetrators (or those who ordered the grave breaches in question) prosecuted or extradited.[210] NGOs and former detainees have repeatedly reported torture at the Bagram air base,[211] where the US has held detainees during the international and the non-international armed conflict phases in Afghanistan. Common Article 3 also prohibits 'cruel treatment and torture' of noncombatants: civilians and combatants who are *hors de combat* from any cause, including detention.

Iraq

2.73 **Classification of the conflict** The international armed conflict in Iraq began with air strikes on 20 March 2003. On 28 June 2004, the Coalition Provisional Authority (CPA) handed over authority to the Iraqi Interim Government.[212] The UN Security Council then passed Resolution 1546 announcing the end of the belligerent occupation in Iraq by 30 June 2004, a commitment to hold democratic elections in January 2005, and confirming that the mandate of the US-led Multinational Force (MNF) would be reviewed by the Iraqi Interim Government one year from the date of that Resolution.[213] Between 20 March 2003 and 28 June 2004 therefore, it is

---

[208] Jonathan Steel, 'Forgotten victims', *Guardian*, 20 May 2002; Carl Conetta, 'Operation Enduring Freedom: Why a Higher Rate of Civilian Bombing Casualties?', Project on Defense Alternatives Briefing Report No 13, 18 January 2002.

[209] First Geneva Convention, Art 49; Second Geneva Convention, Art 50; Third Geneva Convention, Art 129; Fourth Geneva Convention, Art 146; Additional Protocol I, Art 85.

[210] First Geneva Convention, Art 49; Second Geneva Convention, Art 50; Third Geneva Convention, Art 129; Fourth Geneva Convention, Art 146; Additional Protocol I, Art 85.

[211] Physicians for Human Rights—Afghanistan; Human Rights Watch op-ed, 'Memory Loss and Torture', 25 May 2010; BBC News, 'Afghans "Abused at Secret Prison" at Bagram Air Base', 15 April 2010; American Civil Liberties Union (ACLU), 'Unredacted Church Report Documents (Previously Classified)', 11 February 2009.

[212] ICRC, 'Iraq Post 28 June 2004: Protecting Persons Deprived of Freedom Remains a Priority', 5 August 2004.

[213] UN Security Council Resolution 1546, 8 June 2004.

submitted that the IHL of international armed conflict applied to regulate the conduct of hostilities between the US-led MNF and Iraqi armed forces, and that the forces which formed part of the MNF/CPA had the obligations of an occupying power where belligerent occupation was factually established. Subsequent to 28 June 2004, the conflict was a non-international armed conflict, albeit one which involved armed forces from a number of states. This position was set out by the ICRC in 2004.[214] Iraq ratified Additional Protocol I on 1 April 2010, so API did not regulate the international armed conflict phase in Iraq from 2003–04.

Evidence of grave breaches   Successive studies published in the *Lancet* in 2004 **2.74** and 2006 estimated that there had been 100,000 excess deaths as a result of the US-led invasion (in a period roughly comparable to the international armed conflict phase), and a total of 655,000 excess deaths as a result of the ongoing conflict in Iraq (including both international and non-international armed conflict phases) from 2003–06.[215] The parties to international and non-international armed conflicts are obliged to 'search for and collect the wounded and sick',[216] and the dead and wounded.[217] Alongside treaty law, customary IHL provides for the principles of distinction and proportionality, and the prohibition on indiscriminate attacks. Where there is evidence of a grave breach, such as 'wilful killing', states must criminalize these offences, and prosecute or extradite those suspected of being responsible.[218] This same obligation applies to the factually established torture and abuse at Abu Ghraib:[219] as torture is a grave breach, prosecution or extradition is obligatory. Chapter 4 briefly notes the court-martial proceedings against those convicted of involvement in abuse at Abu Ghraib.

Counter-terrorism in belligerent occupation

The IHL of belligerent occupation has applied to the actions of multilateral troop **2.75** coalitions which occupied territory in Afghanistan and Iraq, and is relevant to the West Bank and the Gaza Strip, as this section shows. The factual test for the

---

[214] ICRC, 'Iraq Post 28 June 2004: Protecting Persons Deprived Of Freedom Remains A Priority', 5 August 2004.

[215] Les Roberts, Riyadh Lafta, Richard Garfield, Jamal Khudhairi, and Gilbert Burnham, 'Mortality Before and After the Invasion in Iraq: Cluster Sample Survey' (2004) 364 *The Lancet* 1857–1864; Gilbert Burnham, Riyadh Lafta, Shannon Doocy, and Les Roberts, 'Mortality After the 2003 Invasion in Iraq: a Cross-Sectional Cluster Sample Survey' (2006) 368 *The Lancet* 1421–1428; Reuters AlertNet, 'Iraq Death Toll', 12 October 2006.

[216] First Geneva Convention, Art 15; Common Article 3, para 2.

[217] Fourth Geneva Convention, Art 16.

[218] First Geneva Convention, Art 49; Second Geneva Convention, Art 50; Third Geneva Convention, Art 129; Fourth Geneva Convention, Art 146; Additional Protocol I, Art 85.

[219] US Department of Defense, AR 15-6, Investigation of the Abu Ghraib Prison and 205th Military Intelligence Brigade, Executive Summary & Recommendations (2005); ACLU, 'Documents Obtained by ACLU Provide Further Evidence that Abuse of Iraqi Detainees was Systematic', 19 November 2008.

application of the IHL of belligerent occupation is contained in Article 42 of the Hague Regulations; territory is occupied 'when it is actually placed under the authority of the hostile army. The occupation extends only to the territory where such authority has been established and can be exercised'.[220] The prevention of terrorist attacks is not an explicit obligation in the IHL of belligerent occupation, although it might be read into the obligation to 'take all the measures in his power to restore, and ensure, as far as possible, public order and safety, while respecting, unless absolutely prevented, the laws in force in the country' (Article 43, Hague Regulations). Paragraph 2.07 above gives a brief overview of the obligations of an occupying power, which are balanced in some instances by 'imperative reasons of security'.

Afghanistan

2.76 **Current situation—continued detention post-occupation**   Areas of actual control by ISAF troops in Afghanistan have triggered the obligations of an occupying power, but as there is now a non-international armed conflict in Afghanistan to which Common Article 3 and Additional Protocol II (ratified by Afghanistan in December 2009) applies, the authority to intern protected persons or subject them to assigned residence because of 'imperative reasons of security'[221] no longer applies. When it did apply, those interned were entitled to periodic review of detention.[222] Those interned or subjected to assigned residence are required to be released at the end of occupation.[223] Article 77 of the Fourth Geneva Convention requires that detainees suspected or convicted of criminal offences (including terrorism suspects) be handed over to the authorities of the liberated territory at the close of occupation.[224]

2.77 The continued detention, often in secret,[225] of terrorism suspects in Bagram Air Base is a considerable cause for concern. The ICRC observed that there were 600 detainees in Bagram during October 2009.[226] The ICRC insists that during non-international armed conflict, any detainees should be transferred from US custody to the authorities in Afghanistan: 'No person should be deprived of his freedom or interrogated outside an appropriate legal framework'.[227]

---

[220] Hague Regulations, Art 42.
[221] Fourth Geneva Convention, Art 78.
[222] Ibid.
[223] Ibid.
[224] Fourth Geneva Convention, Art 77.
[225] Joint Study on global practice in relation to secret detention in the context of countering terrorism, A/HRC/13/42, 26 January 2010, para 132. (The Joint Study refers to secret detention in Bagram at para 132—I have amended accordingly.)
[226] ICRC, 'Persons Detained by the US in Relation to Armed Conflict and the Fight Against Terrorism—The Role of the ICRC', Operational Update, 26 October 2009.
[227] Ibid.

Iraq

The belligerent occupation in Iraq lasted from the establishment of Multinational **2.78**
Forces' (MNF-I) authority over Iraqi territory in the summer of 2003 only until 28
June 2004, the date on which the Iraqi Interim Government gave its consent to the
continued presence of MNF-I. This is controversial, as consent from the installed
regime did not remove areas of actual control by MNF-I. Nonetheless, the ICRC
explained that from 28 June 2004, the internment or assigned residence of protected persons under the IHL of belligerent occupation ceased to be regulated by
that law. It recommended that individuals detained prior to 28 June 2004 and held
by MNF-I 'should either be released, charged and tried or placed within another
legal framework that regulates their continued internment'.[228] This statement
reflects the lack of regulation of detention in the IHL of non-international armed
conflicts, even though Common Article 3 prohibits certain acts against those
detained. The ICRC continued by noting that prisoners of war and civilian internees sustain the protection of the Third and Fourth Geneva Conventions until they
are released.[229]

Israel: West Bank and Gaza Strip

Israel has always disputed the application of the IHL of belligerent occupation to **2.79**
the West Bank and the Gaza Strip, arguing that it can only apply to territory which
was 'sovereign' prior to the start of the putative occupation.[230] Moreover, since the
completion of its Disengagement from the Gaza Strip on 12 September 2005,
Israel has argued that it no longer has actual control of the Gaza Strip, despite maintaining an effective blockade of airspace, seaports, and land borders, and making
incursions and air strikes against Hamas targets.[231] Israel has therefore reasoned
that the undisclosed list of 'humanitarian provisions' from the Fourth Geneva
Convention which it aimed to apply de facto in both the West Bank and Gaza Strip
prior to Disengagement no longer apply to the Gaza Strip post-Disengagement.[232]
However, the Fourth Geneva Convention applies in full to all cases of 'partial or
total occupation' of a particular territory,[233] so if it is accepted on the basis of
objective factual criteria that Israel has at least 'partial' control of the West Bank and
the Gaza Strip, then Israel should be bound in full to implement the IHL of
belligerent occupation. It is significant that the Fourth Geneva Convention applies
in full to both partial and total occupation: partial occupation does not lead to
partial applicability of the IHL on belligerent occupation.

---

[228] ICRC, 'Iraq Post 28 June 2004: Protecting Persons Deprived of Freedom Remains a Priority',
5 August 2004, supra, 216.
[229] Ibid.
[230] HPCR Policy Brief, 'Occupation, Armed Conflict, and the Legal Aspects of the Relationship
between Israel, the West Bank, and the Gaza Strip: a Resource for Practitioners', September 2008.
[231] Fact-Finding Mission on the Gaza Conflict, supra, paras 276–280.
[232] Ibid.
[233] Fourth Geneva Convention, Art 2.

2.80 There has been little attention paid to the meaning and scope of partial application in the Fourth Geneva Convention, and the ICRC Commentary on this Article offers no specific guidance. However, it is suggested that the control of a circumference of territory, and of the passage of people and goods in and out of a territory, may amount to 'partial . . . occupation', even without the additional controls of airspace, territorial seas, currency, and taxation which Israel exercises over Gaza, and its regular incursions into Gaza prior to the conflict of 27 December 2008 to 18 January 2009. If the argument based on 'circumference' is accepted, the IDF's policies with regard to the passage of persons and goods must abide by the Fourth Geneva Convention's provisions on humanitarian assistance,[234] the guarantees for protected persons,[235] and prohibitions on collective punishment and intimidation.[236] The grave breaches provisions of the Fourth Geneva Convention also apply.

2.81 The Fact-Finding Mission into Operation Cast Lead (27 December 2008 to 18 January 2009) presented a different argument with the same conclusion. It noted that despite Disengagement, Israel had 'declared a virtual blockade and limits to the fishing zone', continued surveillance by unmanned drone aircraft, occasional incursions into the Gaza Strip, the establishment of no-go zones between Gaza and the Israeli border, and currency, tax, and customs controls as evidence of the actual control required for belligerent occupation, regardless of the existence of a local administration controlled by Hamas.[237] The Fact-Finding Mission found, *inter alia*, that Israel had violated provisions of the IHL of belligerent occupation, in addition to the violations by both Israel and Hamas in the context of Operation Cast Lead. In particular, it concluded that Israel had failed to permit the passage of sufficient humanitarian aid.[238] The section below includes more analysis of Operation Cast Lead, in terms of the IHL on the conduct of hostilities.

Counter-terrorism in non-international armed conflict

2.82 As noted in paragraphs 2.01–2.21 above, armed groups are bound by the IHL on non-international armed conflicts regardless of the nature of their political motivation or methods. Similarly, states which conduct a non-international armed conflict in the name of counter-terrorism must also respect IHL. The following case studies underline the need for states to ratify Additional Protocol II, so that counter-terrorist activity in non-international armed conflicts is trammelled by Additional Protocol II's provisions for the protection of civilians, which are scant compared to those in the IHL of international armed conflict, but nonetheless

---

[234] Fourth Geneva Convention, Arts 55, 59, 62.
[235] Fourth Geneva Convention, Art 27.
[236] Fourth Geneva Convention, Art 33.
[237] Fact-Finding Mission on the Gaza Conflict, paras 276–280.
[238] Fact-Finding Mission on the Gaza Conflict, para 1314.

exceed Common Article 3's minimalist protections. The case studies also highlight the need for clear and unequivocal implementation of IHL in Rules of Engagement (ROE), and the requirement that armed forces and any private military and security companies (PMSCs) accompanying them be trained regularly in IHL, with additional training for those with responsibility for targeting decisions. The ICRC conducts confidential outreach with state armed forces and armed groups, and this can supplement but does not remove the obligation on parties to a conflict to respect IHL. These recommendations are developed more fully in paragraphs 6.18–6.27 and Chapter 7.

Afghanistan

In the non-international armed conflict phase in Afghanistan, Common Article 3 **2.83** bound all parties to the non-international armed conflict between the US, ISAF, and Afghan National Army on the one hand against the Taliban and Al-Qaeda on the other. Common Article 3 binds 'each party to the conflict'. There are no preconditions to being bound to apply Common Article 3, such as the wearing of a uniform, or the existence of 'responsible command', as for the application of Additional Protocol II, where that is ratified. Afghanistan acceded to Additional Protocols I and II only in June 2009, so until then, customary IHL and Common Article 3 applied to regulate the non-international armed conflict phase in Afghanistan.[239] Now Additional Protocol II applies to the non-international armed conflict in Afghanistan, but only between the ISAF troop-contributing countries which have ratified Additional Protocol II and the armed groups fighting the ISAF. The US has not ratified Additional Protocol II, and so it is only bound by the provisions of Additional Protocol II which are considered customary IHL. There may be further difficulties in the enforcement of Additional Protocol II, as the historically disaggregated nature of Al-Qaeda worldwide[240] might mean that it fails to attain the 'responsible command' required before an armed group could be bound by Additional Protocol II. The Taliban may satisfy that requirement, especially where it controls population and territory.[241]

In the non-international armed conflict phase in Afghanistan, civilian casualties **2.84** from terrorist attacks tend to outnumber those from US or ISAF air strikes and artillery fire, but civilians continue to be killed and injured in the course of US or ISAF activity where indiscriminate or disproportionate force is alleged to have been used. Moreover, the statistics vary, and the NGO Afghanistan Rights Monitor has been criticized by the UN Assistance Mission in Afghanistan for the disparity between the former organization's statistics on civilian casualties from insurgent

---

[239] ICRC News Release 129/09, 'Afghanistan Accedes to Additional Protocols I and II in Historic Step to Limit Wartime Suffering', 24 June 2009.

[240] Jason Burke, *Al-Qaeda: The True Story of Radical Islam* (Penguin Books, 2004).

[241] Additional Protocol II, Art 1(1).

attacks and those from Coalition or ISAF bombings.[242] The Afghanistan Independent Human Rights Commission points to conflicting information about a terrorist target which resulted in nine civilians killed and five injured in a series of aerial bombings and artillery attacks by ISAF in March 2007.[243] High rates of civilian casualties have prompted changes in the ROE for US and ISAF troops in Afghanistan, which were a response to increased civilian deaths in 2008 and early 2009.[244] In September 2008, NATO forces limited their resort to immediate air strikes when ground troops come under attack, so as to facilitate better planning and more precise targeting, and to secure approval from the command structure.[245] In June 2009, the newly installed Commander of US and NATO-led troops in Afghanistan adapted the ROE to create a duty to withdraw and not to fire on civilians, even if troops were under attack.[246] ROE should always implement IHL's principles of distinction and proportionality clearly and unequivocally. A new 'civilian-friendly' policy should not have been necessary. Chapter 6 calls for the implementation of IHL in ROE and for thorough training in IHL and IHRL for armed forces engaged in counter-terrorist operations, with an obligation for continuing education being a condition for deployment in the armed forces, and additional training for those responsible for targeting decisions.[247]

Colombia

2.85 The ongoing non-international armed conflict in Colombia is marked by documented instances of hostage-taking by the Revolutionary Armed Forces of Colombia (the FARC) and the National Liberation Army (Ejército de Liberación Nacional, ELN), and allegations of rape and sexual violence against civilians.[248] Monitors have alleged other IHL violations, including the targeting of individual civilians by the army and paramilitary groups, including the United Self-Defence Forces of Colombia.[249] In 2008, the head of the army resigned from his post following the killings of many young people near Soacha.[250] In 2008, the Prosecutor of the International Criminal Court (ICC), Luis Moreno Ocampo, wrote to the Ambassador of Colombia in The Hague to note that while an investigation had not begun at the ICC, the issue of paramilitary killings, and political and military

---

[242] IRIN Asia, 'Afghanistan: UNAMA Raps New Report by Rights Watchdog', 22 January 2009; see also Human Rights Watch, 'Troops in Contact', 8 September 2008, supra, 211.

[243] Afghanistan Independent Human Rights Commission, 'Violations of International Humanitarian Law in Afghanistan: Practices of Concern and Example Cases', Example case, Aerial bombardment in Kapisa province on 14 March 2007, p 3.

[244] Reuters AlertNet, 'US General Vows to Curb Afghan Civilian Casualties', 3 June 2009.

[245] Amnesty International Report 2009—Afghanistan, p 55.

[246] BBC News, 'Shift Needed in Afghan Combat', 25 June 2009.

[247] See paras 6.18–6.27.

[248] Human Rights Council, 10th session, Report of the Working Group on Universal Periodic Review, A/HRC/10/82, 9 January 2009, p 9.

[249] Amnesty International Report 2009—Colombia, p 110.

[250] Ibid.

support for paramilitaries in Colombia, was 'under the analysis' of the Office of the Prosecutor (OTP).[251] Subsequent statements by representatives of Colombia suggest a new willingness to engage with the ICC, and an official investigation has not yet been opened. The Report of the Working Group on Universal Periodic Review of the Human Rights Council noted in December 2008 that Colombia had introduced a national action plan on human rights and IHL, with responsibility on the Ministry of Defence to train armed forces personnel and law enforcement officials in the relevant law.[252] The Office for the High Commissioner for Human Rights (OHCHR) had recommended that specific attention be given to the prevalence of sexual violence against women.[253] Several countries recommended to Colombia that children's rights be better respected, including through programmes to reduce the conscription and enlistment of child soldiers.[254]

The conflict in Colombia is a traditional intra-state non-international armed **2.86** conflict. Colombia acceded to Additional Protocol II in 1995, so both Common Article 3 and Additional Protocol II bind government forces, paramilitaries, and armed groups. Common Article 3 is unequivocal in its prohibitions of 'violence to life and person . . . murder, mutilation, cruel treatment and torture',[255] 'the taking of hostages',[256] 'outrages upon personal dignity'[257] when perpetrated against persons taking no active part in the hostilities (both civilians and former combatants who are wounded, sick, detained, or have laid down their arms).[258] Additional Protocol II expands upon these minimalist protections for civilians and former combatants, with attacks on civilians prohibited in Article 4(2)(a), hostage-taking prohibited by Article 4(2)(c), and rape and indecent assault prohibited in Article 4(2)(e). The ICRC Commentary to Article 4(2) of Additional Protocol II clarifies the ICRC's definition of hostage-taking:

> . . . hostages are persons who are in the power of a party to the conflict or its agent, willingly or unwillingly, and who answer with their freedom, their physical integrity or their life for the execution of orders given by those in whose hands they have fallen, or for any hostile acts committed against them.[259]

It follows that the violations documented by the OHCHR, the ICC's initial analysis, and NGOs are unequivocally prohibited by the applicable IHL treaty law.

---

[251] Global Policy Forum, 'The Para-Uribe Regime, the Extraditions and Justice in Colombia', 22 August 2008.

[252] Human Rights Council, 10th session, Report of the Working Group on Universal Periodic Review, A/HRC/10/82, 9 January 2009, p 9, supra.

[253] Ibid.

[254] Ibid.

[255] Common Article 3, para 1(a).

[256] Common Article 3, para 1(b).

[257] Common Article 3, para 1(c).

[258] Common Article 3, para 1.

[259] ICRC Commentary to Article 4(2) APII, p 1375, para 4537.

Customary IHL also applies, and all parties to the conflict are bound to respect its provisions, independently investigating apparent violations.

Iraq

2.87 The conflict in Iraq, from its international armed conflict phase, which began in 2003, through to the current non-international armed conflict, is thought to have cost approximately 100,000 civilian lives.[260] There may be more: a sample study published in *The Lancet* in 2006 projected 655,000 excess deaths, without a clear differentiation between combatants and civilians.[261] These approximate data indicate the need for thorough investigations into armed forces and armed groups' compliance with IHL in each instance where civilians have been killed. These investigations should address potential breaches of the principles of distinction and proportionality and any apparently indiscriminate attacks, and should also address the types of weapons used to see if they had failed to discriminate between combatants and civilians. The documented instances of torture by US forces in Abu Ghraib,[262] and the reports of civilians targeted and killed by PMSCs, [263] mean that clear, IHL-compliant Rules of Engagement and ongoing training of armed forces and PMSC staff in IHL and IHRL are essential.[264]

2.88 It is submitted that there has been a non-international armed conflict in Iraq since the defeat of Saddam Hussein in 2003. Since that time, multiple armed forces fighting in a US-led Coalition and then a Multi-National Force, subsequently joined by the Iraqi armed forces, have been fighting numerous militant groups at various levels of organization. Although many states are involved, fighting many armed groups, making the conflict arguably 'internationalized', this term has no effect on the applicable treaty law.[265] Although some members of the US-led Coalition, and subsequently Multi-National Force, have ratified both Additional Protocols to the Four Geneva Conventions, the US has not ratified either Additional Protocol, so cannot be bound by Additional Protocol II. Iraq has not ratified Additional

---

[260] Iraq Body Count (web resource); David Brown, 'Study Claims Iraq's "Excess" Death Toll Has Reached 655,000', *Washington Post*, 11 October 2006.

[261] Les Roberts et al, 'Mortality Before and After the 2003 Invasion in Iraq: Cluster Sample Survey' (2004) 364 *The Lancet* 1857–1864; Gilbert Burnham et al, 'Mortality After the 2003 Invasion in Iraq: a Cross-Sectional Cluster Sample Survey' (2006) 368 *The Lancet* 1421–1428.

[262] Jim Garamone, US Department of Defense, 'Report Faults Intelligence Soldiers at Abu Ghraib', 25 August 2004.

[263] Arthur Bright, 'US Soldiers: Blackwater Attacked Fleeing Iraqi Civilians', *Christian Science Monitor*, 12 October 2007; UN Assistance Mission for Iraq (UNAMI), 'Human Rights Report: 1 April–30 June 2007', para 27.

[264] See paras 6.23–6.24.

[265] James Stewart, 'Towards a Single Definition of Armed Conflict in International Humanitarian Law: A Critique of Internationalized Armed Conflict' (2003) 85 *Int'l Rev of the Red Cross* 313–350; Emily Crawford, 'Unequal Before the Law: The Case for the Elimination of the Distinction Between International and Non-international Armed Conflict (2007) 20 *Leiden J of Int'l L* 441–465.

Protocol II, so as the test in Article 1(1) of Additional Protocol II is based on the territory of a state party to Additional Protocol II ('in the territory of a High Contracting Party between its armed forces and dissident armed forces or other organised armed groups . . . '),[266] it cannot apply *de jure*. The ICRC has commented on the inadequacies of applying to Iraq the rudimentary rules of Common Article 3 applicable to non-international armed conflicts, underlining the paucity of protection for civilians which is expressed in IHL treaty law on non-international armed conflicts.[267] Some commentators recommend a reliance on the IHL of belligerent occupation, to provide additional protections for the civilian population in areas controlled by the Multi-National Force in Iraq (MNF-I).[268] However, numerous sectarian armed groups including the Mahdi Army and the Al-Qaeda Organisation in the Land of the Two Rivers (Al-Qaeda in Iraq) can only be bound by the IHL on non-international armed conflict,[269] as armed groups cannot be occupying powers.

The IHL on belligerent occupation can apply alongside a non-international armed conflict, so that armed forces fighting armed groups are fully bound by the IHL relating to non-international armed conflict, and the troops of an occupying power continue to be bound by the Fourth Geneva Convention. In addition, customary IHL binds all parties, so that armed groups and armed forces must implement IHL's principles of distinction, proportionality, and precaution in attack.[270] These require combatants to distinguish between other combatants and civilians, targeting only combatants; to balance military necessity against the risk of civilian harm before each attack; and to take precautions against civilian casualties which outweigh the military necessity anticipated from the attack. **2.89**

Israel–Hamas

From 27 December 2008 to 18 January 2009, in Operation Cast Lead, the Israeli Defence Force (IDF) launched air strikes and a ground invasion of the Gaza Strip with the stated intention of disabling Hamas' armed capacity to launch rockets and mortar strikes on southern Israel. In the hostilities that followed, 13 Israelis, including three civilians, were killed;[271] while the estimates of Palestinians killed range from 1,166 (Israel's estimate) to 1,444 (Hamas' estimate).[272] These figures are in the aggregate: there is no clear indication from the numbers how many of those killed were civilians and how many were Hamas fighters. The Fact-Finding Mission **2.90**

---

[266] Additional Protocol II, Art 1(1).

[267] Knut Dörmann and Laurent Colassis, 'International Humanitarian Law in the Iraq Conflict' (2004) 47 *German Yearbook of International Law* 293–342.

[268] Ibid.

[269] Geneva Academy of International Humanitarian Law and Human Rights (ADH) Rule of Law in Armed Conflicts Project (RULAC)—Iraq.

[270] Henckaerts & Doswald-Beck, supra, Rules 1, 14, 15.

[271] Fact-Finding Mission on the Gaza Conflict, supra, para 31.

[272] Ibid, para 30.

established by the President of the Human Rights Council to investigate Operation Cast Lead noted that NGO findings were 'generally consistent' on the proportion of civilians who were killed in Gaza and that this 'raise[d] very serious concerns' as to Israel's compliance with IHL.[273] As noted in paragraphs 2.30 and 2.81 above, the Fact-Finding Mission found evidence that both Israel and Hamas had committed violations of IHL, including of IHL's specific prohibition on 'terrorism' and 'acts and threat of violence the primary purpose of which was to spread terror among a civilian population'.[274] Independent investigations into the concerns raised by the Fact-Finding Mission report are now long overdue. The weapons used by both Israel and Hamas,[275] and the application of the IHL of belligerent occupation were considered above.[276] This section addresses the appropriate IHL on the conduct of hostilities: whether Operation Cast Lead should be considered an international or a non-international armed conflict.

2.91 The Fact-Finding Mission considered that the IHL of international armed conflicts applied to the hostilities between Israel and Hamas. Reasoning first from the customary international law right of self-determination of peoples, which is enshrined in Article 1 of the UN Charter, and in IHRL,[277] and second from Israel's continued control over the Gaza Strip's borders, airspace, and seaports, the Fact-Finding Mission argues in detail for the full applicability of the IHL of belligerent occupation.[278] The Fact-Finding Mission's report then presented arguments for the increasing convergence in case-law and customary IHL of the IHL relating to international armed conflict and the IHL relating to non-international armed conflict.[279] The Fact-Finding Mission notes that '[i]t is common for armed conflicts to present elements of an international as well as of a non-international character'.[280] After noting the increasing convergence of IHL and IHRL and standards, the Fact-Finding Mission invoked Article 1(4) of Additional Protocol I to ground its argument that the IHL of international armed conflicts should apply to Operation Cast Lead.[281]

2.92 This final argument is the most contentious, and the hardest to apply in practice. It is possible that any conflict between Israel and armed groups within the West Bank and Gaza would reach the threshold of Article 1(4) of Additional Protocol I, with 'peoples . . . fighting against . . . alien occupation'. The Fact-Finding Mission on

---

[273] Ibid.
[274] See para 2.30.
[275] See para 2.30 and 2.61.
[276] See para 2.79–2.81.
[277] Fact-Finding Mission on the Gaza Conflict, supra, para 269.
[278] Ibid, paras 270–280.
[279] Ibid, paras 281–283.
[280] Ibid, para 283.
[281] Ibid, para 308.

Operation Cast Lead accepted this argument,[282] with some nuance.[283] This would make an otherwise non-international armed conflict into an international armed conflict if Additional Protocol I applied. However, Israel has not ratified Additional Protocol I, meaning that it cannot apply to the conflict as a matter of treaty law. The question remains whether Article 1(4) of Additional Protocol I constitutes customary international law. Even though the principle of self-determination in Article 1(4) finds echoes in the UN Charter and in the International Covenant on Civil and Political Rights (ICCPR), proving that the self-determination concept has relevance beyond Additional Protocol I, it is doubtful whether the content and effect of Article 1(4) of Additional Protocol I has a sufficient basis of state practice and *opinio juris* to be customary IHL, binding states which have not ratified Additional Protocol I.

The Fact-Finding Mission's point about the increasing convergence between the **2.93** IHL of international armed conflicts and the IHL of non-international armed conflicts is well-grounded in case law and in customary IHL, as is its argument that the Fourth Geneva Convention continues to apply as a result of Israel's continued control of Gaza's airspace, seaports, and borders (see paragraphs 2.79–2.81 above). However, these points do not fully address the counter-argument that the conflict between Israel and Hamas was between a state armed force and a non-state armed group: ie a non-international and not an international conflict. Hamas cannot be a High Contracting Party to the Four Geneva Conventions, so the threshold of Common Article 2, paragraph 1 has not been met. Although non-state armed groups can enter into 'special agreements' to be bound by IHL,[284] this does not make non-state armed groups into state armed forces which can be bound by the IHL of international armed conflict. Moreover, although the Fourth Geneva Convention may still apply to Gaza post-disengagement on account of Israel's 'partial . . . occupation' of borders, airspace, and seaports, this argument does not remove the possibility that a non-international armed conflict which crossed Israel's boundaries into the Gaza Strip could coexist with a situation of belligerent occupation. The question of the application of the IHL of belligerent occupation is distinct from that of the application of the IHL on the conduct of hostilities.

It may be argued that Operation Cast Lead was regulated by Common Article 3 of **2.94** the Four Geneva Conventions 1949, the Fourth Geneva Convention (by virtue of continued 'partial' occupation—see paragraphs 2.75–2.81 above), and customary IHL, which does transpose many of the protections for civilians found in the IHL of international armed conflicts. Israel has not ratified Additional Protocol II, and as noted above, nor has it ratified Additional Protocol I, so Article 4(1) cannot apply as a matter of treaty law. As noted in paragraphs 2.01–2.21 above, armed

---

[282] Ibid, para 283.
[283] Ibid, para 281–283.
[284] Common Article 3; Additional Protocol I, Art 96(3).

groups, including Hamas, and armed forces, including the IDF, are fully bound by the IHL on non-international armed conflicts. The political aims of armed groups or a 'counter-terrorist' aim for a conflict make no difference to the binding force of IHL. Where evidence suggests violations of IHL by either party to the conflict, there must be independent investigations.

Israel–Hezbollah

2.95 The war in Lebanon between Israel and Hezbollah in July and August 2006 lies at the boundary between international and non-international armed conflict. The hostilities would have been an international armed conflict if the activities of Hezbollah could have been attributed to Lebanon, under the *Tadić* test discussed above,[285] if Hezbollah were integral to the armed forces of Lebanon or if Lebanon as a state had directed Hezbollah's actions. As Hezbollah was a minority party in the Lebanese coalition government at the time of the war, attribution was possible in theory. However, in practice, the Lebanese government disavowed Hezbollah's rocket attacks on Israeli border towns.[286] As a result, it is suggested that the attribution is insufficient for the conflict to be considered an international armed conflict, and that therefore the IHL on non-international armed conflicts applied.[287]

2.96 As Israel is not a party to Additional Protocol II, only Common Article 3 and customary IHL applied to regulate the conflict between Israel and Hezbollah. Nonetheless, Common Article 3's articulation of civilians' immunity from attack is unequivocal, and customary IHL articulates the principle of distinction between combatants and civilians,[288] the principle of proportionality,[289] and the duty to take precautions in attack,[290] including in the means and methods of warfare.[291] According to detailed field research by Amnesty International, Hezbollah is thought to have deliberately targeted civilians in indiscriminate attacks using Katyusha rockets, and Israel is reported to have employed indiscriminate means and methods of warfare, as a means of targeting Hezbollah fighters who were embedded in civilian areas.[292] Pursuant to the principle of distinction and the customary IHL

---

[285] *Prosecutor v Tadić*, supra.

[286] Greg Myer, 'More Airstrikes as Hezbollah Rockets Hit Deeper', *New York Times*, 15 July 2006.

[287] For varied views on the applicable bodies of IHL, see: Human Rights Watch, 'Civilians Under Assault: Hezbollah's Rocket Attacks on Israel in the 2006 War: Legal Standards Applicable to the Conflict', 28 August 2007; Amnesty International USA, 'Israel/Lebanon: Israel and Hizbollah Must Spare Civilians: Obligations under International Humanitarian Law', 25 July 2006, supra; Jonathan Somer, 'Acts of Non-State Armed Groups and the Law Governing Armed Conflict', *ASIL Insight*, Volume 10, Issue 21, 24 August 2006.

[288] Henckaerts & Doswald-Beck, supra, Rule 1.

[289] Ibid, Rule 14.

[290] Ibid, Rule 15.

[291] Ibid, Rule 17.

[292] Amnesty International USA, 'Israel/Lebanon: Israel and Hizbullah Must Spare Civilians: Obligations under International Humanitarian Law', 25 July 2006, supra, 95.

obligation to take precautions in attack, armed groups should differentiate them-selves from the civilian population.[293]

Philippines

The non-international armed conflict in the Philippines principally involves the **2.97** southern island of Mindanao, and includes armed groups fighting for autonomy for the Philippines' Muslim minority (the Moro Islamic Liberation Front or MILF, and the Moro National Liberation Front or MNLF); a group with a pan-Asian Islamist ideology (Abu Sayyaf); and a Maoist group (the New People's Army) which represents the Communist Party of the Philippines.[294] The conflict first flared in the 1960s, and is estimated to have killed 160,000 people and displaced 2 million.[295] The Philippines is a state party to Additional Protocol II, and the armed groups involved satisfy Additional Protocol II's criteria to be bound by its provisions,[296] so the conflict is regulated by both Common Article 3 and Additional Protocol II, with provisions binding both state armed forces and each of the several armed groups.

Abu Sayyaf is alleged to have links to Indonesian jihadist groups, and to have been **2.98** involved in the 2002 Bali bombing.[297] In March 2004, members of Abu Sayyaf were arrested on suspicion of having plotted to bomb the US Embassy in the Philippines.[298] Abu Sayyaf members are also implicated in the hostage-taking of three ICRC delegates in January 2009, all of whom were free by 12 July 2009.[299]

Amnesty International reported 100 civilian deaths in the Mindanao conflict **2.99** in 2008, and raised the issue that these deaths may have resulted from deliberate targeting or indiscriminate attacks by the MILF.[300] There were also reports of hostage-taking by the MILF, and the use of child soldiers.[301] Where the child sol-diers are under 15 years of age, this is prohibited by Article 4(3) of Additional Protocol II, which the Philippines has ratified, and a war crime under Article 8 of the Rome Statute of the International Criminal Court, which the Philippines has signed but not ratified.[302] Hostage-taking and the targeting of civilians in bomb attacks are prohibited absolutely by IHL. Hostage-taking is prohibited by Common Article 3(1)(b) and Article 4(2)(c) of Additional Protocol II, while Article 13 of

---

[293] Henckaerts & Doswald-Beck, supra, Rule 23.
[294] Geneva Academy of International Humanitarian Law and Human Rights (ADH) Rule of Law in Armed Conflicts Project (RULAC), Philippines–Profile.
[295] Reuters AlertNet, Philippines-Mindanao Conflict.
[296] See para 2.08.
[297] Reuters AlertNet, supra.
[298] Reuters AlertNet, supra.
[299] ICRC, 'Switzerland: Freed ICRC Staff Member Eugenio Vagni Arrives in Geneva', 16 July 2009.
[300] Amnesty International Report 2009, Philippines, p 262.
[301] Ibid.
[302] ICRC, International Humanitarian Law, Treaties and Documents by Country, Philippines.

Additional Protocol II articulates civilians' immunity from attack. An attack on parishioners at a Roman Catholic Church in the Philippines in July 2009[303] is a clear violation of Article 13 by the armed group responsible. Government attacks which target civilians are prohibited as absolutely as attacks by armed groups which target civilians. Articles 4 and 13 of Additional Protocol II also prohibit torture and acts or threats of violence to civilians in the course of counter-terrorism policies.

Russian Federation: Chechnya

2.100   There has been a non-international armed conflict in Chechnya, following a declaration of independence in 1991, the first Chechen War of 1994–96, and a second conflict from the summer of 1999. The conflict is non-international because Chechnya's declaration of independence in 1991 was followed by an agreement on autonomy at the end of the first Chechen War, and a Constitution in 2003 which explicitly locates Chechnya within the Russian Federation.[304] The Russian Federation announced an end to its Counter-Terrorism Operation in Chechnya in April 2009,[305] but human rights groups continue to observe enforced disappearances, suicide bombings, and civilian casualties.[306] According to academic analysts, there are no current armed conflicts in Ingushetia and Dagestan, although isolated and sporadic violence continues.[307]

2.101   Insurgents fighting in Chechnya against the pro-federal government led by Ramzan Kadryov are reported to have burned houses and killed law enforcement officials, politicians, and members of their families.[308] Administration and security officials have subjected both insurgents and civilians to enforced disappearances, torture, and unlawful killings, all of which have been the subject of judgments against Russia by the European Court of Human Rights.[309] The Russian Federation's failure to implement these judgments will be considered in depth in the next chapter on IHRL.[310]

2.102   Although the Russian Federation has ratified Additional Protocol II, the violence in Ingushetia and Dagestan does not reach the minimal threshold of intensity for

---

[303] BBC News, 'Bomb Hits Philippine Church-goers', 5 July 2009.

[304] Constitution of the Russian Federation, Art 65.

[305] Michael Schwirtz, 'Russia Ends Operations in Chechnya', *New York Times*, 16 April 2009.

[306] Amnesty International Report 2010, Russian Federation.

[307] Geneva Academy of International Humanitarian Law and Human Rights (ADH) Rule of Law in Armed Conflicts Project (RULAC), Russia—current conflicts.

[308] Human Rights Watch, 'What Your Children Do Will Touch Upon You', Background—Unlawful Tactics Used by Insurgents in Chechnya, 2 July 2009.

[309] European Court of Human Rights, *Isayeva, Yusupova & Bazayeva v Russia*, 24 February 2005; *Khashiyev and Akayeva v Russia*, Application nos 57942/00 and 57945/00; *Bazorkina v Russia* (2006) 46 EHRR 15; *Musayeva v Russia* (2008) 47 EHRR 25; *Ibragimov v Russia*, Application No 34561/03, 29 May 2008.

[310] Human Rights Watch, 'Russia: Complying with European Court Key to Halting Abuse', 27 September 2009; see paras 3.94–3.95.

Additional Protocol II to apply. Some commentators believe that the violence in Chechnya is similarly lacking in intensity such that Additional Protocol II does not apply, while Common Article 3 and customary IHL do still apply.[311]

Common Article 3 expressly prohibits 'violence to life and person, in particular **2.103** murder . . . cruel treatment and torture' and 'outrages upon personal dignity, in particular humiliating and degrading treatment', whether these be perpetrated against civilians or sick, wounded, or detained combatants. Common Article 3 also prohibits the 'taking of hostages'. Common Article 3 also prohibits, in the context of requiring humane treatment, 'any adverse distinction founded on race, colour, religion or faith, sex, birth or wealth, or any other similar criteria'.[312]

Common Article 3 lacks grave breaches provisions, so there is no explicit IHL treaty **2.104** obligation on states parties to enact penal legislation to prohibit violations of Common Article 3, and to prosecute or extradite suspected offenders. Nonetheless, violations of Common Article 3 have been incorporated into the list of war crimes under the jurisdiction of the International Court in Article 8(2)(c) of the Rome Statute of the International Criminal Court (Rome Statute). The Russian Federation has signed but not ratified the Rome Statute.

Somalia

Common Article 3 also applies, alongside customary IHL, to regulate the non- **2.105** international armed conflict in Somalia, where non-state armed groups including the Islamist Al-Shabaab militia are fighting government forces and Ethiopian troops present in Somalia. Somalia has not ratified Additional Protocol II.[313] The activity of pirates from Somalia in the Gulf of Aden is not related to an armed conflict, and IHL therefore does not apply to efforts to counter piracy.

The involvement of Ethiopian troops in the non-international armed conflict in **2.106** Somalia means that it may be a non-international armed conflict which has become international, or an international armed conflict in addition to a non-international armed conflict, following the Appeals Chamber judgment in the *Tadić* case, because '(i) another State [has] intervene[d] in that conflict through its troops'.[314] However, it is suggested that as the Ethiopian forces are not engaged in an inter-state international armed conflict with putative state armed forces of Somalia, then the conflict remains non-international in character. The fact that Somalia has not had a fully functioning state apparatus since 1991, despite the installation of a Transitional National Government in 2000 and the overthrow of the Islamic Courts system

---

[311] Geneva Academy of International Humanitarian Law and Human Rights (ADH) Rule of Law in Armed Conflicts Project (RULAC) Russia.

[312] Four Geneva Conventions, Common Article 3.

[313] ICRC, International Humanitarian Law Treaty Database, Somalia (web resource last checked 16 June 2010).

[314] *Prosecutor v Tadić*, Appeals Chamber, 15 July 1999, supra, para 84.

established in 2006, may add weight to the contention that the conflict in Somalia remains non-international regardless of the analysis in *Tadić*.[315]

2.107 Hostage-taking and wilful killings violate Common Article 3, regardless of whether state armed forces or non-state armed groups are thought to be responsible. According to NGO and IGO reports,[316] these violations have been perpetrated by Al-Shabaab and Hisb-ul-Islam militia groups, forces allied to the Transitional Federal Government (TFG) and Ethiopian forces. The UN High Commissioner for Human Rights considered that war crimes may have been committed.[317] As noted in paragraphs 2.01–2.21 above, the IHL of non-international armed conflicts binds both armed forces and non-state armed groups. Therefore, allegations of IHL violations by the Al-Shabaab militia, by Hisb-ul-Islam and by the TFG and Ethiopian armed forces must all be investigated.

Sri Lanka

2.108 Sri Lanka is not a party to Additional Protocol II,[318] so only Common Article 3 and customary IHL apply to the non-international armed conflict between government armed forces and the Liberation Tigers of Tamil Eelam (LTTE) which lasted well over two decades until mid-2009. A ceasefire from 2002 was formally revoked in January 2008.[319] The Sri Lankan Geneva Conventions Act 2006 provides for the prosecution of war crimes committed inside or outside Sri Lanka. Chapter 3 considers the complex web of emergency regulations, administrative detention under the Prevention of Terrorism Act, and the widespread harassment of human rights defenders and terrorism suspects' defence lawyers.[320]

2.109 During an intensification of the conflict in 2008–09, the ICRC reported that 250,000 displaced civilians were trapped inside an area measuring 250 square kilometres in the north-east of Sri Lanka, unable to escape the fighting.[321] Many thousands were displaced, and humanitarian access greatly reduced. Although the government declared a 'no-fire zone', the ICRC reported many thousands of civilian deaths and injuries from mortar and rocket fire.[322] The ICRC repeatedly

---

[315] Ibid.

[316] Statement by UN High Commissioner for Human Rights, 10 July 2009; Amnesty International Report 2009: Somalia.

[317] UN News, 'Reports from Somalia Suggest Possible War Crimes, Says UN Human Rights Chief', 10 July 2009.

[318] ICRC, International Humanitarian Law Treaty Database, Sri Lanka (web resource—last checked 16 June 2010).

[319] Human Rights Watch World Report 2009, Sri Lanka.

[320] IBA Human Rights Institute, *Justice in Retreat: A Report on the Independence of the Legal Profession and the Rule of Law in Sri Lanka* (May 2009); IBA News release, 'IBAHRI Recommends Protections for a Justice System, Legal Profession and Media in Peril', 26 May 2009; Eminent Jurists Panel of the International Commission of Jurists, 'Eminent Jurists Assess Counter-terrorism Laws in South Asia', 2 March 2007.

[321] ICRC, 'Sri Lanka: Situation of Civilians Nothing Short of Catastrophic', 21 April 2009.

[322] Ibid.

emphasized the obligations in Common Article 3 to treat captured combatants humanely, and to ensure that civilians and other persons who are *hors de combat* are not targeted.[323]

Common Article 3, which binds armed forces and armed groups in a non-interna- **2.110** tional armed conflict, requires that civilians be immune from attack, and provides protections for those who have not or are no longer taking part in hostilities. The bombings of urban areas which have been attributed to the LTTE are prohibited by Common Article 3. According to Human Rights Watch, these bombings left some 70 civilians dead and 250 injured in 2008 alone.[324] The entrapment of civilians in the 'no-fire zone' was a significant concern for the ICRC, which relied on *ad hoc* evacuations of wounded civilians.[325] Common Article 3(2) provides for an unconditional obligation to collect and care for the wounded and sick, which may be more difficult to implement when civilians are trapped in a no-fire zone.

Common Article 3's minimalist obligations do not require state armed forces **2.111** to facilitate humanitarian access, so the government's order in September 2008 for aid agencies to cease their work in the LTTE-controlled Vanni region[326] can be opposed in customary IHL and general principles of law only. If Sri Lanka had ratified Additional Protocol II, Article 18(2) of Additional Protocol II would have required that relief be supplied for populations in need. Rules 31–32 of the ICRC Study on Customary IHL indicate a welter of state practice in the form of military manuals in favour of the respect and protection of humanitarian relief personnel and of objects used in humanitarian relief operations.[327] However, states which have not ratified either of the Additional Protocols should be urged to do so.

After the non-international armed conflict ended in the summer of 2009, it was **2.112** reported that the Sri Lankan authorities continued to hold 280,000 displaced Tamils, including civilians, in internment camps.[328] According to media reports, three-quarters of those interned were resettled in the ten months prior to April 2010.[329] Detention is left largely unregulated in non-international armed conflicts. There is no explicit authority to detain either civilians or combatants in the IHL of non-international armed conflicts. Only in international armed conflicts is there a treaty-based obligation to release both prisoners of war and civilian internees at the

---

[323] Ibid.
[324] Human Rights Watch World Report 2009, Sri Lanka.
[325] ICRC, 'Sri Lanka: Situation of Civilians Nothing Short of Catastrophic', 21 April 2009, supra, 329.
[326] Human Rights Watch World Report 2009, Sri Lanka.
[327] Henckaerts & Doswald-Beck, supra, Rules 31–32.
[328] Human Rights Watch, 'Sri Lanka: Free Civilians from Detention Camps', 28 July 2009.
[329] Jason Burke, 'Sri Lanka's Tamils Freed—But Future Bleak for Those Who Backed Tigers', *Guardian*, 5 April 2010.

close of hostilities.[330] The ICRC Study on Customary IHL indicates in Rule 128 that 'persons deprived of their liberty in relation to non-international armed conflict must be released as soon as the reasons for the deprivation of their liberty cease to exist'.[331] This somewhat circular test should not be interpreted to give extensive discretion to the Sri Lankan state to detain Tamil civilians post-conflict. Despite the absence of an authority to detain in non-international armed conflicts, Common Article 3 and where ratified Additional Protocol II provide numerous protections for those detained. If Sri Lanka had ratified Additional Protocol II, both Article 4(2)(b), which prohibits collective punishment, and Article 5, which provides for certain guarantees of conditions of detention and humane treatment for individuals who have been detained or interned, could apply to protect the 280,000 displaced Tamils in internment camps.

2.113 The IHL of non-international armed conflicts is lacking in detail, especially in those conflicts where Additional Protocol II is not ratified. The principle of distinction between combatants and civilians is articulated only in the ICRC Commentary to Additional Protocol II, rather than being specified in the treaty Articles. This reflects the position that armed groups cannot have a combatant's privilege similar to that in international armed conflict.

The US-led 'war on terror'

2.114 As paragraphs 2.33–2.35 above have noted, the assertion of a 'global war on terror' by then US President George W Bush after the terrorist attacks of 11 September 2001 was accompanied by a selective and often conflicting approach to the applicability of IHL. The Bush administration invoked the number of persons killed in the World Trade Center bombings as evidence that the terrorist attacks were an act of war and not a criminal act.[332] Congress passed the AUMF which gave President Bush almost limitless discretionary powers to 'use all necessary and appropriate force against those nations, organizations, or persons *he determines* planned, authorized, committed, or aided the terrorist attacks that occurred on September 11, 2001, or harboured such organizations or persons'.[333] As noted above, the AUMF said nothing about the applicability of IHL.

2.115 In *Hamdan v Rumsfeld*[334] Common Article 3 was held to be a 'minimum yardstick' for protection of a detainee who had been captured during the international armed conflict phase of the war in Afghanistan, but who was still held at Guantánamo Bay subsequent to that war's arguable transition into a non-international armed conflict

---

[330] Third Geneva Convention, Art 118; Fourth Geneva Convention, Art 133.
[331] Henckaerts & Doswald-Beck, supra, Rule 128.C.
[332] Authorization for the Use of Military Force (AUMF) of 18 September 2001 (Public Law 107-40 [SJ RES.23]), s.2a.
[333] Ibid. (emphasis added).
[334] *Hamdan v Rumsfeld*, 126 S Ct 2749, 548 US 557 (2006).

following the initial defeat of the Taliban.[335] The court opined that the detainees at Guantánamo Bay should receive the procedural protections of Common Article 3(1)(d), ie that there should be no sentences passed 'without previous judgment of a regularly constituted court, affording all the judicial guarantee which are recognized as indispensable by civilized peoples'.[336] The court held that the military commissions established by the Bush administration violated Common Article 3's procedural guarantees. Common Article 3 also requires the humane treatment of a range of individuals affected by non-international armed conflict, including those 'placed *hors de combat* by . . . detention'. Paragraphs 3.113–3.116 and 3.121–3.123 will consider the US habeas corpus case law in some depth.

The current reliance by the Obama administration on targeted killings by CIA **2.116** personnel (who are not combatants) both inside and outside armed conflict and the continued reference to the AUMF are a cause for ongoing concern.[337] Where the US fights non-state armed groups, the treaty and customary IHL of non-international armed conflict should apply, and the US should be urged to ratify Additional Protocol II. Outside armed conflict where IHL cannot apply, IHRL regulates all use of force and firearms. As paragraphs 3.40–3.45 will explain, targeted killings outside armed conflict are arbitrary deprivations of life and extra-judicial executions.[338] Inside armed conflict, there are concerns as to the number of civilian casualties, so the US should be urged to comply rigorously with the principle of proportionality. If drone attacks fall short of the principle of proportionality, as academic analysts suggest,[339] the policy should be stopped.

Conclusion

IHL only regulates terrorism and counter-terrorism during international armed **2.117** conflict, belligerent occupation, or non-international armed conflict. A terrorist attack does not create a situation of war, nor does the use of force in counter-terrorism automatically create an armed conflict to which IHL applies. Although IHL has a context-specific meaning of 'terrorism' and 'acts or threat of violence the primary purpose of which is to spread terror among the civilian population',[340] this meaning relates to IHL's principle of distinction between combatants and civilians, and to civilians' immunity from attack: it should be distinguished from the popular

---

[335] See paras 2.68–2.70, 2.83–2.84.
[336] Four Geneva Conventions, Common Article 3(1)(d).
[337] See paras 2.36–2.37, 2.50–2.52, 2.114–2.116 above.
[338] See paras 2.47–2.48, 3.40–3.45.
[339] David Kilcullen and Andrew MacDonald Exum, 'Death from Above, Outrage Down Below', *New York Times*, 17 March 2009, cited in Mary Ellen O'Connell, 'Unlawful Killing with Combat Drones: A Case Study of Pakistan, 2004–2009', supra.
[340] Fourth Geneva Convention, Art 33; Additional Protocol I, Art 51(2); Additional Protocol II, Arts 4(2)(d) and 13(2).

or media conceptions of the term, and from the many definitions of terrorism offences in domestic criminal legislation.

2.118 While IHL treaty law lacks comprehensiveness in its regulation of non-international armed conflicts,[341] all of IHL is obligatory: unlike IHRL, there can be no temporary suspension of IHL's provisions in war or state of emergency. IHL is also politically neutral. The political motives of an armed group do not excuse or justify violations of IHL committed by that group. Similarly, citing a motive of 'counter-terrorism' does not erase or mitigate any violations of IHL committed by a state. This chapter has revealed the US' inaccurate approaches to IHL, or instances where the US has questioned its applicability or binding force.[342] It has also considered IHL violations committed by both state armed forces and armed groups. Some of these violations encompass grave breaches of the Four Geneva Conventions.[343]

2.119 Chapter 3, which follows, analyses counter-terrorism and IHRL. Subsequent chapters draw on the analysis of IHL in Chapter 2. Chapters 4–6 emphasize the need for accountability for IHL violations,[344] victims' right to reparation under international standards,[345] and measures to prevent future violations of IHL in conflicts fought with a counter-terrorist aim.[346] Chapter 7 includes a set of recommendations to prevent violations of IHL in counter-terrorism operations.

---

[341] See para 2.08.
[342] See paras 2.33–2.37, 2.52, 2.114–2.116.
[343] See paras 2.13, 2.24, 2.71–2.72, 2.74, 2.80.
[344] See paras 4.25–4.26, 4.35–4.36.
[345] See paras 5.12–5.24 and 5.38–5.53.
[346] See paras 6.18–6.27.

3

COUNTER-TERRORISM IN INTERNATIONAL HUMAN RIGHTS LAW

Introduction

IHRL and counter-terrorism

International human rights law (IHRL) regulates state policies in counter-terror- **3.01**
ism, in both peace and war.[1] It binds states to respect and ensure general and specific
civil and political rights;[2] to respect, protect, and fulfil economic, social, and cultural rights;[3] and to secure additional, specific rights for children,[4] women,[5]
members of racial minorities,[6] and migrant workers and members of their families.[7]

---

[1] See paras 2.38–2.40, 3.36–3.45.

[2] International Covenant on Civil and Political Rights 1966 (ICCPR) and its Optional Protocols;
Convention against Torture and Other Cruel, Inhuman or Degrading Treatment or Punishment
1984 (Convention against Torture); International Convention for the Protection of All Persons from
Enforced Disappearance 2006 (not yet in force).

[3] International Covenant on Economic Social and Cultural Rights 1966 (ICESCR).

[4] Convention on the Rights of the Child 1989 (CRC) and its Optional Protocols.

[5] Convention on the Elimination of All Forms of Discrimination against Women 1979
(CEDAW).

[6] International Convention on the Elimination of All Forms of Racial Discrimination 1965
(ICERD).

[7] International Convention on the Protection of the Rights of All Migrant Workers and Members
of their Families 1990 (ICRMW).

As part of these obligations, IHRL requires states to act with due diligence to prevent violations of the right to life by non-state actors,[8] and strictly regulates counter-terrorism law, policy, and practice. State terrorism or state-sponsored terrorism which violates the right to life is a violation of IHRL. Nonetheless, an obligation to protect citizens from terrorist attacks neither excuses nor justifies human rights violations, and it can never oust the application of non-derogable rights.[9]

3.02 The obligations to criminalize, investigate, and prosecute certain terrorist acts come from the subject-specific terrorism conventions outlined in Chapter 1.[10] These establish domestic criminal law as the appropriate accountability mechanism for terrorist attacks committed by non-state actors. The framework and enforcement of IHRL is state-centric, with regional human rights courts, UN treaty bodies, and special procedures calling states to account for their implementation of the treaties which they have ratified. Terrorist attacks present a threat to the implementation of human rights norms,[11] and may amount to crimes against humanity, but they are not human rights 'violations' in the technical sense.[12]

3.03 Unlike IHL, IHRL treaty law permits states to derogate (or temporarily to suspend) certain rights in time of war or public emergency threatening the life of the nation.[13] Such derogations must be 'to the extent strictly required by the exigencies of the situation',[14] must not conflict with other international law obligations, and must not discriminate unlawfully. IHRL also allows for lawful, necessary, and proportionate limitations to certain rights in the pursuit of national security of public order.[15] IHRL treaties include numerous non-derogable and absolute rights, which

---

[8] See paras 3.13–3.14, 3.28–3.35.

[9] See para 3.03.

[10] See paras 1.18–1.20.

[11] UN High Commissioner for Human Rights, Report of the HCHR and Follow-Up to the World Conference on Human Rights, E/CN.4/2002/18, 27 February 2002, para 2.

[12] Wilder Tayler, 'Notes on the Human Rights Movement and the Issue of Terrorism', International Council on Human Rights Policy, 8th Annual International Council Meeting, May 2005; for contrasting perspectives, see: UN Declaration on Measures to Eliminate International Terrorism, General Assembly Resolution 49/60 (9 December 1994), contrast Preamble para 5 and operative para 2; Guidelines of the Committee of Ministers of the Council of Europe on Human Rights and the Fight Against Terrorism, 11 July 2002, Preamble, I; See also, *inter alia*, UN Commission on Human Rights, Human Rights and Terrorism, Res 2003/37; Karima Bennoune, 'Terror/Torture' (2008) 26 *Berkeley Journal of International Law* 1–61.

[13] ICCPR, Art 4; UN Human Rights Committee General Comment No 29, States of Emergency (Art 4), CCPR/C/21/Rev.1/Add/11, 31 August 2001; European Convention for the Protection of Human Rights and Fundamental Freedoms 1951 (ECHR), Art 15; American Convention on Human Rights 1969 (ACHR), Art 27. There is no derogation provision in the African Charter on Human and Peoples' Rights 1981 (ACHPR).

[14] ICCPR, Art 4(1).

[15] ICCPR, Arts 18, 19, 21, 22; ECHR, Arts 8–11; ACHR, Arts 13, 15, 16, 22; ACHPR, Arts 11 and 12.

cannot be the subject of derogation or limitation, but have nonetheless been violated in the course of countering terrorism.

Violations of IHRL in counter-terrorism

The breadth and severity of human rights violations committed in the name of counter-terrorism cannot be adequately documented in a single analytical chapter on the applicable international law. State practice in counter-terrorism has yielded torture, arbitrary detention, enforced disappearances, and extrajudicial executions, with many victims suffering numerous composite human rights violations. Parliamentary, intergovernmental organization (IGO), and non-governmental organization (NGO) research into torture,[16] secret and incommunicado detention, and 'extraordinary rendition' (the unlawful transfer of individuals to interrogation and a risk of torture or enforced disappearance) have indicated that multiple states are complicit in these violations,[17] and that independent investigations are urgently required.[18]   **3.04**

States have attempted to undermine the binding force of IHRL, and its relevance   **3.05**
to counter-terrorism. A number of European states have called for new national security-based exemptions to the prohibition on *refoulement* (the transfer of an individual to another state where there are substantial grounds for believing that he or she will be subject to torture or other ill-treatment).[19] Still other states have argued that IHRL neither applies during armed conflicts fought with a counter-terrorist aim,[20] nor to areas outside a state's territory where that state has

---

[16] UK Joint Committee on Human Rights (JCHR), Twenty-third Report of Session 2008–09, *Allegations of UK Complicity in Torture*, HL Paper 152/HC 230, 4 August 2009, JCHR, 16th Report of Session 2009/10; *Counter-Terrorism Policy and Human Rights (Seventeenth Report): Bringing Human Rights Back In*, 16th Report of Session 2009–10, 9 March 2010; Human Rights Watch, 'Cruel Britannia: British Complicity in the Torture and Ill-Treatment of Terror Suspects in Pakistan', 24 November 2009; Evidence to the Special Committee on the Canadian Mission in Afghanistan, 40th Parliament, 2nd Session, 18 November 2009; Amnesty International USA, 'USA: Normalizing Delay, Perpetuating Injustice, Undermining the "Rules of the Road"', 23 June 2010; International Centre for Transitional Justice, 'Prosecuting Abuses of Detainees in US Counter-terrorism Operations', November 2009.

[17] Parliamentary Assembly of the Council of Europe (PACE), 'Secret Detentions and Illegal Transfers of Detainees Involving Council of Europe Member States: Second Report', Doc 11302 rev, 11 June 2007; Joint Study on Global Practices in Relation to Secret Detention in the Context of Countering Terrorism, A/HRC/13/42, 26 January 2010.

[18] JCHR, *Allegations of UK Complicity in Torture*, supra.

[19] *Saadi v Italy*, European Court of Human Rights (2008) 24 BHRC 123; *Ramzy v Netherlands*, Application No 25424/05 (still pending before a Chamber of the European Court of Human Rights); Observations of the Governments of Lithuania, Portugal, Slovakia, and the United Kingdom Intervening in Application No 25424/05, *Ramzy v Netherlands*; *Chahal v United Kingdom* (1996) 23 EHRR 413.

[20] Human Rights Committee, Concluding Observations on the Initial Report of Israel, CCPR/C/79/Add.93, 18 August 1998, para 10; Concluding Observations on the second periodic report of Israel, CCPR/CO/78/ISR, 21 August 2003, para 11; Committee against Torture, Concluding Observations on the Second Report of the United States of America, CAT/C/USA/CO/2, 25 July 2006, para 14.

effective control.[21] This is at odds with states' acceptance in numerous UN Security Council and General Assembly Resolutions, and in the UN Global Counter-Terrorism Strategy and Plan of Action that successful counter-terrorism and human rights are mutually reinforcing goals: they are not in tension.[22] It also contradicts an emerging consensus in the output of regional human rights courts and UN treaty bodies.[23]

3.06 Overbroad definitions of terrorism in legislation from common law and civil law legal systems,[24] and widely drawn powers to combat it, have been coupled with the US' willingness to define torture narrowly, so that 'enhanced interrogation techniques' which unmistakably cause 'severe pain and suffering, whether mental or physical' were defined as mere ill-treatment and therefore not criminal offences under US law.[25] States have used the threat of terrorism to circumscribe established and incontrovertible definitions of human rights violations so that their counter-terrorist practices are seen to be outside these definitions.

3.07 Alongside the problems of definition, there has been widespread, international secrecy about the prevalence of torture, secret detention, and 'extraordinary rendition' to interrogation, ill-treatment, and enforced disappearances, and about states'

---

[21] Human Rights Committee, Concluding Observations on the Initial Report of Israel, CCPR/C/79/Add.93, 18 August 1998, para 11; Human Rights Committee, Concluding Observations on the Second and Third Periodic Reports of the United States of America, CCPR/C/USA/CO/3, 15 September 2006, para 10; Committee against Torture, Concluding Observations on the Second Report of the United States of America, CAT/C/USA/CO/2, 25 July 2006, para 15; Human Rights Committee, Concluding Observations on the Sixth Periodic Report of the United Kingdom of Great Britain and Northern Ireland, CCPR/C/GBR/CO/6, para 14.

[22] See, *inter alia*, UN Global Counter-Terrorism Strategy and Plan of Action, General Assembly Resolution 60/288, 20 September 2006.

[23] Human Rights Committee General Comment No 31, The Nature of the General Legal Obligation Imposed on State Parties, CCPR/C/21/Rev.1/Add.13, 26 May 2004; *Burgos/Delia Saldias de López v Uruguay*, Inter-American Commission on Human Rights, Communication No 52/1979, UN Doc CCPR/C/OP/1 (1984); *Loizidou v Turkey (Preliminary Objections)*, Application No 15318/89, (1995) 20 EHRR 99, 23 March 1995; *Loizidou v Turkey (Merits)*, Application No 15318/89, (1997) 23 EHRR 513, 28 November 1996; *Xhavara and Others v Italy and Albania*, Application No 39473/98, 11 January 2001; *Cyprus v Turkey*, Application No 2581/94, Judgment of 10 May 2001; *Bankovic v Belgium*, Grand Chamber, European Court of Human Rights (2001) 44 EHRR SE5; *Issa and Others v Turkey (Merits stage)* (2005) 41 EHRR 27, 16 November 2004; *Al-Skeini and Others v Secretary of State for Defence* [2007] UKHL 26.

[24] Pakistan, Anti-Terrorism Act 1997, s 6; Sri Lanka, Prevention of Terrorism (Temporary Provisions) Act 1979, s 2; Malaysia, Internal Security Act 1960, s 2; Swaziland, Suppression of Terrorism Act No 3 of 2008, s 2, see: Amnesty International and International Bar Association, 'Suppression of Terrorism Act Undermines Human Rights in Swaziland', AI Ref: 55/001/2009; Algeria, Code Pénal, s 87; United Kingdom, Terrorism Act 2000, Terrorism Act 2006, s 1; United States of America, PATRIOT Act 2001 (see especially 'material support' for terrorism); Russian Federation, Federal Law No 35-FZ on Counteraction of Terrorism, 6 March 2006, Art 3.

[25] Jay S Bybee, US Assistant Attorney General, US Department of Justice (DOJ), Office of Legal Counsel (OLC), Memorandum for John Rizzo, Acting General Counsel of the Central Intelligence Agency (CIA), 1 August 2002; Steven Bradbury, US Acting Assistant Attorney General, US DOJ OLC, Memorandum for John Rizzo, Senior Deputy General Counsel, CIA, 10 May 2005; Steven Bradbury, US Acting Assistant Attorney General, US DOJ OLC, Memorandum for John Rizzo, Deputy General Counsel, CIA, 30 May 2005.

complicity in these violations.[26] This secrecy feeds into a problem of impunity. As paragraphs 4.42–4.47 consider in depth, states' reliance on a 'state secrets' doctrine to prevent the disclosure of information about complicity in torture and other IHRL violations shuns the international obligation to investigate and prosecute these crimes.[27] It also neglects victims' right to a remedy and reparations for grave violations of IHL and serious violations of IHRL.[28]

Terrorism has also been used as a pretext to repress the activity of human rights **3.08** defenders, and to inhibit the peaceful exercise of the freedoms of expression and assembly. This further diminishes the implementation of IHRL at the national level.[29] IGO and NGO sources have reported direct or indirect discrimination against national, ethnic, and religious minorities, and an often neglected dimension of gender discrimination in many states' counter-terrorism policies.[30]

Methodology

This chapter clarifies the continued application of IHRL to states' counter-terrorism **3.09** laws and practice, and shows the worldwide reach of violations of civil, political, economic, social, and cultural rights in the name of counter-terrorism. It will make reference to findings from IGOs and NGOs, analysis of legislation in translation, and media reports. The chapter considers examples of legislation and state practice in Algeria, China, Indonesia, Israel, Jordan, Pakistan, Peru, the Russian Federation, Spain, Sri Lanka, Swaziland, the UK, the US, Uzbekistan, and Yemen, with brief references to reports of human rights violations elsewhere. As with the case studies in Chapter 2, this chapter uses the findings of NGOs and media reports to give initial factual background, but the legal analysis is done afresh. Each substantive

---

[26] PACE, 'Secret Detentions and Illegal Transfers of Detainees Involving Council of Europe Member States: Second Report', Doc 11302 rev, 11 June 2007.

[27] Convention against Torture, Arts 5–8.

[28] Basic Principles and Guidelines on the Right to a Remedy and Reparation for Victims of Gross Violations of International Human Rights Law and Serious Violations of International Humanitarian Law, General Assembly Resolution 60/147, 16 December 2005.

[29] UN Special Rapporteur on the Situation of Human Rights Defenders, Issues in Focus, Security Legislation, 'Security and Counter-Terrorist Legislation'; Amnesty International, Statement to Working Session 16 of the Organisation for Security and Cooperation in Europe: Fundamental Freedoms II, including: Freedom of Expression, Free Media and Information, HDIM.NGO/396/07, 3 October 2007; Fédération Internationale des Droits de l'Homme (FIDH), 'Turkey: End Human Rights Violations under the Pretext of the "War Against Terrorism"', 22 September 2003; FIDH, Observatory for the Protection of Human Rights Defenders Annual Report 2009, Russian Federation, 18 June 2009.

[30] Open Society Justice Initiative, 'Ethnic Profiling in the European Union: Pervasive, Ineffective and Discriminatory' (2009); Center for Human Rights and Global Justice (CHRGJ) at New York University School of Law, 'Americans on Hold: Profiling, Citizenship, and the "War on Terror"' (2007); Amnesty International, 'Uighur Ethnic Identity Under Threat in China', Repression in the Name of the "War on Terror"', ASA 17/010/2009, April 2009, pp 1–2; Report of the Special Rapporteur on the Promotion and Protection of Human Rights while Countering Terrorism to the 64th Session of the UN General Assembly, III. A gender perspective on countering terrorism, A/64/211, 3 August 2009.

section of this chapter begins with an explanation of the relevant law for non-specialists, before considering examples of apparent violations.

Structure

3.10 Paragraphs 3.11–3.27 explain the framework of IHRL as it relates to terrorism and counter-terrorism. The six sections from paragraphs 3.28–3.169 each include a brief introduction to substantive law, followed by an internationally inclusive selection of case studies and illustrative examples. Paragraphs 3.170–3.184 briefly consider the impact of counter-terrorism practices on economic, social, and cultural rights and non-discrimination norms. The analysis in this chapter has relevance throughout the volume. Chapter 4, considers the gradual, piecemeal accountability processes to address IHRL violations in counter-terrorism;[31] Chapter 5 considers the right to an effective remedy for victims of IHRL;[32] Chapter 6, discusses various measures to prevent violations of IHRL in counter-terrorism;[33] and Chapter 7 distils this analysis in recommendations to states.[34]

The duty to prevent, investigate, and prosecute terrorist attacks

The absence of the term 'terrorism' in IHRL treaties

3.11 IHRL neither defines nor explicitly prohibits terrorism. Nor do IHRL treaties use the term 'terrorism' in a context-specific sense, in contrast to the IHL-specific meaning of the term 'terrorism' which is explored in Chapter 2.[35] While IHRL treaties do require states to criminalize specific human rights violations in their domestic law, such as torture,[36] IHRL is not the source for states' duties to criminalize terrorist violence. States' duties to prevent and repress terrorism, to investigate terrorist crimes, and to prosecute or extradite those suspected of being responsible derive from the subject-specific terrorism conventions and the UN Security Council Resolutions outlined in Chapter 1[37] and considered again in Chapter 6.[38]

IHRL and 'state terrorism'

3.12 Chapter 1 has argued that the absence of 'state terrorism' from the subject-specific terrorism treaties and from the report of the UN High-Level Panel on Threats,

---

[31] See paras 4.25–4.49.
[32] See paras 5.24–5.34.
[33] See paras 6.28–6.41.
[34] See paras 7.12–7.19.
[35] See paras 2.22–2.32.
[36] Convention against Torture, Art 4.
[37] See paras 1.18–1.20.
[38] See para 6.03.

Challenges and Change may not reflect political reality.[39] If terrorist attacks can be attributed to a state under the International Law Commission's (ILC's) Articles on State Responsibility,[40] then that state is responsible for those terrorist attacks, when they are internationally unlawful acts.[41] Where a terrorist attack causes death and where this attribution is possible, this should be investigated as a prima facie violation of the right to life. The individual officials suspected of being responsible for the state terrorist attack in question should be investigated and prosecuted in fair trials. The same conclusion applies to any serious violation of IHRL in counter-terrorism.

IHRL and terrorist attacks by non-state actors

Terrorist acts by non-state actors would seem at first sight to be outside IHRL's **3.13** sphere of influence, being more appropriately regulated by national criminal law. As noted above,[42] IHRL treaties bind states (and only states) which have ratified them. In addition, customary IHRL is formed of widespread *state* practice and *opinio juris*.[43] However, IHRL case law binds states to take measures to prevent, investigate, and prosecute violations of the right to life by non-state actors.[44] States are 'under an obligation to take reasonable and appropriate measures' to protect individuals in their jurisdiction who suffer known threats to their lives. *If* a state's 'failure . . . to act' is 'clearly proven',[45] then this failure may violate the right to security in Article 9 of the International Covenant on Civil and Political Rights (ICCPR).[46] Even where the involvement of state security forces in an individual's death is not proven, states parties to the European Convention on the Protection of Human Rights and Fundamental Freedoms (ECHR) must strive to prevent and to investigate possible unlawful killings.[47] The duty to investigate possible unlawful

---

[39] UN High Level Panel on Threats, Challenges and Change, 'A More Secure World: Our Shared Responsibility', A/59/565, 2 December 2004.

[40] ILC Articles on the Responsibility of States for Internationally Unlawful Acts 2001, adopted by UN General Assembly Resolution 56/83, 12 December 2001.

[41] See paras 1.13–1.15 and 6.07–6.09.

[42] See para 3.02.

[43] International Court of Justice Statute, Art 38(1)(b); Bruno Simma and Philip Alston, 'The Sources of Human Rights Law: Custom, Jus Cogens and General Principles', (1988–89) 12 *Australian Yearbook of International Law* 82; or for an unorthodox approach, see: Isabelle Gunning, 'Modernizing Customary International Law: The Challenge of Human Rights' (1990–1991) 31 *Virginia Journal of International Law* 211.

[44] *Delgado Paez v Colombia*, Communication No 195/1985, CCPR/C/39/D/195/1985, Views, 12 July 1990, para 5.5 (a broad reading of the right to security in ICCPR, Art 9); Inter-American Court of Human Rights, *Velásquez Rodriguez v Honduras* [1989] 28 ILM 291; *Kiliç v Turkey* (2001) 33 EHRR 1357, Judgment of 28 March 2000; *Mahmut Kaya v Turkey*, Application No 22535/93, Judgment of 28 March 2000; *Osman v United Kingdom* (1998) 29 EHRR 245; *Ergi v Turkey* (2001) 23 EHRR 388.

[45] *Delgado Paez v Colombia*, Communication No 195/1985, CCPR/C/39/D/195/1985, Views, 12 July 1990, para 5.5.

[46] Ibid.

[47] *Kiliç v Turkey* (2001) 33 EHRR 1357, Judgment of 28 March 2000.

killings applies both where there is evidence that state security forces may have been involved,[48] and where there is no such evidence.[49]

3.14 Where authorities in ECHR states parties 'knew or ought to have known at the time of the existence of a real and immediate risk to the life *of an identified individual or individuals* from the criminal acts of a third party',[50] they have a due diligence obligation to take 'measures within the scope of their powers which, judged reasonably, might . . . [be] expected to avoid that risk' (*Osman v UK*).[51] However, no violation of the right to life was found on the facts of this case,[52] and the text in italics above strongly suggests that there are limits to states' due diligence obligation to prevent violations of the right to life by non-state actors. Applying this jurisprudence by analogy to terrorist attacks creates some challenges: the bombing of civilians on aircraft or commuter trains and the hijacking of aircraft suggests a random choice of victims, rather than the selection of an 'identified individual or individuals' as victims.

3.15 Nonetheless, the treaties and UN Security Council Resolutions considered in Chapter 1 confer on states an obligation to prevent and repress terrorist attacks. When terrorist attacks occur, the investigatory obligations from the IHRL of the right to life lead to an obligation to investigate and prosecute those suspected of being responsible. However, this does not amount to an absolute duty to prevent terrorist attacks in IHRL (such a conclusion would be not only practically unenforceable but also does not fairly reflect jurisprudence), nor to a statement that terrorist attacks by non-state actors are a human rights violation. Non-state actors, including terrorists whose acts cannot be attributed to a state, are not bound *de jure* by IHRL, but instead should be held to account in domestic criminal trials.[53]

IHRL and counter-terrorism

The obligation to respect IHRL while countering terrorism

3.16 A state's obligation to act with 'due diligence' to prevent, investigate, and prosecute terrorist attacks does not override its obligations to respect, protect, and fulfil all human rights.[54] This echoes the UN Global Counter-Terrorism Strategy, and the UN Security Council Resolutions which emphasize that states must act in

---

[48] *Finucane v UK* (2003) 37 EHRR 29.
[49] *Mahmut Kaya v Turkey*, Application No 22535/93, Judgment of 28 March 2000.
[50] *Osman v United Kingdom* (1998) 29 EHRR 245 (emphasis added).
[51] Ibid.
[52] Ibid.
[53] See paras 4.01–4.02, 4.19–4.24.
[54] Office of the United Nations High Commissioner for Human Rights (OHCHR), 'Human Rights, Terrorism and Counter-Terrorism', Factsheet no 32, p 4.

accordance with IHL, IHRL, and IRL while countering terrorism.[55] As this section will explain, this obligation applies to counter-terrorism laws, policies, and practice, subject to lawful derogation from (a formal suspension of specific articles in a treaty during war or public emergency threatening the life of the nation),[56] or lawful, necessary, and proportionate limitation to certain rights.[57] An obligation to protect citizens from terrorist attacks neither excuses nor justifies human rights violations, and it can never oust the application of non-derogable rights. As noted in Chapter 1, states' obligations to prevent and repress terrorism must be implemented with full respect for IHL, IHRL, and IRL. This is embedded in treaties and UN Security Council and General Assembly documents on terrorism.[58] The full range of states' counter-terrorism policies, legislation, and operations should be scrutinized in terms of their compliance with IHRL. This section analyses the strict parameters IHRL applies to states' counter-terrorism policies, despite the potential for derogation in time of war or public emergency, and for limitations at other times in the name of national security and public order or safety.

Derogation in time of war and public emergency

IHRL permits states to derogate from (temporarily to suspend) certain civil and **3.17** political rights in time of war or public emergency which threaten the life of the nation.[59] Measures taken pursuant to permitted derogations must be proportionate: they must be limited 'to the extent strictly required by the exigencies of the situation';[60] they must be consistent with a state's other international law obligations;[61] under the ICCPR and the American Convention on Human Rights (ACHR), measures taken pursuant to derogations must not discriminate on several enumerated prohibited grounds;[62] the state of emergency must be officially proclaimed,[63] and the notice of derogation deposited with the UN Secretary-General.[64] A notice of withdrawal of the derogation at the end of the state of emergency must be deposited in the same way.[65]

---

[55] See paras 1.01, 1.17, 1.26–1.27, 6.03–6.04, 7.01, 7.08.

[56] ICCPR, Art 4; UN Human Rights Committee General Comment No 29, States of Emergency (Article 4), CCPR/C/21/Rev.1/Add/11, 31 August 2001; ECHR, Art 15; ACHR, Art 27. There is no derogation provision in the ACHPR.

[57] ICCPR, Arts 18, 19, 21, 22; ECHR, Arts 8–11; ACHR, Arts 13, 15, 16, 22; ACHPR, Arts 11 and 12.

[58] UN Global Counter-Terrorism Strategy, annexed to General Assembly Resolution 60/288, 8 September 2006, para 3; UN General Assembly Resolution 60/158, 16 December 2005; UN Security Council Resolution 1624, 14 September 2005, Preamble, para 2.

[59] ICCPR, Art 4(1).

[60] Ibid.

[61] Ibid; ECHR, Art 15.

[62] ICCPR, Art 4(1); ACHR, Art 27.

[63] ICCPR, Art 4(1).

[64] ICCPR, Art 4(3).

[65] Ibid.

3.18 Derogations should not be the mainstay of a state's counter-terrorism policies, and they are rarely used in Europe, with the UK's derogation to Article 5(1)(f) ECHR from 2001–04 being a significant example.[66] Nonetheless, some states argue that the obligation to prevent and repress terrorism justifies long-term states of emergency (whether or not the state in question formally derogates). Longstanding states of emergency, such as those in Egypt[67] and Sri Lanka,[68] cannot justify ongoing human rights violations. The Human Rights Committee and Article 4 of the ICCPR are predicated upon short-term emergencies: and the state of emergency in Egypt, while 'officially proclaimed', has lasted continuously since 1981. Non-derogable rights apply at all times, even during war or public emergency, alongside states' obligations to prevent and repress terrorism.[69]

3.19 The ICCPR specifies that the right to life, the prohibitions on torture and cruel, inhuman, or degrading treatment or punishment, slavery and servitude, imprisonment for debt, retroactive criminal conviction and punishment, the right to recognition everywhere as a person before the law, and the right to freedom of thought, conscience, and religion are all non-derogable.[70] No public emergency can authorize derogation from any of these rights. The list of non-derogable rights also includes the prohibition on the death penalty for those states which have ratified the Second Optional Protocol to the ICCPR.[71] The ACHR and ECHR have their own lists of non-derogable rights.[72]

---

[66] Declaration contained in a *note verbale* from the Permanent Representative of the United Kingdom to the Council of Europe, 18 December 2001; see also *A and Others v Secretary of State for the Home Department* [2004] UKHL 56.

[67] Report of the Special Rapporteur on the promotion and protection of human rights while countering terrorism on his visit to Egypt, A/HRC/13/37/Add.2, 14 October 2009; Human Rights Council, 13th session, Interactive Debate with the Special Rapporteur on Torture and the Special Rapporteur on the promotion and protection of human rights while countering terrorism, 8 March 2010; Fédération Internationale des Droits de l'Homme (FIDH), 'Egypt: Counter-terrorism Against the Background of an Endless State of Emergency', January 2010; Concluding Observations of the Human Rights Committee: Egypt, CCPR/CO/76/EGY, 28 November 2002, para 6; Human Rights Watch, 'Egypt: Cosmetic Changes Can't Justify Keeping Emergency Law', 12 May 2010; *New York Times*, 'Egypt's Emergency Law is Extended for Two Years', 11 May 2010.

[68] Report of the Special Rapporteur on torture and other cruel, inhuman or degrading treatment or punishment, Manfred Nowak, Mission to Sri Lanka, Human Rights Council, 7th session, A/HRC/7/3/Add.6, 26 February 2008; UN Committee against Torture, Conclusions and Recommendations of the Committee against Torture—Sri Lanka, CAT/C/LKA/CO/2, 15 December 2005; International Commission of Jurists, 'Sri Lanka: Briefing Paper—Emergency Laws and International Standards', March 2009.

[69] Statement of the Committee against Torture, CAT/C/XXVII/Misc.7, 22 November 2001.

[70] ICCPR, Art 4(1).

[71] Second Optional Protocol to the ICCPR, aiming at the abolition of the death penalty, Art 6.

[72] ACHR, Art 27(2), ECHR, Arts 3–6, 9, 12, 17–20, 23, and see also Inter-American Court of Human Rights, *Habeas Corpus in Emergency Situations*, Advisory Opinion OC-8 187, 30 January 1987, Series A No 8; ECHR, Arts 2, 3, 4(1), and 7.

Both the Convention against Torture and Other Cruel, Inhuman or Degrading **3.20** Treatment or Punishment (Convention against Torture) and the International Convention for the Protection of All Persons from Enforced Disappearance emphasize that '[n]o exceptional circumstances whatsoever, whether a state of war or a threat of war, internal political stability, or any other public emergency, may be invoked as a justification' for torture or for enforced disappearance.[73]

The Human Rights Committee (HRC), in its General Comment No 29, argues for **3.21** an additional range of rights which continue to apply during public emergencies, even though they are not listed as non-derogable rights in Article 4(2) of the ICCPR.[74] The HRC offers authoritative interpretations of the ICCPR for its states parties. This chapter considers widespread violations of rights which the HRC has identified as non-derogable, including the right of detainees to be treated with humanity and with respect for the inherent dignity of the human person,[75] the prohibition on abductions or unacknowledged detention,[76] the right to take proceedings before a court to determine the lawfulness of detention (habeas corpus or amparo),[77] and the right to a fair trial.[78]

Limitations to certain rights in pursuit of national security or public order

Rights to which limitations are permitted

There is a distinction between derogations in time of a public emergency, and **3.22** 'restrictions or limitations allowed even in normal times' in other ICCPR rights (eg Article 18 on freedom of conscience and religion, or Articles 20 and 21 on the freedoms of peaceful assembly and of association respectively); but both derogations and restrictions or limitations must be proportionate, ie 'required by the exigencies of the situation'.[79] Regional treaties also permit such limitations:

- The ECHR permits limitations on the right to private and family life, the freedom of conscience and religion, freedom of expression, and freedom of peaceful assembly and association.[80]

---

[73] Convention against Torture, Art 2(2); International Convention for the Protection of All Persons from Enforced Disappearance, Art 1(2) (not yet in force).

[74] Human Rights Committee, General Comment No 29, States of Emergency (Article 4), CCPR/C/21/Rev.1/Add.11, 31 August 2001.

[75] Ibid, para 13.

[76] Ibid.

[77] Ibid, para 16; see also Inter-American Court of Human Rights, *Habeas Corpus in Emergency Situations*, Advisory Opinion OC-8 187, 30 January 1987, Series A No 8.

[78] Ibid, para 16.

[79] Ibid.

[80] ECHR, Arts 8(2), 9(2), 10(2), 11(2).

- The ACHR permits restrictions on the grounds of national security, to the freedom of thought and expression, the right of peaceful assembly, the freedom of association, and the freedom of movement and residence.[81]
- The African Charter on Human and Peoples' Rights (ACHPR) has a similar provision for the freedom of assembly: 'The exercise of this right shall be subject only to necessary restrictions provided for by law in particular those enacted in the interest of national security . . .'[82] Restrictions to freedom of conscience are only permitted 'subject to law and order'.[83]

Criteria for lawful restrictions on rights

3.23 The criteria for lawful restriction of rights are found in the text of treaty Articles which permit these restrictions.[84]

- Under the ECHR, any permissible restrictions must be 'prescribed by law and necessary in a democratic society' for one or more specified purposes. '[N]ational security' is specified as a permitted purpose for such restrictions for the right to private and family life,[85] the freedom of expression,[86] and the freedom of assembly and association.[87] No explicit restrictions on grounds of 'national security' are permitted for the freedom of conscience and religion in Article 9,[88] but restrictions are permitted to the 'freedom to manifest one's religion or beliefs . . . in the interests of public safety, for the protection of public order'.[89] Counter-terrorist aims may permit restrictions on the right to private and family life, freedom of expression and freedom of assembly and association under the ground of 'prevention of disorder or crime'.[90] Article 11(2) on the freedom of peaceful assembly and association sets the following parameters: ' . . . this article shall not prevent the imposition of lawful restrictions on the exercise of these rights by members of the armed forces, of the police or of the administration of the State.' All these subparagraphs should be read together with Article 18 ECHR: 'The restrictions permitted under this Convention to the said rights and freedoms shall not be applied for any purpose other than those for which they have been prescribed.'
- The ACHR also permits such restrictions,[91] using a similar formulation: 'No restrictions may be placed on this right other than those imposed in conformity

---

[81] ACHR, Arts 13, 15, 16, 22.
[82] ACHPR, Art 11.
[83] ACHPR, Art 8.
[84] ICCPR, Arts 18, 20, 21.
[85] ECHR, Art 8(2).
[86] ECHR, Art 10(2).
[87] ECHR, Art 11(2).
[88] ECHR, Art 9(2).
[89] Ibid.
[90] ECHR, Arts 8(2), 9(2), 10(2), 11(2).
[91] ACHR, Art 15.

with the law and necessary in a democratic society in the interest of national security, public safety or public order . . . '[92]

Restrictions on rights in case law

In human rights litigation concerning restrictions on particular rights, it is for the **3.24** state to justify the restriction by proving that it was prescribed by law, intended to achieve one of the legitimate objectives specified in the treaty, and, to use the ECHR lexicon, that it was 'necessary in a democratic society'. This includes an IHRL proportionality calculus, which differs from the balancing of military necessity and the risk to civilians in IHL.[93] In the European Court of Human Rights (ECtHR) case law, the state must prove that (a) the interference in a right corresponded to a 'pressing social need', (b) that it was 'proportionate to the aim pursued', and (c) that the state gave 'relevant and sufficient' reasons.[94] The 'necessity' criterion suggests that a high threshold must be reached, or in litigation, that the state must discharge a high burden of proof. However, 'necessity' in this context permits broader restrictions on rights than those permitted through derogation in a time of war or public emergency. Proportionality in IHRL includes an inquiry into the seriousness of the interference in the individual case.

Non-binding standards

Non-binding standards consistently emphasize that limitations on human rights in **3.25** pursuit of national security, or derogations in public emergency, should be rare and strictly limited. The Siracusa Principles on the Limitation and Derogation of Provisions in the ICCPR (Siracusa Principles) are one such example of non-binding standards or soft law.[95] They are highly authoritative and can assist judges and lawyers in their interpretation of the substantive provisions in the ICCPR. However, they are not binding on states as a matter of treaty law. The following extracts from the Siracusa Principles are instructive, and almost prescient, given subsequent violations of IHRL in the name of counter-terrorism:

- '[N]ational security may be invoked to justify measures limiting certain rights only when they are taken to protect the existence of the nation or its territorial integrity or political independence against force or threat of force.'[96]
- National security should not be invoked as a reason to limit rights when the threat to law and order is 'merely local or relatively isolated'.[97]

---

[92] ACHR, Art 15.
[93] See para 2.12.
[94] *Sunday Times v UK* (1979) 2 EHRR 245, para 59.
[95] UN Sub-Commission on Prevention of Discrimination and Protection of Minorities, Siracusa Principles on the Limitation and Derogation of Provisions in the International Covenant on Civil and Political Rights, Annex, UN Doc E/CN.4/1984/4 (1984).
[96] Ibid, para 29.
[97] Ibid, para 30.

- 'National security cannot be used as a pretext for imposing vague or arbitrary limitations and may only be used when there exists adequate safeguards and effective remedies against abuse.'[98]
- 'The systematic violation of human rights undermines true national security and may jeopardise international peace and security.'[99]

The obligation to investigate and prosecute serious human rights violations

3.26 IHRL obliges states not only to criminalize and prevent violations of the right to life, the prohibition on torture, and the prohibition on enforced disappearances, but also to investigate and prosecute those suspected of being responsible.[100] This is a concomitant of victims' right to an effective remedy,[101] but it also emphasizes that impunity in the face of serious human rights violations is unacceptable.[102] The obligation to investigate and prosecute these serious violations of IHRL mirrors the obligation on High Contracting Parties to the Four Geneva Conventions of 1949 to repress grave breaches of the Geneva Conventions, and to prosecute or extradite those suspected of being responsible.[103] Accountability for serious human rights violations committed in counter-terrorism will be considered in Chapter 4.[104]

Victims' rights to a remedy and reparation

3.27 IHRL requires states to provide effective remedies for individuals whose human rights have been violated.[105] This includes an obligation to investigate, prosecute, and punish all serious violations of IHRL,[106] including those which occur in counter-terrorism. Paragraphs 5.25–5.34 consider victims' right to an effective

---

[98] Ibid, para 31.

[99] Ibid, para 32.

[100] Convention against Torture, Arts 2, 4, 12; International Convention for the Protection of All Persons from Enforced Disappearances (Disappearances Convention—not yet in force), Arts 3, 4, 6; European Court of Human Rights, *Mahmut Kaya v Turkey* Judgment of 28 March 2000; *Ergi v Turkey* (2001) 23 EHRR 388; *Finucane v United Kingdom* (2003) 37 EHRR 29; *Isayeva, Yusupova and Bazayeva* (2005) 41 EHRR 39; *Khashiyev and Akayeva* (2005) 42 EHRR 20; Inter-American Court of Human Rights, *Velásquez Rodriguez v Honduras* [1989] 28 ILM 291; *Bámaca Velásquez v Guatemala*, 25 November 2000; *Barrios Altos v Peru*, 14 March 2001; *Goiburú et al v Paraguay*, 22 September 2006; *Almonacid-Arellano et al v Chile*, 26 September 2006.

[101] ICCPR, Art 2(3)(a); Convention against Torture and Other Cruel, Inhuman or Degrading Treatment or Punishment (Convention against Torture), Art 13–14; (Disappearances Convention—not yet in force), Arts 8, 18, 20, 24; ECHR, Art 15; ACHR, Art 25.

[102] See paras 4.25–4.50.

[103] First Geneva Convention, Art 49; Second Geneva Convention, Art 50; Third Geneva Convention, Art 129; Fourth Geneva Convention, Art 146; Additional Protocol I, Art 85; see paras 2.13, 2.34, 2.71–2.72, 2.74, 7.11.

[104] See paras 4.25–4.49.

[105] ICCPR, Art 2(3)(a); Convention against Torture, Arts 13–14; Disappearances Convention (not yet in force), Arts 8, 18, 20, 24; ECHR, Art 15; ACHR, Art 25.

[106] See paras 3.47–3.49, 3.55, 3.69, 3.87, 4.25.

remedy in more depth, with particular reference to terrorism and counter-terrorism.

Arbitrary deprivation of life

The right to life and states' counter-terrorism operations

The following section explores the non-derogable right not to be arbitrarily deprived   **3.28**
of one's life. It analyses potential clashes between IHL and IHRL as regards the
lawfulness of killing combatants in international armed conflict, and the
prohibition on extrajudicial executions in IHRL, with reference to targeted killings
of terrorism suspects by the UK, US, Israel, and Pakistan. It also considers the
status of the death penalty for terrorist crimes, and the obligation to investigate
deaths in custody, whether a death takes place within a state's territory or
extraterritorially.

Treaty law

The right to life must be 'protected by law', and '[n]o-one shall be arbitrarily deprived   **3.29**
of his life'.[107] The right to life is explicitly non-derogable, with the exception of the
ECHR regime, which permits lawful derogations 'in respect of deaths resulting
from lawful acts of war'.[108] States cannot invoke a war or public emergency to justify
the arbitrary deprivation of life in counter-terrorism.[109]

Article 2(2) of the ECHR provides that deprivation of life is not a violation of the   **3.30**
ECHR 'when it results from the use of force which is no more than absolutely
necessary: (a) in defence of any person from unlawful violence; (b) in order to effect
a lawful arrest or to prevent the escape of a person lawfully detained; (c) in action
lawfully taken for the purpose of quelling a riot or insurrection'. The ECHR sets a
high threshold of 'no more than absolutely necessary': Article 2(2) does not permit
states broad discretion to use lethal force wherever there is a risk of unlawful violence, a need to arrest an individual or prevent his or her escape, or where people
assemble in a protest.

Case law

As the European Court of Human Rights (the Court or ECtHR) noted in *McCann*   **3.31**
v United Kingdom, a case which involved the killings of three members of the
Provisional Irish Republican Army (IRA) by UK special forces in Gibraltar, Article
2(2) 'does not primarily define instances where it is permitted intentionally to kill

---

[107] ICCPR, Art 6(1); see also ECHR, Art2; ACHR, Art 4; ACHPR, Art 4.
[108] ECHR, Art 15(2).
[109] ICCPR, Art 4(2); ECHR, Art 15(2); ACHR, Art 27(2): see paras 3.17–3.21.

an individual, but describes the situations where it is permitted to "use force" which may result, as an unintended outcome, in the deprivation of life'.[110] The Court emphasized that 'the use of the term "absolutely necessary" in Article 2(2) indicates that a stricter and more compelling test of necessity must be employed from that normally applicable when determining whether State action is "necessary in a democratic society"' in Articles 8(2)–11(2).[111] A violation of Article 2 was found on the facts of the case, and related to a disproportionate use of force and questions over the level of training received by the marksmen. *McCann* reflects four composite duties for states parties to the ECHR in counter-terrorism operations which use force:

- first, that any use of force is not accompanied by the intention to kill;
- second, that the use of force is 'absolutely necessary' under Article 2(2) ECHR;
- third, that it is strictly proportionate to the aim in Article 2(2)(a); and
- fourth, that counter-terrorism operations be 'planned and controlled by the authorities so as to minimise, to the greatest extent possible, recourse to lethal force'.

3.32 The failure to plan counter-terrorism operations properly, so as to avoid the risk that innocent bystanders will be killed in the cross-fire, can itself amount to a violation of the right not to be arbitrarily deprived of one's life. In *McCann*, the Court 'carefully scrutinise[d] not only whether the force used by the soldiers was strictly proportionate to the aim of protecting persons against unlawful violence but also whether the anti-terrorist operation was planned and controlled by the authorities so as to minimise, to the greatest extent possible, resource to lethal force'.[112] In *Ergi v Turkey,* the ECtHR unanimously found a violation of Article 2 (the right to life) concerning the death of Ms Haava Ergi in a counter-terrorism operation against members of the Workers' Party of Kurdistan (PKK).[113] The Court held that the state had failed to plan and properly to conduct its counter-terrorist operation, and to carry out an adequate and effective investigation into Ms Ergi's death. This was sufficient to find a violation of Article 2, even though there was reasonable doubt as to whether Ms Ergi had been killed by a bullet fired by the security forces or the PKK.[114]

3.33 The killing of Jean Charles de Menezes in south London in July 2005 illustrates the scope for error in any use of intentionally lethal force, and should remind states of the imperative in case law strictly to plan and control any counter-terrorist operation so as to implement IHRL on the right to life. Mr de Menezes, a Brazilian electrician, was followed into Stockwell Underground station by law enforcement

---

[110] *McCann v United Kingdom* (1995) 21 EHRR 97, para 148.
[111] Ibid, para 149.
[112] Ibid, para 194.
[113] *Ergi v Turkey* (2001) 23 EHRR 388.
[114] Ibid, paras 77–86.

officials who mistakenly thought they were pursuing a suicide bomber. He was shot in the head seven times at close range and died at the scene.[115]

Non-binding standards

The Code of Conduct for Law Enforcement Officials (Code of Conduct) and the **3.34** Body of Principles on the Use of Force and Firearms by Law Enforcement Officials (Body of Principles) reflect general principles of international law on the lawful use of lethal force and firearms by law enforcement officials, but are not binding treaty law.[116] Their restrictions are similar to those in *McCann*: Article 3 of the Code of Conduct permits law enforcement officials to 'use force only when strictly necessary and to the extent required for the performance of their duty'. Principles 4 and 5 of the Body of Principles require law enforcement officials to use non-violent means first, opting for the use of force or firearms only if non-violent means are ineffective, and only if the former are used with 'restraint', 'respect for human life', and by 'minimis[ing] damage and injury'. Principle 9 is unequivocal in its controls on the use of firearms, in a passage that reflects Article 2(2) of the ECHR; and that limits the 'intentional lethal use of firearms . . . only . . . when strictly unavoidable in order to protect life'.

Taken together, treaties, case law, and general principles of international law on the **3.35** right to life establish the following points:

- the right not to be arbitrarily deprived of one's life is non-derogable;
- states must take positive measures to protect individuals within their jurisdiction not only from unlawful killings by the state and its agents, but also by non-state actors;
- the circumstances in which the state may use force or firearms, particularly lethal force, are sharply limited and must be construed narrowly;
- counter-terrorist operations which use force must be carefully planned and controlled to avoid the risk of arbitrary deprivation of life; and
- alleged unlawful killings must be investigated.

Adjudicating the IHRL right to life during armed conflict

Paragraphs 2.38–2.40 noted the nuanced position in international law **3.36** concerning the co-applicability of IHL and IHRL, while paragraphs 2.46–2.56 analysed 'targeted killings' policies under IHL. The International Court of Justice Advisory Opinion on the *Legality of the Threat or Use of Nuclear*

---

[115] See paras 3.44, 4.36.
[116] Code of Conduct for Law Enforcement Officials, UN General Assembly Resolution 34/169, 17 December 1979; Body of Principles for the Use of Force and Firearms by Law Enforcement Officials, adopted by the 8th UN Congress on the Prevention of Crime and the Treatment of Offenders, 27 August to 7 September 1990.

Weapons,[117] which otherwise simply asserted the co-applicability of IHL and IHRL, gives an inkling of guidance as to how the apparent conflict between lawful targeting of combatants in IHL and the right to life in IHRL may be resolved. The Court reasoned that in armed conflict, although the right not to be arbitrarily deprived of one's life continues to apply, IHL applies as *lex specialis* so that '[t]he test of what is an arbitrary deprivation of life . . . falls to be determined by . . . the law applicable in armed conflict'.[118] At least for targeting decisions and the choice of weapons in armed conflict, IHL therefore sets the meaning of 'arbitrary' in IHRL treaty law, so that any targeting must respect the IHL principle of distinction between combatants and civilians, the prohibition on indiscriminate means and methods of warfare, the duty to take precautions in attack to avoid civilian casualties, and the principle of proportionality between military necessity and the risk of harm to civilians.[119]

3.37   Regional human rights courts and UN treaty bodies have been willing to adjudicate on violations of the right to life committed during armed conflict,[120] even though IHL is not part of their subject-matter jurisdiction. In the words of the Inter-American Court of Human Rights, the application of IHL does not 'exonerate[e]' states from their obligation to 'respect and guarantee human rights': the existence of an armed conflict 'in fact oblige[s states] . . . to act in accordance with those obligations'.[121] The Inter-American Commission on Human Rights has noted that the 'common nucleus' of non-derogable rights in IHL and IHRL means that in armed conflict both bodies of law 'protect the lives of civilians, combatants placed *hors de combat*, and to some extent the lives of combatants taking part in the hostilities'.[122]

3.38   The ECtHR applied IHRL to cases of killings in Chechnya, with brief reference to IHL's prohibition on indiscriminate attacks. In *Isayeva v Russia*,[123] military planes dropped explosives over a highly populated area in Chechnya, where militants were holding hostage many civilians, and from which the applicant and her relatives were trying to escape. The applicant's son and three nieces were killed. The Court

---

[117] International Court of Justice, *Legality of the Threat or Use of Nuclear Weapons*, Advisory Opinion, ICJ Reports 1996.

[118] Ibid, para 25.

[119] See para 2.10.

[120] Inter-American Commission on Human Rights, *Las Palmeras v Argentina (Preliminary Objections)*, Inter-American Court of Human Rights, 4 February 2000; *Juan Carlos Abella v Argentina*, Report No 55/97, Case 11.137, 18 November 1997; Inter-American Court of Human Rights, *Bemaca Velásquez v Guatemala*, 25 November 2000; European Court of Human Rights, *Isayeva, Yusupova & Bazayeva v Russia*, 24 February 2005.

[121] Inter-American Court of Human Rights, *Bemaca Velásquez v Guatemala*, 25 November 2000, para 207.

[122] Inter-American Commission on Human Rights, Report on Terrorism and Human Rights, OEA/Ser.l/V/II.116, Doc 5, rev 1, corr, 22 October 2002, 3 The Right to Life and Terrorism, para 108.

[123] European Court of Human Rights, *Isayeva, Yusupova & Bazayeva v Russia*, 24 February 2005.

found a violation of Article 2, as the government forces should have had the 'primary aim' of 'protect[ing] lives from unlawful violence', but that instead, they employed a 'massive use of indiscriminate weapons' which was incompatible with 'the standard of care' required for the use of lethal force by state agents.[124]

In the case of the 'Dirty War' in Colombia, a non-international armed conflict,[125] **3.39** the UN Human Rights Committee found a violation of Article 6(1).[126] This was because Colombian law enforcement officials opened fire on suspected rebels, despite having discovered that the suspected rebels had not taken hostages, as had been previously thought. This amounted to an arbitrary deprivation of life, because the use of force was disproportionate, and arrest could have been used instead.[127] This approach is consistent with the Body of Principles on the Use of Force and Firearms by Law Enforcement Officials, and with the Principles on the Effective Prevention and Investigation of Extra-legal, Summary and Arbitrary Executions, which prohibit killings in circumstances including '*internal armed conflict*, excessive or illegal use of force by a public official or other person acting in an official capacity or by a person acting at the instigation, or with the consent or acquiescence of such person, and situations in which deaths occur in custody'.[128] The existence of an armed conflict neither excuses nor justifies arbitrary deprivation of life in IHRL.

Extrajudicial executions of terrorism suspects

Cross-border strikes and drone attacks

Targeted killings outside armed conflict are presumptively 'extrajudicial executions', which Amnesty International defines as 'unlawful or deliberate killings, carried out by order of a government or with its complicity or acquiescence'.[129] The term 'extrajudicial executions' has no explicit definition in treaty law or non-binding standards.[130] According to one scholarly analysis of the term 'extrajudicial executions' in the context of Israel's targeted killings policy, it can cover any arbitrary deprivation of life in treaty law.[131] The UN Special Rapporteur on extrajudicial, summary, or arbitrary executions has noted his concern at the regular resort to

---

[124] Ibid, para 191.

[125] Expert Meeting on the Right to Life in Armed Conflicts and Situations of Occupation, The University Centre for International Humanitarian Law, Geneva, 1–2 September 2005, p 9.

[126] Human Rights Committee, *Guerrero v Colombia,* Communication No 45/1979, Views, 31 March 1982.

[127] Ibid.

[128] Principles on the Effective Prevention and Investigation of Extra-Legal, Summary and Arbitrary Executions, ECOSOC Resolution 1989/65, 24 May 1989 (emphasis added).

[129] Amnesty International, '14-point Program for the Prevention of Extrajudicial Executions'.

[130] Principles on the Effective Prevention and Investigation of Extra-Legal, Summary and Arbitrary Executions, supra.

[131] David Kretzmer, 'Targeted Killings of Suspected Terrorists: Extra-Judicial Executions or Legitimate Means of Defence?' (2005) 16 *European Journal of International Law* 171–212 at 176.

targeted killings in states' counter-terrorism policies, and has called for investigations into the killings of civilians where the US has targeted suspected terrorists.[132]

3.41 As the analysis in paragraphs 2.48–2.49 demonstrates, any targeted killing which occurs outside armed conflict, including those by US drone attacks in Pakistan, and the US's first targeted killing in Yemen in 2002, is not regulated by IHL, but falls to be analysed by IHRL.[133] As a result, only IHRL applies to determine whether these killings are an arbitrary deprivation of life, just as IHRL alone applies to decide upon the lawfulness of killing terrorism suspects by law enforcement officials in peacetime. The Bush Administration's invocation of a 'global war on terror'[134] does not create new rules for law enforcement officials as regards the use of force and firearms in counter-terrorism.

US: 'kill-capture-detain' orders

3.42 In 2007, the Parliamentary Assembly of the Council of Europe (PACE) produced a report indicating that the United States Central Intelligence Agency's (CIA) network of secret detention centres aimed to 'kill, capture, and detain' 'high-value' terrorism suspects; that two of those secret detention centres were located in Poland and Romania; and that lawyers in the US Justice Department, the CIA, and in the Administration of then President George W Bush had authorized 'Kill-Capture-Detain' or 'K-C-D' orders against certain 'high-value detainees'.[135] Margaret Satterthwaite notes that 'the exact number and identities of people subject to "K-C-D orders" are still unconfirmed',[136] and that disclosures by the US about CIA secret detention centres have not included any further information about the 'kill' component of the alleged "K-C-D orders".[137] As a result, it is unknown how many suspected terrorists may have been killed subsequent to the 'K-C-D orders'. Where there was no ongoing armed conflict at the time a suspected terrorist was killed, any killings which may have taken place subsequent to a 'K-C-D order' should be investigated as extrajudicial executions, and analysed under IHRL alone. National inquiries and accountability processes within the US should press for the

---

[132] UN Special Rapporteur on extrajudicial, summary or arbitrary executions, Report to the 64th session of the General Assembly, A/64/187, 29 July 2009, para 13.

[133] See paras 2.46–2.52; Christian Tomuschat, 'Human Rights and International Humanitarian Law' (2010) 21 European J of Int'l L 15–23.

[134] President George W Bush, Address to US Congress, 21 September 2001; *Washington Post*, 'Global War on Terror is Given New Name', 25 March 2009.

[135] Parliamentary Assembly of the Council of Europe (PACE), 'Secret Detentions and Illegal Transfers of Detainees Involving Council of Europe Member States: Second Report', Doc. 11302 rev, 11 June 2007, paras 7, 64.

[136] Margaret L Satterthwaite, 'The Story of *El Masri v Tenet*: Human Rights and Humanitarian Law in the "War on Terror"', in D R Hurwitz, M L Satterthwaite, and D B Ford (eds), *Human Rights Advocacy Stories* (Foundation Press, 2009), pp 535–577.

[137] Margaret L Satterthwaite, 'The US Program of Extraordinary Rendition and Secret Detention: Past and Future', in European Center for Constitutional and Human Rights (ECCHR) (ed), *CIA Extraordinary Rendition Flights, Torture and Accountability: A European Approach* (ECCHR, 2008), pp 27–59.

release of information about the targeted killings of terrorism suspects and their identities.

Pakistan

As noted in paragraphs 3.29–3.35 above, IHRL and standards only permit the **3.43** intentional use of lethal force when absolutely necessary to prevent loss of life. In *Mehram Ali et al v Federation of Pakistan*, the Supreme Court of Pakistan declared that section 5(2)(a)(i) of the Anti-Terrorism Act 1997 was invalid because it authorized the police, armed forces, or civil armed forces to open fire or to order the opening of fire upon 'any person who is committing, or in all probability is likely to commit a terrorist act or a scheduled offence', merely with a requirement to give 'prior warning', to use 'necessary and appropriate' force, and to consider all circumstances.[138] The statutory authorization to use firearms on terrorism suspects precedes the obligation to arrest 'without warrant' any such suspect (section 5(2)(ii)), or to search premises (section 5(2)(iii)), suggesting that the Pakistan Anti-Terrorism Act 1997 saw the use of force and firearms as a measure of first resort in counter-terrorism.

UK: Jean Charles de Menezes

The killing of Jean Charles de Menezes, a Brazilian electrician who was mistakenly **3.44** identified as a terrorism suspect, indicates the risks of error where a state permits targeted killings of terrorism suspects. The circuitous and inadequate accountability processes which followed his death are considered in paragraph 4.36 below. Where the ECHR applies, the exceptions in Article 2(2)(a)–(c) ECHR should guide states' policies in counter-terrorism. Unless a use of force passes the high threshold of absolute necessity and proportionality as developed in *McCann*, the targeted killing of a terrorism suspect is a violation of the right to life.

As the ICCPR lacks the explicit exceptions developed in Article 2(2)(a)–(c) ECHR, **3.45** it is submitted that any intentional use of lethal force against a terrorism suspect in states where the ECHR does not apply is a violation of the right to life, unless that use of lethal force is absolutely necessary to prevent an imminent terrorist attack.

Deaths in custody

Deaths of terrorism suspects in custody: China, Russian Federation, US

Terrorism detainees have been reported to have died in custody in China,[139] and in **3.46** the Russian Federation.[140] NGO investigations have revealed compelling evidence

---

[138] *Mehram Ali et al v Federation of Pakistan* [1998] PLD SC 1445, 1461–62, 1465.
[139] Radio Free Asia, 'China: Standoff over Death in Custody', 19 September 2009; Xinhua News Agency, 'Police Prevent Terrorist Attacks in Xinjiang', 3 August 2009.
[140] Amnesty International, 'Rule Without Law: Human Rights Violations in the North Caucasus', EUR/46/012/2009, 30 June 2009.

of multiple deaths of terrorism suspects in US custody outside the US. By Human Rights First's calculations, more than 100 terrorism suspects have died in US custody in Bagram Air Base, Afghanistan, at Guantánamo Bay, and in Iraq.[141] Human Rights Watch and Human Rights First have each called upon the US authorities to investigate these deaths.[142] Three apparent suicides in one night were reported to have occurred at Guantánamo Bay detention facility in June 2006. A heavily redacted but apparently contradictory account of their deaths by the US Naval Criminal Investigation Service has been the subject of scrutiny by Seton Hall Law School,[143] and sceptical media analysis.[144]

The duty to investigate deaths in custody

3.47 These NGO and media accounts underscore the need for independent and comprehensive investigations into all deaths in custody. The IHRL on the right to life imposes a duty to prevent and investigate, and where evidence suggests, also prosecute those alleged to be responsible for deaths in custody: a duty which links strongly to the absolute prohibition on torture and cruel, inhuman, or degrading treatment or punishment.

3.48 Where investigations are incomplete, or documents from these investigations are classified or redacted, this duty has not been discharged. States must not impede accountability and victims' right to a remedy and reparations where deaths in custody may have been as a result of a human rights violation. The US Department of Justice filed a brief in 2009 to suggest that the Military Commissions Act 2006, considered in paragraph 3.122 below, stripped federal courts of jurisdiction to hear a case brought by the relatives of two men who died, allegedly by suicide at Guantánamo Bay.[145]

The death of Baha Mousa in UK custody in Iraq

3.49 The duty to investigate apparent violations of the right to life applies to all deaths in custody which occur within a state's jurisdiction, including when a state has 'effective control' of a person held extraterritorially. This duty is consistent with the UN Human Rights Committee's General Comment No 31, which confirmed that states parties to the ICCPR must ensure ICCPR rights to all persons within their

---

[141] Human Rights First, 'Command's Responsibility: Detainee Deaths in US Custody in Iraq and Afghanistan', February 2006.

[142] Ibid; Human Rights Watch, 'US: Release the Full Report into Guantanamo Deaths', 7 December 2009.

[143] Mark Denbeaux and Joshua Denbeaux, 'Report: June 10th Suicides at Guantanamo: Government Words and Deeds Compared', 21 August 2006.

[144] Scott Horton, 'The Guantánamo "Suicides": A Camp Delta Sergeant Blows the Whistle', *Harper's Magazine*, 18 January 2010.

[145] Human Rights Watch, 'US: Release the Full Report into Guantanamo Deaths', 7 December 2009.

custody and control, even if that person is not within that state's territory.[146] Case law has established that IHRL can apply extraterritorially (a) to individuals held in a state's custody outside the territorial state,[147] and (b) to areas of territory subject to the 'effective control' of the state in question.[148]

Although Israel,[149] the US,[150] and the UK dispute the extraterritorial effect of IHRL   **3.50** treaties in general, in the case concerning the deaths of Iraqi civilians in UK custody in Iraq, the UK government's counsel conceded a limited extraterritorial effect of Article 2 ECHR, relating to point (a) above. While the UK government continues to argue that jurisdiction under the ECHR is primarily territorial, the UK admitted it was bound by Article 2 ECHR in relation to the death of the Iraqi civilian Baha Mousa in UK custody in Iraq in September 2003.[151] The House of Lords found that Article 2 ECHR, incorporated into the UK's three legal systems by the Human Rights Act 1998, applied only to the death of Mr Mousa in British military custody, and not to other Iraqi civilians killed in crossfire.[152] Paragraph 4.36 will consider the court-martial and public inquiry procedure into the death of Baha Mousa.

Death penalty

The ICCPR, ECHR, and ACHR provide for certain limited exceptions to the   **3.51** right to life for those states which have not abolished the death penalty,[153] although the Second Optional Protocol to the ICCPR (ICCPR-OP2),[154] and Protocols No 6 and 13 of the ECHR oblige states which have ratified them to abolish the

---

[146] Human Rights Committee General Comment No 31, The Nature of the General Legal Obligation Imposed on State Parties, CCPR/C/21/Rev.1/Add.13, 26 May 2004, para 10; see also Committee Against Torture, General Comment No 2, para 16.

[147] *Burgos/Delia Saldias de López v Uruguay*, Inter-American Commission on Human Rights, Communication No 52/1979, UN Doc CCPR/C/OP/1 (1984); *Issa and Others v Turkey (Merits)* (2005) 41 EHRR 567, 16 November 2004.

[148] *Loizidou v Turkey (Preliminary Objections)*, Application No 15318/89, (1995) 20 EHRR 99, 23 March 1995; *Loizidou v Turkey (Merits)*, Application No 15318/89 (1997) 23 EHRR 513, 28 November 1996; *Xhavara and Others v Italy and Albania*, Application No 39473/98, 11 January 2001; *Cyprus v Turkey*, Application No 2581/94, Judgment of 10 May 2001.

[149] Human Rights Committee, Concluding Observations on the initial report of Israel, CCPR/C/79/Add.93, 18 August 1998, para 11.

[150] Human Rights Committee, Concluding Observations on the second and third periodic reports of the United States of America, CCPR/C/USA/CO/3, 15 September 2006, para 10; Committee against Torture, Concluding Observations on the second report of the United States of America, CAT/C/USA/CO/2, 25 July 2006, para 15; Steven Bradbury, US Acting Assistant Attorney General, US DOJ OLC , Memorandum for John Rizzo, Deputy General Counsel, CIA, 30 May 2005.

[151] *Al Skeini and Others v Secretary of State for Defence* [2007] UKHL 26, para 97.

[152] *Al Skeini and Others v Secretary of State for Defence* [2007] UKHL 26.

[153] ICCPR, Art 6(2), (4)–(6) ECHR, Art 2(1); ACHR, Art 4 (2)–(6).

[154] Second Optional Protocol to the International Covenant on Civil and Political Rights, aiming at the abolition of the death penalty (ICCPR-OP2).

death penalty.[155] Protocol No 13 to the ECHR extends the abolition of the death penalty so that it cannot be imposed, and people cannot be sentenced to death, in any circumstance. Protocol No 6 to the ECHR did not exclude the application of the death penalty in relation to acts committed 'in time of war or of imminent threat of war'.[156] The ACHR is supplemented by a Protocol to the American Convention on Human Rights to Abolish the Death Penalty.

3.52   China,[157] India,[158] Pakistan,[159] Iraq,[160] Morocco,[161] Saudi Arabia,[162] and the US[163] are among the states which maintain the death penalty for those convicted of terrorist crimes, despite the increasing tendency towards moratoria and abolition of the death penalty worldwide.[164] Those states which have ratified the Second Optional Protocol to the ICCPR aiming at the abolition of the death penalty, or its regional equivalents, are bound to abolish the death penalty. However, the legal analysis of the right to life in IHRL permits the continued use of the death penalty, with multiple specific controls, for those states which have not ratified specific

---

[155] Protocol No 6 to the Convention for the Protection of Human Rights and Fundamental Freedoms Concerning the Abolition of the Death Penalty; Protocol No 13 to the Convention for the Protection of Human Rights and Fundamental Freedoms Concerning the Abolition of the Death Penalty in All Circumstances.

[156] Protocol No 13 to the Convention for the Protection of Human Rights and Fundamental Freedoms Concerning the Abolition of the Death Penalty in All Circumstances; Protocol No 6 to the Convention for the Protection of Human Rights and Fundamental Freedoms concerning the Abolition of the Death Penalty.

[157] Criminal Law of the People's Republic of China, Order No 83, 14 March 1997, s 5; Decision Regarding the Severe Punishment of Criminals Who Seriously Endanger Public Security, Order No 3, Decision of 2 September 1983; International Bar Association Human Rights Institute, 'China: Call for Abolition of Death Penalty', 25 February 2009.

[158] India, Prevention of Terrorism Act 2002, Act No 15 of 2002, 28 March 2002, s 3(2)(a); *Devender Pal Singh v State of NCT of Delhi* 2002 (1) SC (Cr) 209; the Special Court of India passed a death sentence on Mohammed Ajmal Kasab, the surviving perpetrator of the Mumbai terrorist attacks in November 2008; see: *Los Angeles Times*, 'Mumbai Gunman Sentenced to Hang', 7 May 2010.

[159] Pakistan, Anti-Terrorism Act 1997 (as amended), s 7(1), 22.

[160] Iraqi Penal Code 1969 (Law 111 of 1969, as amended), Anti-Terrorism Act 2005, Art 4, quoted in Amnesty International, 'Unjust and Unfair: The Death Penalty in Iraq', MDE 14/014/2007, 20 April 2007.

[161] Morocco, Dahir (Law) no 03.03, quoted in Youssef El Bouhairi, 'The Fight Against Terrorism: Between the Reason of State and the Human Rights. Special Reference to Morocco', in Pablo Antonio Fernández-Sánchez (ed), *International Legal Dimension of Terrorism* (Martinus Nijhoff, 2009), p 47; Dahir no 1-59-413 of 26 November 1962, as amended, Art 218-7, specifies that the death penalty can be imposed for acts of terrorism.

[162] Amnesty International, 'Countering Terrorism with Repression', MDE 23/025/2009, August 2009, 43–55.

[163] Department of Justice, 'Departments of Justice and Defense Announce Forum Decisions for Ten Guantanamo Bay Detainees', 13 November 2009; CNN, 'Accused New York Plotter Faces New York Trial', 13 November 2009.

[164] UN Commission on Human Rights Resolution 2004/67; Amnesty International, 'Rwanda Abolishes Death Penalty', 2 August 2007; IBA Council Resolution on the Abolition of the Death Penalty, adopted 15 May 2008; IBA Human Rights Institute 2009 Annual Report (notes moratorium on the death penalty in the Russian Federation, November 2009), pp 4 and 29.

treaties to abolish it. These include a requirement that the death penalty only be imposed for the most serious crimes,[165] after a final judgment by a competent court,[166] and that it never be imposed on those who were under 18 at the time of their crime, nor on pregnant women.[167] Those sentenced to death must be permitted to seek pardon or commutation of the sentence.[168]

Nonetheless, the cruelty and inhumanity of capital punishment cannot be overstated. The imperative of a fair trial cannot be more urgent where there is a risk of capital punishment. There should be serious concern when the death penalty has been imposed after politically motivated trials in special security courts, and in a context of widespread discrimination on racial or religious grounds.[169]   **3.53**

Torture and cruel, inhuman, or degrading treatment or punishment

The prohibition of torture and ill-treatment in IHRL

This section emphasizes the peremptory (*jus cogens*) nature of the prohibition of torture, and of states' obligations to prevent, investigate, and prosecute acts of torture, regardless of the identity of the perpetrator; and to provide fair compensation to victims. It scrutinizes case studies of so-called 'extraordinary rendition' to torture and secret detention; the increased use of 'diplomatic assurances' to transfer terrorism suspects to other states, including where there are substantial grounds for believing that they may face torture; and the use of evidence (which is established to have been obtained) as a result of torture—in courts, contrary to Article 15 of the Convention against Torture, and also by intelligence agencies.   **3.54**

Torture is the intentional infliction of severe mental or physical pain or suffering, for one of four prohibited purposes, by or with the consent or acquiescence of a public official or another person acting in an official capacity.[170] Torture, and cruel, inhuman, or degrading treatment or punishment are absolutely prohibited in international human rights treaty law.[171] The prohibition on torture is also a   **3.55**

---

[165] ICCPR, Art 6(2).

[166] Ibid, Art 6(2).

[167] Ibid, Art 6(5).

[168] Ibid, Art 6(4).

[169] Amnesty International, 'Unjust and Unfair: The Death Penalty in Iraq', MDE 14/014/2007, 20 April 2007; Amnesty International, 'China: Briefing for the UN Committee on the Elimination of Racial Discrimination', 75th session, August 2009, 1 June 2009.

[170] Convention against Torture, Art 1(1).

[171] ICCPR, Art 7; Convention against Torture and Other Cruel, Inhuman or Degrading Treatment or Punishment; ECHR, Art 7; ACHR, Art 5(2); ACHPR, Art 5; Committee against Torture (CAT), General Comment No 2, CAT/C/GC/2, 24 January 2008, para 6 (emphasizing that the prohibition on cruel, inhuman, or degrading treatment or punishment is also absolute and non-derogable).

peremptory (*jus cogens*) norm in customary international law.[172] The prohibition on both torture and cruel, inhuman, or degrading treatment or punishment is non-derogable, and '[n]o exceptional circumstances whatsoever, whether a state of war or a threat of war, internal political instability or any other public emergency, may be invoked as a justification of torture'.[173] States are obliged to criminalize, prevent, investigate, and prosecute acts of torture, or to extradite suspected offenders, regardless of the identity of the perpetrator; and to provide fair compensation to victims.[174]

3.56 States have a range of pragmatic preventive obligations as part of the international legal prohibition of torture. In addition to criminalizing torture, attempted torture, and complicity or participation in torture ,[175] states parties must train 'law enforcement personnel, civil or military, medical personnel, public officials and other persons who may be involved in the custody, interrogation or treatment of any individual subjected to any form of arrest, detention or imprisonment' in the prohibition of torture, and include this prohibition in the 'rules or instructions' issued to them.[176]

3.57 Other obligations to prevent torture, which require states to submit places of detention to inspection by an expert body, are found in the Optional Protocol to the Convention against Torture and Other Cruel, Inhuman or Degrading Treatment or Punishment (OP-CAT), and the European Convention for the Prevention of Torture and Inhuman or Degrading Treatment or Punishment. The Inter-American Convention to Prevent and Punish Torture echoes the obligation of the UN Convention against Torture for member states of the Organization of American States (OAS).

3.58 Under Article 3 of the Convention against Torture, states must not transfer an individual to another state if 'there are substantial grounds for believing that he would be in danger of being subjected to torture'.[177] This *non-refoulement* obligation, which is distinct from the obligation of the same name in international refugee law,[178] has been threatened by states' increasing reliance on diplomatic assurances or on Memoranda of Understanding. These purport to provide guarantees that a particular terrorism suspect will not be tortured if transferred to the custody of a state where he or she is at risk of torture.

3.59 Article 15 of the Convention against Torture provides for the inadmissibility in any proceedings of 'any statement which is established to have been made as a result

---

[172] CAT, General Comment No 2, supra, para 1.
[173] Convention against Torture, Art 2(2).
[174] Ibid, Arts 4, 5–9, 12–14.
[175] Ibid, Art 4.
[176] Ibid, Art 10.
[177] Ibid, Art 3.
[178] Convention relating to the Status of Refugees 1951, Arts 1(F) and 33; see paras 1.27–1.28.

of torture'. The only exception is if the proceedings in question are a prosecution for torture, in which case the statement may be admitted as evidence.[179]

States must prevent cruel, inhuman, or degrading treatment or punishment; include **3.60** its prohibition in the training of officials; keep interrogation rules under review to prevent such treatment; investigate allegations; and provide victims with a right to complain to the authorities and to have their case promptly and independently examined, while being protected against ill-treatment and intimidation.[180] Case law suggests that conduct which in the past would have been considered cruel, inhuman, or degrading treatment or punishment may now be considered torture.[181] Case law has emphasized the non-derogable nature of the prohibition against torture and ill-treatment, regardless of national security concerns;[182] and the centrality of this norm to IHRL.

Torture in states' counter-terrorism operations

While the torture of detainees at Abu Ghraib prison in Iraq in 2004,[183] at Bagram **3.61** Air Base in Afghanistan,[184] and of 'high-value detainees' held in US custody in the 'war on terror',[185] may be the most widely known examples of torture against those detained in counter-terrorism operations, the torture and ill-treatment of terrorism detainees recurs region-by-region, and is not a new phenomenon. The following examples are listed chronologically, with additional findings from UN treaty bodies and special procedures and legislative analysis listed alphabetically:

* The European Commission of Human Rights found that the 'five techniques' of wall-standing, hooding, subjection to continuous hissing noise, deprivation of food, and deprivation of sleep used by UK officials against detainees from the IRA constituted not only inhuman and degrading treatment or punishment but also torture.[186] The ECtHR in 1978 found a clear violation of Article 3 ECHR, finding the 'five techniques' to be inhuman or degrading.[187]
* Prior to the end of the Dirty War in 1983, Argentina established 280 internment camps, and used torture and execution in its own state terrorism against non-state

---

[179] Convention against Torture, Art 15.

[180] Ibid, Art 16 and cf Arts 10–13.

[181] European Court of Human Rights, *Ireland v United Kingdom* (1978) 2 EHRR 25; *Aksoy v Turkey* (1996) 23 EHRR 553; *Selmouni v France* (1999) 29 EHRR 403.

[182] *Aksoy v Turkey* (1996) 23 EHRR 553; CAT, General Comment No 2, supra.

[183] Human Rights Watch, 'The Road to Abu Ghraib', 8 June 2004.

[184] Human Rights Watch, 'Enduring Freedom: Abuses by US Forces in Afghanistan', 7 March 2004.

[185] ICRC Report on the Treatment of Fourteen 'High Value Detainees' in CIA Custody, February 2007 (released 2009).

[186] *Ireland v United Kingdom* (1976) *Yearbook of European Human Rights Law* 512.

[187] *Ireland v United Kingdom* (1978) 2 EHRR 25.

militants in the 1980s: 9,000 cases of enforced disappearances were documented by a national commission.[188]

- Algeria was found to have tortured security detainees in its war of independence from France, and in the conflict during the 1990s.[189] NGOs have noted with concern the risks of lasting impunity for these and subsequent acts of torture as a result of amnesty laws.[190]

- Widespread resort to torture has been documented in China, where rules of evidence permit the use of confessions obtained through torture,[191] and where punishments and 'preventive measures' allow for legislation to be applied flexibly according to the urgency of the situation.[192]

- In Israel, case law used to permit the use of sleep deprivation in interrogation and a defence of necessity for public officials who use coercion in a 'ticking bomb' situation.[193] In 1999, the Supreme Court of Israel ruled that the system of interrogation recommended by the Landau Commission of Inquiry and in operation from 1987–99 was unlawful, and that the defence of necessity could not apply.[194]

- In Jordan, the UN Special Rapporteur on torture and other cruel, inhuman, or degrading treatment or punishment found that torture is 'routine' in interrogations by the General Intelligence Directorate (GID), and the Criminal Investigations Department (CID).[195]

- Torture in Pakistan has been extensively documented, including the extent to which intelligence services from the US and the UK are complicit in torture by

---

[188] *Nunca Más: Informe sobre la desaparición de personas* (Editorial Universitaria de Buenos Aires, 1983), cited in William C Banks and Alejandro D Carrió, 'Terrorism in Argentina', in Victor V Ramraj, Michael Hor, and Kent Roach (eds), *Global Anti-Terrorism Law and Policy* (Cambridge University Press, 2005), pp 609–625, at p 613 and note 17.

[189] Report of the Committee against Torture, General Assembly 52nd session, Supplement No 44, A/52/44, Concluding Observations: Algeria, 18 November 1996, paras 70–80.

[190] Amnesty International, 'Algeria: Unrestrained Powers: Torture by Algeria's Military Security', MDE 28/004/2006, 9 July 2006.

[191] Report of the Special Rapporteur on torture and other cruel, inhuman or degrading treatment or punishment, Manfred Nowak, Mission to China, Commission on Human Rights 62nd session, E/CN.2/2006/6/Add.6, p 2.

[192] People's Republic of China, Macau Special Administrative Region, Prevention and Suppression of the Crimes of Terrorism, Law No 3/2006, chapters 3 and 4, 'Preventative provisions'; Peoples' Republic of China, Decision Regarding the Severe Punishment of Criminals who Seriously Endanger Public Security, Order No 3, Decision of 2 September 1983.

[193] Supreme Court of Israel sitting as the High Court of Justice, *The Public Committee against Torture in Israel v The State of Israel*, HCJ 5100/94 53(4) PD 817; see also Conclusions and Recommendations of the Committee against Torture: Israel, CAT/C/XXVII/Concl.5, 23 November 2001, para 6.

[194] Yuval Ginbar, *Why Not Torture Terrorists? Moral, Practical and Legal Aspects of the 'Ticking Bomb' Justification for Torture* (OUP, 2008), chs 12 and 14; see also Conclusions and Recommendations of the Committee against Torture: Israel, CAT/C/XXVII/Concl.5, 23 November 2001, para 6.

[195] Report of the Special Rapporteur on torture and other cruel, inhuman or degrading treatment or punishment, Manfred Nowak, Mission to Jordan, Human Rights Council, 4th session, A/HRC/4/33/Add.3, p 2.

Pakistan's security services.[196] Terrorism suspects who were subsequently released report being questioned after their fingernails had been extracted, and at least one suspect was forcibly drugged.[197]

- The Committee against Torture has found that the Russian Federation tortured and subjected to enforced disappearances those suspected of involvement in alleged militant activities in Chechnya and Ingushetia.[198] At the time of the Second Chechen War, Article 2 of the Russian Federation Federal Law on Counter-Terrorism 1998 affirmed basic principles in counter-terrorism including the 'inevitability of punishment for terrorist activity', 'minimum concessions to terrorists', and 'minimum disclosure of technical methods and tactics for the conduct of counterterrorist operations': creating an institutional secrecy in which torture could flourish.[199] Similar principles are contained in Article 2 of the Russian Federation Federal Law on the War against Terrorism 2006 which replaced the 1998 Federal Law and is currently in force.[200] Statutes do not regulate *zachistka* (roughly translated as 'thorough cleaning' or 'mop-up operations'), which are federal law enforcement actions which block entry and exit to individual villages, and interrogate and torture civilians. In one such *zachistka* in Tevzeni, Vvedensky district, Chechnya, in August 2002, 70 people were summarily detained for several days and tortured with electric shocks.[201] The ECtHR found violations of Articles 2, 3, and 13 in respect of a *zachistka* carried out in Chechnya in 2000.[202]
- The prevalence of Emergency Regulations in Sri Lanka has yielded 'routine' torture of terrorism detainees.[203] The UN Committee against Torture and the International Commission of Jurists have each urged Sri Lanka to bring administrative detainees promptly before a judge to check the lawfulness of their

---

[196] Human Rights Watch, 'Cruel Britannia: British Complicity in the Torture and Ill-Treatment of Terror Suspects in Pakistan', 24 November 2009.

[197] Ibid.

[198] Committee against Torture, Conclusions and Recommendations on the fourth periodic report of the Russian Federation, CAT/C/RUS/CO/4, 6 February 2007, paras 22 et seq.

[199] Russian Federation Federal Law on Counter-Terrorism No 130-FZ, 25 July 1998, Art 2.

[200] Russian Federation Federal Law on the War against Terrorism, No 35-FZ of 6 March 2006 (as amended on 27 July 2006, and on 8 November, 22 December, and 30 December 2008), Art 2(4), (10), and (11).

[201] 'Counterterrorism Operation' by the Russian Federation in the Northern Caucasus throughout 1999–2006', Brief Overview by the Human Rights Center *Memorial* submitted to the Eminent Jurists Panel on Terrorism, Counter-Terrorism and Human Rights, 2007, pp 12–14.

[202] European Court of Human Rights, *Khashiyev and Akayeva v Russia*, Application nos 57942/00 and 57945/00, quoted in '"Counterterrorism Operation" by the Russian Federation in the Northern Caucasus throughout 1999–2006', Brief Overview by the Human Rights Center *Memorial* submitted to the Eminent Jurists Panel on Terrorism, Counter-Terrorism and Human Rights, 2007, p 12.

[203] Report of the Special Rapporteur on torture and other cruel, inhuman or degrading treatment or punishment, Manfred Nowak, Mission to Sri Lanka, Human Rights Council, 7th session, A/HRC/7/3/Add.8, 26 February 2008, p 3.

detention, not only to protect the right to liberty and security of the person, but also as an important safeguard against torture and enforced disappearances.[204]

- Uzbekistan systematically tortures dissidents and those charged with 'terrorism',[205] and has been an important ally in the US-led 'war on terror'.[206] This brief global survey is far from an exhaustive list.

'Extraordinary rendition' to torture

3.62 'Extraordinary rendition' is not a legal term of art, but is media shorthand for a range of overlapping human rights violations: arrest or abduction by state agents, a denial of lawful process in detainee transfer, secret or incommunicado detention, torture and ill-treatment, and enforced disappearances. It is a modified version of the kidnapping rather than extradition formalized by US President Reagan's 'rendition to justice' in National Security Decision Directive 207. [207]

3.63 The practice of 'extraordinary rendition' shows the complicity of multiple states in lawless counter-terrorism practices. A Council of Europe inquiry established that several European states violated their IHRL obligations '[i]n at least ten cases, in relation to seventeen victims' of extraordinary rendition; that those violations were 'a *determining factor* for the viability of the operations' which should engage state responsibility for internationally unlawful acts.[208] Such findings should give rise to investigations and prosecutions for alleged complicity in torture, or the extradition of those alleged to be responsible, as required by the Convention against Torture.

3.64 Participation in 'extraordinary renditions' where a detainee is transferred to a risk of torture may also violate the *non-refoulement* obligation in Article 3 of the Convention against Torture. The Committee against Torture found a violation of Article 3 in the case of Ahmed Agiza, an Egyptian national who had been summarily

---

[204] UN Committee against Torture, Concluding Observations on Sri Lanka, CAT/C/LKA/CO/2, 15 December 2005, para 8; International Commission of Jurists, 'Sri Lanka: Briefing Paper—Emergency Laws and International Standards', March 2009.

[205] Report of the Special Rapporteur on torture and other cruel, inhuman or degrading treatment or punishment, Manfred Nowak, Addendum, Follow-up to the recommendations made by the Special Rapporteur's country visits, Uzbekistan, E/CN.4/2006/6/Add.2, 21 March 2006.

[206] Jane Mayer, *The Dark Side: The Inside Story of How the War on Terror Turned into a War on American Ideals* (Anchor Books, 2009), pp 131–132; Rosemary Foot, *Human Rights and Counter-Terrorism in America's Asia Policy* (International Institute for Strategic Studies, Adelphi Paper 363, 2004), pp 34–42.

[207] Margaret L Satterthwaite, 'The Story of *El Masri v Tenet*: Human Rights and Humanitarian Law in the "War on Terror"', in D R Hurwitz, M L Satterthwaite, and D B Ford (eds), *Human Rights Advocacy Stories* (Foundation Press, 2009), pp 535–577.

[208] Amnesty International, *Partners in Crime: Europe's Role in US Renditions*, EUR 01/008/2006, 13 June 2006, Parliamentary Assembly of the Council of Europe (PACE) Resolution 1507 (2006), *Alleged Secret Detention and Unlawful Inter-State Transfer of Detainees involving Council of Europe Member States*, quoted in Nuria Arenas-Hidalgo, 'The International Responsibility of the EU in US "Extraordinary Renditions" of Suspected Terrorists', in Pablo Antonio Fernández-Sánchez (ed), *International Legal Dimension of Terrorism* (Martinus Nijhoff, 2009), pp 113–130, at p 115 (emphasis in original).

expelled from Sweden to Egypt following his unsuccessful asylum claim. Ahmed Agiza was subsequently held in solitary confinement in an Egyptian prison with his hands and feet bound, deprived of access to a toilet, and subjected to torture by electric shocks.[209] The Committee against Torture held that the Swedish authorities knew or should have known, at the time of Ahmed Agiza's removal to Egypt, that there were substantial grounds for believing that he would be in danger of torture there.[210] The widespread use of torture in Egypt was well-known, especially against terrorism suspects, and the Swedish authorities considered Ahmed Agiza a terrorism suspect.[211] As Ahmed Agiza was transferred to Egypt subject to diplomatic assurances, which the Committee against Torture viewed as insufficient to discharge Sweden's obligations under Article 3 of the Convention against Torture, his case is also relevant to paragraphs 3.74–3.80 below.

Dual Canadian–Syrian national, Maher Arar, was detained in New York in **3.65** September 2002 and transferred without full legal process first to Jordan and then on to Syria, where he was detained incommunicado and tortured, on the basis of inaccurate information shared with US intelligence agents by Canadian officials. The US was fully aware of the endemic torture practised by Syrian Military Intelligence (SMI), as the US State Department had itself reported on the torture and resort to incommunicado detention practised by the SMI.[212] A Canadian inquiry into the events surrounding the case of Maher Arar found that some Canadian consular officials who visited Mr Arar in Syria operated under the 'working assumption' that he had been tortured,[213] indicating Canada's complicity in torture by Syrian officials. The Canadian public inquiry declared Mr Arar innocent of all involvement in terrorism, apologized and awarded monetary compensation. In November 2009, the Second Circuit Court of Appeals dismissed Maher Arar's appeal owing to a lack of standing to obtain declaratory relief for torture committed outside the US,[214] and Arar has appealed to the Supreme Court.[215] In June 2010, the US Supreme Court declined to grant certiorari, without giving reasons, precluding any possibility that his case will ever be heard by a US court.[216]

The UK resident Binyam Mohamed was subjected to 'extraordinary rendition' on a **3.66** flight from Morocco to Afghanistan in 2004. In February 2010, seven previously

---

[209] Committee against Torture, Decision, *Agiza v Sweden*, CAT/C/34/D/233/2003, 20 May 2005.
[210] Ibid, para 13.4.
[211] Ibid, paras 13.2–13.4.
[212] US State Department, Country Reports on Human Rights Practices, 2001, Syria, 4 March 2002.
[213] Commission of Inquiry into the Actions of Canadian Officials in Relation to Maher Arar, *Report of the Events relating to Maher Arar: Analysis and Recommendations*, 5.3.2.
[214] *Arar v Ashcroft et al*, US 2nd Court of Appeals, 06-4216-cv, 2 November 2009.
[215] *Arar v Ashcroft et al*, Petition for Writ of Certiorari to the US Supreme Court, 1 February 2010.
[216] *Arar v Ashcroft, Former Attorney-General*, 09-923, US Supreme Court Order List 560 US, 14 June 2010.

redacted paragraphs from an earlier judgment which showed evidence of British complicity in the 'cruel, inhuman and degrading' treatment of Mr Mohamed were finally published.[217] They revealed that 'at some stage during [a] further interview process by the United States authorities',[218] Binyam Mohamed was subjected to sustained sleep deprivation, which was likely to have been worsened by having been shackled throughout the interviews.[219] He was threatened with being subjected to enforced disappearance.[220] Binyam Mohamed was placed under supervision lest he harm himself, as evidence of the mental suffering that this ill-treatment caused.[221] The Court of Appeal ruled that the treatment suffered by Binyam Mohamed 'if it had been administered on behalf of the United Kingdom, would clearly have been in breach of the undertakings given . . . in 1972',[222] following the judgment of the ECtHR in *Ireland v UK*. Paragraph 4.46 will consider the secrecy and complicity in torture revealed by this case.

3.67 Human Rights Watch collected evidence of the 'extraordinary rendition' of Kenyan nationals to interrogation and torture in Ethiopia in 2007.[223] The report details the beatings and injuries suffered by Ismael Noor, who was unlawfully transferred to Ethiopia from Kenya with the collusion or encouragement of US intelligence officials, and detained for 14 months.[224] As yet there has been no criminal investigation or prosecution of those involved in the abduction and unlawful transfer of Kenyan nationals to Ethiopia and Somalia, and the arbitrary detention and torture of security detainees and political opponents in Ethiopia continues.[225]

3.68 The case of Abu Omar is a single example of successful prosecution and limited accountability for 'extraordinary rendition' to torture, as paragraphs 4.25–4.49 will discuss. In this Italian prosecution, 22 CIA operatives and one military officer were found guilty *in absentia* in November 2009. They were sentenced to prison terms, for involvement in the abduction in 2003 of Abu Omar from Milan to Ramstein Air Base in Germany. Abu Omar was then transferred on to Egypt, where he was detained for four years and tortured. Two Italian security personnel were also convicted of complicity in Abu Omar's abduction.[226] It should be noted in this context

---

[217] *R v Secretary of State for Foreign and Commonwealth Affairs, ex parte Binyam Mohamed* [2010] EWCA Civ 158, 26 February 2010.

[218] Previously redacted para (v).

[219] Paragraph (vi)–(vii).

[220] Paragraph (vi).

[221] Paragraph (viii).

[222] Paragraph (x)

[223] Human Rights Watch, '"Why Am I Still Here?" The 2007 Horn of Africa Renditions and the Fate of Those Still Missing', October 2008.

[224] Ibid, pp 22–27.

[225] Human Rights Watch, Universal Periodic Review mechanism Submission, Ethiopia, April 2009.

[226] Spiegel Online International, 'Abu Omar Case: Italian Court Delivers Damning Verdict on CIA Renditions', 4 November 2009; Francesco Messineo, '"Extraordinary Renditions" and State Obligations to Criminalize and Prosecute Torture in the Light of the Abu Omar Case in Italy' (2009) 7 *Journal of International Criminal Justice* 1023–1044.

that in general trials *in absentia* are considered a violation of the right to a fair trial under international law except in limited circumstances, for example where the accused has been informed of the proceedings against him and declines to exercise his right to be present.[227]

As an essential component of the prohibition against torture, states should crimin- **3.69** alize, investigate, and prosecute any involvement in the arrest or abduction and unlawful transfer of any suspect to another jurisdiction where there are substantial grounds for believing that he or she will be in danger of torture or cruel, inhuman, or degrading treatment or punishment. As *Agiza v Sweden* above and paragraphs 3.74–3.80 below show, 'diplomatic assurances' are paltry reassurance that an individual will not be tortured. Memoranda of Understanding or 'diplomatic assurances' cannot extricate a state from its obligation to inquire whether there are substantial grounds for believing that an individual will face a risk of torture if transferred, nor from the obligation not to transfer that individual if there are such substantial grounds.

Attempts to shrink the definition of torture: the US Department of Justice 'Torture Memos'

IHRL prohibits absolutely both torture and cruel, inhuman, or degrading treat- **3.70** ment or punishment: the dual prohibition is non-derogable and cannot be justified or excused by terrorism. Nonetheless, the distinction between torture and cruel, inhuman, or degrading treatment or punishment may be exploited in jurisdictions where the criminal prohibition of cruel, inhuman, or degrading treatment or punishment is lacking or unclear, and where there are few, if any, prosecutions of torture. Lawyers must act to uphold the rule of law and IHRL: duties which are reflected in UN standards.[228] This subsection examines the attempts of lawyers in only one jurisdiction, the US.

Until President Obama's Executive Order revoking all previously authorized CIA **3.71** interrogation practices and requiring that interrogations comply with the US Army Field Manual,[229] lawyers in the Bush Administration had attempted to define interrogation policies as lawful by minimizing the definition of torture in federal criminal law. In 2002 and 2005, lawyers of the Office of Legal Counsel of the US Department of Justice wrote a series of classified memoranda for the CIA which considered

---

[227] General Comment No 13: Equality before the courts and the right to a fair and public hearing by an independent court established by law (Art 14), 13/04/1984; *Daniel Monguya Mbenge v Zaire*, Communication No 16/1977, UN Doc CCPR/C/OP/2 at 76 (1990); see also Report of the Secretary-General Pursuant to Paragraph 2 of Security Council Resolution 808, UN Doc S/25704, para 101.
[228] Basic Principles on the Role of Lawyers, 8th United Nations Conference on the Prevention of Crime and the Treatment of Offenders, Havana, Cuba, 27 August to 7 September 1990.
[229] Executive Order, Ensuring Lawful Interrogations, 22 January 2009.

whether the interrogation techniques which the CIA intended to use on detainees would amount to torture under US federal criminal law.[230]

- The first such memorandum was written on 1 August 2002, but released in a partially redacted form only after a successful Freedom of Information Act request by the American Civil Liberties Union (ACLU). It reveals ten interrogation techniques modelled on the Survival, Evasion, Resistance, Escape (SERE) simulations used in training by the US armed forces. Jay S Bybee, the author of the memorandum and the then Assistant Attorney-General, authorized ten interrogation methods which were used on Abu Zubaydah, one of the CIA's 'high-value detainees'. The ten techniques were: '(1) attention grasp, (2) walling [pushing the detainee's upper body against a false wall], (3) facial hold, (4) facial slap, (5) cramped confinement, (6) wall standing, (7) stress positions, (8) sleep deprivation, (9) insects placed in confinement box, and (10) the waterboard [simulated drowning].' The techniques were to be used 'as-needed' and 'in some sort of escalating fashion'.

- The 1 August 2002 memorandum attempts to shrink the definition of torture as prohibited by US federal criminal law.[231] Its author separates mental and physical pain and suffering, and concludes that as previous communications between the Department of Justice and the CIA had suggested that 'severe . . . physical pain and suffering' would be the equivalent of burning a detainee or beating him or her with clubs, none of the interrogation techniques proposed would constitute 'severe . . . physical pain and suffering': the then definition of torture in US criminal law.

- The 1 August 2002 memorandum also considers waterboarding, or simulated drowning, as follows:

  > The waterboard, which inflicts no pain or actual harm whatsoever, does not in our view inflict 'severe pain and suffering'. Even if one were to parse the statute more finely to attempt to treat 'suffering' as a distinct concept, the waterboard could not be said to inflict severe suffering. The waterboard is simply a controlled acute episode, lacking the connotation of a protracted period of time generally given to suffering.[232]

Considering that elsewhere in the memorandum there is discussion of the likely physiological response of a heightened carbon dioxide level in the detainee's blood as a result of the 'waterboarding', and acknowledgement that the detainee will experience the sensation of drowning, the reasoning that such treatment

---

[230] Jay S Bybee, US Assistant Attorney General, US DOJ OLC, Memorandum for John Rizzo, Acting General Counsel, CIA, 1 August 2002; Steven Bradbury, US Acting Assistant Attorney General, US DOJ OLC, Memorandum for John Rizzo, Senior Deputy General Counsel, CIA, 10 May 2005; Steven Bradbury, US Acting Assistant Attorney General, US DOJ OLC, Memorandum for John Rizzo, Deputy General Counsel, CIA, 30 May 2005.

[231] 18 USC ss 2340–2340A.

[232] Jay S Bybee, US Assistant Attorney General, US DOJ OLC, Memorandum for John Rizzo, Acting General Counsel, CIA, 1 August 2002, p 11.

would not constitute 'severe mental or physical pain and suffering' is unsustainable. The definition of torture in Article 1 of the Convention against Torture would include the severe mental and physical suffering inflicted by waterboarding.

- A subsequent memorandum, written by the then Acting Assistant Attorney General, Steven Bradbury, on 10 May 2005, assesses the compliance of other interrogation techniques, used singly and in combination with that criminal statute as redefined by the Department of Justice.[233] This memorandum is notable for its admission that the prolonged sleep deprivation of detainees (for up to 180 hours) may cause swelling, impaired brain function, a drop in body temperature, 'impairment to coordinated body movement, difficulty with speech, nausea and blurred vision'. However, it notes that close supervision to remove shackles if swelling developed would be sufficient to bring the physical pain experienced below the statutory threshold of 'severe . . . physical pain', and that the element of 'physical . . . suffering' that would result would not be 'severe'.[234] '[S]evere mental . . . pain and suffering' is defined narrowly and is assumed only to result from the 'infliction or threatened infliction of severe physical pain and suffering' or a 'threat of imminent death'. The memorandum's author concludes that this extended sleep deprivation would not amount to 'severe mental . . . pain and suffering' for the purposes of the statute.[235]

- Applying a dual requirement of intensity and duration to the undefined notion of 'severe physical suffering' in the statute, the memorandum concludes that controlled and supervised use of waterboarding cannot amount to torture under the statute, and that it cannot cause 'pain'. Despite the 'threat of imminent death' experienced by a detainee undergoing waterboarding, which is sufficient to amount to 'severe mental pain or suffering' under the statute, the memorandum's author argues that waterboarding applied only for 40 seconds at a time cannot amount to the 'prolonged mental harm' which is an alternative criterion for 'severe mental pain or suffering'.[236] This reasoning ignores the logically obvious traumatic consequences of repeated simulated drowning, and the definition of torture in Article 1 of the Convention against Torture, which includes severe mental and physical suffering.

Since these memoranda were written, and before they were all released, the Detainee **3.72** Treatment Act[237] confirmed that terrorism detainees may not be subjected to torture or to cruel, inhuman, or degrading treatment or punishment, 'regardless' of that detainee's 'nationality or physical location'.[238] This prohibition was endorsed

---

[233] Steven Bradbury, US Acting Assistant Attorney General, US DOJ OLC, Memorandum for John Rizzo, Senior Deputy General Counsel, CIA, 10 May 2005.
[234] Ibid, p 37.
[235] Ibid, p 39.
[236] Ibid, p 43.
[237] Detainee Treatment Act of 2005, Title X, Public Law 109-148.
[238] Detainee Treatment Act of 2005, s 1003.

by the Military Commissions Act 2006, despite that Act's introduction of military commission procedures which violate IHRL on fair trials.[239] The Detainee Treatment Act endorses the application of the *de minimis* protections of Common Article 3 to the Four Geneva Conventions to detainees held in the 'war on terror', which the Supreme Court had affirmed in *Hamdan v Rumsfeld*.[240] However, the statutory definition of 'cruel, inhuman or degrading treatment or punishment' is dependent on US constitutional law on cruel and unusual punishment, and on US reservations and understandings to the UN Convention against Torture, rather than the pronouncements of the Committee against Torture and regional human rights bodies. The geographic extent of the prohibition of cruel, inhuman, or degrading treatment or punishment in the Detainee Treatment Act of 2005 is in sharp contrast with the Department of Justice memorandum of 30 May 2005. This was also written by Stephen Bradbury, and proffers the unconvincing argument that no CIA interrogation method can violate Article 18 of the Convention against Torture if it takes place outside US territory.[241]

3.73 The fallacious reasoning in the Department of Justice legal memoranda directly facilitated the torture of the CIA's 'high-value detainees'. As a result, the lawyers who are responsible for this reasoning may be complicit in torture, and under Article 4 of the Convention against Torture, they should face investigation and prosecution.[242] As Chapter 4 will note, after the case of *Rasul v Myers*,[243] and in light of the narrow mandate of the Special Prosecutor appointed by Attorney-General Eric Holder, any such prosecution may be dependent on proving that the legal advisers did not write the memoranda in good faith.[244] Thus far, an internal investigation by the Department of Justice Office of Professional Responsibility has noted merely that the lawyers showed 'poor judgment'.[245] Chapter 4 on accountability will consider these arguments in more depth.

Diplomatic assurances and non-refoulement

3.74 Under Article 3 of the Convention against Torture, states must not transfer an individual to another state if 'there are substantial grounds for believing that he would

---

[239] Military Commissions Act of 2006, Public Law 109-366.

[240] *Hamdan v Rumsfeld*, 126 S Ct 2749, 548 US 557 (2006).

[241] Steven Bradbury, US Acting Assistant Attorney General, US DOJ OLC, Memorandum for John Rizzo, Deputy General Counsel, CIA, 30 May 2005.

[242] See para 4.39.

[243] *Rasul v Myers*, US Court of Appeals for the DC Circuit, No 06-5209, 11 January 2008.

[244] Basic Principles on the Role of Lawyers, 8th United Nations Conference on the Prevention of Crime and the Treatment of Offenders, Havana, Cuba, 27 August to 7 September 1990, Principle 20.

[245] Department of Justice, Office of Professional Responsibility Report, Investigation into the Office of Legal Counsel's Memoranda Concerning Issues Relating to the Central Intelligence Agency's Use of 'Enhanced Interrogation Techniques' on Suspected Terrorists, 29 July 2009 (partially redacted, released 2010).

be in danger of being subjected to torture'.[246] This obligation of *non-refoulement* is distinct from that in Article 33 of the Convention on the Status of Refugees 1951, in IRL, although concerns relating to both types of *non-refoulement* may arise in the same case.[247] The case law of the ECtHR and CAT General Comment No 2 have extended this obligation so that no state may transfer another individual to a risk of either torture or of inhuman or degrading treatment or punishment, which is also prohibited by international law.[248] The 'war on terror' has led some states to argue, so far unsuccessfully,[249] that a national security 'balancing test' should be read into the ECHR and its case law as regards the *non-refoulement* obligation,[250] and that 'diplomatic assurances' might be used to circumvent this obligation.

Current law before the ECtHR resists these attempts. In a unanimous judgment in *Saadi v Italy*, the Grand Chamber of the European Court of Human Rights remarked that despite the 'immense difficulties' posed by terrorism, states' duty to protect their citizens from terrorist attacks 'must not . . . call into question the absolute nature of Article 3'.[251] Before the Grand Chamber, the UK had intervened as a third party to argue that there should be a national security exception to the *non-refoulement* obligation as it applies to a risk of ill-treatment on transfer. **3.75**

'Diplomatic assurances' involve a non-binding agreement between the sending state and the receiving state that persons subject to transfer will not be tortured once transferred. The UK has concluded more specific agreements, Memoranda of Understanding (MoU), with Ethiopia, Jordan, and Lebanon. The UK's MoU with Libya has been struck down in litigation, prohibiting the return of Libyan nationals under the MoU's terms.[252] The House of Lords upheld the ad hoc diplomatic assurances given in an exchange of letters between the UK and Algeria.[253] Following the judgment of the House of Lords in the conjoined appeals on diplomatic assurances with Algeria and Jordan,[254] Omar Othman's (Abu Qatada's) application is pending before the ECtHR in relation to the UK's MoU with Jordan.[255] Similarly, at the time of writing, both RB and U's lawyers have made applications to the ECtHR regarding the Algerian MoU. **3.76**

---

[246] Convention against Torture, Art 3.

[247] European Court of Human Rights, *Ismoilov v Russia*, Application No 2947/06, 24 April 2008.

[248] European Court of Human Rights, *Soering v United Kingdom* (1989) 11 EHRR 439; *Chahal v United Kingdom* (1996) 23 EHRR 413.

[249] European Court of Human Rights, *Saadi v Italy* (2008) 24 BHRC 123.

[250] European Court of Human Rights, Application No 25424/04, Observations of the Governments of Lithuania, Portugal, Slovakia and the United Kingdom Intervening in Application No 25424/04, *Ramzy v Netherlands*.

[251] European Court of Human Rights, *Saadi v Italy* (2008) 24 BHRC 123 at para 137.

[252] *DD and AS v Secretary of State for the Home Department* [2008] EWCA Civ 289.

[253] *RB and U (Algeria) v Secretary of State for the Home Department and Secretary of State for the Home Department v OO (Jordan)* [2009] UKHL 10.

[254] Ibid.

[255] *Omar Othman v UK*, Application No 8139/09 (request for interim measures granted).

3.77 Although the House of Lords ruled in the *Al-Skeini* case that Baha Mousa was within the jurisdiction of the UK when he died in UK custody in Iraq,[256] this ruling has not been extended to cases involving MoUs where a detainee is transferred out of UK custody. In *R v Hassan*, the deceased had been transferred from UK to US custody subject to a MoU. The High Court of England and Wales ruled that he was not within UK jurisdiction at the time of his death, because a MoU 'amounts to a legal regime in which the detaining power [the UK] has no substantial control over the day to day living conditions of the individual in question'.[257]

3.78 Diplomatic assurances and MoU are inadequate to fulfil states' *non-refoulement* obligation in IHRL.

- First, they cannot guarantee that a person will not be tortured or ill-treated on return: the case of *Agiza v Sweden* before the Committee against Torture, that of Mohamed Al-Zari before the Human Rights Committee, and Maher Arar's case above provide compelling evidence of this.[258]
- Second, they ignore the language of Article 3 of the Convention against Torture, which simply forbids states from transferring a detainee 'where there are substantial grounds for believing that he would be in danger of being subjected to torture'.[259] The Convention on Torture prohibits torture and ill-treatment absolutely: there is no discretion for states to make special arrangements in an individual case.
- Third, diplomatic assurances are not legally binding, so any post-return monitoring that they may provide cannot be enforced by the sending state. As Human Rights Watch argues strongly, a receiving state where torture is known to be practised has little incentive to comply with non-binding diplomatic assurances: 'It is unlikely that governments that practice torture unconstrained by international legal commitments will rein in abuse on the basis of non-binding assurances.'[260]
- Fourth, as diplomatic assurances relate to the treatment of individual detainees, the sending state fails in its obligations to condemn the general practice of torture in the receiving state, and to act (in pursuit of its prosecute or extradite obligation, and in international diplomacy) to prevent that torture as regards other detainees.

3.79 Diplomatic assurances have also been used for the transfer of detainees from the custody of a Coalition or ISAF member state in Iraq and Afghanistan into the

---

[256] *Al-Skeini and Others v Secretary of State for Defence* [2007] UKHL 26.

[257] *R (Hassan) v Secretary of State for Defence* [2009] EWHC 309 (Admin) at para 32.

[258] Committee against Torture, *Agiza v Sweden*, CAT/C/34/D/233/2003, 20 May 2005; Human Rights Committee, *Alzery v Sweden*, CCPR/C/88/D/1416/2005, 10 November 2006; see also Human Rights Watch, 'Cases involving Diplomatic Assurances against Torture: Developments since May 2005', January 2007.

[259] Convention against Torture, Art 3.

[260] Human Rights Watch, 'Still at Risk: Diplomatic Assurances No Safeguard against Torture', 14 April 2005.

custody of the territorial state. The lack of access granted to the ICRC by Afghan authorities was one of many concerns voiced by the NGO community in relation to Canada's Memorandum of Understanding with Afghanistan on detainee transfers.[261] The transfers of detainees by the UK to Iraqi custody on the expiry of the UN mandate for the Multi-national Force (MNF) in Iraq at the end of 2008 was the subject of litigation in the UK,[262] and subsequently before the ECtHR. The two detainees, Faisal Al-Saadoon and Khalaf Hussain Mufdi, were transferred to Iraqi custody regardless of interim measures to stay the transfer ordered by the ECtHR.[263] The Court of Appeal reasoned that with the expiry of the MNF mandate in Iraq, international law required the transfer of the two detainees; and it applied a precedent from refugee law which was arguably wrongly decided. This case, *R (B) v Secretary of State for the Home Department*,[264] permitted the grant of political asylum rather than an inter-state transfer of the claimants only if it was 'clear . . . that the receiving state intends to subject the fugitive to treatment so harsh as to constitute a crime against humanity'. When applied to IHRL, this narrows into absurdity the clear obligation under Article 3 of the Convention against Torture, and in case law on Article 3 ECHR.

In March 2010, the ECtHR found unanimously that there had been a violation of Article 3 ECHR's *non-refoulement* provisions, and held by six votes to one that there had been violations of Article 13 and 34, the ECHR's provisions for an effective remedy and just satisfaction.[265] *Al-Saadoon and Mufdhi* is one of a series of recent judgments from the ECtHR in which the Court has ruled against the use of diplomatic assurances in the national security context.[266]   **3.80**

Use of evidence obtained by torture

International law is unequivocal that evidence obtained by torture is inadmissible in court, unless the case in question is a prosecution of torture, in which case the evidence may be used 'against a person accused of torture as evidence that the statement was made'.[267] Case law supports this prohibition on the inadmissibility of   **3.81**

---

[261] Human Rights Watch, 'Canada/Afghanistan: Investigate Canadian Responsibility for Detainee Abuse', 27 November 2009.

[262] *R (Al Saadoon and Mufdhi) v Secretary of State for Defence* [2009] EWCA Civ 7.

[263] *Al Saadoon and Mufdhi v The United Kingdom*, Application No 61498/08, Provisional Measures, December 2008.

[264] *R (B) v Secretary of State for the Home Department* [2005] QB 643.

[265] *Al-Saadoon and Mufdhi v UK*, Application No 61498/08, Judgment of 2 March 2010.

[266] European Court of Human Rights, *Saadi v Italy* (2008) 24 BHRC 123; *Ismoilov v Russia*, Application No 2947/06, 24 April 2008; *Ryabikin v Russia*, Application No 8320/04, 19 June 2008; *Ben Khemais v Italy*, Application No 246/07, 24 February 2009; *Klein v Russia*, Application No 24268/08, 1 April 2010; see Amnesty International, *Dangerous Deals: Europe's Reliance on 'Diplomatic Assurances' Against Torture,* April 2010, AI Index EUR/01/012/2010, pp 13–15.

[267] Convention against Torture, Art 15.

evidence obtained by torture.[268] In the UK, the House of Lords rejected the argument of the government and the Court of Appeal that the inadmissibility rule applied only to torture by UK public officials. In a significant reaffirmation of the prohibition against torture, the House of Lords remarked that to admit in evidence statements obtained through torture would have the 'effect' of encouraging torture, regardless of the government's rhetorical opposition to the practice. However, the House of Lords set a high burden of proof for the inadmissibility of evidence obtained by torture: a court or tribunal should find evidence inadmissible only where it has been 'established' on the balance of probabilities that it had been obtained under torture. Where there was a risk that a statement had been obtained under torture, but that the fact of torture was not 'established', the evidence could be admitted, but should be given somewhat less weight.[269] Such a stringently literal interpretation of Article 15 of the Convention against Torture is problematic. It sets the bar too high, whereas the aim of the article is to prevent torture by removing the incentive to rely upon its results in court.

3.82 The Convention against Torture is silent on whether evidence obtained by torture can be used in intelligence-gathering. However, the incompatibility between IHRL's absolute prohibition on torture and the subsequent use of the results of torture is evident. The willing receipt and use of data obtained by torture feeds a demand for torture in interrogation. If the state receiving information obtained by torture has also forwarded questions asked to a detainee while he or she is being tortured, then this complicity is particularly striking, as the case of Binyam Mohamed makes clear. The use of evidence obtained by torture is incompatible with the prohibition on torture, and should be considered complicity in torture.[270] Treaty law obliges states to criminalize, investigate, and prosecute that complicity.

3.83 States must prohibit all transfers of terrorism suspects where there are substantial grounds for believing that they may face torture or other ill-treatment upon transfer. Intelligence officials must be trained so that they perceive and act upon a duty to intervene to prevent torture in interrogations held outside a state's boundaries. As Chapter 6 argues, states should develop formal mechanisms for civilian and legislative oversight of intelligence services, for militias, and members of the armed forces which conduct counter-terrorism operations.

---

[268] *A and Others v Secretary of State for the Home Department (No 2)* [2005] UKHL 71, 9 December 2005.

[269] Ibid; see also Helen Duffy, 'Human Rights Litigation and the "War on Terror"' [2008] 90 *International Review of the Red Cross* 573–597 at 587.

[270] JCHR, *Counter-Terrorism Policy and Human Rights (Seventeenth Report): Bringing Human Rights Back In*, 16th report of session 2009–10, 9 March 2010; Human Rights Watch, 'Cruel Britannia: British Complicity in the Torture and Ill-Treatment of Terror Suspects in Pakistan', 24 November 2009.

Enforced disappearances

The prohibition of enforced disappearances in international law

Enforced disappearances[271] are a composite violation of IHRL: they involve **3.84** abduction; secret and incommunicado detention, both of which are prohibited unequivocally by IHRL; denial of the right to challenge the lawfulness of detention before a judge; the placing of an individual outside the protection of the law; and a violation of the right to trial within a reasonable time or release. An enforced disappearance increases the risk of torture and may result in the victim's death in custody, or in an extrajudicial killing. Enforced disappearances also violate a peremptory or *jus cogens* norm of international law: they are contrary to IHL, and where they are perpetrated as part of a widespread or systematic attack on a civilian population with knowledge of the attack, they may amount to a crime against humanity.[272] Family members suffer when a state refuses to acknowledge the whereabouts of the person subjected to an enforced disappearance. This section reveals the widespread nature of enforced disappearances in the name of counter-terrorism, and considers the complicity of many states in secret detention and the unlawful transfers known as 'extraordinary rendition'. 'Extraordinary rendition' in the US-led 'war on terror' and the practice of detention in secret CIA 'black sites' have led to enforced disappearances of persons,[273] as well as to torture, and arbitrary and secret detention. There is compelling evidence that Sri Lanka, China, and the Russian Federation have also been responsible for enforced disappearances in the context of countering terrorism.

Enforced disappearances are the subject of the new International Convention for **3.85** the Protection of All Persons from Enforced Disappearance, which at present has 18 of the 20 states parties required for it to enter into force. Existing multilateral and regional instruments prohibit the components of enforced disappearances,[274] but the new Convention will be the first universal convention to codify the

---

[271] Inter-American Convention on Forced Disappearance of Persons; Declaration on the Protection of All Persons from Enforced Disappearance, adopted by General Assembly resolution 47/133 of 18 December 1992; International Convention for the Protection of All Persons from Enforced Disappearance (not yet in force).

[272] Rome Statute, Art 7(1)(i).

[273] Report of the Working Group on Enforced and Involuntary Disappearances (WGEID), Report to the E/CN.4/2006/56, 27 December 2005; Amnesty International, Cageprisoners, Center for Constitutional Rights, Center for Human Rights and Global Justice at New York University School of Law, Human Rights Watch & Reprieve, 'Off the Record: US Responsibility for Enforced Disappearances in the "War on Terror"'.

[274] ICCPR, Convention against Torture, Inter-American Convention on Forced Disappearance of Persons; Declaration on the Protection of All Persons from Enforced Disappearance, adopted by General Assembly resolution 47/133 of 18 December 1992.

prohibition on enforced disappearances. Chapters 6 and 7 include a recommendation to states swiftly to ratify the new Convention on Enforced Disappearances.[275]

3.86 When the new Convention enters into force, it will impose a *non-refoulement* obligation which closely traces that in Article 3 of the Convention against Torture.[276] It will also include a prohibition on secret detention,[277] with a series of guarantees intended to specify the grounds on which a person may be deprived of liberty, and the locations in which detainees may be held. It will oblige states to allow 'competent and legally authorised authorities' to access places of detention, and to allow family members, counsel, or representatives of a suspected victim of enforced disappearance to bring proceedings before a court. This will test the lawfulness of that person's deprivation of liberty, so that the person may be released if he or she is found to be unlawfully detained.[278] States parties will have to maintain registers showing, *inter alia*, the identity of the person detained and his or her location.[279]

3.87 The new Convention will engage states' duty to investigate apparent enforced disappearances,[280] to criminalize enforced disappearances,[281] to hold criminally responsible those who perpetrate, attempt, or are complicit in enforced disappearances, or superiors who are responsible for them;[282] to punish the offence with appropriate penalties;[283] and to guarantee victims the right to an effective remedy during any limitation period.[284] It will impose an obligation to prosecute or to extradite or surrender any suspected offender, reflecting the international criminal law on enforced disappearances and the potential for universal jurisdiction.[285] Enforced disappearances should not be considered a political offence and should be included in bilateral extradition treaties.[286] States parties will be obliged to offer mutual legal assistance in criminal trials,[287] and in assisting victims of enforced disappearances, including in identifying the whereabouts of those detained, and in exhuming the remains of victims of enforced disappearances who have been unlawfully killed.[288]

---

[275] See paras 6.28 and 7.12.
[276] International Convention for the Protection of All Persons from Enforced Disappearance, Art 16.
[277] Ibid, Art 17(1).
[278] Ibid, Art 17(2)(e)–(f).
[279] Ibid, Art 17(3)(a)–(h).
[280] Ibid, Arts 3 and 12.
[281] Ibid, Art 4.
[282] Ibid, Art 6.
[283] Ibid, Art 7.
[284] Ibid, Art 8(2).
[285] Ibid, Arts 9 and 11.
[286] Ibid, Art 13.
[287] Ibid, Art 14.
[288] Ibid, Art 15.

States will be obliged to take measures in their domestic law to ensure that all vic- **3.88** tims, as defined in Article 24(1), have 'the right to obtain reparation and prompt, fair and adequate compensation'. Reparation is defined in Article 24(4) as '(a) Restitution; (b) Rehabilitation; (c) Satisfaction, including restoration of dignity and reputation; (d) Guarantees of non-repetition'.

Enforced disappearances in counter-terrorism

'Extraordinary rendition' in the US-led 'war on terror' and the practice of detention **3.89** in secret CIA 'black sites' have led to enforced disappearances of persons,[289] as well as to torture, and arbitrary and secret detention. Yet enforced disappearances constitute a serious human rights violation of global proportion not only involving the complicity of several states in the US-led 'war on terror', but also encompassing state and state militias' repression of dissidents, whether or not they were alled 'terrorists'. This latter practice occurred in Argentina, Chile, Colombia, Peru, and South Africa during the 1970s, 1980s, and/or 1990s; and in Sri Lanka, Philippines, and the Russian Federation, to name but three states, in modern 'counter-terrorist' operations. This section will examine enforced disappearances in the US-led 'war on terror', before considering cases of or case law on enforced disappearances in the Horn of Africa, China, Chechnya and Ingushetia, Turkey, and Sri Lanka.

Enforced disappearances in the US-led 'war on terror'

There remain 'unresolved allegations' about Council of Europe member states' **3.90** complicity in enforced disappearances and secret detention in the context of the US 'extraordinary rendition' programme. The Swiss parliamentarian Dick Marty strongly criticized European states' refusal to supply information upon request for his two reports for the Parliamentary Assembly of the Council of Europe (PACE).[290] The US, Poland, Romania, Macedonia, Italy, Germany, and the Russian Federation were singled out for criticism in this regard, and the report considered it 'factually established' that Poland and Romania had hosted CIA secret detention centres.[291] A Lithuanian parliamentary inquiry subsequently concluded in December 2009 that a secret prison was constructed in Lithuania following an agreement between the CIA and Lithuanian intelligence agencies of which the Lithuanian government

---

[289] Report of the Working Group on Enforced and Involuntary Disappearances (WGEID), Report to the E/CN.4/2006/56, 27 December 2005; Amnesty International, Cageprisoners, Center for Constitutional Rights, Center for Human Rights and Global Justice at New York University School of Law, Human Rights Watch & Reprieve, 'Off the Record: US Responsibility for Enforced Disappearances in the "War on Terror"'

[290] PACE Committee on Legal Affairs and Human Rights, 'Secret detentions and illegal transfers of detainees involving Council of Europe member states: second report', Doc 11302 rev, 11 June 2007, para 26.

[291] Ibid, Summary, paras 5 and 1.

had been unaware. The inquiry was unable to confirm whether any detainees had been held there following transfer by the CIA,[292] but a criminal investigation into that possibility is underway.

Horn of Africa

3.91 Human Rights Watch has documented prolonged enforced disappearances following the CIA's 'extraordinary rendition' programme in the Horn of Africa 2007. Human Rights Watch concluded that the governments of Ethiopia (where unacknowledged detentions continued through 2009), Kenya, the US, and the Transitional Government of Somalia all have responsibility, *inter alia*, for the enforced disappearances of persons arbitrarily arrested and detained in Kenya and Somalia and unlawfully transferred outside the protection of the law to Somalia or Ethiopia.[293]

China

3.92 Members of the Uighur community in China have been subjected to enforced disappearances. Human Rights Watch investigated the enforced disappearance of at least 43 Uighur men and boys following inter-ethnic tensions in Urumqi, Xinjiang in July 2009.[294] The organization noted that the number of victims was probably higher, but a fear of retaliation, among other factors, prevented further investigations.[295]

Russian Federation

3.93 The Committee against Torture and the ECtHR have each found violations of IHRL in respect of enforced disappearances perpetrated against suspected militants in Chechnya and Ingushetia by the Russian Federation, as paragraphs 3.74–3.80 note.[296] The *zachistkas* in the Second Chechen War were left unregulated by Russian domestic law,[297] so that the arbitrary detention, beatings, torture, looting, and enforced disappearances were all extra-legal counter-terrorism operations. This may be a reflection of the statutory provision of 'special legal regimes' which can apply without further definition to counter-terrorism operations.[298] These 'special

---

[292] Amnesty International, News, 'Lithuania Admits Existence of Secret Prison', 22 December 2009.

[293] Human Rights Watch, '"Why Am I Still Here?" The 2007 Horn of Africa Renditions and the Fate of Those Still Missing', October 2008, p 4.

[294] Human Rights Watch, '"We Are Afraid to Even Look for Them": Enforced Disappearances in the Wake of Xinjiang's Protests', October 2009.

[295] Ibid, p 5.

[296] Committee against Torture, Conclusions and Recommendations on the fourth periodic report of the Russian Federation, CAT/C/RUS/CO/4, 6 February 2007, paras 22 et seq; see para 2.77.

[297] Brief Overview by the Human Rights Center *Memorial* submitted to the Eminent Jurists Panel on Terrorism, Counter-Terrorism and Human Rights, 2007, p 12.

[298] Russian Federation Federal Law No 35-FZ on Counteraction of Terrorism, 6 March 2006, Art 11.

legal regimes' indicate an official discretion which is incompatible with the principle of legality. In addition, Russian federal law provides for immunities from prosecution for those participating in counter-terrorism operations in the Russian Federation.[299] This shuns IHRL's duty to investigate and prosecute human rights violations and to provide reparations to victims. The human rights organization Memorial estimates that 3,000–5,000 individuals have been subjected to enforced disappearance in Chechnya, with around 50 documented victims in neighbouring Ingushetia.[300] The organization notes that since the 'Chechenisation' of the conflict, where pro-Russian Chechen officials carried out raids in Chechen villages, arbitrary detention continued, but extrajudicial killings of those detained have declined.

The ECtHR has found the Russian Federation responsible for violations of the **3.94** ECHR more than 80 times in the context of the Chechen conflict, with 60 of these cases involving enforced disappearances.[301] The systemic failure of the Russian state to investigate cases of enforced disappearances is itself a violation of the procedural obligations in Article 2 of the ECHR. In the line of cases beginning with *Bazorkina v Russia*, and applying the ruling from *Salman v Turkey*, the Court has responded effectively to the climate of official impunity surrounding enforced disappearances by shifting the burden of proof to the state to provide a plausible explanation as to the victim's fate or whereabouts.[302] The Court has drawn negative inferences from limited evidence which suggests state involvement in an enforced disappearance, and from the frequent failure of the Russian Federation to deliver the criminal case file to the Court.[303] Where the state failed to conduct a prompt and effective investigation into a case of enforced disappearance the suffering of the victim's relatives that resulted amounted to inhuman or degrading treatment, in violation of Article 3.[304]

The Russian Federation has failed to implement these judgments:[305] both as regards **3.95** the obligation to conduct an adequate domestic investigation of the enforced disappearances, and as regards the 'general measures' to prevent future violations. The Committee of Ministers of the Council of Europe has urged the Russian Federation to improve the training of security officials, to reform legislation and the security

---

[299] Russian Federation Federal Law No 130-FZ, 25 July 1998, Art 20 (left intact by the 2006 Federal Law).

[300] Brief Overview by the Human Rights Center *Memorial* Submitted to the Eminent Jurists Panel on Terrorism, Counter–Terrorism and Human Rights, 2007, p 22.

[301] Human Rights Watch, 'Update on European Court of Human Rights Judgments against Russia regarding Cases from Chechnya', 20 March 2009.

[302] *Bazorkina v Russia* (2008) 46 EHRR 15; applying *Salman v Turkey* (2002) 34 EHRR 17.

[303] *Musayeva v Russia* (2008) 47 EHRR 25.

[304] *Ibragimov v Russia*, Application No 34561/03, 24 May 2008.

[305] Human Rights Watch, 'Russia: Complying with European Court Key to Halting Abuse', 27 September 2009; Joseph Barrett, 'Chechnya's Last Hope: Enforced Disappearances and the European Court of Human Rights' (2009) 22 *Harvard Human Rights Journal* 133–143.

sector, to improve access to domestic remedies, and finally to cooperate with the ECtHR (eg by sending case files).[306]

Turkey

3.96 The ECtHR's case law on enforced disappearances by Turkey, which largely precedes its jurisprudence on Chechnya, has also emphasized the state's duty to investigate cases of enforced disappearances.[307]

3.97 In *Varnava and Others v Turkey*,[308] the Grand Chamber of the Court found violations of the ECHR in a conjoined case relating to nine enforced disappearances in Cyprus in 1974. Although the nine men were killed in Turkish military custody in the context of the Turkish occupation of northern Cyprus rather than in a counter-terrorism operation, this case is instructive for its emphasis on the ongoing nature of violations in enforced disappearances, such that the complaint could not be time-barred; the continued insistence on investigatory duties under Article 2; the finding of a violation of Article 3 as a result of the state's decades-long 'indifference' towards the applicant relatives of those subjected to enforced disappearances; and the continuing violation of Article 5 in respect of two of the nine men whose detention was recorded on an ICRC detainee list, but whose fate and whereabouts had never been clarified by the Turkish authorities.[309]

Sri Lanka

3.98 In its views on *Jegatheeswara Sarma v Sri Lanka*, the Human Rights Committee noted the 'large scale disappearances of youth' in Northern and Eastern areas of Sri Lanka in 1989 and 1990. The Committee attributed the security forces' power 'to dispose of the bodies without post mortem or inquest' to the Emergency Regulations which have characterized Sri Lanka's operations against the Liberation Tigers of Tamil Eelam (LTTE).[310] The Human Rights Committee found violations of Articles 7 and 8 of the ICCPR in respect of the applicant's son, who had been subjected to an enforced disappearance, and of Article 7 of the ICCPR in respect of the author and his wife.[311] The Human Rights Committee emphasized a variety of obligations on Sri Lanka: to prevent enforced disappearances in the future, to expedite criminal proceedings concerning the enforced disappearance, and to provide an 'effective remedy, including a thorough and effective investigation . . . immediate

---

[306] Committee of Ministers of the Council of Europe, 'Actions of the security forces in the Chechen Republic of the Russian Federation: general measures to comply with the judgments of the European Court of Human Rights' CM/Inf/DH(2008)33, 11 September 2008.

[307] *Kurt v Turkey* (1999) 27 EHRR 373; *Avsar v Turkey* (2003) 37 EHRR 53; *Tas v Turkey* (2001) 33 EHRR 15; *Salman v Turkey* (2002) 34 EHRR 17.

[308] *Varnava and Others v Turkey*, Grand Chamber of the European Court of Human Rights, 18 September 2009.

[309] Ibid.

[310] *Jegatheeswara Sarma v Sri Lanka*, Communication No 950/2000, 31 July 2003, para 8.2.

[311] Ibid, para 10.

release if he is still alive, adequate information resulting from its investigation, and adequate compensation'.[312]

There is ongoing evidence that enforced disappearances have continued in Sri **3.99** Lanka, up to and including the stated end of the conflict between the government and the LTTE in 2009, targeting Tamil civilians, suspected members of the LTTE, journalists, and human rights defenders.[313] The Universal Periodic Review of Sri Lanka by the UN Human Rights Council yielded several calls by the Czech Republic, France, the Holy See, and Sweden for the authorities in Sri Lanka to prevent, investigate, and prosecute enforced disappearances, and to submit to a visit by the UN Working Group on Enforced and Involuntary Disappearances as well as to ratify the new Convention on Enforced Disappearances.[314] It is unfortunate and to its discredit that the Human Rights Council failed to accede to these appropriate calls.

Conclusion

The case law considered briefly here shows the global reach of enforced disappear- **3.100** ances both during and outside armed conflict. It demonstrates the climate of impunity which leads not only to violations of IHRL's obligation to investigate and prosecute enforced disappearances, but also to treatment amounting to a violation of the prohibition on cruel, inhuman, or degrading treatment or punishment as regards the relatives of the 'disappeared'. Enforced disappearance in counter-terrorism operations remains a serious composite human rights violation, which is neither excused nor justified by states' obligations to prevent and repress terrorism (see Chapter 1). The framework of derogations and limitations in IHRL cannot apply to enforced disappearances, which are prohibited by non-derogable and absolute rules of international law.

As the prohibition on enforced disappearances is a *jus cogens* or peremptory norm, **3.101** states are obliged to cooperate to bring enforced disappearances to an end. Existing law establishes beyond doubt states' obligations to conduct a prompt and effective investigation into enforced disappearances, to prosecute those suspected of being responsible, and to respect victims' rights to a remedy and to reparation. When the Convention on Enforced Disappearances is in force, states will be obliged to prosecute or extradite individuals who are suspected of having committed, ordered, attempted, aided, or abetted enforced disappearances.

Chapter 4 which follows will consider a range of criminal investigations, civil **3.102** suits, and national and intergovernmental inquiries into 'extraordinary rendition':

---

[312] Ibid, para 11.
[313] Amnesty International, 'Enforced Disappearance: Stephen Sunthararaj', 14 May 2009.
[314] Report of the Working Group on the Universal Periodic Review on Sri Lanka, 8th session of the Human Rights Council, A/HRC/8/46, 5 June 2008.

torture, enforced disappearances, and unlawful transfer of detainees. Chapters 6 and 7 address a number of measures to prevent enforced disappearances in counter-terrorism.[315]

Arbitrary detention

The right to liberty and security of the person

3.103 Paragraphs 3.104–3.109 explain the substantive and procedural elements of the right to liberty and security of the person in international human rights treaty law. Paragraphs 3.110–3.118 offer case studies of prolonged detention without charge or trial, in Yemen, Indonesia, at Guantánamo Bay and in CIA 'black sites', and in the regime of internment established by the UK Anti-Terrorism, Crime and Security Act 2001, and modified following a judgment of the House of Lords.[316] Paragraphs 3.119–3.123 study litigation on the right to challenge the lawfulness of detention, otherwise known as habeas corpus or amparo, with detailed consideration of US case law. Paragraphs 3.124–3.126 detail evidence of secret detention in the counter-terrorism context; and paragraphs 3.127–3.128 consider incommunicado detention in Spain. Paragraphs 3.129–3.133 consider the point at which control orders in the UK and Canada, and compulsory residence orders in France and Italy, may amount to a deprivation of liberty, while noting the concerns relating to the right to a fair hearing and to secret evidence which ground control orders in the UK. Control orders may also violate the right to private and family life, freedom of movement, and the freedoms of expression and assembly.

3.104 The right to liberty and security of the person is provided in Article 9 of the ICCPR, Article 5 ECHR, Article 7 of the ACHR, and Article 6 of the ACHPR. The right comprises:

- a prohibition on arbitrary arrest and detention;[317]
- the requirement that any deprivation of liberty be 'on such grounds and in accordance with such procedure as are established by law';[318]
- the requirement to inform individuals at the moment of arrest of the reasons for that arrest, and to be promptly informed of any charges against them;[319]

---

[315] See paras 6.28, 6.34–6.38, 7.12, 7.16.

[316] *A (FC) and Others (FC) v Secretary of State for the Home Department* [2004] UKHL 56.

[317] ICCPR, Art 9(1); ECHR, Art 5(1); ACHR, Art 7(3) and (2) ; ACHPR, Art 6.

[318] ICCPR, Art 9(1), with similar provisions in ECHR, Art 5(1), which enumerates permissible grounds for detention; ACHR, Art 7(2), which makes specific reference to a state's constitution and to constitutional law; ACHPR, Art 6.

[319] ICCPR, Art 9(2); ECHR, Art 5(2) (in addition, a detainee must be so informed in a 'language he understands'); ACHR, Art 7(4).

- the obligation to bring a detainee promptly before a judge or 'other officer authorised by law to exercise judicial power', and the detainee's entitlement to 'trial within a reasonable time or to release';[320]
- a provision that pre-trial detention 'not be the general rule';[321]
- the right 'to take proceedings before a court, in order that that court may decide without delay on the lawfulness of . . . detention and order . . . release if the detention is not lawful' (habeas corpus or amparo);[322] and
- 'an enforceable right to compensation' for victims of unlawful arrest or detention.[323]

Although the right to liberty and security of the person is omitted from the lists of **3.105** non-derogable rights in treaty law, the ACHR provides that 'recourse to a competent court . . . may not be restricted or abolished'.[324] General Comment No 29 of the UN Human Rights Committee emphasizes that this right is non-derogable, so states cannot invoke an emergency relating to terrorism to justify the suspension of this right.[325] The Inter-American Court of Human Rights reached the same conclusion in its Advisory Opinion on Habeas Corpus in Emergency Situations.[326] The peremptory norm against enforced disappearances suggests that its component prohibitions on secret and incommunicado detention should also be non-derogable.[327]

The paradigmatically lawful deprivation of liberty occurs after conviction following **3.106** a fair trial in a competent, independent, and impartial court. However, preventive detention may be permitted under narrow circumstances, and with procedural guarantees.[328] The Human Rights Committee in its General Comment No 8 provides:

> [i]f so-called preventive detention is used, for reasons of public security . . . it must not be arbitrary, and must be based on grounds and procedures established by law ([Article 9] para.1), information of the reasons must be given (para.2), and court control of the detention must be available (para.4), as well as compensation in the case of a breach (para.5). And if, in addition, criminal charges are brought in such cases, the full protection of article 9(2) and (3), as well as article 14, must also be granted.[329]

---

[320] ICCPR, Art 9(3); ECHR, Art 5(3); ACHR, Art 7(5).

[321] ICCPR, Art 9(3); ECHR, Art 5(3); ACHR, Art 7(5).

[322] ICCPR, Art 9(4); ECHR, Art 5(4): the ECHR provides in addition that the lawfulness of detention be determined 'speedily'; ACHR, Art 7(6): the ACHR further specifies that the right to 'recourse to a competent court . . . may not be restricted or abolished'.

[323] ICCPR, Art 9(5); ECHR, Art 5(4).

[324] ACHR, Art 7(6).

[325] Human Rights Committee, General Comment No 29, States of Emergency (Article 4), CCPR/C/21/Rev.1/Add.11, 31 August 2001, para 16.

[326] Inter-American Court of Human Rights, *Habeas Corpus in Emergency Situations*, Advisory Opinion OC-8 187, 30 January 1987, Series A No 8.

[327] See paras 3.124–3.128.

[328] See paras 6.39–6.40.

[329] Human Rights Committee, General Comment No 8, Right to liberty and security of persons (Article 9), 16th session, 1982, 30 June 1982, para 4.

3.107   Article 5(1)(b)–(f) ECHR detail enumerated grounds of lawful detention other than the deprivation of liberty following 'conviction by a competent court' (Article 5(1)(a)). The most relevant to counter-terrorism is that relating to detention 'when it is reasonably considered necessary to prevent [a detainee] committing an offence' in Article 5(1)(c). None of the enumerated grounds of detention in Article 5(1) ECHR permits states to ignore any or all of the procedural and substantive guarantees elsewhere in Article 5. General Comment No 8 and the ECHR both support the conclusion that administrative detention in IHRL is far removed from a 'legal black hole' of detention without charge, without trial, and without the right to challenge the lawfulness of detention before a court.[330]

3.108   In its determination of individual complaints, the UN Working Group on Arbitrary Detention (WGAD) has developed three categories of arbitrary detention:

- Category I: 'When it is clearly impossible to invoke any legal basis justifying the deprivation of liberty';
- Category II: 'When the deprivation of liberty results from the exercise of [specifically enumerated] rights or freedoms' in the Universal Declaration of Human Rights (UDHR) or the ICCPR;[331] and
- Category III: 'When the total or partial non-observance of the international norms relating to the right to a fair trial . . . is of such gravity as to give the deprivation of liberty an arbitrary character.'[332]

Category III points to the intersection between arbitrary detention and the right to a fair trial. It should be considered in the light of detention pursuant to secret evidence, which a detainee and his or her counsel cannot challenge, or after proceedings in military commissions or state security courts where detainees may not be able to challenge the evidence against them.[333]

3.109   The sections which follow consider states' responsibilities to respect and ensure all aspects of the right to liberty and security of the person in their counter-terrorism policies. The kidnap or hostage-taking of individuals by non-state terrorist groups is not considered, as non-state groups are not bound *de jure* by IHRL.[334] Arbitrary detention by paramilitary groups allied to the state or by private companies carrying out state functions could engage state responsibility for violations of the right to liberty and security of the person.[335]

---

[330] Lord Steyn, 'Guantanamo Bay: The Legal Black Hole', 27th FA Mann Lecture, British Institute of International and Comparative Law and Herbert Smith, Lincoln's Inn Old Hall, 25 November 2003.

[331] UDHR, Arts 7, 13, 14, 18–21; ICCPR, Arts 12, 18, 19, 21, 22, 25–27.

[332] Working Group on Arbitrary Detention, Individual Complaints, Urgent Appeals, Deliberations, I. Investigation of Individual Cases.

[333] See paras 3.146–3.148.

[334] See paras 3.02, 3.13.

[335] Report of the UN Special Rapporteur on Extralegal, Summary and Arbitrary Executions to the 61st session of the UN Commission on Human Rights, E/CN.4/2005/7, para 69; Report of the UN

Prolonged detention without charge or trial in counter-terrorism

IHRL guarantees the right to trial within a reasonable time or to release pending **3.110** trial, while pre-trial or 'remand' detention should be the exception rather than the rule.[336] However, the importance of combating terrorism has led many states to legislate for prolonged detention before charge or trial, or for lengthy periods of internment without charge or trial. This is prima facie a violation of the right to liberty and security of the person: case law has established this in the UK context, and regional human rights organizations have noted their concern at prolonged detention without charge or trial at Guantánamo Bay and in France's new preventive detention statute.

France

France passed a new law in 2008 which authorized indefinite preventive detention, **3.111** in renewable terms of one year. This law is not exclusive to France's criminal justice measures against terrorism, as it can apply to anyone considered 'dangerous', even after they have completed a criminal sentence.[337] The Commissioner for Human Rights of the Council of Europe, and the UN Human Rights Committee both noted their concern at this discretionary violation of the right to liberty and security of the person.[338]

Indonesia

The Indonesian Anti-Terrorism Law of 2002 permits seven days' detention without **3.112** charge, on the basis of a court appearance to check the validity of a warrant against a terrorism suspect.[339] Detention can last for one day and still be considered an arrest, before authorization must be obtained for the detention phase to begin.[340] Article 25(2) of the Anti-Terrorism Law permits detention for six months 'for the purpose of investigation and prosecution',[341] where investigation can last four months and prosecution two months.[342] This practice is in part compatible with state practice on remand detention, but the seven days pre-charge detention is a concern.

Special Rapporteur on Extralegal, Summary and Arbitrary Executions to the 60th session of the UN Commission on Human Rights, E/CN.4/2004/7.

[336] ICCPR, Art 9(3); ECHR, Art 5(3); ACHR, Art 7(5).

[337] Loi No 2008-174 du 25 février 2008 relative à la rétention de sureté et à la déclaration d'irresponsabilité pénale pour cause de trouble mental; cited in Amnesty International Report 2009, France, p 149.

[338] Memorandum by Thomas Hammarberg, Council of Europe Commissioner for Human Rights, following his visit to France from 21–23 May 2008; Human Rights Committee, Concluding Observations on the fourth periodic report of France, CCPR/C/FRA/CO/4, 31 July 2008, para 16.

[339] Simon Butt, 'Indonesian Terrorism Law and Criminal Process', University of Sydney, Sydney Law School, Legal Studies Research Paper, No 09/30, May 2009, p 15 (available on SSRN).

[340] Ibid, p 14, citing Code of Criminal Procedure (KUHAP), Art 19(1).

[341] Ibid, p 18, citing Anti-Terrorism Law, Art 25(2).

[342] Ibid, p 18, citing Elucidation of Anti-Terrorism Law, Art 25(2).

US: Guantánamo Bay

3.113 The most infamous example of detention without charge or trial in global counter-terrorism is that at the US-run Guantánamo Bay detention facility in Cuba. It should be noted, however, that many more detainees (an undisclosed number) are thought to be held at the Bagram Air Base in Afghanistan,[343] and prior to President Obama's Executive Order that the CIA detention facilities be closed,[344] an indeterminate number have been held in secret detention in CIA 'black sites'.[345] The 'Torture Memos' considered above indicate that these forms of administrative detention were instituted to gather intelligence through the torture and ill-treatment of 'high-value detainees', in violation of the prohibition on torture and the right to liberty and security of the person.

3.114 In 2002, the Inter-American Commission on Human Rights (IACHR) issued Precautionary Measures relating to the indefinite detention without charge or trial of the then 254 detainees at Guantánamo Bay.[346] The IACHR called upon the US to take all the 'urgent measures necessary to have the legal status of detainees at Guantánamo Bay determined by a competent tribunal'. The US responded by rejecting the IACHR's jurisdiction over the case, arguing unpersuasively that IHRL did not apply to a 'war on terror' to which only IHL should apply as *lex specialis*.[347] The IACHR in its turn responded by reiterating the force of its Precautionary Measures and noting its disagreement with the US government's position.[348] The Precautionary Measures were reiterated in March 2003,[349] reiterated in 2004,[350] and extended in 2005, with particular reference to the detention of juveniles, the prohibition on the use of evidence obtained by torture in legal proceedings, on the investigation of allegations of torture and other cruel, inhuman, or

---

[343] ACLU, 'DOD Refuses to Turn Over List of Bagram Detainee Information', 13 August 2009.

[344] Executive Order, Ensuring Lawful Interrogations, 22 January 2009.

[345] A US Freedom of Information Act lawsuit by a number of NGOs, *Amnesty International v CIA, et al*, has yielded multiple documents marked 'Top Secret' where '[t]here is no meaningful, segregable portion of the document that can be released'. *Amnesty International USA, Center for Constitutional Rights, and Washington Square Legal Services Inc v Central Intelligence Agency, Department of Defense Department of Homeland Security et al*, 07-CV-05435-LAP, filed 20 November 2007.

[346] IACHR, Precautionary Measures on Guantánamo Bay, Communication of 12 March 2002 from IACHR President Juan E Méndez to US Secretary of State Colin Powell, (2002) 96 *American Journal of International Law* 730: the chronology of IACHR and US government communications in this paragraph are cited from Brian D Tittemore, 'Guantánamo Bay and the Precautionary Measures of the Inter-American Commission on Human Rights: A Case for International Oversight in the Struggle against Terrorism' (2006) 6 *Human Rights Law Review* 378–402.

[347] US Government Response to the IACHR Precautionary Measures on Guantánamo Bay, 12 April 2002.

[348] IACHR, Precautionary Measures on Guantánamo Bay, Communication of 23 July 2002 from IACHR President Juan E Méndez to US Secretary of State Colin Powell.

[349] IACHR, Precautionary Measures on Guantánamo Bay, Communication of 18 March 2003 from the IACHR to US Secretary of State Colin Powell.

[350] IACHR, Precautionary Measures on Guantánamo Bay, Communication of 29 July 2004 from the Executive Secretary of the IACHR to US Secretary of State Colin Powell.

degrading treatment or punishment, and the obligation of *non-refoulement*.[351] In 2006, the IACHR issued a resolution to call for the closure of the detention facility at Guantánamo Bay.[352]

Although President Obama announced his intention to close the detention camp   **3.115** at Guantánamo Bay in January 2010,[353] he admitted in November 2009 that this deadline would not be met.[354] In late 2009, the US Department of Justice and Department of Defense recommended that 35 Guantánamo Bay detainees should face trial or military commission, and that ten Guantánamo Bay detainees should face trial in federal court.[355] In early 2010 a final report by President Obama's Guantánamo Review Task Force found that '48 detainees were determined to be too dangerous to transfer but not feasible for prosecution. They will remain in detention pursuant to the government's authority under the Authorization for the Use of Military Force passed by Congress in response to the attacks of 11 September 2001. Detainees may challenge the legality of their detention in federal court and will further review within the Executive Branch'.[356]

In a document placed in the public domain in April 2010, the Joint Task Force   **3.116** Guantánamo Mission noted that '[t]he current detainee population is approximately180…[and m]ore than 520 have been transferred or released'.[357] Afghanistan, Albania, Belgium, Bermuda, Bulgaria, Chad, France, Germany, Georgia, Italy, Latvia, the Maldives, Palau, Portugal, Republic of Ireland, Slovakia, Spain, Somaliland, Sweden, Switzerland, and the UK are among the states which have received or expressed willingness to receive former Guantánamo Bay detainees.[358] The Obama Administration's attempt to transfer some remaining Guantánamo Bay detainees to a US federal prison in Illinois may be delayed. In May 2010, the US House of Representatives passed the National Defense Reauthorisation Act for Fiscal Year 2011, with the proviso that the Obama Administration present detailed cost-benefit analyses to Congress on the construction and maintenance of such a facility.[359]

---

[351] IACHR, Extension of Precautionary Measures on Guantánamo Bay, 2 November 2005.

[352] IACHR, Resolution No 2/06 on Guantánamo Bay Precautionary Measures, 28 July 2006.

[353] Closure of Guantánamo Detention Facilities, Executive Order-Review and Disposition of Individuals Detained at the Guantánamo Bay Naval Base and Closure of Detention Facilities, 22 January 2009.

[354] BBC News, 'Obama Admits Delay on Guantánamo', 18 November 2009.

[355] Department of Justice, 'Departments of Justice and Defense Announce Forum Decisions for Ten Guantánamo Bay Detainees', 13 November 2009.

[356] Final Report, Guantánamo Review Task Force, 22 January 2010, p 2, Executive Summary.

[357] Joint Task Force Guantánamo Mission, Fact Sheets, Detainees, p 3 (web resource).

[358] JURIST—Paper Chase, 'Italy Agrees to Take Two More Guantánamo Bay Detainees', 26 May 2010.

[359] House Armed Services Committee, HR 5136 National Defense Authorization Act for Fiscal Year 2011.

UK

3.117 In 2009, the ECtHR largely endorsed a judgment by the UK House of Lords that the statutory provision for the internment of non-nationals by Part IV of the Anti-Terrorism Crime and Security Act (ATCSA) 2001 was a violation of Article 5 of the ECHR, despite the UK government's temporary derogation from that provision under Article 15 of the ECHR. The Court also held that this was discriminatory on the ground of national origin under Article 14 ECHR.[360] The Grand Chamber found that four appellants had suffered violations of Article 5(4) ECHR while five others did not suffer that violation. Specifically on the imperative to combat terrorism, the Grand Chamber said the following:

> The Court does not accept the Government's argument that Article 5(1) permits a balance to be struck between the individual's right to liberty and the State's interest in protecting its population from terrorist threat . . . [paras a–f] are exhaustive] If detention does not fit within the confines of the paragraphs as interpreted by the Court, it cannot be made to fit by an appeal to the need to balance the interests of the State against those of the detainee.[361]

Yemen

3.118 In November 2009, the Committee against Torture (CAT) issued its Concluding Observations in respect of Yemen's second periodic report on its implementation of the Convention against Torture. The Committee noted with alarm cases of enforced disappearances, torture in detention, deportation in violation of the *non-refoulement* obligation, and prolonged periods of detention without charge or trial.[362] Detainees in state security detention must obtain a prior written authorization from the body which authorized their detention before they can receive visits from family members or their lawyer.[363] The CAT noted the plethora of institutions which can arrest individuals, often without a warrant, and emphasized the link between a lack of judicial oversight of detention and an increased risk of torture.[364]

The right to challenge the lawfulness of detention

Treaty law

3.119 The right to take proceedings before a court 'in order that that court may decide without delay on the lawfulness of . . . detention' is the fulcrum of much litigation

---

[360] *A and Others v Secretary of State for the Home Department* [2004] UKHL 56; European Court of Human Rights, Grand Chamber, *A and Others v United Kingdom* (2009) EHRR 301.

[361] European Court of Human Rights, Grand Chamber, *A and Others v United Kingdom* (2009) EHRR 301 at para 171.

[362] Committee against Torture, Concluding Observations on the second periodic report of Yemen, CAT/C/YEM/CO/2, 19 November 2009.

[363] Ibid, para 9.

[364] Ibid, para 13.

on counter-terrorism and human rights, dating from the first case before the ECtHR.[365] Following the Human Rights Committee's General Comment No 29 and the Advisory Opinion of the Inter-American Court of Human Rights on Habeas Corpus in Emergency Situations, the right to challenge the lawfulness of detention is non-derogable, although it is not in the specifically enumerated list of non-derogable rights in the ICCPR or the ECHR.[366] Article 27 of the ACHR guarantees the judicial processes required to make non-derogable rights effective.

Case law: European Court of Human Rights

In *Aksoy v Turkey*,[367] the applicant was detained for a period of 14 days prior to being brought before a judge to test the lawfulness of his detention. The ECtHR therefore found a violation of Article 5(3) ECHR, reasoning that 14 days of detention before that right could be discharged did not conform to the exigencies of the public emergency identified by Turkey in its derogation under Article 15 ECHR. The UK also derogated from Article 5 ECHR with respect to the internment of non-national terrorist suspects prior to the judgment of the House of Lords in *A and Others*,[368] and the subsequent judgment of the Grand Chamber of the ECtHR.[369] Part IV of ATCSA 2001 permitted review of the indefinite detention of terrorism suspects only by the Special Immigration Appeals Tribunal (SIAC), a special court for national security cases which provided only administrative review and representation by Special Advocates, not review by a judge of the lawfulness of detention. However, the Grand Chamber focused its analysis on the discriminatory and disproportionate nature of the detention regime in *A and Others*, not on the mechanisms by which detainees might challenge that detention.

3.120

Case law: US

Both the Bush and Obama Administrations have fought against the grant of habeas corpus rights in the 'war on terror'. The Bush Administration repeatedly cited the Congressional Authorization for the Use of Military Force (AUMF),[370] the *lex specialis* application of IHL which reportedly ousted the application of the right to liberty and security of the person under IHL,[371] and the refusal to countenance the extraterritorial application either of the US Constitution or of IHRL.[372]

3.121

---

[365] *Lawless Case (Merits)*, Judgment of 1 July 1961.

[366] See paras 3.17–3.21, 3.105.

[367] *Aksoy v Turkey* (1996) 23 EHRR 553.

[368] *A and Others v Secretary of State for the Home Department* [2004] UKHL 56.

[369] European Court of Human Rights, Grand Chamber, *A and Others v United Kingdom* (2009) EHRR 301.

[370] US House of Representatives and US Senate, Joint Resolution, Authorization for the Use of Military Force of 18 September 2001, Public Law 107-40 [SJ RES.23].

[371] US Government Response to the IACHR Precautionary Measures on Guantánamo Bay, 12 April 2002.

[372] Human Rights Committee, Concluding Observations on the second and third periodic reports of the United States of America, CCPR/C/USA/CO/3, 15 September 2006, para 10.

US Department of State Legal Adviser Harold Koh has referred to the AUMF, 'self-defence' (a concept from *jus ad bellum* rather than IHL), the 'law of war', and the ICRC Interpretive Guidance on the Direct Participation of Civilians in Hostilities (which refers to targeting rather than detention) to ground the Obama Administration's counter-terrorism detention policies.[373]

Habeas corpus for Guantánamo Bay detainees

3.122   A litany of case law and Congressional responses marked the years between 2001 and 2008, the year in which the US Supreme Court finally acknowledged the constitutional right of detainees at Guantánamo Bay to bring a habeas corpus suit:[374]

- In *Rasul and Others v Bush*,[375] the Supreme Court decided that non-nationals detained at Guantánamo Bay had only statutory, not constitutional *habeas corpus* rights.
- The government responded with a 'jurisdiction-stripping' provision in the Detainee Treatment Act 2005,[376] which precluded federal courts from hearing habeas petitions from Guantánamo Bay detainees.
- The Supreme Court in *Hamdan v Rumsfeld*, in addition to holding that Common Article 3 of the Four Geneva Conventions of 1949 applied to 'war on terror' detainees, also decided that section 1005(e) of the Detainee Treatment Act 2005 did not have retrospective effect to preclude federal courts from hearing habeas petitions which were already pending when the Act was passed.[377]
- The US Congress responded with an absolute provision to oust federal court jurisdiction, in section 7 of the Military Commissions Act of 2006.[378]
- The judgment of the Supreme Court in *Boumediene v Bush* reasoned that section 7 of the Military Commissions Act was an unconstitutional suspension of the constitutional writ of *habeas corpus*, and that the designation of the petitioners as 'enemy combatants' did not remove their constitutional right to seek a judicial review of the lawfulness of their detention.[379]

Habeas corpus for detainees at Bagram Air Base

3.123   In 2009, a District Court judge ruled that habeas corpus rights also apply to detainees at Bagram Air Base, Afghanistan,[380] but in May 2010, this was overturned on

---

[373] Harold Hongju Koh, Legal Adviser, US Department of State, 'The Obama Administration and International Law', ASIL Annual Meeting, 25 March 2010; see paras 2.36–2.37, 2.52.

[374] US Supreme Court, *Boumediene v Bush*, US 128 S Ct 2229, 2262, 171 L.Ed. 2d 41 (2008).

[375] *Rasul and et al v Bush*, 542 US 466 (2004).

[376] Detainee Treatment Act 2005, s 1005(e).

[377] *Hamdan v Rumsfeld*, 126 S Ct 2749, 548 US 557 (2006); see paras 2.35 and 2.115.

[378] Military Commissions Act, Pub L No 109–366, 120 Stat 2600, 17 October 2006.

[379] US Supreme Court, *Boumediene v Bush*, 128 S Ct 2229, 2262, 171 L.Ed. 2d 41 (2008).

[380] US District Court for the District of Columbia, *Fadi al Maqalch et al v Robert Gates et al*, 06–1669, Judgment of 2 April 2009.

appeal,[381] leaving detainees at Bagram without the right to challenge the lawfulness of their detention before a judge. In the US District Court for the District of Columbia, Judge John Bates ruled in *Al Maqaleh v Gates* that the constitutional right to habeas corpus applied also to detainees at Bagram, as a result of *Boumediene's* invalidation of section 7 of the Military Commissions Act 2006.[382] However, this has been subsequently overturned on appeal.[383] Before the District Court, the US government had argued unsuccessfully for the territorial restriction of habeas rights, on the basis that if they were held to apply to detainees in Afghanistan, they would apply 'to the four corners of the earth'.[384]

Secret detention

Links between secret detention and enforced disappearances

Paragraphs 3.84–3.102 above have noted the close correlation between enforced **3.124**
disappearance and secret detention. The new Convention for the Protection of All Persons from Enforced Disappearance codifies international law's prohibition on secret detention. The monitoring of places of detention (one means of preventing torture) would be stymied if detainees were held in secret or unauthorized places of detention.[385] In January 2010, a strongly worded joint report of the UN Special Rapporteur on promotion and protection of human rights while countering terrorism, the UN Special Rapporteur on Torture, the WGAD, and the Working Group on Enforced and Involuntary Disappearances, pointed to the links between secret detention in counter-terrorism and enforced disappearances.[386] The experts received 44 replies to questionnaires sent to states, and interviewed 30 detainees and family members.[387] They reasoned that 'secret detention is irreconcilably in violation of IHRL including during states of emergency and armed conflict. Likewise, it is in violation of IHL during any form of armed conflict.'[388] The experts also argued that secret detention itself amounted to enforced disappearance based on the cases they studied. The Joint Report also found the UK to have been

---

[381] US Court of Appeals for the District of Columbia Circuit, *Fadi al Maqaleh et al v Robert Gates et al*, 09-5265, Judgment of 21 May 2010.

[382] US District Court for the District of Columbia, *Fadi al Maqaleh et al v Robert Gates et al*, 06-1669, Judgment of 2 April 2009.

[383] US Court of Appeals for the District of Columbia Circuit, *Fadi al Maqaleh et al v Robert Gates et al*, 09-5265, Judgment of 21 May 2010.

[384] Argument of the respondents, cited in *Fadi al Maqaleh et al v Robert Gates et al*, 06-1669, Judgment of 2 April 2009, section E, p 45.

[385] See paras 6.18–6.27 and 7.15–7.16.

[386] Joint Study on global practice in relation to secret detention in the context of countering terrorism, A/HRC/13/42, 26 January 2010.

[387] Ibid.

[388] Ibid, Executive Summary, p 2.

complicit in the torture and ill-treatment of several of its residents during the US-led 'war on terror'.[389]

Evidence of CIA secret detention centres in Europe

3.125   Despite the patent risks of torture and ill-treatment as a result of secret detention, there is compelling evidence that the US CIA operated secret detention sites in Romania,[390] Poland,[391] and Lithuania.[392] Those held were subject to enforced disappearances while their fate or whereabouts was unknown. Parliamentary questions and an NGO investigation have pointed to the possible complicity of the UK in relation to secret detention at the US air base in the British overseas territory of Diego Garcia.[393] Enforced disappearances in China, the Russian Federation, and during the 'extraordinary rendition' programme in the Horn of Africa also violate the right to liberty and security of the person.

Current US policy on secret and unacknowledged detention

3.126   Although the final report of the US Detention Policy Task Force is still classified, it should reinforce IHRL's prohibition on secret and incommunicado detention, consistently with President Obama's Executive Order to revoke all 2001–08 Executive Orders relating to the detention of terrorism suspects, including those 'issued to or by' the CIA.[394] Despite these changes in policy immediately upon Obama's Inauguration, the US government continues to refuse to publish the names of those detained in Bagram Air Base, Afghanistan.[395] There were also reports in 2010 of an additional, secret detention facility at Bagram.[396]

Incommunicado detention

3.127   Incommunicado detention is defined by the detainee's inability to communicate with 'anyone other than his or her captors and perhaps his co-detainees'.[397] It can be

---

[389] Joint Study on global practice in relation to secret detention in the context of countering terrorism, A/HRC/13/42, 26 January 2010; *Guardian*, 'Britain "Complicit in Mistreatment and Possible Torture", Says UN', 27 January 2010.

[390] Amnesty International Report 2009, Romania, notes that 'prisoner-shaped parcels' were seen near Constanta, p 268.

[391] Parliamentary Assembly of the Council of Europe (PACE), 'Secret detentions and illegal transfers of detainees involving Council of Europe member states: second report', Doc 11302 rev, 11 June 2007, paras 5 and 1; *Guardian*, 'Poland Admits Role in CIA Rendition Programme', 22 February 2010.

[392] Amnesty International, News, 'Lithuania Admits Existence of Secret Prison', 22 December 2009.

[393] Written question to UK Government, *Hansard*, HC Deb, Vol 430, Col 917 W, 18 January 2005; Reprieve, 'Ghost Detention on Diego Garcia', 20 May 2009.

[394] Executive Order, Ensuring Lawful Interrogations, 22 January 2009, s 1.

[395] ACLU, 'DOD Refuses to Turn Over List of Bagram Detainee Information', 13 August 2009.

[396] BBC News, 'Red Cross Confirms Second Jail at Bagram', 11 May 2010.

[397] Association for the Prevention of Torture (APT), 'Incommunicado, Unacknowledged and Secret Detention under International Law', 2 March 2006, p 1.

distinguished from secret detention, unacknowledged detention, and unannounced detention.[398] It is technically possible for a detainee to be prevented from contacting family members, lawyers, medical staff, or a judge while the fact of his or her detention and his or her whereabouts has been acknowledged or communicated to one or more of those individuals. However, the Joint Study on global practices in secret detention in counter-terrorism equates incommunicado and secret detention.[399] The definition of enforced disappearances in Article 2 of the new Convention on Enforced Disappearances only requires that the detainee's fate or whereabouts be unknown or that the deprivation of liberty be unacknowledged.[400] When it enters into force, Article 17(d) of the new Convention will require states parties to 'guarantee' certain communication rights for every detainee, as a means of preventing enforced disappearances.[401] Incommunicado detention risks other human rights violations, including torture and other ill-treatment, and would preclude the exercise of *habeas corpus* or the right to challenge the lawfulness of detention before a judge. It is prohibited by IHRL, and states should cease the use of incommunicado detention in their counter-terrorism practices.

In December 2009, the Committee against Torture noted recent reforms in Spain's **3.128** detention policies, but emphasized its concerns that suspects can be held incommunicado for up to 13 days.[402] While there is no separate regime of detention and trial for terrorism suspects in Spain, incommunicado detention can be specifically authorized by a judge.[403] The period of preventative arrest can last five days.[404] The Committee called for Spain to review the practice of incommunicado detention with a view to its abolition, and listed a number of guarantees which should be provided for detainees.[405]

Control orders

Overview

Methods of control short of detention have been employed in counter-terrorism. **3.129** Pakistan's Anti-Terrorism (Amendment) Ordinance 2002 allows for a system of sureties which controls the movement of individuals listed as alleged members

---

[398] Ibid.

[399] Joint Study on global practice in relation to secret detention in the context of countering terrorism, A/HRC/13/42, 26 January 2010.

[400] Convention on Enforced Disappearances, Art 2.

[401] Ibid, Art 17(d).

[402] Committee against Torture, Concluding Observations on the fifth periodic report of Spain, CAT/C/ESP/CO/5, 9 December 2009, para 12.

[403] International Bar Association, Case Study—Spain, January 2008 (web resource–archive with IBA).

[404] Ibid.

[405] Committee against Torture, Concluding Observations on the fifth periodic report of Spain, CAT/C/ESP/CO/5, 9 December 2009, para 12.

of terrorist or sectarian groups; compulsory residence orders have been approved by the ECtHR in some instances in France[406] and Italy, [407] while control orders in the UK[408] and Australia[409] do not require those subjected to them to have been convicted of a terrorist crime in a court.[410] Control orders can include an obligation to report to the authorities at regular intervals, prolonged curfews, and restrictions on use of telecommunications and on contact with other individuals.[411]

3.130 Control orders have the potential to limit a subject's freedom of movement and potential infringements of the right to private and family life, and the freedoms of expression, assembly, and association. Paragraphs 3.152–3.154 will consider the fair hearing aspects of the imposition of control orders in the UK, including reliance on secret evidence which the individual subjected to control orders was not allowed to see. This section focuses on when these methods of control amount to a deprivation of liberty under IHRL, with particular reference to the UK.

UK control orders: case law and legislative background

3.131 In *A and Others* ('the Belmarsh case'),[412] the House of Lords issued a Declaration of Incompatibility between the impugned statutory provision and ECHR rights under section 4 of the UK Human Rights Act 1998. As a result, the government replaced the system of internment with a framework of derogating and non-derogating control orders in the Prevention of Terrorism Act 2005 (as amended in the Counter-Terrorism Act 2008). 'Derogating' means that the control order would involve such a deprivation of liberty or other infringement of rights under the ECHR that the UK would have to derogate from a specific article citing a public emergency.[413] If the UK were to derogate again from Article 5 ECHR, this might authorize a 'derogating' control order which imposed house arrest, in contrast to the curfews of 16 and 18 hours a day examined in the case law below. By May 2010, only non-derogating control orders had been created. The control orders can involve restrictions on a person's freedom of movement, a home-based curfew, electronic tagging, and communication restrictions.

---

[406] UN Human Rights Committee, *Salah Karker v France*, Communication No 833/1998, CCPR/C/70/D/833/1998, 2000 (no violation found on the facts of the case).

[407] Law no 1423 of 27 December 1956 (as amended); *Guzzardi v Italy* (1981) 3 EHRR 333 at para 95 (compulsory residence order did amount to a deprivation of liberty under Art 5).

[408] Prevention of Terrorism Act 2005.

[409] Australian Anti-Terrorism Act (No 2) 2005; *Thomas v Mowbray* [2007] HCA 33.

[410] *Thomas v Mowbray* [2007] HCA 33.

[411] Amnesty International, Control Orders Briefing, September 2009.

[412] *A and Others v Secretary of State for the Home Department* [2004] UKHL 56.

[413] See paras 3.03 and 3.17–3.18.

Control orders are executive, not judicial powers. The Home Secretary must have   **3.132**
reasonable grounds:

- to suspect that the individual concerned is involved in 'terrorism-related activity';[414] and
- to believe that the restrictions to be imposed by the control order are necessary to protect the public (public safety or public order).[415]

Control orders may be confirmed by a court, after a full hearing, if the court is satisfied on the balance of probabilities that the person subjected to the order 'is or has been involved in terrorism-related activity'.[416] Considering the stringent restrictions which are possible under control orders, it would be more appropriate to require the higher criminal standard of proof of beyond reasonable doubt. As Chapter 7 recommends, control orders should only be imposed after conviction of a terrorist crime in a fair trial.[417] The Special Immigration Appeals Tribunal (SIAC) hears appeals against the imposition of control orders. This is a special court set up to hear terrorism-related cases, including those on deportations and transfers of terrorism suspects.[418] Paragraphs 3.152–3.154 below will consider case law from June 2009 which ruled that the closed procedures and secret evidence used in control orders cases were unlawful.[419]

UK case law: does the control order amount to a deprivation of liberty?

In *Secretary of State for the Home Department v JJ and Others*, the UK House of   **3.133**
Lords found that the 18-hour curfew established on the appellants by 'non-derogating' control orders under the UK Prevention of Terrorism Act 1995 amounted to a deprivation of liberty which might violate the right to liberty and security of the person.[420] The case on closed hearings examined in paragraphs 3.152–3.154 involved a control order which imposed a 16-hour curfew,[421] which was not ruled to be a violation of Article 5 ECHR. However, in June 2010 the UK Supreme Court confirmed that other conditions can be taken into account in holding that a control order is a deprivation of liberty under Article 5. In *Secretary of State for the Home Department v AP*[422] the Supreme Court allowed the appeal of a man subjected to a 16-hour curfew combined with confinement to a flat in the

---

[414] Prevention of Terrorism Act 2005, s 2(1)(a); for definitions of 'terrorism-related activity', see Prevention of Terrorism Act 2005, s 1(9), as amended by Counter-Terrorism Act 2008, s 79.
[415] Prevention of Terrorism Act 2005, s 2(1)(b).
[416] Ibid, s 4(7)(a).
[417] See para 7.18.
[418] House of Commons Constitutional Affairs Committee, 7th report, 22 March 2005.
[419] *Secretary of State for the Home Department v AF (FC) and Another* [2009] UKHL 28.
[420] *Secretary of State for the Home Department v JJ and Others* [2007] UKHL 45.
[421] *Secretary of State for the Home Department v AF (FC) and Another* [2009] UKHL 28.
[422] *Secretary of State for the Home Department v AP* [2010] UKSC 24 (16 June 2010).

Midlands 150 miles away from his family. The Supreme Court restored the order of the High Court, on the bases that the overall effect of a 16-hour curfew and separation from family constituted a violation of Article 5.[423] Any challenge to a control order which establishes the fact of a deprivation of liberty which is a violation of Article 5 ECHR may trigger the finding of a Declaration of Incompatibility under section 4 of the UK Human Rights Act 1998, ie a finding by the court that a provision of the Prevention of Terrorism Act 2005 is incompatible with an ECHR right. Such a Declaration can lead to legislative reform.[424]

Unfair trials

The right to a fair trial in IHRL

3.134 Paragraphs 3.135–3.136 introduce the main elements of the right to a fair trial and to a fair hearing in IHRL. Paragraphs 3.137–3.143 examine excessive breadth in the definition of terrorist crimes in states' criminal law, and in the powers of counter-terrorism officials, contrary to the requirement of precision in the principle of legality. These paragraphs also consider risks to the independence of judges and lawyers in a state of emergency. Paragraphs 3.144–3.148 look at violations of defendants' rights to a fair trial in criminal cases, with particular reference to the use of military or state security courts to try terrorism suspects. The latter are insufficiently independent and impartial to satisfy the right to a fair trial, and often use secret evidence which the defendant cannot challenge in practice. Paragraphs 3.149–3.154 consider violations of the right to a fair hearing in civil cases, including the failure to give reasons and to permit a meaningful appeal where an individual has been subjected to 'blacklisting' and asset-freezing by UN or regional organizations; and the impossibility of challenging control orders based on secret evidence.

Treaty law

3.135 The right to a fair trial in criminal cases is bolstered by the principle of equality before the law,[425] and includes for criminal defendants: the right to be informed, promptly, in a language they understand, of the charges against them;[426] the right to adequate time and facilities for the preparation of a defence and the right to a lawyer of the defendant's own choosing,[427] and the right to be informed of this right;[428] the right to the provision of free legal advice or representation for those

[423] Ibid, per Lord Brown at para 12.
[424] UK Human Rights Act 1998, s 4 (cf s 19).
[425] ICCPR, Art 14(1).
[426] ICCPR, Art 14(3)(a); ACHR, Art 8(2)(b); ECHR, Art 6(3)(a).
[427] ICCPR, Art 14(3)(b); ACHR, Art 8(2)(c) and (d); ECHR, Art 6(3)(b) and (c).
[428] ICCPR, Art 14(2)(d).

who cannot afford it;[429] the right to trial by a competent, independent, and impartial tribunal established by law,[430] within a reasonable time,[431] and with the defendant present;[432] the presumption of innocence;[433] to call and examine witnesses;[434] to the free assistance of an interpreter if necessary;[435] not to be compelled to testify against oneself or to confess guilt;[436] and to trial and judgment in public unless there are important competing interests.[437] IHRL also protects the right to appeal of a criminal conviction,[438] the right to compensation if a person has been wrongfully convicted following a miscarriage of justice,[439] and a prohibition on double jeopardy.[440] There are additional protections for juvenile defendants, in treaty and soft law.[441]

In civil cases, equality before the courts must be respected, and everyone is entitled **3.136** to a fair and public hearing by a competent, independent and impartial tribunal established by law,[442] although the hearing may be held *in camera* where there are important competing interests.[443]

Counter-terrorism legislation and the rule of law

Terrorism has also been used as a pretext to repress the activity of human rights **3.137** defenders[444] and legitimate forms of peaceful protest, further diminishing the implementation of IHRL at the national level.[445] States' counter-terrorism legislation has

---

[429] ICCPR, Art 14(2)(d); ECHR, Art 6(3)(c).

[430] ICCPR, Art 14(1); ACHR, Art 8(1); ECHR, Art 6(1).

[431] ECHR, Art 6(1); ACHPR, Art 7(1)(d); ICCPR, Art 14(2)(c)—'without undue delay'.

[432] ICCPR, Art 14(2)(d).

[433] ICCPR, Art 14(2); ACHR, Art 8(2); ECHR, Art 6(2); ACHPR, Art 7(1)(b).

[434] ICCPR, Art 14(3)(e); ACHR, Art 8(2)(f); ECHR, Art 6(3)(d).

[435] ICCPR, Art 14(3)(f); ECHR, Art 6(2)(e).

[436] ICCPR, Art 14(3)(g); ACHR, Art 8(2)(g).

[437] ICCPR, Art 14(1); ACHR, Art 8(5); ECHR, Art 6(1).

[438] ICCPR, Art 14(5); ACHR, Art 8(2)(h).

[439] ICCPR, Art 14(6).

[440] ICCPR, Art 14(7); ACHR, Art 8(4)—only if the conviction was 'an unappealable judgment'.

[441] ICCPR, Art 14(4); Standard Minimum Rules for the Administration of Juvenile Justice, General Assembly Resolution 40/33, 29 November 1985.

[442] ICCPR, Art 14(1); ACHR, Art 8(1); ECHR, Art 6(1); ACHPR, Art 7(1) and (1)(a).

[443] ICCPR, Art 14(1); ACHR, Art 8(5); ECHR, Art 6(1).

[444] Declaration on the Right and Responsibility of Individuals, Groups and Organs of Society to Promote and Protect Universally Recognised Human Rights and Fundamental Freedoms, annexed to UN General Assembly Resolution A/RES/53/144, 8 March 1999.

[445] UN Special Rapporteur on the Situation of Human Rights Defenders, Issues in Focus, Security Legislation, 'Security and Counter-Terrorist Legislation'; Amnesty International, Statement to Working Session 16 of the Organisation for Security and Cooperation in Europe: Fundamental Freedoms II, including: Freedom of Expression, Free Media and Information, HDIM.NGO/396/07, 3 October 2007; Fédération Internationale des Droits de l'Homme (FIDH), 'Turkey: End Human Rights Violations under the Pretext of the "War Against Terrorism"', 22 September 2003; FIDH, Observatory for the Protection of Human Rights Defenders Annual Report 2009, Russian Federation, 18 June 2009.

violated the rule of law's requirements of precision and prospectivity. There is a lack of precision and an excessive breadth in:

- the definition of terrorism or terrorist crimes, meaning that many non-criminal actions, the peaceful expression of dissent, or the activity of human rights defenders, may be criminalized as 'terrorism';[446] and
- an excessive breadth, secrecy, or mass of overlapping regulations to define the powers of law enforcement officials, armed forces, and the intelligence services in counter-terrorism. Multiple emergency laws and their overlapping regulations present risks to the independence of the judiciary and the role of lawyers.

Overbroad definitions of terrorist crimes

3.138   Section 2 of Malaysia's Internal Security Act 1960 includes in its broad definition of 'terrorist' a person who 'demands, collects or receives any supplies for the use of any person who intends or is about to act, or has recently acted, in a manner prejudicial to public safety or the maintenance of public order'. This has the potential to criminalize lawful transactions, and defines terrorism not by reference to politically or ideologically motivated acts of violence, but as the broadest possible threat to public safety and public order. This risks a disproportionate interference in the exercise of freedoms of expression, assembly, and association, and in the activities of human rights defenders.

3.139   In Pakistan, section 6 of the Anti-Terrorism Act 1997 defines 'terrorism' as a 'threat of action' which takes one of several forms. While the statute specifically enumerates several forms of terrorist attack which cause death or grievous bodily harm, or which result in kidnap or hostage-taking, terrorism also constitutes any action which 'is designed to disrupt the provision of a public service', or which 'involves intimidation of a public servant in his official capacity'. The latter two forms of 'threat of action' may criminalize strike action by public service workers, or letters of protest by human rights defenders, and therefore risk a disproportionate interference in labour rights and the freedom of expression and assembly. There is also a risk of discrimination, as any threat of terrorism must be used to advance a 'religious, sectarian or ethnic cause'. This latter concern is related to the legislation's inadequate breadth as to the motivation for a terrorist attack, as it omits terrorism for political or ideological ends other than those linked to religious, sectarian, or ethnic causes.

---

[446] Pakistan, Anti-Terrorism Act 1997, s 6; Sri Lanka, Prevention of Terrorism (Temporary Provisions) Act 1979, s 2; Malaysia, Internal Security Act 1960, s 2; Swaziland, Suppression of Terrorism Act No 3 of 2008, s 2; see Amnesty International and International Bar Association, 'Suppression of Terrorism Act Undermines Human Rights in Swaziland', 2009; Algeria, Code Pénal, s 87; United Kingdom, Terrorism Act 2000, Terrorism Act 2006, s 1; United States of America, PATRIOT Act 2001 (see especially 'material support' for terrorism); Russian Federation, Federal Law No 35-FZ on Counteraction of Terrorism, 6 March 2006, Art 3.

Amnesty International and the International Bar Association have noted their concerns at the breadth of the definition of terrorist crimes in section 2 of Swaziland's Suppression of Terrorism Act No 3 of 2008.[447] The organizations noted that the definition of terrorism is not restricted to the threatened or actual use of violence against civilians, or to an ideological motivation for such threatened or actual use of violence against civilians. Moreover, the organizations believe that the law fails to adhere to the accessibility, non-retroactivity, non-discrimination, and precision inherent in the principle of legality.[448] **3.140**

In Russia, a 2006 definition of terrorism includes 'the ideology of violence and the practice of influencing the adoption of a decision of public authorities, local self-government bodies, or international organisations connected with frightening the population (or) other forms of violent actions'.[449] An 'ideology of violence' is both hard to prove, and imprecise. The criminalization of 'the practice of influencing the adoption of a decision of public authorities' is likely to imperil the activities of human rights defenders, especially given the assassination and harassment of human rights defenders in the Russian Federation.[450] The definition of terrorism in Article 205 of the Criminal Code of the Russian Federation, as amended in 2004, uses a more restrictive definition of 'terrorism', which comprises 'the perpetration of an explosion, arson or any other action endangering the lives of people and causing sizable property damage or entailing other socially dangerous consequences'. **3.141**

Excessive scope of counter-terrorism powers

The Russian Federation also broadly defines counter-terrorism powers, which can include the imposition of special measures or special law to cover counter-terrorism operations.[451] This suggests a secrecy and imprecision which violates not only equality before the law (terrorism suspects facing a special regime would be treated differently from those facing federal criminal charges) but also the precision required in the principle of legality. Before recent statutory amendments, Russian law provided for the 'certainty of punishment' for terrorism,[452] suggesting an erosion of the presumption of innocence. Russian law also provides **3.142**

---

[447] Amnesty International and International Bar Association, 'Suppression of Terrorism Act Undermines Human Rights in Swaziland', 2009.

[448] Ibid.

[449] Russian Federation, Federal Law No 35-FZ on Counteraction of Terrorism, 6 March 2006 (as amended by Federal Law No 321-FZ, which came into force on 1 January 2010), Art 3.

[450] Fédération Internationale des ligues de Droits de l' Homme (FIDH), Observatory for the Protection of Human Rights Defenders Annual Report 2009, Russian Federation, 18 June 2009; Amnesty International, 'Human Rights Activist Natalia Estemirova Murdered in Russia', 16 July 2009.

[451] Russian Federation, Federal Law No 35-FZ on Counteraction of Terrorism, 6 March 2006 (as amended by Federal Law No 321-FZ, which came into force on 1 January 2010), Art 11.

[452] Russian Federation, Report to the UN Counter-Terrorism Committee on the implementation of Security Council Resolution 1625 (2005).

immunity in relation to the death or injury of 'terrorists' for those who participate in counter-terrorism operations.[453] This is a particular concern when considered alongside the Russian Federation's failure to comply with a litany of judgments against it from the European Court of Human Rights.[454]

3.143   States' counter-terrorism actions must safeguard the independence of the judiciary and the role of lawyers. The Basic Principles on the Independence of the Judiciary require states to guarantee the independence of the judiciary and enshrine it in legislation or the constitution;[455] and provide that '[t]here shall not be any inappropriate or unwarranted interference with the judicial process'.[456] Judges' freedom of expression and of association must be respected.[457] The states of emergency in Pakistan (prompted by counter-terrorism policies) and in Sri Lanka (caused by the conflict between the state and the LTTE) have created overlapping and overbroad legislative provisions on counter-terrorism. They have also led to erosions of the independence of the judiciary and several cases of intimidation of lawyers.[458]

Right to a fair trial in criminal cases

Treaty law

3.144   The right to a fair trial includes the right to a fair and public hearing by a competent, independent, and impartial tribunal established by law. The independence criterion relates to the separation of powers, and to the judges' freedom from interference from the legislative and executive branches of the state. Impartiality relates to the court's capacity to decide the case before it without bias, and implies a lack of undue influence which might create bias. Hearings may be held *in camera* where there are important competing concerns, as provided by Article 14(1) of the ICCPR, but the general presumption is for public hearings, so trials in secret should be avoided.

Basic principles on the role of lawyers

3.145   Defence counsel must have 'prompt' access to detainees, and governments should ensure 'effective and equal access to lawyers'.[459] Lawyers should have an opportunity

---

[453] Russian Federation Federal Law No 130-FZ, 25 July 1998, Art 20 (still in force despite later legislation).

[454] See paras 3.93–3.95.

[455] Basic Principles on the Independence of the Judiciary, General Assembly Resolutions 40/32 of 29 November 1985 and 40/146 of 13 December 1985, Principle 1.

[456] Ibid, Principle 4.

[457] Ibid, Principles 8 and 9.

[458] International Bar Association, 'Justice in Retreat: A Report on the Independence of the Legal Profession and the Rule of Law in Sri Lanka', 2009; International Bar Association, 'The Struggle to Maintain an Independent Judiciary: A Report on the Attempt to Remove the Chief Justice of Pakistan', July 2007; International Bar Association, 'A Long March to Justice: A Report on Judicial Independence and Integrity in Pakistan', September 2009.

[459] Basic Principles on the Role of Lawyers, 8th UN Congress on the Prevention of Crime and the Treatment of Offenders, 27 August to 7 September 1990, Principles 1 and 2.

to challenge evidence against defendants, in order to assist them to prepare a defence. Where lawyers cannot mount an effective challenge as a result of secret evidence which is either not disclosed to the defendant, or not disclosed to the defendant's lawyer, the 'equality of arms' between prosecution and defence is undermined. This is especially so given the disparity in resources between prosecution and defence. Governments must also ensure that lawyers 'are able to perform all of their professional functions without intimidation, harassment or improper interference'.[460] They should further ensure that lawyers 'shall not suffer, or be threatened with, prosecution or administrative, economic or other sanctions for any action taken in accordance with recognised professional duties, standards and ethics'.[461]

Military courts or military commissions

The Basic Principles on the Independence of the Judiciary provide that '[e]veryone **3.146** shall have the right to be tried by ordinary courts or tribunals using established legal procedures'. [462] Yet Egypt,[463] Jordan,[464] Syria,[465] Turkey,[466] and the US[467] all rely on special security courts or military commissions for the prosecution of some terrorism suspects.[468] Counter-terrorism state practice in the Middle East and in the US shows a reliance on military courts or military commissions, with questionable independence from the executive and restricted rights of a defendant. This is contrary to international law and standards on the right to a fair trial in criminal matters, and the UN Human Rights Committee has opposed the general use of military courts to try civilians, finding a violation of Article 14 of the ICCPR in its Views on *Madani v Algeria*.[469] The Human Rights Committee reasoned that while military and special courts are not prohibited by the ICCPR, only 'exceptional circumstances' that rendered it 'unavoidable' for a civilian to be tried by a military court would be acceptable, in addition to full guarantees as to the implementation of Article 14.[470] The Inter-American system has also criticized military courts.[471]

---

[460] Ibid, Principle 16(a).

[461] Ibid, Principle 16(c).

[462] Basic Principles on the Independence of the Judiciary, General Assembly Resolutions 40/32 of 29 November 1985 and 40/146 of 13 December 1985, Principle 4.

[463] Human Rights Watch, 'Egypt: Transfer Zeitoun Trial to Criminal Court', 14 February 2010.

[464] Amnesty International, Submissions to the Universal Periodic Review Mechanism: Jordan, 2008, MDE 16/004/2008.

[465] Human Rights Watch, 'Syria: Dissolve the State Security Court', 24 May 2009.

[466] Amnesty International, 'Turkey: Justice Delayed and Denied: The Persistence of Protracted and Unfair Trials for Those Charged under Anti-Terrorism Legislation', EUR 44/013/2006, 5 September 2006.

[467] Military Commissions Act 2009.

[468] See para 4.24.

[469] *Abbasi Madani v Algeria*, Communication No 1172/2003, CCPR/C/89/D1172/2003, Views, 28 March 2007.

[470] Ibid.

[471] *Loayza Tamayo v Peru*, Inter-American Court of Human Rights (Reparations), 27 November 1998, Ser C No 42 (1998).

3.147 Jordan's Special Security Court has also raised concerns as to independence and impartiality: while there is one civilian among two military officials, the military officials are not independent judges. There is a right of appeal to the Court of Cassation, but cross-examination of witnesses is at the judges' discretion.[472] The court has jurisdiction over a variety of 'security offences', black marketeering, and drug-trafficking, not only terrorism. Coupled with the broad definition of terrorism in Jordanian law,[473] this court has tried civilians for crimes including attacks on tourists.

3.148 Military commissions were first established to try suspects detained in the US-led 'war on terror' by President Bush's Military Order of 2001, which was subsequently declared unconstitutional by the Supreme Court in *Hamdan v Rumsfeld*.[474] The Military Commissions Act 2006 largely reinstated the provisions of the Military Order of 2001, but infringed the right to mount an effective defence owing to the prevalence of classified evidence, and did not provide for the inadmissibility of evidence obtained by torture or ill-treatment. President Obama did state an intention to resume military commissions for remaining detainees at Guantánamo Bay,[475] although a number of detainees will now be tried in federal court.[476] President Obama announced that he would introduce 'improve[ments]' to the Bush-era military commissions, by including fair procedures, precluding the admissibility of evidence obtained by torture, tightening the rules on hearsay evidence, and allowing for review of military commissions decisions.[477] However, even with relatively increased procedural protections for defendants in the new proposed military commissions, including the inadmissibility of evidence obtained through coercion, Human Rights Watch has expressed concern at military commissions' lack of independence from the larger military structure.[478]

Right to a fair hearing in civil cases

3.149 IHRL protects equality before the courts and the right to a fair hearing in civil matters. All persons have the right to a fair hearing before a competent, independent, and impartial tribunal established by law.[479] These rights have been eroded in the context of intergovernmental 'listing' and assets-freezing orders against suspected

---

[472] Amnesty International, Submissions to the Universal Periodic Review Mechanism: Jordan, 2008, MDE 16/004/2008.

[473] Prevention of Terrorism Act 2006; see Amnesty International, 'Challenging Repression: Human Rights Defenders in the Middle East and North Africa', MDE 01/001/2009, 11 March 2009.

[474] *Hamdan v Rumsfeld*, 126 S Ct 2749, 548 US 557 (2006).

[475] Military Commissions Act 2009; National Defence Reauthorisation Act for FY 2010, s 1031.

[476] Department of Justice, 'Departments of Justice and Defense Announce Forum Decisions for Ten Guantanamo Bay Detainees', 13 November 2009; see para 4.24.

[477] President Barack H Obama, 'Protecting Our Security and Our Values', National Archives Museum, Washington DC, 21 May 2009.

[478] Human Rights Watch, 'US: Revisions Can't Fix Military Commissions', 8 July 2009.

[479] ICCPR, Art14(1); ACHR, Art 8(1); ECHR, Art 6(1).

terrorists by the UN, the EU, and individual governments; and by the use of secret evidence to ground control orders in the UK.

Terrorism 'listing' and assets-freezing

Prior to the reforms of UN Security Council Resolution 1904 of 17 December   **3.150**
2009, which introduced an Ombudsperson to be appointed by the Secretary-General in consultation with the UN Sanctions Committee to hear delisting requests,[480] both the UN Human Rights Committee, and the European Court of Justice noted the erosion of the right to a fair hearing in the context of terrorism 'listing' and the freezing of assets pursuant to UN Security Council Resolution 1267 (1999).

- In *Nabil Sayadi & Patricia Vinck v Belgium*,[481] the Human Rights Committee found violations of the freedom of movement and the right to protection from arbitrary and unlawful interference with privacy, family, home, and correspondence. However, the Human Rights Committee found that the applicants had an effective remedy in Belgium, and they were eventually removed from the terrorism list by the UN Sanctions Committee. The Human Rights Committee did not find a violation of Article 14 of the ICCPR in that case.
- In the *Kadi* line of cases before the CFI and ECJ,[482] the right to a fair hearing in EC law was ruled to be fully applicable to sanctions cases,[483] and while an initial freezing order may be applied without the opportunity to make representations, a person subject to such an order must subsequently have the right to make representations.[484] There is a duty to give reasons in the decision to impose an assets-freezing order.[485] This is analogous to a right to know the reasons for a judicial decision, but it is far less than is required by the right to a fair hearing before a competent, independent, and impartial tribunal established by law.

The Financial Action Task Force, in its Best Practices on the Freezing of Terrorist   **3.151**
Assets, recommends the insertion of due process guarantees, including communication of the reasons for listing, and the establishment of an adversarial procedure

---

[480] See paras 1.21–1.22, 6.13.

[481] Human Rights Committee, *Nabil Sayadi and Patricia Vinck v Belgium*, Communication No 1472/2006, CCPR/C/94/D/1472/2006, Views, 22 October 2008.

[482] European Court of Justice and Court of First Instance of the European Communities, Joined Cases C-402/05P and C-415/05P, *Kadi and Al Barakaat International Foundation v Council of the European Union and Commission of the European Communities*, 3 September 2008; *Organisation des Modjahedines du people d'Iran v Council* [2006] ECR II-4665 ('*OMPI 1*'), T-256/07 23 ('*OMPI 2*') October 2008.

[483] *Organisation des Modjahedines du people d'Iran v Council* [2006] ECR II-4665 ('*OMPI 1*').

[484] *Kadi and Al Barakaat International Foundation v Council of the European Union and Commission of the European Communities*, Joined Cases C-402/05P and C-415/05P, 3 September 2008, at para 331.

[485] *Organisation des Modjahedines du people d'Iran v Council* [2006] ECR II-4665 ('*OMPI 1*'), paras 143–148.

to challenge the listing of individuals or legal persons.[486] As paragraphs 1.21–1.22 note, the recent reforms of Resolution 1904 fall short of an adversarial procedure. Chapter 7 recommends rapid reform of the UN and EU listing processes to ensure merits-based review by an independent and impartial court.[487]

UK case law: control orders and the right to a fair hearing[488]

3.152 Litigation on control orders in the UK has emphasized the failure to implement the right to a fair hearing in Article 6 ECHR,[489] especially in relation to the secrecy of the allegations against the person subjected to a control order.[490] As noted in paragraph 3.131 above, the Home Secretary has discretion to impose control orders based on two grounds. The Special Immigration Appeals Commission (SIAC) has power to review the imposition of a control order. The SIAC can use closed procedures, in which the individual subject to a control order is not permitted to hear evidence in open court, or to know the substance of the intelligence which alleges that he or she is involved in 'terrorist-related activity'. Where secret evidence is used, the individual subject to a control order is represented by a court-appointed Special Advocate,[491] who has the task of representing the individual's interests, but the individual cannot hear arguments on the secret evidence.

3.153 In a criminal context, the use of secret evidence would infringe the right to know the substance of the charges and to mount a meaningful defence. This is particularly concerning given the litigation on Article 5 ECHR before the UK House of Lords discussed in paragraph 3.133 above, which considered an 18-hour curfew in a control order to be a deprivation of liberty.[492] There are strong commonalities between a custodial sentence, usually only applied after conviction for a criminal offence, and the extensive restrictions on individual liberty imposed by a control order.

3.154 Judges in the UK are increasingly willing to challenge closed procedures. In June 2009, the House of Lords held that those subject to a control order have the right to understand the substance of the allegations against them.[493] In December 2009, the High Court extended this principle to bail applications in

---

[486] Financial Action Task Force (FATF-GAFI), International Best Practices for the Freezing of Terrorist Assets, July 2009; for recent case law quashing 'listing' and freezing orders in the UK, see *Treasury v Mohammed al-Ghabra; R (Hani El Sayed Sabaeri Youssef) v HM Treasury* [2010] UKSC 2.

[487] See para 7.18.

[488] See paras 3.130 et seq above.

[489] *Secretary of State for the Home Department v MB (FC)* [2007] UKHL 46; *Secretary of State for the Home Department v AF (FC) and Another* [2009] UKHL 28.

[490] *Secretary of State for the Home Department v JJ and Others* [2007] UKHL 45; *Secretary of State for the Home Department v MB* [2007] UKHL 46, per Lord Bingham of Cornhill.

[491] House of Commons Constitutional Affairs Committee, 7th report, 22 March 2005.

[492] *Secretary of State for the Home Department v AF (FC) and Another* [2009] UKHL 28.

[493] Ibid.

the counter-terrorism context.[494] In May 2010, the Court of Appeal held that closed procedures could not be used in a civil case concerning allegations of UK complicity in torture.[495]

Synthesis

Individuals have a right to a fair and public hearing before a competent, independ- **3.155**
ent, and impartial tribunal established by law. This right applies to terrorism suspects facing trial, and requires that they be tried in civilian criminal courts, as recommended in Chapter 7. This right also applies outside the criminal context: in challenges to the imposition of sanctions and assets-freezing orders, and to control orders. Litigation on control orders in the UK has pointed to a failure to implement the right to a fair hearing in Article 6 ECHR, although recently, the use of secret evidence was considered sufficient grounds to quash a control order.

Disproportionate interference with civil and political rights

Limitations on certain rights in counter-terrorism

IHRL permits limitations to certain rights, *inter alia*, in pursuit of national security, **3.156**
public order, and public safety if the limitations chosen are prescribed by law, neces-sary in a democratic society, and proportionate to (or no more than absolutely nec-essary for) the aim in question.[496] These limitations cannot be applied to so-called absolute rights, including the right to life and the prohibition on torture or cruel, inhuman, or degrading treatment or punishment. Instead, they relate to the right to private and family life, the freedom of conscience and religion, the freedom of expres-sion, and the freedom of assembly and association. The Protocols to the ECHR permit similar restrictions on the freedom of movement, and to procedural safe-guards relating to the expulsion of non-nationals.[497] The exact scope of the tests of necessity and proportionality has been set by the UN Human Rights Committee, the European Court of Human Rights, and the Inter-American human rights system.

Right to private and family life

The right to private and family life may be undermined when a control order or **3.157**
assets-freezing order is imposed, or through the deportation or transfer of terrorism suspects. The Human Rights Committee found a violation of this right where individuals had been incorrectly placed on a terrorism sanctions list by the UN

---

[494] *R v Upper Tribunal, SIAC and Others v XC and Others (Carts and Others)* [2009] EWHC 3052 (Admin).
[495] *Al-Rawi and Others v The Security Service and Others* [2010] EWCA Civ 482; see para 4.47.
[496] See paras 3.03, 3.22–3.25.
[497] Protocol No 4 to the ECHR, Art 2; Protocol No 7, Art 1.

Sanctions Committee and the Belgian authorities.[498] Litigation on control orders pursuant to the UK Prevention of Terrorism Act 2005 has thus far focused on the right to liberty and security of person[499] and the right to a fair hearing under Article 6 ECHR.[500] However, lawyers for persons subject to control orders can present arguments based on a disproportionate impact on the right to private and family life under Article 8 ECHR in an attempt to persuade a court to modify or quash an order. Conversely, in *Secretary of State for the Home Department v AP*, the UK Supreme Court confirmed that even conditions which are justified and proportionate restrictions of Article 8 rights can be relevant to a judge's determination of whether a control order constitutes a deprivation of liberty under Article 5 ECHR. These Article 8 restrictions can be a 'decisive factor—capable of tipping the balance' between a control order that does constitute a deprivation of liberty and one which does not.[501]

3.158   In *Al-Nashif v Bulgaria*,[502] the ECtHR found a violation of Article 8 ECHR. In this case, a stateless Palestinian was detained and deported from Bulgaria, where he was legally resident with his wife and children, to Syria. According to the Bulgarian government, Mr Al-Nashif's teaching activities presented a threat to national security, and this justified his deportation. Mr Al-Nashif's wife and children remained in Bulgaria following the deportation, but later joined him in Jordan. The Court also found violations of Article 5(4) and Article 13, as Mr Al-Nashif had been prevented from challenging the lawfulness of his detention, and had been denied an effective remedy for the violation of his rights.

Freedom of conscience and religion

3.159   The freedom of conscience and religion is not included in the list of treaty rights for which there can be limitations in pursuit of national security, although treaty law does permit restrictions on the manifestation of religion and belief. These restrictions must be prescribed by law, necessary in a democratic society for 'the protection of public safety, public order, health or morals, or the protection of the rights and freedoms of others', and proportionate to the aim pursued.[503] Counter-terrorist policies which infringe detainees' or other individuals' freedom of conscience and religion are justified only if they can be shown to be the most minimal intrusion possible on that right in pursuit of these enumerated grounds. *Newsweek* reported in 2005 that US military guards at Guantánamo Bay had desecrated a copy of

---

[498] Human Rights Committee, *Nabil Sayadi & Patricia Vinck v Belgium*, Communication No 1472/2006, CCPR/C/94/D/1472/2006, Views, 22 October 2008.
[499] *Secretary of State for the Home Department v JJ and Others* [2007] UKHL 45; *Secretary of State for the Home Department v MB* [2007] UKHL 46, per Lord Bingham of Cornhill.
[500] *Secretary of State for the Home Department v AF and Another* [2009] UKHL 28.
[501] *Secretary of State for the Home Department v AP* [2010] UKSC 24, para 2, per Lord Brown.
[502] *Al-Nashif v Bulgaria* (2003) 36 EHRR 37.
[503] ECHR, Art 9(2); see also ICCPR, Art 18(3).

the Qur'an.[504] This report was then retracted, but an internal Department of Defense inquiry concluded that there had been 'mishandling' of the Qur'an.[505] There is no indication that these incidents were part of a policy which was prescribed by law for any of the permitted purposes in treaty law. If there were such a policy, it would almost certainly violate the freedom of conscience and religion of the detainees. There is no evidence that the bans on the hijab or other Islamic head coverings in Europe have been justified by reference to national security or counter-terrorism. In France and Turkey, the laicity of the state is the principal reason for the ban on wearing the hijab in public places.[506] Whatever the reason adduced for the limitation, the state must still justify the legality, necessity, and proportionality of any restriction on the right to manifest a religious belief.

Freedom of expression and the role of the media

Terrorist attacks can have a chilling effect on freedom of expression when they target academics,[507] human rights defenders and journalists,[508] and judges and lawyers,[509] through assassinations[510] or threats. States should exercise their due diligence obligation to prevent terrorist attacks, and where possible to protect citizens from erosions of their freedom of expression from non-state actors. Nonetheless, states' counter-terrorism policies should protect the 'freedom to seek, receive and impart information and ideas of all kinds, regardless of frontiers'.[511] States which cite national security to block transmission signals or to curb Internet use need to adduce strong justifications or their actions are likely to be a disproportionate interference in the freedom of expression.   **3.160**

The freedom of expression is a somewhat limited right in IHRL, and carries 'special duties and responsibilities'.[512] Examples of potentially lawful restrictions would be court orders to prevent the publication or transmission of conclusions which may prejudice the result of a trial, particularly as regards the presumption of innocence; or the prohibition of incitement to racial hatred.[513] However, states must still prove that limitations on that right in pursuit of national security are necessary   **3.161**

---

504 CNN, 'Newsweek Retracts Quran Story', 17 May 2005.

505 *Washington Post*, 'Pentagon Details Abuse of Koran', 4 June 2005.

506 Human Rights Watch, 'France: Headscarf Ban Violates Religious Freedom', 27 February 2004; 'Turkey: Headscarf Ban Stifles Academic Freedom', 28 June 2004.

507 *Houston Chronicle*, 'Dimming the Future', 15 November 2006, quoted in Scholars at Risk Network publication; Azzaman.com, '340 Academics and 2,334 Women Killed in 3 Years, Human Rights Ministry Says', 1 July 2008.

508 Press Statement by Security Council President on Attempted Assassination of Lebanese Journalist, 28 September 2005.

509 Associated Press, 'Two Gunmen Kill Judge in Spain's Basque Country: ETA Separatists Suspected', 11 July 2001.

510 Scholars at Risk Network, Iraq (email listserv).

511 ICCPR, Art 19.

512 Ibid.

513 International Convention for the Elimination of All Forms of Racial Discrimination, Art 4.

and proportionate. The non-binding Johannesburg Principles on National Security, Freedom of Expression and Access to Information may offer some guidance to states planning counter-terrorism policies which may impact on freedom of expression.[514]

3.162 Some restrictions on media freedom may be considered necessary and proportionate, especially if they are enumerated in treaty provisions which specify permissible grounds for restriction on the freedom of expression. Courts have noted that national security concerns may in principle justify restrictions on the media; however these restrictions must not sweep too broadly. In *Sürek v Turkey (No 4)*, a majority of the Grand Chamber of the European Court of Human Rights found a violation of Article 10 ECHR on the grounds of disproportionate criminal penalties imposed in a case where a journalist wrote in a 'literary and metaphorical tone' to compare current politicians with renowned Kurdish separatists.[515]

3.163 Definitions of terrorism as broad as that in Bahrain, where terrorism can amount to 'threats to national unity'[516] or as circular as that in Swaziland, where terrorism can include 'an act or omission which constitutes an offence under this Act'[517] fail to respect the precision required for criminal legislation in the principle of legality, and risk criminalizing political speech, contrary to the freedom of expression. In *Holder v Humanitarian Law Project*[518] the US Supreme Court risked criminalizing training in international law when it declared constitutional a federal law banning 'material support' to foreign organizations which are designated as 'terrorist'.[519] In that case, 'material support' for terrorism was construed to include the provision of assistance or expert advice regarding international law, on the questionable basis that 'material support meant to promote peaceable, lawful conduct can be diverted to advance terrorism in multiple ways'.[520] The court held that the statute did not violate the US Constitution's First Amendment protections on freedom of speech.[521] Training non-state terrorist groups in IHL applicable to non-international armed conflicts is intended to increase compliance with IHL, and to

---

[514] Article IX & University of Witwatersrand, Johannesburg Principles on National Security, Freedom of Expression and Access to Information, 1 October 1995.

[515] Grand Chamber of the European Court of Human Rights, *Sürek v Turkey (No 4)*, Application No 24762/94, Judgment of 8 July 1999, para 58.

[516] International Freedom of Expression Exchange (IFEX), 'Counter-Terrorism Bill Threatens Freedom of Expression', 4 September 2006.

[517] Swaziland, Suppression of Terrorism Act No 3 of 2008, s 2; see Amnesty International and International Bar Association, 'Suppression of Terrorism Act Undermines Human Rights in Swaziland', AFR 55/001/2009, January 2009.

[518] *Holder, Attorney General, et al v Humanitarian Law Project et al*, No 08–1498, United States Supreme Court, 21 June 2010.

[519] 18 USC s 2339B(a)(1).

[520] *Holder, Attorney General, et al v Humanitarian Law Project et al*, No 08–1498, United States Supreme Court, 21 June 2010, p 25.

[521] Ibid, pp 20–34.

reduce civilian casualties.[522] The judgment may reduce IHL compliance by armed groups, as US-based organizations will no longer be able to offer training in international law to these armed groups lest they be criminalized under the 'material support' statute.[523]

Incitement to terrorism; apologie du terrorisme

UN Security Council Resolution 1624 (2005) requires states to '[p]rohibit by law **3.164** incitement to commit a terrorist act or acts'.[524] There is some tension between the strict necessity and proportionality tests in IHRL on the one hand, and states' obligations from UN Security Council Resolutions and new regional treaties to criminalize incitement to terrorism on the other. The new Council of Europe Convention on the Prevention of Terrorism, adopted in 2005, will oblige its states parties to criminalize 'public provocation to commit a terrorist offence',[525] which Ben Saul notes is an 'an amalgam of two concepts: "*apologie du terrorisme*" and "incitement to terrorism"'.[526] Apologism for terrorism may cover a broader range of expression than incitement, which is more compatible with established criminal law outside the counter-terrorism context.[527] Nonetheless, as for all limitations on the freedom of expression, states must be ready to justify the lawfulness, necessity, and proportionality of their counter-terrorism policies. The UN Human Rights Committee noted that the offence of 'encouragement of terrorism' in section 1 of the UK's Terrorism Act 2006 risked disproportionate interference with the freedom of expression, and recommended that the provision be amended.[528]

Prosecution of journalists and attacks on the media

However, assaults on or harassment of journalists and the use of the criminal law **3.165** to curb all peaceful expression of dissent would be unnecessary in a democratic society and disproportionate to the aim of protecting national security. The International Bar Association researched freedom of expression, and the activity of journalists, lawyers, judges, and human rights defenders in Sri Lanka. It concluded that government interference in the media, coupled with the 'use of

---

[522] Dietmar Klenner, 'Training in International Humanitarian Law' (2000) 839 *International Review of the Red Cross* 653–661.

[523] Association for Conflict Resolution, 'Understanding the Impact of *Holder v. Humanitarian Law Project*. A Conversation with David Cole', 12 July 2010, summary, at http://www.alliance-forpeacebuilding.org/news/45435/Advocacy-News-Understanding-the-impact-of-Holder-v.-Humanitarian-Law-P. html.

[524] UN Security Council Resolution 1624 (2005), S/RES/1624 (2005), 14 September 2005, para 1(a).

[525] Council of Europe Convention for the Prevention of Terrorism, Art 5(2).

[526] Ben Saul, 'Speaking of Terror: Criminalising Incitement to Violence', University of Sydney, Sydney Law School, Legal Studies Research Paper, No 08/112, October 2008, p 2.

[527] Ibid.

[528] Human Rights Committee, Concluding Observations on the United Kingdom of Great Britain and Northern Ireland, CCPR/C/GBR/CO/6, 30 July 2008, para 26.

repressive criminal legislation to prosecute journalists [including the overlapping Emergency Regulations and the Prevention of Terrorism Act], and an increase in attacks against the media, have had a chilling effect on freedom of expression in Sri Lanka'.[529] The report also noted that the freedom of expression of lawyers and judges had been systematically curtailed.[530]

Freedom of assembly

3.166 Counter-terrorism policies and the use of counter-terrorism as a pretext to repress human rights defenders and national minorities have eroded freedom of assembly in a number of states:

- In the Russian Federation, counter-terrorism law criminalizes 'organizing extremist communities'.[531] This provision may be used both to discriminate unlawfully on the grounds of race or religion, and to erode freedom of assembly for 'communities' deemed 'extremist'.
- In 2003 in Uzbekistan, the Committee of Ministers cited counter-terrorism as grounds to restrict freedom of assembly following cross-border incursions from Kyrgyzstan and Tajikistan.[532] In May 2005, the then President of Uzbekistan Islam Karimov attempted to portray the protesters killed by security forces in Andijan as 'an attempt by Islamist terrorists to destabilize the country'.[533]
- In Pakistan, gatherings of four or more people are prohibited without police authorization, under section 144 of the Criminal Procedures Code, despite the freedom of assembly being guaranteed by the Constitution of Pakistan.[534] The International Federation of Human Rights (FIDH) concluded that under former President Musharaff, the pretext of cooperation in the US-led 'war on terror' had led to progressive failures to respect and ensure the freedom of expression, the freedom of association (particularly relevant for the functioning of NGOs), and the freedom of assembly.[535]

Disproportionate curbs on freedom of assembly repress the activity of human rights defenders, and endanger the full implementation of human rights norms.

---

[529] International Bar Association, 'Justice in Retreat: A Report on the Independence of the Legal Profession and the Rule of Law in Sri Lanka', 2009, para 7.34.

[530] Ibid.

[531] Criminal Code of the Russian Federation, No 63-FZ, 13 June 1996, Art 282.1.

[532] Human Rights First, 'The Uzbekistan Crisis: Assessing the Impact and Next Steps Hearing of the Commission on Security and Cooperation in Europe' (United States Helsinki Commission), Written Testimony of Human Rights First, 29 June 2005, Persecution of Human Rights Defenders in the Wake of the Andijan Crisis.

[533] Human Rights Watch, 'The Andijan Massacre: One Year Later, Still No Justice', Briefing Paper, 11 May 2006, p 3.

[534] Constitution of Pakistan, s 16.

[535] FIDH, 'In Mala Fide: Freedoms of Expression, Association and Assembly in Pakistan', 17 January 2005.

Freedom of association

States have invoked national security to justify the prohibition of political parties **3.167**
which they deem to be linked to terrorist groups. In a line of cases on the dissolution
of political parties in Turkey, the ECtHR has found a violation of Article 11 ECHR,
read together with Article 10, where a domestic court ruled that the aims of the
Freedom and Democracy (Ozdep) party were incompatible with the unity and
secular nature of the Turkish state.[536] However, the dissolution of a party which
aimed to implement Sharia law in Turkey was prescribed by law, and presented a
proportionate and therefore lawful interference in Article 11 rights. The Grand
Chamber held that the threat to Turkey's democratic system was sufficiently
immediate and serious to justify the interference in the right.[537]

The Court showed a similar level of deference to Spain in a judgment rendered in **3.168**
2009: it found that there was a sufficient link between the dissolved political parties
and the Basque separatist group ETA to find their dissolution proportionate to a
'pressing social need' of national security.[538] Accordingly, there was no violation of
Article 11.[539] This case raises some concerns, especially as the closure of the political
party was accompanied by the closure of some Basque newspapers.[540] While the
latter was beyond the scope of the Court's inquiry, it may have led to a disproportionate intrusion in the freedom of expression for individuals in the Basque region.
A successful challenge on these grounds would be likely in the light of the same
newspaper executives' successful appeal in April 2010, in which national court
judges found that they had no links with ETA.[541]

Synthesis

Any restrictions on these rights must be necessary in a democratic society and pro- **3.169**
portionate to the aim of national security, public order, or public safety. The tests
for necessity and proportionality are strict: political platitudes and cooperation
with other states in counter-terrorism should not be allowed to shield states from
appropriate scrutiny in their human rights records. As noted in Chapter 7, states
should amend or repeal counter-terrorism legislation which criminalizes the peaceful exercise of the freedoms of expression, assembly, or association.

---

[536] *Freedom and Democracy Party (Ozdep) v Turkey* (2001) 31 EHRR 27, applying *Socialist Party v
Turkey* (1999) 27 EHRR 51.
[537] *Refah Partisi (Welfare) Party v Turkey (No 2)* (2003) 37 EHRR 1.
[538] *Herri Batasuna and Batasuna v Spain*, Application Nos 25803/04 and 25817/04, Judgment of
30 June 2009, not yet reported.
[539] Ibid.
[540] *Independent*, 'Basque Newspaper Closed Over Alleged Links With Eta', 21 February 2003.
[541] *Guardian*, 'Court Clears Basque Newspaper Bosses of Eta Membership', 12 April 2010.

Economic, social, and cultural rights

Treaty law

3.170 States cannot formally derogate from their obligation to respect, protect, and fulfil economic, social, and cultural rights in time of war or public emergency. Nor can they derogate from the obligations of mutual assistance and cooperation, to assist other states in the respect, protection, and fulfilment of economic, social, and cultural rights.[542] The right to form a trade union and join a trade union of one's choice in Article 8(1)(a) of the International Covenant on Economic, Social and Cultural Rights (ICESCR), and the right of trade unions to function freely in Article 8(1)(c), can be limited on the grounds of national security. These limitations must satisfy tests of necessity and proportionality similar to those detailed above.

3.171 The absence of a derogation clause in the ICESCR, the very few permissible limitations on right on grounds of national security, and the limited concessions but continuing obligations to developing countries and regardless of the circumstances all strongly indicate that states must continue to implement their obligations under the ICESCR, regardless of their coexistent obligations to prevent terrorist attacks. The obligation of mutual assistance and cooperation also continues to apply, regardless of the importance of preventing terrorism. As a corollary of these obligations, states should consider the impact on economic, social, and cultural rights of their counter-terrorism policies domestically and internationally.

Intergovernmental statements on economic, social, and cultural rights and terrorism

3.172 The UN High Commissioner for Human Rights (the High Commissioner) has emphasized the circular causal relationship between counter-terrorism policies which erode economic, social, and cultural rights and the poverty and social exclusion which may encourage the recruitment of terrorists.[543] The High Commissioner argued strongly that:

> It is only by addressing human rights issues, including economic, social and cultural rights, through the lens of the conditions that lead to the spread of terrorism, such as socio-economic marginalization and exclusion, ethnic, national and religious discrimination, political exclusion and lack of good governance, that [the goal of eliminating terrorism] can be achieved.[544]

---

[542] International Covenant on Economic, Social and Cultural Rights (ICESCR), Art 2(1).
[543] Report of the High Commissioner on Human Rights to the 12th session of the UN Human Rights Council, A/HRC/12/22, 2 September 2009, paras 7, 17.
[544] Ibid, para 7.

The Human Rights Council's Resolution 10/15 urged states to 'bear . . . in mind that certain counter-terrorism measures may have an impact on the enjoyment of . . . [economic, social, and cultural] rights'.[545]

Counter-terrorism and violations of economic, social, and cultural rights

The Special Rapporteur on the promotion and protection of human rights while **3.173** countering terrorism has reported on the restrictions on charitable aid as a result of legislation to prevent the financing of terrorism;[546] the impact of 'military action, armed insurgency and terrorist acts' in Iraq and Afghanistan on the delivery of humanitarian aid;[547] and in particular the impact on economic, social, and cultural rights of Israel's policies against the Palestinians, particularly the creation of the 'Wall' in the West Bank,[548] and the impact of counter-terrorism legislation on indigenous communities in Chile and Peru.[549] In addition, the money available for international development aid has been constricted as a result of the funds allocated for military and intelligence operations in the course of the US-led 'war on terror'.[550] Scholars have noted that international aid in counter-terrorism has all too often been directed at military cooperation, with little heed paid to the human rights records of the countries in receipt of aid money, nor to the human rights violations which may be facilitated as a result of military and strategic cooperation in the US-led 'war on terror'.[551]

Right to housing

The right to housing as a component of the right to an adequate standard of living **3.174** is protected by Article 11(1) of the ICESCR, but the destruction of homes may violate other human rights. In *Bilgin v Turkey*,[552] the ECtHR found a violation of Article 3 ECHR, the prohibition on torture or inhuman or degrading treatment or punishment, for the inhuman treatment suffered by the applicant when his home and possessions were destroyed by security forces. The applicant also suffered violations of the right to private and family life in Article 8 ECHR; of the right to the peaceful enjoyment of possessions, in Protocol I to the ECHR; and of the right to

---

[545] Human Rights Council Resolution 10/15, para 6, cited in Report of the High Commissioner on Human Rights to the 12th session of the UN Human Rights Council, A/HRC/12/22, 2 September 2009, para 4.

[546] Report of the Special Rapporteur on the Promotion and Protection of Human Rights while Countering Terrorism to the 6th session of the UN Human Rights Council, A/HRC/6/17, 21 November 2007, section IV.B.

[547] Ibid, para 47.

[548] Ibid, paras 23 and 72(c).

[549] Ibid, section IV.D.

[550] Ngaire Woods, 'The Shifting Politics of Foreign Aid' (2005) 81 *International Affairs* 393–409.

[551] Rosemary Foot, *Human Rights and Counter-Terrorism in America's Asia Policy* (International Institute for Strategic Studies, Adelphi Paper 363, 2004).

[552] *Bilgin v Turkey* (2003) 36 EHRR 50.

an effective remedy in Article 13 ECHR, owing to the inadequate investigation of the destruction of the applicant's home.[553]

3.175 The ECtHR's analysis cannot apply *de jure* to the demolition of homes in the West Bank by Israeli security forces, but it is a strong analogy in terms of the facts involved. The UN has documented the destruction of over 600 Palestinian homes in 2009, in the West Bank and East Jerusalem, in violation of Article 11(1) of the ICESCR.[554] The Supreme Court of Israel has emphasized that Palestinians have the right to petition the court for a hearing prior to the demolition of their homes; that changes in state policy against and later in favour of so-called 'punitive house demolitions' trigger a right to another hearing; and that the destruction of a home gives applicants the right to challenge the decision to demolish the home before the Supreme Court.[555] Israel's policy of punitive house demolitions was reinstated by a judgment of the Supreme Court of Israel in February 2009.[556]

Due diligence: girls' right to education

3.176 States owe an obligation of due diligence, as part of their obligations to respect economic, social, and cultural rights to prevent violations of those rights. Abuses of the right to education by non-state groups' terrorist attacks on girls' schools in Pakistan's Swat Valley is a strong example which triggers this due diligence obligation,[557] which is related to states' obligation of due diligence to prevent violence against women.[558] States should also act in due diligence to maintain the security of pupils and students attending school. Such attacks present a threat to the right to education, which is guaranteed by Article 13 of the ICESCR.

Freedom of movement, right to health, right to education

3.177 Counter-terrorism policies which restrict freedom of movement also have an impact on the right to the best attainable standard of physical and mental health,[559] and the right to education.[560] The Supreme Court of Israel barred a cohort of occupational therapy students from Gaza from travelling to the West Bank, owing to travel restrictions imposed with an ostensibly counter-terrorist aim.[561] This policy impacts upon the freedom of movement, guaranteed in Article 13 of the ICCPR, as well as

---

[553] Ibid.

[554] Human Rights Watch, 'Israel: Stop East Jerusalem Home Demolitions', 6 November 2009.

[555] Supreme Court of Israel sitting as the High Court of Justice, *Nasser v IDF West Bank Military Commander*, HCJ 7733/04.

[556] Supreme Court of Israel sitting as the High Court of Justice, *Abu-Dahim v Commander of the Rear Forces*, HCJ 9353/08, Judgment of 5 January 2009.

[557] Reuters, 'Pakistani Taliban Blow Up Schools in Swat', 19 January 2009.

[558] Committee on the Elimination of All Forms of Discrimination against Women (CEDAW), General Recommendation No 19, 11th session, 1991.

[559] ICESCR, Art 12.

[560] ICESCR, Art 13.

[561] Supreme Court of Israel sitting as the High Court of Justice, *Hamdan v GOC Southern Command*, HCJ 11120/05 and other conjoined cases, Judgment of 25 July 2007.

the right to education, and the right to health of those in need of occupational therapy in the Gaza Strip. Palestinian civilians have suffered delays in travel past checkpoints for essential medical treatment in Israel. In 2009, the Committee against Torture urged Israel to ensure that checkpoint personnel be trained, that an urgent complaints mechanism be set up, and that 'consideration be given as a matter of urgency to the availability of emergency medical personnel to assist persons in need'.[562] The fact that the Committee against Torture considered it sufficiently important to engage with this issue indicates that violations of the right to health may in certain circumstances amount to a violation of the prohibition on torture or of cruel, inhuman, or degrading treatment or punishment.

General Comment No 14 (2000) of the Committee on Economic, Social and **3.178** Cultural Rights (CESCR) reasserts that the right to health is non-derogable, and calls for the right to health to be respected for 'prisoners or detainees, minorities, asylum-seekers, illegal immigrants'. Those detained in counter-terrorism must have their health rights respected, and a public emergency caused by a threat of terrorism does not entitle states to derogate from economic, social, and cultural rights.[563]

Summary

Economic, social, and cultural rights are non-derogable, meaning that states' obli- **3.179** gations to respect, protect, and ensure these rights and to offer inter-state assistance continue to apply despite a threat of terrorism. States should monitor the impact of counter-terrorism policies on economic, social, and cultural rights domestically and internationally. They should also direct development aid where possible to reduce the threat of terrorism, such as in the good governance programmes considered in Chapter 6, and to mitigate the impact of counter-terrorism policies on economic, social, and cultural rights.

Counter-terrorism and discrimination

Non-discrimination and IHRL

International human rights treaty law protects the right to be free from discrimina- **3.180** tion in five main respects:

- First, measures derogating from certain human rights 'in time of war or public emergency threatening the life of the nation'[564] must be (a) restricted 'to the extent strictly required by the exigencies of the situation'; (b) compatible with the

---

[562] Committee against Torture, 42nd session, Concluding Observations, Israel, CAT/C/ISR/CO/4, 23 June 2009, para 31.
[563] CESCR, General Comment No 14, The right to the highest attainable standard of health, E/C.12/2000/4, 11 August 2000, para 34.
[564] See paras 3.17–3.21.

state's other international law obligations; and (c) must 'not involve discrimination solely on the grounds of race, colour, sex, language, religion or social origin'.[565]

- Second, IHRL's protection of equality before the law, a core element of the rule of law, entitles all persons 'to the equal protection of the law' 'without any discrimination'.[566] As a result, Article 26 of the ICCPR requires that states parties' domestic law 'shall prohibit any discrimination and guarantee to all persons equal and effective protection against discrimination on any ground such as race, colour, sex, language, religion, political or other opinion, national or social origin, property, birth or other status'.[567] The ACHR includes a similar provision.[568]

- Third, states' obligations to respect and ensure rights in the ICESCR, ACHR, and ECHR are conditional on a principle of non-discrimination, on a list of enumerated grounds.[569] This is not a free-standing right to be free of all discrimination, especially as regards the ICESCR and ECHR, which lack an Article specifying the right to equal protection of the law. Instead, this is a duty of equality in the full implementation of the human rights detailed in each treaty.

- Fourth, 'any reason based on discrimination of any kind' is one of the four prohibited purposes in the definition of torture in Article 1 of the Convention against Torture.[570] This shows that the norm of non-discrimination is not merely peripheral in IHRL, but is one aspect of the peremptory or *jus cogens* prohibition on torture. The Committee on the Elimination of Racial Discrimination (CERD) has stated that the right not to be discriminated against on the grounds of race is also a *jus cogens* norm.[571]

- Fifth, IHRL provides both specific treaties and specific provisions in international and regional treaties to eliminate discrimination on the grounds of race[572] and gender,[573] and to provide for the rights of children,[574] migrant workers and members of their families,[575] and persons with a disability.[576] There are

---

[565] ICCPR, Art 4(1); see also ACHR, Art 27(1).

[566] ICCPR, Art 26.

[567] ICCPR, Art 26.

[568] ACHR, Art 24.

[569] ACHR, Art 1; ECHR, Art 14 and Protocol No 12; ICESCR, Art 2(2).

[570] Convention Against Torture and Other Cruel, Inhuman or Degrading Treatment or Punishment, Art 1(1).

[571] CERD, Statement on Racial Discrimination and Measures to Combat Terrorism, cited in Office of the United Nations High Commissioner for Human Rights (OHCHR), 'Human Rights, Terrorism and Counter-Terrorism', Fact sheet no 32, p 4.

[572] International Convention on the Elimination of All Forms of Racial Discrimination (ICERD).

[573] Convention on the Elimination of All Forms of Discrimination Against Women (CEDAW); ACHPR, Art 18(3).

[574] Convention on the Rights of the Child; ICCPR, Art 24(1); ICESCR, Art 10(3).

[575] International Convention on the Protection of the Rights of All Migrant Workers and Members of their Families.

[576] Convention on the Rights of Persons with Disabilities.

restrictions on the freedom of expression to prevent '[a]ny advocacy of national, racial or religious hatred that constitutes incitement to discrimination'.[577]

However, some unequal policies may nonetheless be lawful in the context of coun- **3.181** tering terrorism, if they are prescribed by law, necessary, and proportionate. The Office of the High Commissioner of Human Rights (OHCHR) has observed that the practice of profiling in counter-terrorism law enforcement 'may, in principle, be a permissible means of investigation and can be an important law enforcement tool'.[578] However, after reviewing the jurisprudence of the Inter-American Court of Human Rights,[579] and General Comment No 30 of CERD,[580] both of which note that the right to non-discrimination can be a *jus cogens* norm and the output of varied regional and intergovernmental bodies on the subject of racial profiling, the OHCHR urged that '[p]rofiling or similar devices must strictly comply with the principles of necessity, proportionality and non-discrimination; they should be subject to close judicial scrutiny and should be periodically reviewed'.[581]

Discrimination on the grounds of race, religion, ethnicity, or national origin

Despite the clarity and multi-faceted nature of the norm against discrimination in **3.182** IHRL, prohibited discrimination on the grounds of race, religion, ethnicity, and national origin has been a feature of states' counter-terrorism policies.

- A judgment of the ECtHR found 'clear risks' of a disproportionate impact of 'stop and search' powers under sections 44–47 of the Terrorism Act 2000 on the UK's Afro-Caribbean and South Asian communities.[582]
- Research by the Center for Human Rights and Global Justice (CHRGJ) at New York University School of Law indicates that 'shoot-to-kill' and airport security policies may be 'a proxy for racial, ethnic, religious or nationality profiling in violation of Articles 2 and 26 of the ICCPR'.[583]

---

[577] ICCPR, Art 20.

[578] Office of the United Nations High Commissioner for Human Rights (OHCHR), 'Human Rights, Terrorism and Counter-Terrorism', Fact sheet no 32, p 37.

[579] See Inter-American Court of Human Rights, Advisory Opinion OC-18/03 on the juridical condition and rights of the undocumented migrants, 17 September 2003, para 101, cited in OHCHR, 'Human Rights, Terrorism and Counter-Terrorism', Fact sheet no 32, p 37.

[580] CERD, General Recommendation No 30, Discrimination against Non-Citizens, 1 October 2004, cited in OHCHR, 'Human Rights, Terrorism and Counter-Terrorism', Fact sheet no 32, p 37.

[581] OHCHR, 'Human Rights, Terrorism and Counter-Terrorism', Fact sheet no 32, p 38.

[582] European Court of Human Rights, *Gillan and Quinton v UK*, Judgment of 13 January 2010 (not yet reported—the judgment found a violation of Art 8 ECHR and 'clear risks of discrimination' in relation to ss 44–47 of the UK Terrorism Act 2000).

[583] CHRGJ, Written Submission to the Human Rights Committee, 87th session, July 2006, 'Racial Profiling and Lethal Force in the "War on Terror"', paras 13, 14.

- The Open Society Institute has researched the use of racial profiling in counter-terrorism policies in European states, and concluded that there was no evidence of efficacy for the use of racial and/or religious profiling for measures including 'stop and search', discriminatory arrest, and detention.[584]
- NGO research indicates that discrimination on the grounds of race and ethnicity is a recurrent element in China's 'counter-terrorism' activity against the Muslim Turkic Uighurs of Xinjiang.[585]
- In Peru, in June 2009, up to 79 members of indigenous communities were placed in police and military custody, some on charges of terrorism. This had followed the quashing of 50 days of violent demonstrations by indigenous Peruvians against plans for mining and other resource exploitation in the Amazon.[586] The violent protests are thought to be unrelated to the ongoing activities of the Maoist Shining Path.[587]

Counter-terrorism and gender discrimination

3.183 Although terrorist attacks have been noted to have a gender dimension, such as attacks on girls en route to school in Afghanistan and Pakistan following orders by the Taliban to close all girls' schools,[588] and sexual violence against hostages by FARC rebels in Colombia,[589] the subject of gender discrimination, whether direct or indirect, has been largely ignored until a recent report of the Special Rapporteur on the promotion and protection of human rights while countering terrorism.[590] This report notes not only violence against women and girls by terrorist groups, but also the repression of women's human rights defenders as a result of overly broad counter-terrorism policies, and 'gender-based violence and gendered economic, social and cultural rights violations' where terrorism and counter-terrorism yields humanitarian crises, and where legislation to prevent the financing of terrorism curbs the ability of aid agencies to mitigate the effects of these violations.[591] The report notes 'the use of collective sanctions against female relatives of suspected terrorists by which women not suspected of terrorism-related offences are unlawfully detained and ill-treated to either gain information about male family members or

---

[584] Open Society Institute, 'Ethnic Profiling in the European Union: Pervasive, Ineffective and Discriminatory', IV. Ethnic Profiling in Counterterrorism since 9/11, 2009.

[585] Human Rights Watch, '"We Are Afraid to Even Look for Them": Enforced Disappearances in the Wake of Xinjiang's Protests', October 2009, p 10; see para 3.92.

[586] Amnesty International, 'Peru: Fear for Safety', AMR 46/009/2009, 9 June 2009.

[587] International Crisis Group, *Crisis Watch No 66*, 1 February 2009, Peru.

[588] Reuters, 'Pakistani Taliban Force Girls' Schools to Close', 17 January 2009; Reuters, 'Pakistani Taliban Blow Up Schools in Swat', 19 January 2009.

[589] Human Rights Council, 10th session, Report of the Working Group on Universal Periodic Review, A/HRC/10/82, 9 January 2009, p 9.

[590] Report of the Special Rapporteur on the Promotion and Protection of Human Rights while Countering Terrorism to the 64th session of the UN General Assembly, A/64/211, 3 August 2009.

[591] Ibid, Summary, pp 2–3.

to compel male terrorism suspects to provide information or confessions'.[592] The report notes what might be called intersectional discrimination, where stereotypes about Muslim women are employed in racial profiling practices.[593]

Counter-terrorism operations and people with disabilities

The Fact-Finding Mission established by the UN Human Rights Council to investi- **3.184**
gate Operation Cast Lead reasoned that Israel's counter-terrorism policies have unlawfully discriminated against Palestinians not only on the grounds of race, ethnicity, or national origin,[594] but also against people with disabilities. Israel had not provided sufficient bomb shelters for persons with disabilities.[595] Israel's restrictions on freedom of movement in and out of Gaza were found to have affected not only people with disabilities but also the right to health.[596]

Conclusion

States' obligation to prevent and repress terrorist attacks neither excuses nor jus- **3.185**
tifies human rights violations, and it can never oust the application of non-derogable rights. States have sought to erode the absolute prohibition on torture and ill-treatment through fallacious definitions of the crime. Many hundreds of detainees have suffered either secret or incommunicado detention, or prolonged detention without charge or trial. Still others have been subjected to 'extraordinary rendition'—unlawful transfers to detention and a risk of torture in another state. Terrorism has been used as a pretext to repress the activity of human rights defenders[597] and legitimate forms of peaceful protest, further diminishing the implementation of IHRL at the national level.[598] States'

---

[592] Ibid, Summary, p 2.

[593] Ibid, Summary, p 3.

[594] Report of the United Nations Fact-Finding Mission on the Gaza Conflict, UN Doc A/HRC/12/48, 15 September 2009, para 1577.

[595] Ibid, paras 1285–1286.

[596] B'Tselem, 'Infringement of the Right to Medical Treatment in the West Bank' (web resource, last accessed 30 May 2010).

[597] Declaration on the Right and Responsibility of Individuals, Groups and Organs of Society to Promote and Protect Universally Recognised Human Rights and Fundamental Freedoms, annexed to UN General Assembly Resolution A/RES/53/144, 8 March 1999.

[598] UN Special Rapporteur on the Situation of Human Rights Defenders, Issues in Focus, Security Legislation, 'Security and Counter-Terrorist Legislation'; Amnesty International, Statement to Working Session 16 of the Organisation for Security and Cooperation in Europe: Fundamental Freedoms II, including: Freedom of Expression, Free Media and Information, HDIM.NGO/396/07, 3 October 2007; Fédération Internationale des Droits de l'Homme (FIDH), 'Turkey: End Human Rights Violations under the Pretext of the "War Against Terrorism"', 22 September 2003; FIDH, Observatory for the Protection of Human Rights Defenders Annual Report 2009, Russian Federation, 18 June 2009.

counter-terrorism legislation has violated the rule of law's requirements of precision and prospectivity in overbroad definitions of terrorist crimes and in an excessive breadth or complexity in counter-terrorism legislation or emergency regulations. Chapter 4 traces the scope for prosecuting terrorist crimes, and the piecemeal approach to accountability for violations of IHRL in counter-terrorism, with reference to intergovernmental and national inquiries, criminal investigations, and civil suits.

4

ACCOUNTABILITY FOR TERRORIST ATTACKS AND FOR VIOLATIONS COMMITTED IN COUNTER-TERRORISM

Introduction

In this chapter, 'accountability' is shorthand for criminal trials, civil suits, independ- **4.01**
ent national investigations, and intergovernmental reports: procedures which can
address impunity, combat secrecy, and fulfil victims' right to truth and right to
justice.[1] The obligation to investigate and prosecute terrorist crimes derives from the
multilateral treaties and UN Security Council Resolutions examined in Chapter 1.[2]
As the International Criminal Court lacks jurisdiction over the crime of terrorism,[3]
states' domestic criminal courts will be the main forum for prosecution of terrorist
crimes. Accountability for state terrorism and state-sponsored terrorism may be
established through the non-binding ILC Articles on State Responsibility, as
Chapters 1 and 6 explain,[4] but the gold standard of accountability remains a fair
trial in domestic criminal civilian courts.[5]

---

[1] UN Basic Principles and Guidelines on the Right to a Remedy and Reparation for Victims of
Gross Violations of International Human Rights Law and Serious Violations of International
Humanitarian Law, adopted by UN General Assembly Resolution 60/147, A/Res/60/147, 16
December 2005, Principles 24 and 11; see paras 5.38–5.53.

[2] See paras 1.01, 1.18, 1.20.

[3] See para 4.05.

[4] ILC Articles on the Responsibility of States for Internationally Unlawful Acts 2001, adopted by
UN General Assembly Resolution 56/83, 12 December 2001; see paras 1.14–1.15, 6.09.

[5] See paras 3.135, 3.144.

4.02 While states are obliged to investigate and prosecute terrorist crimes, they must also ensure that their counter-terrorism policies and practices comply in full with IHL, IHRL, and IRL.[6] It follows that accountability mechanisms should be even-handed: states should criminalize, investigate, and prosecute certain terrorist offences, but they should also criminalize, investigate, and prosecute serious violations of IHL and IHRL committed in counter-terrorism operations. Chapter 2 has explained states' obligations to criminalize grave breaches of the Four Geneva Conventions, and to prosecute and extradite those suspected of perpetrating or ordering these crimes.[7] IHL also provides for 'enquiries' into other violations of the Four Geneva Conventions, so that states may cooperate to bring those violations to an end.[8] Chapter 3 has demonstrated the obligation to investigate and prosecute serious violations of IHRL, including extrajudicial killings, torture, and enforced disappearances.[9] In some cases, human rights bodies have held that the failure to investigate and prosecute serious IHRL violations amounts to a violation in itself.[10]

4.03 Although states are developing a welter of jurisprudence on the prosecution of terrorism suspects,[11] they show far less willingness to establish accountability for violations of IHL and IHRL committed in their efforts to counter terrorism. Despite a small number of court-martial convictions for unlawful killings and prisoner abuse in the UK and US, there has been only one *in absentia* conviction in Italy (of 22 CIA operatives and one military officer) of crimes relating to 'extraordinary rendition'.[12] There are three interrelated themes:

- *complicity* of many states in IHL and IHRL violations in counter-terrorism;
- *secrecy*: the assertion of state secrets doctrines to prevent the disclosure of information about state actors' involvement in these violations; and
- *impunity* for violations owing to government secrecy and failure to commence or to cooperate in inquiries and/or investigations.

---

[6] See paras 1.01, 1.17–1.18, 1.26–1.28, 6.03–6.04, 7.01, 7.08.

[7] First Geneva Convention, Art 49; Second Geneva Convention, Art 50; Third Geneva Convention, Art 129; Fourth Geneva Convention, Art 146; Additional Protocol I, Art 85; see paras 2.13, 2.34, 2.71–2.72, 2.74, 7.11.

[8] Fourth Geneva Convention, Art 149; see paras 2.13, 2.24, 7.09, 7.11.

[9] Convention against Torture, Arts 2, 4, and 12; International Convention for the Protection of All Persons from Enforced Disappearances (not yet in force), Arts 3, 4, 6; Inter-American Court of Human Rights, *Velásquez Rodríguez v Honduras* [1989] 28 ILM 291; *Bámaca Velásquez v Guatemala*, 25 November 2000; *Barrios Altos v Peru*, 14 March 2001; *Goiburú et al v Paraguay*, 22 September 2006; *Almonacid-Arellano et al v Chile*, 26 September 2006.

[10] Human Rights Committee General Comment No 31 [80], The Nature of the General Legal Obligation Imposed on States Parties to the Covenant, CCPR/C/21/Rev.1/Add.13, 26 May 2004, para 18; *Mahmut Kaya v Turkey* (28 March 2000), *Ergi v Turkey* (2001) 23 EHRR 388; *Finucane v United Kingdom* (2003) 37 EHRR 29; *Isayeva, Yusupova and Bazayeva* (2005) 41 EHRR 39; *Khashiyev and Akayeva* (2005) 42 EHRR 20. See paras 3.26, 3.32, 3.55, 3.94, 3.97, and 3.100.

[11] For a general overview, see UN Office on Drugs and Crime (UNODC), *Digest of Terrorism Cases*, May 2010.

[12] See below paras 4.26, 4.32–4.33.

While criminal prosecutions are the gold standard of accountability both for terror- **4.04**
ist attacks and for violations of international law in counter-terrorism, states should
ensure a gamut of accountability mechanisms are in place, fully to respect victims'
rights to a remedy and reparation. These mechanisms include civil suits, the right
of individual petition to UN treaty bodies and regional human rights courts, independent national inquiries, and truth commissions. Independent national inquiries
and intergovernmental investigations can also establish accountability for committing, aiding, or abetting violations of IHL and IHRL in counter-terrorism, under
the non-binding ILC Articles on State Responsibility.[13] However, these mechanisms can only be supplementary to criminal investigations and prosecutions.
States must ensure individual criminal responsibility in their domestic law both for
terrorist attacks and for crimes committed in counter-terrorism operations.

Accountability for terrorist attacks

Prosecuting terrorism in international criminal law

The absence of a defined crime of terrorism in international criminal law

There is no specifically enumerated, defined crime of terrorism in international **4.05**
criminal law (ICL). Terrorism is absent from the lists of war crimes, crimes against
humanity, and genocide in the jurisdiction of the International Criminal Court
(ICC).[14] A number of states had been in favour of including terrorism as a crime in
the Rome Statute of the International Criminal Court (Rome Statute), but the lack
of a single accepted definition of terrorism in international law and the political
sensitivity surrounding the definition of terrorism prevented it from being included.[15] Resolutions E and F of the Rome Conference Final Act had announced an
intention to consider the definitions of aggression, terrorism, and drug-trafficking
at the first Review Conference of the Rome Statute[16] in May–June 2010. However,
discussions at the 8th meeting of the Assembly of States Parties (ASP) of the Rome
Statute of the International Criminal Court did not yield sufficient support for the
Review Conference to consider the inclusion of a crime of terrorism in the Rome
Statute.[17] Delegates at the 8th ASP meeting considered that the inclusion of a crime

---

[13] ILC Articles, supra, Art 16; John Cerone, 'Re-examining International Responsibility:
"Complicity" in the Context of Human Rights Violations' (2008) 14 *ILSA Journal of International &
Comparative Law* 525–534.

[14] Rome Statute of the International Criminal Court, Arts 6–8.

[15] Roberta Arnold, 'Terrorism as a Crime against Humanity under the ICC Statute', in Giuseppe
Nesi (ed), *International Cooperation in Counter-Terrorism* (Martinus Nijhoff, 2006), pp 121–139 at
p 131.

[16] Resolution E and F, Final Act of the United Nations Diplomatic Conference of Plenipotentiaries
on the Establishment of an International Criminal Court, A/CONF.183/10, 17 July 1998.

[17] Assembly of States Parties to the Rome Statute of the International Criminal Court (ICC-ASP),
8th session, 29 November 2009, Resolution ICC-ASP/8/Res.6, para 2.

of terrorism in the ICC's jurisdiction would have to wait for agreement on the definition of terrorism at the United Nations.[18] The future definition of a crime of terrorism is likely to be one of the possible amendments to the Rome Statute considered at an ASP Working Group on Amendments, which will begin work at the Ninth ASP meeting in December 2010.[19]

4.06 Terrorism is also absent from the crimes enumerated in the Statutes of the International Criminal Tribunals for the former Yugoslavia (ICTY) and Rwanda (ICTR), and that of the Special Court for Sierra Leone (SCSL). The Special Tribunal for Lebanon (STL) is an exception to this trend, as it was established with the purpose of prosecuting 'persons responsible for the attack of 14 February 2005 resulting in the death of Prime Minister Rafik Hariri and in the death or injury of other persons'.[20] However, the STL's substantive jurisdiction derives from the crimes in the Lebanese Criminal Code.[21] The STL's jurisprudence will not create a crime of terrorism in international criminal law.

Indictments and case law which refer to 'terror'

4.07 However, selected indictments and some judgments of the International Military Tribunal (IMT) at Nuremberg, the ICTY, the ICTR, and the SCSL have referred to 'terror'. A close analysis of the indictments and case law suggest that they refer to 'terror' as a facet of other crimes within the jurisdiction of these courts, rather than a *sui generis* crime of terrorism which would enable the prosecution of terrorist bombings or other terrorist violence before an international criminal tribunal.

- The jurisprudence of the IMT at Nuremberg refers to a 'Nazi reign of terror', and to a 'system of terror', but it is left unexplained whether terrorism exists as a specific crime per se, and if it does not, whether it constitutes a war crime or a crime against humanity.[22] The jurisprudence of the IMT indicates that state officials were themselves guilty of 'terror',[23] reflecting the notion of state terrorism and state sponsorship of terrorism considered in Chapter 1.
- In July 1947, a court martial in the Netherlands East Indies (NEI) convicted Japanese armed forces personnel of 'systematic terrorism' for acts which included mass arrests on the basis of rumour only, and 'repeated, regular and lengthy torture and/or ill-treatment' which had resulted in the death or severe physical and

---

[18] ICC-ASP, Annex II, Report of the Working Group on the Review Conference, ICC-ASP/8/20, para 44.

[19] ICC-ASP, Resolution ICC-ASP/8/Res.6, para 4.

[20] Statute of the Special Tribunal for Lebanon, UN Security Council Resolution 1757 (2007).

[21] Ibid, Art 2.

[22] Roberta Arnold, 'Terrorism as a Crime against Humanity under the ICC Statute', supra, pp 127–129.

[23] International Military Tribunal (IMT), Judgment, 30 September 1946, p 421.

mental suffering of some of the detainees.[24] 'Systematic terror' was prosecuted as a war crime under the NEI court martial's statute. However, the language of the indictment, in referring to severe physical and mental suffering, to torture and ill-treatment, and to 'systematic' acts, predicts future developments in the definition of torture in IHRL, and to the contextual requirement for crimes against humanity in Article 7 of the Rome Statute of the ICC: a 'widespread or systematic attack directed against a civilian population with knowledge of the attack'.

- Multiple indictments before the ICTY refer to 'terrorism' and 'terror'.
  - The Amended Indictment against Milan Martic refers to 'a campaign of terror designed to drive [non-Serb civilians] out of the territory'.[25] There is no reference to a crime of terror in the Trial Chamber's judgment of 12 December 2007, nor in the later Appeals Chamber judgment which affirmed Milan Martic's conviction on multiple counts.[26]
  - The Third Amended Indictment of Radovan Karadzic refers in count 9 to a 'crime of terror', suggesting a standalone crime which is not clearly related to war crimes, crimes against humanity, or genocide,[27] despite 'terror' not being included in the Statute of the ICTY. The Indictment also refers to a campaign of sniping and shelling 'to spread terror among the civilian population of Sarajevo'.[28] This language is more clearly related to war crimes and to the language of Article 51(2) of Additional Protocol I than to a stand-alone crime of 'terror'.
  - The Second Amended Indictment for Slobodan Milosevic did not consider 'terror' as a specific crime, but mentioned a campaign of terror against the civilian population as a contextual factor only.[29] Other indictments and judgments of the ICTY have considered 'terrorism' and 'terror' in the context of war crimes and crimes against humanity.
- In ICTY case law, *Prosecutor v Kunarac* considered rape in the context of terror,[30] and expulsion of civilians as a crime of terror.[31] The sole case in which the meaning of 'terrorism' is explored is *Prosecutor v Stanislav Galic*.[32] The judgment provides a historical survey of the crime of 'unlawfully inflicting terror upon

---

[24] *Motomura et al*, cited in ICTY, *Prosecutor v Galic*, Case No IT-98-29-T, Judgment of the Trial Chamber, 5 December 2003, paras 114–115.

[25] ICTY, *Prosecutor v Milan Martic*, Case No IT-95-11, Amended Indictment, 9 September 2003, p 5.

[26] ICTY, *Prosecutor v Milan Martic*, Case No IT-95-11, Appeals Chamber Judgment, 8 October 2008.

[27] ICTY, *Prosecutor v Radovan Karadzic*, Case No IT-95-5/18-PT, Third Amended Indictment, 27 February 2009, count 9, paras 46, 58–60, 76 et seq.

[28] Ibid, paras 8, 15, 19, 62, 65, 77.

[29] ICTY, *Prosecutor v Slobodan Milosevic*, Case No IT-02-54-T, Second Amended Indictment 'Croatia', 28 July 2004, para 68.

[30] ICTY, *Prosecutor v Dragoljub Kunarac et al*, Case No IT-96-23-T, Judgment of the Trial Chamber, 22 February 2001.

[31] Ibid, para 579.

[32] *Prosecutor v Galic*, supra, paras 63–138.

civilians' in international criminal jurisprudence. It clarifies that the actual creation of an emotional state of terror (defined in the prosecution's case as 'extreme
fear') is not part of the *actus reus* for the crime. To prove terror, it is sufficient to
show that the defendant intended to create a state of terror among the civilian
population, and that this intention was accompanied by acts which violated the
laws of war. The judgment in *Galic* locates 'terror' as part of an attack on a civilian
population, in violation of IHL. 'Terror' is a war crime, or a set of war crimes, in
Galic, not a crime against humanity or genocide. *Galic* recalls IHL's specific
meaning of 'terrorism'[33] and 'acts or threat of violence the primary purpose of
which is to spread terror among a civilian population'.[34] It does not indicate a
crime of terrorist bombings committed during peacetime, nor does it link to the
specific terrorist offences which states must criminalize, investigate, and prosecute under the multilateral conventions considered in Chapter 1.

• In *The Prosecutor of the Special Court v Alex Tamba Brima et al*, the Appeals
Chamber of the SCSL upheld convictions for 'acts of terrorism', a 'common plan
to carry out a campaign of terrorising and collectively punishing the civilian
population of Sierra Leone . . . in order to achieve the ultimate objective of gain-
ing and exercising political power and control over the territory'. [35] The SCSL
coupled terrorism with collective punishments, echoing the language of Article
33 of the Fourth Geneva Convention. The Appeal Chamber's judgment affirms
the Trial Chamber's conviction for terrorism for acts which included amputa-
tions, burning civilians alive in a house, and forcibly extracting a foetus from the
womb of a pregnant woman. The Trial Chamber had held that such acts could
only have been committed with the specific purpose of spreading terror among a
civilian population.[36]

4.08 The ICTY in *Galic,* and the SCSL in *Brima,* both suggest that a specific purpose
of spreading terror among a civilian population can be a component in the *mens rea*
of one or more war crimes. The case law does not indicate that there is a definable
actus reus of terrorism, nor a specific war crime with the same name. Nonetheless,
the analytical framework is that of IHL's specific meaning of terrorism, which refers
to the principle of distinction between combatants and civilians, and violations of
civilians' immunity from attack.[37] This case law is not authority that there is a
crime of terrorism in its broadest sense in international criminal law, nor is it
authority to ground a prosecution of terrorist attacks before international courts or
tribunals.

---

[33] Fourth Geneva Convention, Art 33; Additional Protocol I, Art 4(2)(d); Additional Protocol II,
Art 13(2).
[34] Additional Protocol I, Art 51(2); Additional Protocol II, Art 13(2).
[35] Special Court for Sierra Leone, *The Prosecutor of the Special Court v Alex Tamba Brima et al*, Case
No SCSL-2004-16-A, Judgment of the Appeals Chamber, 22 February 2008, pp 22–23.
[36] Ibid, p 23.
[37] See paras 2.22–2.32.

The relevance of 'terrorism' to crimes against humanity and genocide is barely **4.09** considered in ICL case law. However, it is possible that terrorist attacks perpetrated after 1 July 2002, when the Rome Statute entered into force, might be prosecuted as crimes against humanity or genocide before the ICC, if all other jurisdictional hurdles are overcome. This would echo the statement by Mary Robinson, the then High Commissioner for Human Rights, that the terrorist attacks on the US of 11 September 2001 might amount to a crime against humanity if other contextual elements had been made out.[38] The following paragraphs consider these possibilities.

Prosecuting acts of terrorism as genocide

One judgment of the ICTR cautiously notes that acts of terrorism may amount to **4.10** the *actus reus* of causing severe mental harm as a component of genocide, but that this must be settled on a case-by-case basis.[39] The judgment in *Prosecutor v Kayishema and Ruzindana* considers only whether terrorist acts may amount to the infliction of severe mental harm, as part of the *actus reus* of genocide, and after concluding that this is technically possible and must be determined on a case-by-case basis, there is no further guidance on the criteria which might be applied in this case-by-case analysis. However, it is technically possible that a terrorist attack which killed members of a group may qualify as genocide if it was committed 'with intent to destroy, in whole or in part, a national, ethnical, racial or religious group'. This would amount to the *actus reus* and *mens rea* of genocide in Article 6(a) of the Rome Statute of the ICC. Serious injuries or trauma which resulted from a terrorist attack committed with the same specific intent might be the *actus reus* of genocide under Article 6(b). It is technically possible to prosecute future terrorist attacks as genocide before the ICC, if the specific intent is present and if all jurisdictional requirements are met.

Prosecuting terrorist attacks as crimes against humanity

Article 7 of the Rome Statute defines a list of acts which constitute crimes against **4.11** humanity when committed as part of a 'widespread or systematic attack against a civilian population with knowledge of the attack'. The 'widespread or systematic attack against a civilian population' is considered a contextual requirement, while the 'knowledge' of that attack is part of the *mens rea*. The list of crimes in Article 7 differs slightly from the list of acts which may be crimes against humanity in the Statutes of

---

[38] Press Briefing, High Commissioner for Human Rights, 25 September 2001, cited in William A Schabas, 'Is Terrorism a Crime against Humanity?' in Harvey Langholtz, Boris Kondoch, and Alan Wells (eds), *International Peacekeeping: The Yearbook of International Peace Operations*, Vol 8 (Martinus Nijhoff, 2003), pp 255–262.

[39] ICTR, *Prosecutor v Kayishema and Ruzindana*, Case No ICTR-95-1-T, Judgment of the Trial Chamber, 21 May 1999, paras 107, 110.

the ICTY, the ICTR, and the SCSL, reflecting the lack of a single international law definition of crimes against humanity. Under the Rome Statute of the ICC, crimes against humanity may be prosecuted whether their constituent acts are committed in peace or war: only the reference to 'a civilian population' complicates the prosecution of crimes against humanity committed in peacetime. A prosecution of terrorist attacks as crimes against humanity would require evidence of a 'State or organisational policy to commit' a widespread or systematic attack on a civilian population.[40] The defendants could be either state actors or acting on behalf of a non-state terrorist organization, which 'actively promote[s] or encourage[s] such an attack against a civilian population'.[41] A prosecution for several of the acts which may amount to crimes against humanity is plausible in the terrorism context, such as:

- murder (Article 7(1)(a) of the Rome Statute, which the Elements of Crimes define as 'kill[ing]' or 'caus[ing] death');[42]
- 'other severe deprivation of liberty in violation of fundamental rules of international law' (Article 7(1)(e)): this could include hostage-taking, although the Elements of Crimes do not specify this);[43]
- torture (Article 7(1)(f)—it should be noted that unlike in IHRL, torture in ICL does not require that the defendant be a public official or someone acting with the support or acquiescence of a public official, only that the crime be carried out pursuant to a 'State or organisational policy', and that the victim be in the 'custody or control' of the perpetrator);[44]
- 'rape . . . or any other form of sexual violence of comparable gravity' (Article 7(1)(g));[45]
- 'persecution' (Article 7(1)(h)—if the victims were targeted 'by reason of the identity of [their] group or collectivity');[46]
- 'enforced disappearance of persons' (Article 7(1)(i));[47] and
- 'other inhumane acts of a similar character intentionally causing great suffering, or serious injury to body or to mental or physical health' (Article 7(1)(k)—this could cover injuries caused by terrorist bombings if other contextual and mental elements were present).

---

[40] Elements of Crimes of the Rome Statute of the International Criminal Court, Article 7—Crimes against humanity, Introduction, para 3.

[41] Ibid, and note 6.

[42] Elements of Crimes of the Rome Statute of the International Criminal Court , Article 7—Crimes against humanity, Introduction, note 7; Statement by UN High Commissioner for Human Rights at the Opening of the 58th Session of the Commission on Human Rights, Geneva, 10 March 2002.

[43] Elements of Crimes of the Rome Statute of the International Criminal Court, Article 7(1)(e)—Crime against humanity of imprisonment or other severe deprivation of physical liberty, para 1.

[44] Ibid, Article 7—Crimes against humanity, Introduction, para 3 and Article 7(1)(f)—Crime against humanity of torture, para 2.

[45] See paras 2.85–2.86.

[46] Elements of Crimes, supra, Article 7(1)(h)—Crime against humanity of persecution, para 2.

[47] See paras 3.84–3.88.

In any prosecution for a crime against humanity, the contextual and mental ele- **4.12**
ments must be established in addition to the component acts. This presents
challenges to the prosecution of single, isolated terrorist attacks. Where two or
more attacks are coordinated to occur on the same day, such as the attacks on the
US on 11 September 2001, on the London transport system on 7 July 2005, and
on the Moscow metro on 29 March 2010, the attack would appear 'systematic' and
possibly even 'widespread'. The 'widespread' criterion might also be extended to
cover all terrorist attacks committed by a certain terrorist group worldwide. As
these conditions are disjunctive, a crime against humanity may have been perpetrated in each of these instances, leaving aside the jurisdictional hurdles of
prosecution for crimes against humanity in domestic courts or before the ICC. A
terrorist bombing of civilians which is widespread in the sense of being more than
just a single, isolated attack, or systematic in the sense of being part of a state or
organizational policy, may amount to the crime against humanity of murder in
Article 7(1)(a). If the same contextual factors are in place, a terrorist bombing which
causes serious injuries but no deaths may qualify as the crime against humanity of
'other inhumane acts' (Article 7(1)(k)).

However, the absence of terrorism per se from current definitions of crimes against **4.13**
humanity would give rise to a challenge to any such prosecution on the basis of
nullum crimen sine lege.[48] Such a challenge is likely, given the longstanding interpretive principle that criminal legislation, and therefore the Rome Statute, be
narrowly construed.[49] This principle is reflected in Article 22(2) of the Rome
Statute: 'The definition of a crime shall be strictly construed and *shall not be extended
by analogy*' (emphasis added). It is only through reasoning by analogy that it appears
feasible to prosecute terrorist attacks as one or more component crimes against
humanity, as defined by Article 7 of the Rome Statute. Some authors believe that
terrorism can be prosecuted directly as a crime against humanity, without there
being any need to introduce a specific crime of terrorism within the jurisdiction of
the ICC,[50] and without such a prosecution failing for *nullum crimen sine lege*.
However, these arguments may prove unconvincing in practice. The ASP's unwill-
ingness to consider the inclusion of a crime of terrorism at the Review Conference
on the Rome Statute in May–June 2010 underlines that there remains no specific
crime of terrorism in ICL. A defence lawyer's arguments based in *nullum crimen*
may ultimately prove more convincing than a prosecutor's zeal in prosecuting
terrorist attacks as crimes against humanity.

---

[48] Rome Statute, Art 22.
[49] Elements of Crimes, supra, Article 7—Crimes against humanity, Introduction, para 1.
[50] Vincent-Joël Proulx, 'Rethinking the Jurisdiction of the International Criminal Court in the
Post-September 11th Era: Should Acts of Terrorism Qualify as Crimes against Humanity' (2004) 19
American University International Law Review 1009–1089; Roberta Arnold, supra, pp 121–139 at
p 134.

4.14 Nonetheless, where states parties to the Rome Statute have implemented it into domestic law, it is possible to investigate and prosecute terrorist attacks as war crimes or crimes against humanity where they satisfy the relevant substantive, contextual, and mental elements. *Nullum crimen* objections may still be raised, but prosecutions may be grounded in domestic criminal law in the alternative. Chapter 7 recommends that states prosecute terrorist attacks in their domestic courts (see paragraphs 4.23–4.24 below) and that they also do so where the crimes in question qualify as war crimes or crimes against humanity.[51]

Prosecuting terrorist attacks in ad hoc international criminal tribunals

4.15 Without a defined crime of terrorism in the Rome Statute, the ICC is very unlikely to be a forum for prosecution of terrorist attacks. However, the STL may be such a forum. It is the only current example of an ad hoc international criminal tribunal being established specifically to investigate a terrorist attack and the circumstances leading to it. The STL, based in The Hague, was established to prosecute the 'persons responsible for the attack of 14 February 2005 resulting in the death of Prime Minister Rafik Hariri and in the death or injury of other persons'.[52] However, while the STL is a 'tribunal of international character',[53] the Lebanese Criminal Code is the applicable law: the relevant crime of 'terrorism' within the jurisdiction of the STL derives from domestic law and not international criminal law,[54] although both Lebanese and international judges sit at the STL. The STL may enlarge its temporal jurisdiction to cover . . . 'other attacks that occurred in Lebanon between 1 October 2004 and 12 December 2005, or any later date decided by the Parties and with the consent of the Security Council, [which] are connected in accordance with the principles of criminal justice and are of a nature and gravity similar to the attack of 14 February 2005'.[55]

4.16 The case work of the STL began on 1 March 2009. Following the detention in Lebanon of a number of suspects in the *Hariri* case, the STL Office of the Prosecutor requested that the Lebanese authorities recognize the jurisdiction of the STL. The Lebanese authorities handed to the STL their investigatory documents and the STL became officially seized of the case on 10 April 2009.[56] There have been concerns that the STL may lead to 'politically selective' justice as the Statute for the Special Tribunal for Lebanon has a very narrow range of subject-matter jurisdiction until or unless its temporal jurisdiction is extended as anticipated

---

[51] See para 7.20.
[52] Statute of the Special Tribunal for Lebanon, UN Security Council Resolution 1757 (2007).
[53] Ibid, Preamble.
[54] Ibid, Art 2(a)—Art 2(a) is the substantive criminal law.
[55] Ibid, Art 1.
[56] STL: Order Assigning Matter to Pre-Trial Judge, CH/PRES/2010/01, 15 April 2010, para 4.

above.[57] Amnesty International has also called on Lebanon to repeal the amnesty laws of 1991 and 2005.[58]

The hijack and bombing of Pan Am flight 103 over the Scottish town of Lockerbie **4.17** in 1988 was the subject of an ad hoc criminal trial in 2001, following a deadlock over extradition from 1992 onwards. In 1992, the US and Scotland both indicted Abdelbaset Ali Mohamed Al Megrahi and Al Amin Khalifa Fhimah. The UK and the US sought the extradition of these two suspects from Libya, citing Articles 7 and 8 of the Convention for the Suppression of Unlawful Acts against the Safety of Civil Aviation. Libya claimed that the duty to prosecute in Article 7 had precedence over the duty to extradite in Article 8, and argued that the two men would not face a fair trial, and brought suit against the US and UK at the ICJ.[59] In response, the UK and US sought UN Security Council Resolution 731, which was passed in 1992 and required Libya to surrender the two suspects to the US and UK. As a result, the ICJ never pronounced on the dispute.[60] The prosecution was held in the Netherlands, but used Scots criminal law and rules of procedure. Both suspects were extradited, following lengthy legal and political wrangling, but only Al Megrahi was convicted.[61] While his conviction was deeply controversial,[62] Al Megrahi withdrew his appeal after the Scottish government made a decision to release him on compassionate grounds.[63]

These examples indicate that while political sensitivities and concerns about sub- **4.18** ject-matter jurisdiction remain, ad hoc tribunals may continue to prosecute those suspected of involvement in terrorist attacks. It is suggested that ad hoc tribunals may be more likely than the ICC to prosecute terrorist attacks, given the lack of a single, defined crime of terrorism in the Rome Statute of the ICC.

---

[57] Amnesty International, 'The Special Tribunal for Lebanon: Selective Justice', MDE 18/001/2009, 27 February 2009.

[58] Ibid, 6, Conclusion and Recommendations.

[59] M Chérif Bassiouni, 'The Duty to Prosecute and/or Extradite: *Aut Dedere Aut Judicare*', in M Chérif Bassiouni (ed), *International Criminal Law*, Vol III (Martinus Nijhoff, 2008), pp 35–45 at pp 43–44.

[60] Ibid.

[61] In the High Court of Justiciary at Camp Zeist, *HM Advocate v Abdelbaset Ali Mohmed Al Megrahi and Al Amin Khalifa Fhimah*, Judgment, Case No 1475/99, 31 January 2001: the decision was upheld on appeal, but Abdelbaset Ali Al Megrahi was released from detention on compassionate grounds in 2009.

[62] Scottish Criminal Cases Review Commission (SCCRC), News Release, Abdelbaset Ali Mohmed Al Megrahi, 28 June 2007.

[63] The Scottish Government, Cabinet Secretary for Justice Kenny MacAskill, 'Decisions on the applications for prisoner transfer and compassionate release in relation to Abdelbaset Ali Mohmed Al Megrahi', 20 August 2009.

Prosecuting terrorist attacks in domestic criminal courts

Obligations under terrorism conventions and UN Resolutions

4.19 Under the multilateral terrorism conventions outlined in Chapter 1, states must criminalize specific acts, and prosecute or extradite suspected offenders.[64] States must prevent and repress aircraft hijackings,[65] hostage-taking by terrorist groups,[66] attacks against the safety of sea vessels,[67] and the proliferation of nuclear weapons to terrorist groups.[68] States parties to these treaties must prosecute or extradite terrorism suspects,[69] denying them safe haven,[70] and exercising jurisdiction on the basis of territory or nationality. The crimes defined in these subject-specific treaties must not be considered political offences: a class of crimes for which suspects cannot be extradited.[71]

4.20 Security Council Resolution 1373 (2001) requires states not only to ratify the subject-specific terrorism treaties outlined in Chapter 1, including those which provide for an obligation to prosecute or extradite offenders; but also to cooperate in criminal investigations and prosecutions, affording each other the greatest possible measure of assistance in trials on the financing or support of terrorist crimes.[72] In the UN Global Counter-Terrorism Strategy, which is considered in depth in Chapter 6, states resolved to conclude and implement extradition agreements and agreements on mutual legal assistance (MLA), and to strengthen cooperation between law enforcement agencies.[73] As the UN Global Counter-Terrorism Strategy also emphasizes that states must counter terrorism in full compliance with existing IHL, IHRL, and IRL, it follows that inter-state cooperation in law enforcement and criminal cases must comply in full with the right to a fair trial, the prohibition

---

[64] See Chapter 1, nn 1 and 2.

[65] Convention on Offences and Certain Other Acts Committed on Board Aircraft 1963; Convention for the Suppression of Unlawful Seizure of Aircraft 1970; Convention for the Suppression of Unlawful Acts against the Safety of Civil Aviation 1971, and its Protocol 1988.

[66] International Convention against the Taking of Hostages 1979.

[67] Convention for the Suppression of Unlawful Acts against the Safety of Maritime Navigation 1988, and its Protocol 2005.

[68] Convention on the Physical Protection of Nuclear Material 1980, as amended 2005; International Convention for the Suppression of Acts of Nuclear Terrorism 2005.

[69] International Convention for the Suppression of Terrorist Bombings 1997; International Convention for the Suppression of Acts of Nuclear Terrorism 2005.

[70] UN Security Council Resolution 1373, 28 September 2001, para 2(c).

[71] Convention for the Suppression of Unlawful Seizure of Aircraft 1970, Art 7; Convention for the Suppression of Unlawful Acts against the Safety of Civil Aviation 1971, Art 7; Convention on the Prevention and Punishment of Crimes against Internationally Protected Persons 1973, Art 3(2); International Convention against the Taking of Hostages 1979, Art 5(2); International Convention for the Suppression of Terrorist Bombings 1997, Art 7(2); International Convention for the Suppression of the Financing of Terrorism 1997, Art 7(4); International Convention for the Suppression of Acts of Nuclear Terrorism 2005, Art 9(4); see para 1.18.

[72] UN Security Council Resolution 1373, 28 September 2001, operative para 2(f).

[73] UN Global Counter-Terrorism Strategy, annexed to General Assembly Resolution 60/288, 8 September 2006, II, Measures to prevent and combat terrorism; see also: UN Convention on Transnational Organised Crime 2000; EU Convention on Mutual Assistance in Criminal Matters 2000.

on torture and other ill-treatment, and the prohibition on *refoulement* where there are substantial grounds for believing that a person would suffer torture or ill-treatment if transferred.[74] The UN Office on Drugs and Crime has published an informative manual for international cooperation in criminal prosecutions of terrorism, which explains extradition and mutual legal assistance in counter-terrorism in the context of applicable IHL, IHRL, and IRL.[75]

Types of jurisdiction

As criminal jurisdiction is primarily territorial, prosecutions should take place **4.21** wherever possible in the territorial state where terrorist attacks occur, even if the acts were on board sea vessels and aircraft, and in the airspace or territorial seas of a state. Where an offence takes place on a ship on the high seas, the flag state can exercise jurisdiction. Extraterritorial jurisdiction in criminal cases can be exercised on the basis of active personality, where the defendant is a national of the prosecuting state. Less commonly, criminal jurisdiction may be exercised extraterritorially under the protective principle—where a state seeks to defend a national interest, including a national security interest, which is reputedly threatened by the commission of a criminal offence. Passive personality jurisdiction is more controversial but increasingly accepted. States can exercise extraterritorial criminal jurisdiction under the passive personality principle if the victims of an offence were nationals of the prosecuting state.[76] The Convention on Offences and Certain Other Acts Committed on Board Aircraft 1963 calls on its states parties to use passive personality jurisdiction in the prosecution of offences detailed therein,[77] and US federal criminal law now encompasses this ground of jurisdiction.[78]

Universal jurisdiction is the most controversial of the five principles of jurisdic- **4.22** tion, and is based on the theory that certain crimes are crimes against the international legal order, such that they may be tried by any court anywhere in the world. This type of jurisdiction does not require a link between the crime and the territorial state, or the nationality of the defendant or victims.[79] There is insufficient authority in treaty or custom to ground a duty to exercise universal jurisdiction to prosecute terrorist attacks: the subject-specific terrorism conventions outlined in Chapter 1 tend to rely on a duty to prosecute or extradite an offender (*aut dedere aut judicare*) rather than universal jurisdiction.[80] The several expanded grounds for

---

[74] See paras 3.05, 3.58, 3.64, 3.74–3.80, 3.86, 3.114, 3.118, and 7.12.

[75] UNODC, *Manual on International Cooperation in Criminal Matters Related to Terrorism*, 2009.

[76] DJ Harris, *Cases and Materials on International Law* (6th edn, Sweet and Maxwell, 2004).

[77] Convention on Offences and Certain Other Acts Committed on Board Aircraft 1963.

[78] *US v Yunis* (1988) 82 Int'l L Rep 344.

[79] International Center for Transitional Justice, 'Universal Jurisdiction: the "War on Terror"', 17 April 2009.

[80] Convention for the Suppression of Unlawful Seizure of Aircraft 1970, Art 7; Convention for the Suppression of Unlawful Acts against the Safety of Civil Aviation 1971, Art 7; Convention on

extraterritorial criminal jurisdiction over terrorist bombings in Article 6 of the International Convention for the Suppression of Terrorist Bombings 1997 fall short of true universal jurisdiction.[81]

Prosecuting terrorist crimes in domestic criminal courts

4.23 Numerous states have investigated and prosecuted terrorist attacks as crimes in their domestic criminal courts. The UNODC notes the forensic challenges and prolonged investigatory capacity which is often required for terrorism prosecutions.[82] In its *Digest of Terrorism Cases* the UNODC notes prosecutions of terrorism attacks in Colombia, Egypt, France, Ireland, Italy, Kenya, the Russian Federation, Spain, and the UK, among others.[83] Nonetheless, some states insist upon trying terrorism suspects in special military or security courts which lack the necessary independence from the executive to ensure a fair trial.[84] In the context of a debate on the creation of a national security court, the NGO Human Rights First reasoned in 2008 that terrorism trials both could and should take place in US federal criminal courts.[85] That simple proposition was balanced with some caveats, which noted the complexities of the multilateral terrorism treaties, evidentiary challenges, and the need for a multifaceted approach to counter terrorism—comprising military, intelligence, diplomatic, economic, and law enforcement mechanisms.[86] The study examined prosecutions under the US' 'material support' for terrorism statutes[87] and prosecutions for terrorism-related homicide and conspiracy.[88]

4.24 These two studies point to precedents for the prosecution of terrorist crimes in domestic courts. However, Egypt,[89] Jordan,[90] Syria,[91] Turkey,[92] and the US,[93] among

---

the Prevention and Punishment of Crimes against Internationally Protected Persons 1973, Art 3(2); International Convention against the Taking of Hostages 1979, Art 5(2); International Convention for the Suppression of Terrorist Bombings 1997, Art 7(2); International Convention for the Suppression of the Financing of Terrorism 1997, Art 7(4); International Convention for the Suppression of Acts of Nuclear Terrorism 2005, Art 9(4).

[81] International Convention for the Suppression of Terrorist Bombings 1997, Art 6(1) and (2).

[82] UNODC, *Digest of Terrorism Cases,* supra, IV. A, Characteristic Investigative Obstacles.

[83] Ibid, VI.

[84] See paras 3.146–3.148.

[85] Richard B Zabel and James J Benjami Jnr, 'In Pursuit of Justice: Prosecuting Terrorism Cases in the Federal Courts', *Human Rights First,* May 2008.

[86] Ibid, p 2.

[87] See *Holder, Attorney-General, et al v Humanitarian Law Project et al,* No 08–1498, United States Supreme Court, 21 June 2010, at para 3.163.

[88] Richard B Zabel and James J Benjami Jnr, 'In Pursuit of Justice: Prosecuting Terrorism Cases in the Federal Courts', *Human Rights First,* May 2008, p 6.

[89] Human Rights Watch, 'Egypt: Transfer Zeitoun Trial to Criminal Court', 14 February 2010.

[90] Amnesty International, 'Jordon: Submission to the UN Universal Periodic Review, 4th Session of the UPR Working Group of the Human Rights Council', AI Index: MDE 16/004/2008, 1 September 2008.

[91] Human Rights Watch, 'Syria: Dissolve the State Security Court', 24 February 2009.

[92] Amnesty International, 'Turkey: Justice Delayed and Denied: The Persistence of Protracted and Unfair Trials for Those Charged under Anti-Terrorism Legislation', EUR 44/013/2006, 5 September 2006.

[93] Military Commissions Act 2009.

others, all rely on special security courts or military commissions for the prosecution of some terrorism suspects. Trials in similar courts have been found to violate the right to a fair hearing before a competent, independent, and impartial tribunal established by law.[94] In November 2009, the US Attorney-General Eric Holder announced that the Department of Justice intended to pursue prosecutions of five suspects in the 11 September 2001 attacks on the US in federal court in the Southern District of New York.[95] As military commissions charges against Khalid Sheikh Mohammed, Walid Bin Attash, Ramzi Bin al Shibh, Ali Abdul Aziz Ali, and Mustafa Ahmed Adam al Hawsawi were dropped as a result, these prosecutions mark a first step in reform of the US' approach to high-profile terrorism trials. Prior to this announcement, Ahmed Ghalani, who is suspected of involvement in the 1998 US Embassy bombings in East Africa, had been transferred from Guantánamo Bay to New York for a trial in federal court.[96] Other cases are pending, including the prosecutions of Umar Farouk Abdulmutallab[97] and Faizal Shahzad,[98] suspected of terrorism offences in December 2009 and May 2010 respectively. In April 2010, hearings before military commissions resumed in the US for Guantánamo detainees. At the time of writing the trial for Omar Khadr was due to begin in July 2010.[99]

Accountability for violations in counter-terrorism

Introduction

Although states are developing a welter of jurisprudence on the prosecution of ter- **4.25**
rorism suspects,[100] they show far less willingness to establish accountability for violations of IHL and IHRL committed in counter-terrorism. This is in spite of the duties to criminalize, prosecute, and extradite in the Geneva Conventions' grave breaches provisions,[101] the duty to investigate alleged violations of grave human rights abuses, such as torture and ill-treatment, and the case law which establishes that a failure to investigate violations of IHRL can amount to a violation in its

---

[94] *Abbasi Madani v Algeria*, Communication No 1172/2003, Views, 28 March 2007, CCPR/C/89/D1172/2003, p 4.

[95] Department of Justice, 'Departments of Justice and Defense Announce Forum Decisions for Ten Guantanamo Bay Detainees', 13 November 2009.

[96] Ibid.

[97] Reuters, 'Not Guilty Plea Entered for Nigerian Bomb Suspect', 8 January 2010.

[98] William K Rashbaum and Benjamin Weiser, 'Times Square Bombing Suspect Appears in Court', *New York Times*, 18 May 2010.

[99] Amnesty USA, 'Military Commission Proceedings Against Omar Khadr Resume, as USA Disregards its International Human Rights Obligations', AI Index: AMR 51/029/2010, 26 April 2010.

[100] UNODC, *Digest of Terrorist Cases*, supra.

[101] See n 7.

own right.[102] The duty to provide an 'effective remedy' for all violations of IHRL is embedded in the structure of IHRL treaties.[103] The European Court of Human Rights has held that torture and ill-treatment should be followed by a thorough and effective investigation which is capable of identifying and punishing those responsible.[104] The Inter-American Court has held that investigations must be carried out 'in a serious manner and not as a mere formality preordained to be ineffective'.[105] States which neglect accountability for violations of IHL and IHRL committed in their counter-terrorism operations undermine the enforcement of IHL and IHRL treaties. As UN Security Council Resolutions and the UN Global Counter-Terrorism Strategy emphasize that states must prevent and repress terrorism in full compliance with IHL, IHRL, and IRL, impunity for violations in counter-terrorism shows disdain for this obligation, and disrespect for victims. Failures to provide judicial and administrative sanctions may also deny victims satisfaction—one of the types of reparations in international standards.[106]

4.26 Thus far, accountability for these violations is gradual and piecemeal. Despite a small number of court-martial convictions for unlawful killings and prisoner abuse in the UK and US,[107] there has been only one *in absentia* conviction for crimes relating to 'extraordinary rendition',[108] although further criminal investigations are pending. The insufficiency of national accountability processes has led some victims to seek justice in supranational and intergovernmental bodies. Impunity remains, in part because of the complicity of several states in IHRL violations, and the invocation of state secrets doctrines to prevent the disclosure of evidence of this complicity in open court. However, case law in the UK in particular has begun to challenge this pervasive secrecy and impunity. National inquiries in Lithuania and Poland into secret detention have led to information and factual admissions and there are ongoing criminal investigations. There are also nascent criminal investigations into secret detention in a number of other European states.

4.27 This section delineates findings by intergovernmental bodies of violations of IHRL in counter-terrorism, before considering pending and past criminal investigations, civil suits, and national inquiries into violations of IHL and IHRL committed in counter-terrorism operations.

---

[102] See n 10.

[103] ICCPR, Art 2(3)(a); Convention against Torture and Other Cruel, Inhuman or Degrading Treatment or Punishment (CAT), Arts 13–14; International Convention for the Protection of All Persons from Enforced Disappearance (Disappearances Convention—not yet in force), Arts 8, 18, 20, 24; European Convention on Human Rights (ECHR), Art 15; American Convention on Human Rights 1969 (ACHR), Art 25.

[104] *Selmouni v France* (1999) 29 EHRR 403, para 79.

[105] *Vélasquez-Rodríguez*, supra, para 177.

[106] Basic Principles and Guidelines, Principle 22.

[107] See paras 4.35–4.36.

[108] See para 4.32.

Intergovernmental organizations

As Chapter 3 demonstrates, a Joint Report of four UN Special Procedures of the   **4.28**
Human Rights Council parsed the composite violations inherent in the practice of
secret detention.[109] Their report excoriated the conduct of states which participated
in the secret detention and 'proxy detention' (transfers to another state for the
purpose of coercive interrogation), and alleged that the UK, Germany, Poland,
Lithuania, Romania, and Macedonia were complicit in the torture of an unknown
number of individuals in the course of the US-led 'war on terror'.[110]

In its 2007 report, the Parliamentary Assembly of the Council of Europe (PACE)   **4.29**
similarly condemned the practice of secret detention in CIA prisons; noted the
complicity of a number of European states in 'extraordinary rendition' flights,[111]
and the state secrets doctrines which states invoked when refusing to disclose details
of their involvement; and concluded that it was 'factually established' that CIA
detention facilities had been located in Poland and Romania.[112] These findings triggered subsequent investigations in Poland, Lithuania, and Romania, and a number
of Freedom of Information Act proceedings.[113]

In 2005, the UN Committee against Torture found Sweden in violation of Article   **4.30**
3 of the Convention against Torture for having deported Ahmed Agiza[114] to Egypt
in December 2001, in violation of the prohibition on *refoulement*. Prior to his failed
asylum claim in Sweden, Ahmed Agiza had been tried and convicted of terrorism
offences *in absentia;* and sentenced to penal servitude for life.[115] Sweden rejected his
asylum claim prior to the deportation, received diplomatic assurances from Egypt
that he would not face torture if returned, and allowed a CIA aeroplane to transport
Agiza to Egypt.[116] In 2002, Agiza reported torture and ill-treatment in Egyptian
custody, including the application of electric shocks.[117] The Committee against

---

[109] Human Rights Council, 'Joint Study on global practice in relation to secret detention in the
context of countering terrorism', A/HRC/13/42, 26 January 2010; see para 3.123.

[110] Ian Cobain, 'Britain "complicit in mistreatment and possible torture", says UN', *Guardian*, 27
January 2010.

[111] For a definition of aiding and abetting internationally unlawful acts (a definition of complicity
in international standards), see the ILC Articles on State Responsibility, Art 16.

[112] Parliamentary Assembly of the Council of Europe (PACE), 'Secret Detentions and Illegal
Transfers of Detainees Involving Council of Europe Member States: Second Report', Doc 11302 rev,
11 June 2007; see also John Cerone, 'Re-examining International Responsibility: "Complicity" in the
Context of Human Rights Violations' (2008) 14 *ILSA J Int'l & Comp L* 525–534; see paras 3.42, 3.89.

[113] Wolfgang Kaleck, 'Justice and Accountability in Europe—Discussing Strategies' in European
Centre for Constitutional and Human Rights (ed), *CIA—Extraordinary Rendition: Flights, Torture
and Accountability—A European Approach,* March 2008, pp 13–27, at p 13 ('ECCHR Rendition
Report').

[114] Committee against Torture, Decision, *Agiza v Sweden*, CAT/C/34/D/233/2003, 20 May
2005.

[115] Ibid, para 2.4.

[116] Ibid, paras 10.2, 11.13, 13.4.

[117] Ibid, para 2.6.

Torture found that the Swedish authorities knew or should have known about the 'consistent and widespread' use of torture against security detainees in Egypt;[118] and that the interests of two foreign states in interrogating Ahmed Agiza should have put Sweden on notice as to the real risk of torture he would face upon expulsion.[119] The Committee found that there had been treatment amounting to a violation of Article 16 of the Convention by foreign agents acting with the collusion of Swedish authorities prior to Ahmed Agiza's expulsion,[120] and that as a result of all these combined factors, the Swedish authorities transferred Ahmed Agiza in violation of Article 3's prohibition on *refoulement*.

4.31 The UN Human Rights Committee made an analogous finding, in relation to the case of Mohamed Alzery, a second Egyptian national expelled by Sweden to Egypt with the collusion of foreign agents. The Committee found Sweden in violation of the prohibition on *refoulement* implicit in Article 7 of the ICCPR.[121] The Committee noted that the Swedish authorities actually witnessed the ill-treatment of Mohamed Alzery at the hands of foreign agents at Bromma airport, so that they were thoroughly aware of the real risk of torture and ill-treatment upon transfer, such that those acts should have been imputed to Swedish authorities through their consent or acquiescence.[122] Moreover, the Committee made pointed criticisms of Sweden's failure to ensure individual criminal responsibility for the violation of Article 7 of the ICCPR: in the Committee's view, Sweden should have investigated and prosecuted both Swedish and foreign agents.[123] The *non-refoulement* point in Alzery's case also involved an apparent risk of a manifestly unfair trial in Egypt, although the Committee did not make a separate finding on this issue.[124] There had been substantial grounds for believing that both men would face a risk of torture upon transfer, and in both cases, the diplomatic assurances offered were inadequate to prevent the violations of Article 3 of the Convention against Torture and Article 7 of the ICCPR respectively. The Decision of the Committee against Torture in Agiza's case was the first UN accountability mechanism to note the insufficiency of diplomatic assurances in counter-terrorism transfers.[125]

Prosecuting IHL and IHRL violations in domestic criminal courts

Italy: Abu Omar

4.32 In contrast to this record of useful investigations by supranational bodies, there has been only one successful prosecution to date for involvement in an enforced

---

[118] Ibid, para 13.4.
[119] Ibid.
[120] Ibid.
[121] Views of the Human Rights Committee, *Alzery v Sweden*, CCPR/C/88/D/1416/2005, 10 November 2006.
[122] Ibid, para 11.6.
[123] Ibid, para 11.7.
[124] Ibid, para 11.9.
[125] *Agiza v Sweden*, supra, para 13.4.

disappearance in the 'war on terror'. In the Abu Omar case discussed in Chapter 3,[126] 23 US nationals were convicted of involvement in the abduction of Abu Omar from Milan to Ramstein Air Base in Germany, from where he was transferred to four years of detention and torture in Egypt. Two Italian security personnel were also convicted of complicity in Abu Omar's abduction.[127]

Although the prosecution was successful, the case belies an inter-state reluctance to **4.33** bring the perpetrators of serious human rights violations to justice. The 22 CIA operatives (and one US military officer) were convicted and sentenced *in absentia*, and 'successive Italian Justice Ministers refused to transmit' arrest warrants to the US government.[128]

Germany and Spain: Khaled El-Masri

The German government has not implemented a January 2007 court decision to **4.34** issue 13 arrest warrants for CIA agents alleged to have been involved in the abduction of German citizen Khaled El-Masri.[129] As Germany does not permit trials *in absentia,* this precludes a criminal trial in Germany in relation to human rights violations suffered by El-Masri. El-Masri was abducted while on holiday in Macedonia, interrogated and threatened, and after 23 days of detention, blindfolded and subjected to an 'extraordinary rendition' flight, injected with drugs, and flown to Iraq and then Afghanistan.[130] When officials are unwilling to process an extradition request to the US,[131] the trial is very unlikely to proceed. In Spain, prosecutors have sought arrest warrants for 13 CIA agents alleged to have been involved in the abduction, interrogation, and unlawful transfer of El-Masri. However, the US refuses to identify the CIA personnel involved.[132]

In 2004–05, 11 US armed forces personnel were convicted of involvement in tor- **4.35** ture and ill-treatment at the Abu Ghraib detention facility in Iraq. Convictions have been confirmed on appeal, most recently by the US Court of Appeals for the

---

[126] See para 3.68.
[127] Britta Sandberg, 'Abu Omar Case: Italian Court Delivers Damning Verdict on CIA Renditions', Spiegel Online International, 11 May 2009; Francesco Messineo, '"Extraordinary Renditions" and State Obligations to Criminalize and Prosecute Torture in the Light of the *Abu Omar* Case in Italy' (2009) 7 *Journal of International Criminal Justice* 1023–1044.
[128] Amnesty International, 'Convictions in Abu Omar Case a Step Toward Accountability', 5 November 2009.
[129] Wolfgang Kaleck and Andreas Schüller, 'Litigating Extraordinary Renditions', *INTERIGHTS Bulletin*, Vol 16, No 1 (2010), 34–35.
[130] Case Summary, Khaled El-Masri, in 'ECCHR Rendition Report', supra, at 106–107; Margaret L Satterthwaite, 'The Story of *El Masri v Tenet*: Human Rights and Humanitarian Law in the "War on Terror"', in D R Hurwitz, M L Satterthwaite, and D B Ford (eds), *Human Rights Advocacy Stories* (Foundation Press, 2009), pp 535–577.
[131] Wolfgang Kaleck, 'Justice and Accountability in Europe—Discussing Strategies', in ECCHR Rendition Report, supra, pp 13–27 at 21.
[132] The Lift weblog, 'Spanish Prosecutors Seek the Arrest of 13 CIA Agents', 13 May 2010.

Armed Forces in Washington.[133] One conviction has been overturned on appeal: that of the only officer convicted at the courts martial in 2004–05.[134]

4.36   In contrast, the court-martial of Corporal Donald Payne led to quite limited accountability for the death of Baha Mousa in UK custody in Iraq, even when coupled with a public inquiry which is still ongoing at the time of writing.[135] Corporal Donald Payne entered a guilty plea to a charge of inhumane treatment of Baha Mousa at a court-martial hearing on Baha Mousa's death. The court-martial acquitted all other defendants, and acquitted Corporal Payne of the more serious charge of manslaughter.[136] As Baha Mousa suffered 93 injuries before his death,[137] and as a pathologist testified that he had died from asphyxiation caused by a ligature on his neck and a subsequent struggle,[138] these acquittals suggest that there should be further investigations and prosecutions of other suspects thought to be responsible. At a public inquiry convened in 2008 and still ongoing at the time of writing, other armed forces personnel were granted immunity from prosecution for giving evidence.[139] The surviving members of Baha Mousa's family accepted $3 million in damages for his death, in fulfilment of the obligation to provide a remedy and reparations to victims of grave violations of IHL and serious violations of IHRL.[140] The case of Jean Charles de Menezes (see paragraphs 3.33, 3.44, and 5.32) resulted in a prosecution only under health and safety legislation. There was no prosecution for the unlawful killing of Mr de Menezes.

Criminal investigations and special prosecutors

Incomplete prosecutions

4.37   Criminal investigations which do not reach the prosecution stage, for example because extradition requests are not fulfilled, can nonetheless provide information and begin to furnish victims with a right to truth.[141] As Wolfgang Kaleck notes, the two requests to the German Federal Prosecutor under universal jurisdiction for the trials of Donald Rumsfeld, former CIA Director George Tenet, and others, 'directly challenge . . . an entire policy' in counter-terrorism. It appears to be Kaleck's position that attempted accountability is better than no accountability

---

[133] *US v Harman,* CAAF, 27 April 2006; *US v Smith,* CAAF, 4 February 2010.

[134] *Guardian,* 'US Army Rejects Court Martial of Abu Ghraib Commander', 11 January 2008.

[135] See para 3.50.

[136] Redress, 'Court Martial Acquittals in Baha Mousa Case: The Full Truth of What Happened Remains Unknown', Statement, 14 March 2007.

[137] BBC News, 'Baha Mousa Inquiry: Chief Officer "Punched Detainee"', 19 January 2010.

[138] The Baha Mousa Public Inquiry, Witness Statement of Ian Rowland Hill, 22 May 2009, para 12.

[139] The Baha Mousa Public Inquiry:<http://www.bahamousainquiry.org>.

[140] Rachel Stevenson and Matthew Weaver, 'Timeline: Baha Mousa Case', *Guardian,* 13 July 2009.

[141] See para 5.04.

at all.[142] However, truncated prosecutions do not fully implement victims' rights to a remedy and reparation. In Spain, April 2009 amendments to universal jurisdiction legislation[143] may preclude a prosecution of torture crimes at Guantánamo and other overseas detention facilities.[144] It may also stop a prosecution of the authors of the Department of Justice 'Torture Memos'.[145] However, accountability processes seem to be ongoing as of May 2010, as Spanish prosecutors have asked a judge to issue arrest warrants for 13 CIA agents whom they believe were involved in 'extraordinary rendition'.[146]

Delayed prosecution of anonymous intelligence officer

Of the criminal investigations ongoing in the UK, one case is that of Witness B, a **4.38** current or former MI5 intelligence officer who testified that he had acted pursuant to the orders of his superiors when supervising the interrogation and torture of Binyam Mohamed. Since 2009, this case has been before the Attorney-General and Director of Public Prosecutions, for a decision as to whether it is in the public interest to prosecute.[147]

Investigation into US Department of Justice 'Torture Memos'

In the spring of 2009, President Obama granted Attorney-General Eric Holder a **4.39** mandate to establish a Special Prosecutor to investigate the disappearance of 72 CIA interrogation tapes from the Bush-era, and to investigate any torture which occurred which was more serious than that authorized in the Department of Justice 'Torture Memos' which were analysed in depth in Chapter 3.[148] Human Rights Watch wrote an open letter to Attorney-General Holder, critiquing the very narrow mandate for the Special Prosecutor, and noting that reform cannot be effective until there has been a comprehensive investigation into the authorization of torture, and

---

[142] *Center for Constitutional Rights et al v Donald Rumsfeld et al*, 10 February 2005, (2006) 45 ILM 115, discussed in Wolfgang Kaleck, 'Justice and Accountability in Europe—Discussing Strategies', in ECCHR Rendition Report, supra, pp 13–27, at pp 22–23.

[143] Art 23.4 of the Organic Law of the Judicial Branch, amended by Spanish Congress of Deputies on 25 June 2009.

[144] CNN, 'Spanish Judge Orders Guantánamo Torture Probe', 29 April 2009; Ignacio de la Rasilla del Moral, 'The Swan Song of Universal Jurisdiction in Spain' (2009) 9 *International Criminal Law Review* 777–808.

[145] David Cole, 'Getting Away with Torture', NYRB, 16 December 2009, pp 39–42, at p 42; Kai Ambos, 'Prosecuting Guantánamo in Europe: Can and Shall the Masterminds of the "Torture Memos" be Held Criminally Responsible on the Basis of Universal Jurisdiction?' (2009) 42 *Case Western Journal of International Law* 405–448.

[146] The Lift weblog, 'Spanish Prosecutors Seek the Arrest of 13 CIA Agents', 13 May 2010.

[147] UK Intelligence and Security Committee, 'Alleged Complicity of the UK Security and Intelligence Agencies in Torture or Cruel, Inhuman or Degrading Treatment or Punishment', 17 March 2009, p 2:< http://www.cabinetoffice.gov.uk/media/143156/090317_alledged.pdf>, accessed 21 June 2010.

[148] See paras 3.70–3.73.

into those who ordered it.[149] The narrow mandate for this investigation mirrors the weak findings of the internal Office of Professional Responsibility inquiry into the Department of Justice 'Torture Memos'.[150] A partially-redacted version of this document concluded that the authors of the memos had exercised 'poor judgment': language which shows no awareness on the part of the authors of the absolute and *jus cogens* nature of the prohibition on torture, and of the requirement to criminalize not only its commission, but also complicity in torture.[151] Attorney-General Holder has said that he will not prosecute interrogators who 'acted in good faith' in reliance on the 'Torture Memos'.[152] This is an unprincipled position given the imperative of ensuring accountability for torture crimes, yet it seems to have affected the US judiciary as well as the executive. In *Rasul v Myers*, the US Court of Appeals for the District of Columbia refused to prosecute an apparent crime of torture, because at the time the applicant alleged the acts in question, it was 'not clearly established that [they were] unlawful'.[153]

Failed prosecution of Blackwater/Xe

4.40 Also in the US, a recent prosecution of the Blackwater/Xe private military and security company for unlawful killings in Iraq faltered because prosecutors had compelled witnesses to give testimony regardless of the constitutional Fifth Amendment privilege against self-incrimination.[154] The company reached a civil settlement with the alleged victims in January 2010,[155] but as Chapter 5 makes clear, reparation is more than just monetary compensation. Under the UN Basic Principles and Guidelines on the Right to a Remedy and Reparation for Victims of Gross Violations of IHL and Serious Violations of IHRL, reparations can take the form of restitution, compensation, rehabilitation, satisfaction, and guarantees of non-repetition.[156] A separate criminal prosecution of two Blackwater guards accused of murdering two Afghan civilians in May 2009 is also ongoing.[157]

---

[149] Human Rights Watch, Open Letter to Attorney-General Eric Holder, 22 July 2009, p 3, available at HRW, Letter to Holder Supporting Criminal Prosecution for Counterterrorism Abuses, 20 July 2009.

[150] Department of Justice, Office of Professional Responsibility Report, 'Investigation into the Office of Legal Counsel's Memoranda Concerning Issues Relating to the Central Intelligence Agency's Use of "Enhanced Interrogation Techniques" on Suspected Terrorists', 29 July 2009 (partially redacted, released 2010).

[151] See paras 3.70–3.73.

[152] Human Rights Watch, 'US: Lawyers' Misconduct Shows Need for Torture Inquiry', 19 February 2010.

[153] *Rasul v Myers*, US Court of Appeals for the District of Columbia, 14 December 2009 (the Supreme Court later denied *certiorari* to review the case).

[154] *United States v Slough*, US District Court for the District of Columbia, Criminal Action 08-0360 (RMU), 31 December 2009.

[155] BBC News, 'Two Former Blackwater Guards Charged with Afghan Murder', 7 January 2010.

[156] See paras 5.38 et seq.

[157] Mike Baker, 'Blackwater Settles Series of Civil Lawsuits', *The Huffington Post*, 7 January 2010.

Civil suits

Canada: complicity in torture

The Guantánamo Bay detainee Omar Khadr was subjected to sleep deprivation in   **4.41**
the 'frequent flyer' programme established by the CIA. A Canadian national who
was a minor at the time of his transfer to and initial detention in Guantánamo Bay
in 2002, Khadr was interrogated in the presence of Canadian employees of the
Department of Foreign Affairs and International Trade (DFAIT) and the Canadian
Security and Intelligence Service (CSIS) in 2003, even though those security
employees had been made aware of the sleep deprivation and planned isolation to
which Khadr was being subjected.[158] Khadr brought a judicial review application
to challenge the Prime Minister's decision not to seek his repatriation from
Guantánamo Bay, and at first instance, the Federal Court held that the Canadian
government had a duty to protect Khadr under section 7 of the Canadian Charter
of Rights and Freedoms. The Federal Court ordered the government to seek Khadr's
repatriation. This order was upheld by the Federal Court of Appeal, which found
that the breach of section 7 arose from the DFAIT and CSIS employees' knowledge
of the ill-treatment to which Omar Khadr had been subjected.[159] The Federal Court
of Appeals held that section 7 applied to a regime operated by the US which was
found to have violated international law.[160] Before the Supreme Court of Canada
in January 2010, the Prime Minister's appeal was allowed in part. Again, Canada
was found complicit in the ill-treatment of Omar Khadr at Guantánamo Bay, and
his liberty and security had been found to have been violated. The Supreme Court
of Canada ruled that Khadr was entitled to a remedy under section 24(1) of the
Canadian Charter for the violations of his rights, but the court left the issue to the
government's discretion 'to decide how best to respond'.[161] This is a sorry failure of
accountability processes for complicity in ill-treatment and deprivation of liberty.
The Canadian government could respond well to the judgment by initiating its
own investigation and prosecution of individuals who are suspected on the balance
of probabilities of being complicit in torture or other ill-treatment, and by using all
diplomatic means to secure the release of Omar Khadr from Guantánamo Bay and
his repatriation to Canada.

State secrets

State secrets doctrines have been invoked by governments in court proceedings as a   **4.42**
means of excluding certain evidence on the basis of an asserted risk that the revelation of that evidence could endanger national security. In the US, the successful

---

[158] Supreme Court of Canada, *Prime Minister of Canada, Minister of Foreign Affairs, Director of the
Canadian Security Intelligence Service and Commissioner of the Royal Canadian Mounted Police v Omar
Ahmed Khadr*, 29 January 2010, Summary, para 1.
[159] Ibid.
[160] Ibid, Summary, para 2.
[161] Ibid, para 39.

invocation of a state secrets doctrine prevents the court from hearing the case. In the UK, disputes over secret evidence relate to specific parts of a party's case, or particular paragraphs in a judgment, as in the Binyam Mohamed litigation. Italy also invokes state secrets. Despite having provided the only successful conviction, albeit *in absentia*, for crimes relating to 'extraordinary rendition', state secrets led to an earlier suspension in the trial because of the risk of revealing Italy's alleged complicity in the abduction of Abu Omar.[162]

4.43 The US Supreme Court refused to hear Khaled El-Masri's civil suit against George Tenet, the former Director of the CIA responsible for the extraordinary rendition programme.[163] Having exhausted domestic remedies in the US, he has now petitioned the Inter-American Commission on Human Rights.[164] State secrets doctrines also precluded Maher Arar's civil suit in the US District Court of Appeals and in February 2010 the US Supreme Court denied *certiorari*, without giving reasons.[165]

4.44 Both the Bush and Obama Administrations consecutively argued in *Mohamed et al v Jeppesen Dataplan, Inc*[166] that the entire subject matter of the case falls under a state secrets doctrine. In that case, for which a decision on a rehearing *en banc* is pending before the US 9th Circuit Court of Appeals, the American Civil Liberties Union (ACLU) brought suit under the Alien Tort Claims Act (ATCA) on behalf of five victims of extraordinary rendition against Jeppesen Dataplan Inc. They argued that the company knowingly participated in extraordinary rendition flights *inter alia* to torture, by its provision of logistical support and flight plans. Binyam Mohamed and Ahmed Agiza are among the plaintiffs.

4.45 UK jurisprudence on state secrets is slowly turning the tide on impunity. In the case of Shaker Aamer, the last British resident to be held at Guantánamo Bay, the Divisional Court of England and Wales ruled in December 2009 that the government must disclose to the Guantánamo Review Task Force documents held by the UK security and intelligence services in which there could be evidence that Mr Aamer had been tortured while in detention in Afghanistan or Guantánamo Bay.[167] Lloyd Jones J reasoned that the UK had become mixed up in the tort to the extent of facilitating it (the *Norwich Pharmacal* test). The judge granted relief and

---

[162] Statewatch, 'Interpretation of "State Secret" Leads to Suspension of Abu Omar Trial', 3 December 2008.

[163] *Khaled El-Masri v United States of America*, No 06-1613.

[164] ACLU, 'Petition Alleging Violations of the Human Rights of Khaled el-Masri by the United States of America with a Request for an Investigation and Hearing on the Merits', 9 April 2008.

[165] *Arar v Ashcroft et al* (S Ct, 14 June 2010) (denying cert); Human Rights Watch, 'Denying Arar Opportunity for Redress Undermines US Justice System', 6 February 2010; Amnesty USA, 'Amnesty International "Deeply Disappointed" by Supreme Court's decision to Reject Arar Appeal', 14 June 2010.

[166] *Mohamed v Jeppesen Dataplan Inc*, 563 F.3d 992, 1000 (9th Cir 2009).

[167] *Shaker Aamer v Secretary of State for Foreign and Commonwealth Affairs* [2009] EWHC 3316 (Admin), 15 December 2009.

disclosed the documents to Mr Aamer's lawyers, rejecting the government's submission that the documents could be shared confidentially with the Guantánamo Review Task Force. Only with access to the documents alleging torture could Mr Aamer meaningfully present his case for release to the Guantánamo Review Task Force. However, the judgment was subject to future challenges on statutory prohibitions on disclosure and public interest immunity.[168]

The Binyam Mohamed litigation, noted in paragraph 3.66, ultimately resulted in **4.46** the release of seven previously redacted paragraphs from a judgment of the Divisional Court. The Divisional Court had made a *Norwich Pharmacal* order to make public the seven paragraphs, quashing the Secretary of State's refusal to provide information to Binyam Mohamed about his detention, treatment, and rendition on which he had intended to rely in his defence against military commission charges in the US—prior to his release from Guantánamo Bay in 2009. The redacted paragraphs related to accounts given by US intelligence agents to UK intelligence agents about Binyam Mohamed's treatment in custody, and also related to an interview by an UK intelligence agent (Witness B). The Divisional Court held that, in part, because the information was already in the public domain as a result of Binyam Mohamed's litigation in the US, the redacted paragraphs should be released as the risk to national security was not serious and there was an overwhelming public interest in their disclosure. The Secretary of State for Foreign and Commonwealth Affairs (Foreign Secretary) then appealed unsuccessfully to the Court of Appeal against the decision of the Divisional Court to publish seven paragraphs which had been redacted from a previous judgment of the Divisional Court. This was despite the Foreign Secretary's statement in a public interest immunity certificate that the publication of the redacted paragraphs would risk serious harm to UK national security. The Court of Appeal rejected the Foreign Secretary's appeal in February 2010.[169] It held that the control principle (when intelligence is shared between states, the state disclosing the information holds confidentiality) is not a principle in English law; Binyam Mohamed had a personal interest in seeing the Divisional Court's full reasoning and there was a public interest in disclosure.

A central thesis of this book is that state secrets doctrines should not be invoked **4.47** to prevent accountability for violations of IHL or IHRL in counter-terrorism operations. This principle has now been recognized as regards closed hearings (a procedure for dealing with secret evidence) in the UK. In May 2010, the Court of Appeal in England and Wales held in *Al-Rawi and Others* that there could be no closed proceedings, with secret evidence hidden from the plaintiffs, in civil suits about IHRL violations in counter-terrorism. Previously, these closed procedures had been used only in Special Immigration Appeals Commission (SIAC) hearings

---

[168] Ibid.
[169] *R v Secretary of State for Foreign and Commonwealth Affairs, ex parte Binyam Mohamed* [2010] EWCA Civ 158, 26 February 2010; see para 3.66.

on deportations and control orders.[170] Lord Neuberger MR reasoned that explicit statutory authority would have been required to justify closed procedures in the context of civil proceedings. In the absence of that statutory authority, 'a litigant's right to know the case against him and to know the reasons why he has lost is fundamental to the notion of a fair trial: an irreducible minimum requirement of an ordinary civil trial.'[171]

National inquiries into CIA secret detention

4.48 National inquiries in Lithuania and Poland into secret detention have led to information and factual admissions, and there are ongoing criminal investigations into secret detention in Poland, Lithuania, Bosnia-Herzegovina, and Macedonia,[172] and additional Freedom of Information Act requests pending in Poland, Macedonia, Albania, and Romania.[173] In contrast to the discoveries in Lithuania and Poland about CIA secret detention centres, the German parliamentary inquiry into the 'extraordinary rendition' of Khaled El-Masri exonerated all German officials who had been alleged to be involved.[174] Likewise, a recent Romanian parliamentary inquiry concluded there had been no Romanian complicity in the operation of the CIA's secret prisons.[175]

4.49 Although this analysis of accountability processes reveals far more impunity, secrecy, and complicity at the national level than at the level of regional courts and supranational institutions, the tide is turning against impunity and secrecy, particularly in UK case law, and in pending investigations on secret detention in Europe. The sweeping state secrets doctrine, and the narrow mandate of Attorney-General Holder's Special Prosecutor, show that comprehensive accountability processes have barely begun in the US. As many of the European cases and inquiries are pending, a full assessment of accountability for IHL and IHRL violations in counter-terrorism will need to wait several years.

Conclusion

4.50 While some precedents exist for the prosecution of terrorism (as defined by IHL) in international criminal law, the International Criminal Court cannot be a forum for

---

[170] *Al-Rawi and Others v Security Service and Others* [2010] EWCA Civ 482.

[171] Ibid, para 30.

[172] Wolfgang Kaleck, 'Justice and Accountability in Europe—Discussing Strategies', in ECCHR Rendition Report, supra, pp 13–27, at p13.

[173] Denise Bentele, Kamil Majchrzak, and Georgios Sotiriadis, in ECCHR Rendition Report, supra, p 59.

[174] Amnesty International Report 2010, Germany.

[175] Human Rights Council, 'Joint Study on the Global Practices in Relation to Secret Detention' A/HRC/13/42, 20 May 2010, para 112, note 189.

prosecuting a defined crime of terrorism. Ad hoc international criminal tribunals may be convened for this purpose, but states retain their obligation from the treaties and UN Security Council Resolutions, discussed in Chapter 1, to prosecute suspected offenders or to extradite them for trial elsewhere. This is subject to prohibitions on *refoulement* in IHRL, and the requirements of a fair trial. Suspects should be tried in civilian criminal courts rather than military courts or commissions. Investigating and prosecuting terrorist attacks is vital not only to combat impunity, and fully to implement states' obligation to prevent and repress terrorism, but also to ensure victims' rights to a remedy and reparation: the subject of Chapter 5.

Ensuring individual criminal responsibility for terrorist attacks is imperative. **4.51** Equally imperative is the obligation to establish individual criminal responsibility for violations of international law committed in counter-terrorism. States must criminalize in their domestic law and prosecute (or extradite for prosecution) those suspected of having perpetrated, ordered, aided, or abetted grave breaches of IHL and serious violations of IHRL, including extrajudicial executions, torture, enforced disappearances, secret detention, and incommunicado detention. States must adhere to IHRL's prohibition on *refoulement* in their extradition practices, and all prosecutions must adhere to international law and standards on the right to a fair trial.

While criminal prosecutions are the gold standard of accountability both for terror- **4.52** ist attacks and for violations in counter-terrorism, states should ensure a full gamut of accountability mechanisms are in place, fully to respect victims' rights to a remedy and reparation. These mechanisms include civil suits, independent national inquiries or truth commissions, the right of individual petition to UN treaty bodies and regional human rights courts, and an open invitation to UN special procedures, the ICRC and regional special mechanisms to document conditions in places of detention and to prevent torture and other ill-treatment. Each of these mechanisms helps to prevent future violations, as Chapter 6 will explain, or respects and ensures victims' rights to a remedy and reparation, as laid out in Chapter 5. However, truth commissions and public inquiries can only be ancillary means of establishing accountability for terrorist attacks and for crimes committed in counter-terrorism operations: they cannot displace states' duties to investigate and prosecute suspected offenders. Whatever the jurisdictional barriers to prosecution, and the inchoate nature of international law on state responsibility, states must ensure individual criminal responsibility in their domestic law both for terrorist attacks and for crimes committed in counter-terrorism operations.

5

VICTIMS' RIGHTS TO A
REMEDY AND REPARATION

Introduction, definitions, and sources

Introduction

As Chapter 3 has shown, victims of human rights violations have a right to an **5.01** effective remedy, and this right is embedded in the structure of IHRL treaties.[1] Under IHRL, victims of torture, arbitrary detention, and enforced disappearance, and the family members of those killed unlawfully, should receive fair compensation.[2] Chapter 4 has documented the scant enforcement of this right as regards the victims of extrajudicial executions, torture, and 'extraordinary rendition' committed in counter-terrorism.[3] Although IHL treaties are silent on whether reparations for violations should be paid to individuals or states,[4] subsequent developments in

---

[1] International Covenant on Civil and Political Rights (ICCPR), Art 2(3); Optional Protocol to the International Covenant on Civil and Political Rights (OP-ICCPR); European Convention for the Protection of Human Rights and Fundamental Freedoms (ECHR), Arts 13, 34; American Convention on Human Rights, Art 63; Convention against Torture and Other Cruel, Inhuman or Degrading Treatment or Punishment, Art 14; International Convention for the Protection of All Persons from Enforced Disappearance (not yet in force as at May 2010), Art 8.

[2] See paras 5.25–5.26; see n 1, supra.

[3] See paras 4.25–4.49.

[4] For a single exception, see Third Geneva Convention, Art 68.

international criminal law[5] and in non-binding standards[6] provide for a right to a remedy and reparation for victims of gross violations of IHL. The right to a remedy and reparation can be understood in several components: the right to truth, the right to justice, and the right to reparation, all of which are defined in the paragraphs below. This chapter examines the development of victims' rights to a remedy and reparation in international law and standards, and examines IHL, IHRL, international criminal law, and the Basic Principles and Guidelines on the Right to a Remedy and Reparation for Victims of Gross Violations of International Human Rights Law and Serious Violations of International Humanitarian Law (Basic Principles and Guidelines).[7]

5.02   Victims of terrorist attacks and victims of violations committed in counter-terrorism all have a right to remedy and reparation, although the legal grounds for these rights differ, and political considerations may affect the award of damages in this area.[8] As explored in Chapter 4, cases such as that of Ahmed Agiza suggest that victims may be better protected by regional human rights courts and international treaty bodies than at the national level. Khaled El-Masri's right to a remedy and reparation was not implemented by domestic courts, although his pending complaints before the European Court of Human Rights (against Macedonia) and the Inter-American Commission on Human Rights (against the US) may be successful.[9] There are some counter-examples, including the controversial 'Eye that Cries' memorial for victims of terrorism and of violations in counter-terrorism in Peru,[10] and the even-handed approach to reparations in the Philippines Comprehensive Agreement on Respect for Human Rights and International Humanitarian Law.[11]

In the counter-terrorism context, the generally poor enforcement of victims' rights to a remedy and reparation is closely linked to the inchoate investigations, state secrecy, and impunity explored by Chapter 4. Although judicial discretion should remain as to the quantum of damages, and as to whether a finding of a violation constitutes just satisfaction,[12] victims' rights to a remedy and to reparation are

---

[5] Rome Statute of the International Criminal Court, Arts 68, 75, 79.

[6] UN Basic Principles and Guidelines on the Right to a Remedy and Reparation for Victims of Gross Violations of International Human Rights Law and Serious Violations of International Humanitarian Law (Basic Principles and Guidelines), adopted by UN General Assembly Resolution 60/147, A/Res/60/147, 16 December 2005.

[7] *Ibid.*

[8] *McCann v United Kingdom* (1995) 21 EHRR 97, para 219; *A and Others v United Kingdom*, Grand Chamber of the European Court of Human Rights, Application No 3455/05, 19 February 2009 (not yet reported), para 252; see para 5.28 below.

[9] For details of the petition before the European Court of Human Rights, see <*http://*www.soros. org/initiatives/justice/litigation/macedonia> and before the Inter-American Commission on Human Rights, see <*http://*www.aclu.org/national-security/el-masri-v-tenet>.

[10] See para 5.52.

[11] Philippines Comprehensive Agreement on Respect for Human Rights and International Humanitarian Law 1998 (Comprehensive Agreement); see para 5.20.

[12] Ibid.

grounded in law and persuasive standards, and should not be stymied by political expediency. In addition to investigating and prosecuting terrorist attacks and crimes committed in counter-terrorism, states should encourage victims' participation in criminal proceedings, civil suits, and public inquiries relating to terrorist attacks and violations of international law committed in counter-terrorist operations. States should make judicial remedies available to victims, and should legislate to implement in enforceable judgments the five types of reparation detailed in the Basic Principles and Guidelines.[13] States should inform victims of the progress of criminal investigations and prosecutions. Where domestic law allows, states should enable victims to participate as parties in criminal proceedings, removing any barriers to the initiation of civil suits for damages and establishing public inquiries into terrorist attacks and allegations of violations of international law committed in counter-terrorist operations. States should consider establishing national compensation funds, supported by UN-administered escrow funds for victims of terrorism, and another for victims of IHL and IHRL violations committed in the course of countering terrorism. These recommendations should be considered alongside the arguments on accountability and reform developed in Chapters 4 and 6 respectively.

Definitions

Victim

The UN Declaration of Basic Principles of Justice for Victims of Crime and Abuse **5.03** of Power emphasizes that the definition of a 'victim' (a) is not dependent upon the arrest, prosecution, or conviction of the perpetrator of a specific crime or abuse of power, (b) may extend to the family members or dependents of a primary victim, and (c) to those who have intervened to assist the victim or prevent his or her victimization.[14] While this UN Declaration is not binding as a matter of treaty law, it was adopted by consensus by the UN General Assembly and can offer useful guidance to judges. While states' obligations (a) to investigate and prosecute serious violations of IHRL,[15] and (b) to search for suspected perpetrators of grave breaches of IHL, prosecuting them or extraditing them,[16] are compatible with victims' right to a remedy and reparation, the definition in the UN Declaration emphasizes that victims have a right to redress even where this duty has not been discharged. The UN Declaration's broadening of the status of 'victim' to include family members or dependants of a primary victim[17] is reflected in established IHRL on the right

---

[13] Basic Principles and Guidelines, Principle 19 (restitution), Principle 20 (compensation), Principle 21 (rehabilitation), Principle 22 (satisfaction), and Principle 23 (guarantees of non-repetition).

[14] UN Declaration of Basic Principles of Justice for Victims of Crime and Abuse of Power, adopted by General Assembly Resolution 40/34 of 29 November 1985, section A(2).

[15] See paras 3.26–3.27, 4.02, 4.25

[16] See paras 2.13 2.71–2.72, 2.74.

[17] See n 14, supra.

to life.[18] The international jurisprudence on enforced disappearance and the new Convention on Enforced Disappearances (which at the time of writing awaits two more ratifications before it can enter into force) also establish that the family members of victims of enforced disappearance can be victims of the right not to be subjected to torture and other cruel, inhuman, or degrading treatment or punishment due to the pain and anguish caused to them by the enforced disappearance.[19] The third broadening[20] of the category of victim beyond the primary victim to include those to intervene to help the victim or prevent his or her victimization is progressive development, and goes beyond existing case law.

Right to truth; right to justice

5.04 Victims' right to a remedy includes the right to know the truth about violations of international law, and about the circumstances surrounding those violations.[21] The right to truth has both an individual and a collective dimension. Individual victims and their families, in addition to society as a whole, have the right to the truth about the causes, facts, circumstances, and identity of the perpetrators of the violations concerned.[22] An individual right to truth can relate to the right of a family member of a victim of enforced disappearance or arbitrary deprivation of life to know the truth about that victim's fate or whereabouts,[23] while a collective right to truth can be fulfilled by an independent and well-resourced public inquiry or truth commission.[24] This requires that the state provide a general (collective) truth as to the structure and mechanisms that enabled the violations to be committed as

---

[18] *McCann v United Kingdom* (1995) 21 EHRR 97 (although relief was denied on other grounds); *Kurt v Turkey* (1999) 27 EHRR 373.

[19] International Convention for the Protection of All Persons from Enforced Disappearance (not yet in force as at May 2010), Art 24(1); see paras 3.84–3.102; see also, *Madoui v Algeria*, UN Human Rights Committee, CCPR/C/94/D/1495/2006 (1 December 2008) at para 7.5; *El Hassy v The Libyan Arab Jamahiriya*, UN Human Rights Committee, CCPR/C/91/D/1422/2005 (13 November 2007) at para 6.11; *El Alwani v The Libyan Arab Jamahiriya,* UN Human Rights Committee, CCPR/C/90/D/1295/2004 (29 August 2007) at para 6.6.

[20] UN Declaration of Basic Principles of Justice for Victims of Crime and Abuse of Power, adopted by General Assembly Resolution 40/34 of 29 November 1985, section A(2), see 14, supra.

[21] UN Basic Principles and Guidelines on the Right to a Remedy and Reparation for Victims of Gross Violations of International Human Rights Law and Serious Violations of International Humanitarian Law, adopted by UN General Assembly Resolution 60/147, A/Res/60/147, 16 December 2005, Principle 24.

[22] Human Rights Council, Resolution 9/11, 'Right to Truth'.

[23] International Convention for the Protection of All Persons from Enforced Disappearance, Art 24(2).

[24] Updated Set of Principles for the Protection and Promotion of Human Rights Through Action to Combat Impunity, submitted to the 61st session of the UN Commission on Human Rights on 8 February 2005, E/CN.4/Res/2005/81, Principle 2, cited in Amnesty International, 'Morocco/Western Sahara: Broken Promises—The Equality and Reconciliation Commission and its Follow-up', MDE 29/001/2010, p 24.

well as an individualized truth about the fate and whereabouts of each victim.[25] A state can fulfil its duty to provide the truth through judicial mechanisms in addition to non-judicial processes such as truth and reconciliation commissions or public inquiries.[26]

Unlike the right to truth, which operates '[i]rrespective of any legal proceedings',[27]   **5.05** the right to justice is dependent on the availability of formal court proceedings. Where a victim of human rights violations is denied access to a court, as Khaled El-Masri has been in the US,[28] or where a lawsuit is blocked because of a state secrets doctrine, as in Maher Arar's case before the Second Circuit Court of Appeals in 2009,[29] this violates his or her right to an effective remedy in IHRL,[30] and risks impunity for human rights violations.[31] The Supreme Court denied *certiorari* of Maher Arar's case before the Second Circuit Court of Appeals in June 2010, without giving reasons.[32] The right to justice is reflected in the provisions for victims' participation in proceedings before the International Criminal Court (ICC).[33] Principle 11 of the Basic Principles and Guidelines provide for victims '(a) Equal and effective access to justice; (b) Adequate, effective and prompt reparation for harm suffered; [and] (c) Access to relevant information concerning violations and reparation mechanisms'.[34]

Reparation

The Rome Statute of the International Criminal Court provides for three types of   **5.06** reparation for victims in Article 75(1): restitution (or the return, as far as possible,

---

[25] International Convention for the Protection of All Persons from Enforced Disappearance, Art 24(2).

[26] Updated Set of Principles for the Protection and Promotion of Human Rights Through Action to Combat Impunity, submitted to the 61st session of the UN Commission on Human Rights on 8 February 2005, E/CN.4/Res/2005/81, Principle 2, cited in Amnesty International, 'Morocco/ Western Sahara: Broken Promises—The Equality and Reconciliation Commission and its Follow-up', MDE 29/001/2010, p 24.

[27] Ibid, Principle 4.

[28] *El-Masri v Tenet*, supra; see para 4.43.

[29] *Arar v Ashcroft et al*, US 2nd Court of Appeals, 06-4216-cv, 2 November 2009.

[30] International Covenant on Civil and Political Rights (ICCPR), Art 2(3); Optional Protocol to the International Covenant on Civil and Political Rights (OP-ICCPR); European Convention for the Protection of Human Rights and Fundamental Freedoms (ECHR), Arts 13, 34; American Convention on Human Rights, Art 63; Convention against Torture and Other Cruel, Inhuman or Degrading Treatment or Punishment, Art 14; International Convention for the Protection of All Persons from Enforced Disappearance (not yet in force as at May 2010), Art 8; UN Declaration on the Protection of All Persons from Enforced Disappearance, Art 19.

[31] Brief for the Redress Trust as *Amicus Curiae* in Support of Plaintiff-Appellant Urging Reversal, *Arar v Ashcroft*, 06-4216-CV, in the US Court of Appeals for the 2nd Circuit (*Arar v Ashcroft*, Redress Trust *amicus curiae* brief).

[32] *Arar v Ashcroft, Former Attorney-General*, 09-923, US Supreme Court Order List 560 US, 14 June 2010.

[33] Rome Statute, Art 68.

[34] Basic Principles and Guidelines, Principle 11.

to the state the victim was in prior to the crime in question); compensation (monetary sums for material and moral damages, to be financed by a Victims Trust Fund);[35] and rehabilitation (covering medical and psycho-social assistance for victims of crimes within the jurisdiction of the ICC).[36]

5.07 The UN Basic Principles and Guidelines have a longer list of reparations: not only restitution (which can include restoration of liberty for a victim of arbitrary detention), compensation, and rehabilitation, but also satisfaction (such as cessation of ongoing violations, an acknowledgement of a violation through a public memorial, an official apology, an investigation and prosecution, or administrative or penal sanctions against the person responsible for the violation), and guarantees of non-repetition (measures to prevent the violations occurring).[37] The Basic Principles and Guidelines also expand rehabilitation to include legal and social assistance to the victim. The Principles and Guidelines insist that victims receive 'full and effective reparation', either with one type of reparation or a combination thereof, in enforceable judgments, which are 'proportional to the gravity of the violation and the circumstances of each case'.[38]

5.08 When it enters into force, the new Convention on Enforced Disappearances will also provide for compensation (referred to in the Convention as 'moral and material damages') and 'where appropriate' the full gamut of reparations considered in the Basic Principles and Guidelines.[39] In the Convention on Enforced Disappearances, 'satisfaction' specifically 'include[s] restoration of dignity and reputation'.[40] When the Convention enters into force, this provision may be used to provide reparation for a victim of enforced disappearance in the context of counter-terrorism, against whom all allegations of involvement in terrorism were untrue.

5.09 All three documents show that reparation is not simply a question of financial compensation, but can be multi-faceted and suited to the needs of an individual victim. States should bear this in mind in their policy-making for victims, and should legislate to make the full range of reparations available to victims of terrorist attacks and to victims of violations of IHL and IHRL committed in the context of counter-terrorism.

Sources

5.10 The right to inter-state reparation has a long history in general international law: in 1928, the Permanent Court of International Justice (PCIJ) held that inter-state

---

[35] Rome Statute, Art 79.
[36] Rome Statute, Art 75.
[37] Basic Principles and Guidelines, Principle 25.
[38] Basic Principles and Guidelines, Principle 18.
[39] International Convention for the Protection of All Persons from Enforced Disappearance, Art 24(4)–(5).
[40] Ibid, Art 25(5)(c).

reparation must be paid for any violation of international law, and that 'there is no necessity [for the duty to pay reparation] to be stated in the convention itself'.[41] States have a responsibility to pay compensation for violations of the IHL relating to international armed conflict, though the treaties are silent on whether compensation should be paid to individual victims or to states.[42] The International Law Commission Articles for the Responsibility of States for Internationally Unlawful Acts (ILC Articles on State Responsibility) do not specify remedies for individual victims.[43] Article 33(2) provides that inter-state reparation is without prejudice to 'any rights, arising from the international responsibility of a State, which may accrue directly to any person or entity other than a State'.[44] Reparation 'shall take the form of restitution, compensation and satisfaction, either singly or in combination'.[45]

In contrast victims' right to an effective remedy for violations of IHRL is embedded **5.11** in the structure of international human rights treaties and in the courts and treaty bodies which supervise their enforcement.[46] The Inter-American Commission of Human Rights has emphasized that protecting victims and implementing victims' right to reparation is central to the 'objective of international human rights law'.[47] This emphasis on victims' right to a remedy and reparation for serious violations of international law can also be found in the Rome Statute of the ICC,[48] and the Basic Principles and Guidelines,[49] supported by the earlier UN Declaration of Basic Principles of Justice for Victims of Crime and Abuse of Power (Basic Principles of Justice).[50] This range of sources suggests the following:

- the duty to provide an effective remedy for violations of IHRL is fully binding on states parties to IHRL treaties;
- the duty to provide reparation for victims of war crimes, crimes against humanity, and genocide as defined by the Rome Statute of the ICC is binding only in relation to cases before the ICC, and to states parties to the Rome Statute; and

---

[41] Permanent Court of International Justice, *Factory at Chorzow (Claim for Indemnity) Case (Germany v Poland)*, Merits, PCIJ Series A, No 17, 1928, pp 21 and 29.

[42] Hague Convention (IV) respecting the Laws and Customs of War on Land, Art 3; Protocol Additional to the Four Geneva Conventions of 12 August 1949, and relating to the Protection of Victims of International Armed Conflicts (Additional Protocol I), Art 91.

[43] ILC Articles on the Responsibility of States for Internationally Unlawful Acts, General Assembly Resolution 56/83, UN Doc A/CN.4/L.602/Rev.1, 26 July 2001, Annex.

[44] Ibid, Art 33(2).

[45] Ibid, Art 34.

[46] See paras 5.25–5.28.

[47] Inter-American Commission on Human Rights, *Juan Carlos Abella v Argentina*, Report No 55/97, Case 11.137, 18 November 1997, para 198.

[48] Rome Statute, Art 75.

[49] Basic Principles and Guidelines.

[50] UN Declaration of Basic Principles of Justice for Victims of Crime and Abuse of Power, adopted by General Assembly resolution 40/34 of 29 November 1985, section A(2).

- the Basic Principles and Guidelines and the earlier Basic Principles of Justice are not binding as a matter of treaty law. The Basic Principles and Guidelines do not create new international law, but instead 'identify mechanisms . . . for the implementation of existing legal obligations' under IHL and IHRL.[51] M Chérif Bassiouni, who drafted the final version of the Basic Principles and Guidelines, finds historic authority for his contention that the notion of 'redress of wrongs' is binding as both a general principle of law and as customary international law 'recognised and applied in all legal systems'.[52] However, this does not establish that the Basic Principles and Guidelines are themselves binding as customary international law. Customary international law requires evidence of widespread and consistent state practice and *opinio juris,* or the subjective belief that the norms in question are binding as law. While the Basic Principles and Guidelines were adopted by the General Assembly, this endorsement does not suggest that UN member states hold the *opinio juris* that the Basic Principles and Guidelines are binding as customary international law. There is very little state practice implementing the Basic Principles and Guidelines, so the required elements of customary international law are not met. The analysis below suggests that some elements of the Basic Principles and Guidelines are progressive development of international law.

Reparation for violations of IHL

IHL and individual remedies

5.12 The responsibility of states for violations of IHL relating to international armed conflicts is found in the text of Article 3 of the Hague Convention (IV) respecting the Laws and Customs of War on Land of 1907, which is almost exactly replicated in Article 91 of Protocol Additional to the Four Geneva Conventions of 12 August 1949 and relating to the Protection of Victims of International Armed Conflicts (Additional Protocol I).[53] These Articles provide that a belligerent or party to an international armed conflict which violates IHL, 'shall be responsible for all acts committed by persons forming part of its armed forces'[54] and 'shall, if the case demands, be liable to pay compensation'.[55] This is a reference to monetary compensation only, for any violations of applicable IHL by any member of the armed forces

---

[51] Basic Principles and Guidelines, preambular para 7.
[52] M Chérif Bassiouni, 'International Recognition of Victims' Rights' (2006) 6 *Human Rights Law Review* 203–279 at 207.
[53] Space precludes discussion of restitution for violations of the Hague Convention for the Protection of Cultural Property 1954, contained within its Protocol, cited by Emanuela-Chiara Gillard (2003) 85 *International Review of the Red Cross* 529–553 at 533.
[54] Additional Protocol I, Art 91.
[55] Ibid.

of a party to the conflict: not only violations of IHL which are ordered by a central command. The treaty articles are silent on whether this compensation should be paid to the other party to the conflict or to individual victims. Although a duty to pay reparation features in the Second Protocol to the Hague Convention on the Protection of Cultural Property,[56] there is no explicit duty to pay reparation in IHL treaty law relating to non-international armed conflicts. The International Committe of the Red Cross (ICRC) Study on Customary IHL indicates a number of examples from state practice where reparations have been sought from either state armed forces or armed groups, in international and non-international armed conflicts.[57]

The ICRC Commentary to Article 91 of Additional Protocol I indicates that indi- **5.13** vidual victims were contemplated by this wording. At the Hague Conference which led to the adoption of Hague Convention (IV), it was noted that 'any recourse by wronged persons was considered illusory if this could not be exercised against the government of the perpetrators of those violations, through their own government'.[58] M Chérif Bassiouni believes that the Hague Conventions are authority for the right of the state of nationality of a victim of an IHL violation to request compensation on behalf of their citizens, as distinct from an individual right to a remedy against a state for a violation of IHL.[59] Bassiouni sees this as 'damages based on the injuries of individuals', which do not 'give rise to an individual right of legal action against a state'.[60]

Christian Tomuschat agrees that IHL provides no individual right to reparation. **5.14** Tomuschat sceptically notes the 'scarce' state practice on reparation compiled by the ICRC Study on Customary International Humanitarian Law.[61] A closer look at the relevant pages in the ICRC Customary IHL Study shows numerous examples of individual reparations post-conflict, in the Ethiopia–Eritrea Claims Commission, the UN Compensation Commission established to grant damages for losses resulting from Iraq's invasion of Kuwait in 1991, and numerous post-Second World War reparations policies in Austria, Germany, and France. The key difference is that few of these examples of state practice relate reparations explicitly to a breach of IHL.

The ICRC Commentary notes that the article makes 'no distinction . . . between **5.15** the victor and the vanquished, nor between a Party which is presumed to have resorted to force unlawfully and a Party which is believed only to have exercised its

---

[56] Jean Marie Henckaerts and Louise Doswald-Beck, *Customary International Humanitarian Law, Volume 1: Rules* (International Committee of the Red Cross and Cambridge University Press, 2005), p 537.
[57] Ibid, Rule 150.
[58] J Pictet (ed), *ICRC Commentary*, Art 91, p 1054.
[59] M Chérif Bassiouni, 'International Recognition of Victims' Rights' (2006) 6 Hum Rts L Rev 203–279 at 213.
[60] Ibid.
[61] Henckaerts and Doswald-Beck, supra, pp 541–545, cited in Christian Tomuschat, *Human Rights: Between Idealism and Realism* (2nd edn, OUP, 2008), pp 367–368.

right to self-defence'.[62] This emphasizes that reparations are due from any state which violates IHL. IHL authorizes neither one-sided 'victor's justice', nor reparations relating to the international law on the use of force (*jus ad bellum*). Emanuela-Chiara Gillard emphasizes the all-inclusive phrasing of Article 3 of Hague Convention (IV) and Article 91 of Additional Protocol I: reparations are due from all violations of IHL relating to international armed conflict, not just from the grave breaches which trigger the obligation to prosecute or extradite suspected offenders.[63]

5.16 The remaining paragraphs of this section consider potential reparations under IHL for victims of IHL's specific meaning of the term 'terrorism' and 'acts or threat of violence the primary purpose of which is to spread terror among the civilian population', and victims of violations of IHL committed in counter-terrorism operations. Paragraphs 5.35–5.37 below will examine the potential for reparations for violations of IHL in non-international armed conflict where such violations amount to genocide, war crimes, or crimes against humanity.

Reparations for victims of 'terrorism' and 'spread[ing] terror among a civilian population'

5.17 Chapter 2, paragraphs 2.22–2.32 explored the meaning of 'terrorism' and 'acts or threat of violence the primary purpose of which is to spread terror among the civilian population' in IHL, noting that these terms are used in a context-specific, particular way in IHL; that they apply in international and non-international armed conflict,[64] and reflect the principle of distinction between combatants and civilians. In IHL, 'terrorism' is prohibited where it is perpetrated by state armed forces in international armed conflicts or by either state armed forces or organized armed groups in non-international armed conflicts regulated by Additional Protocol II. While 'terrorism' is not listed as a grave breach in Article 147 of the Fourth Geneva Convention, it remains a violation of IHL.

5.18 States responsible for 'terrorism' and 'acts or threat of violence the primary purpose of which is to spread terror among the civilian population', as these concepts are defined in IHL, should pay 'compensation' under Article 3 of Hague Convention (IV) and Article 91 of Additional Protocol I. The only question is whether that 'compensation' should be paid directly to an individual or to a government on behalf of its citizens who are the victims of the violation. For this argument to succeed, victims litigating for damages would have to invoke both

---

[62] J Pictet (ed), *ICRC Commentary*, Art 91, p 1055.

[63] Emanuela-Chiara Gillard, 'Reparations for Violations of International Humanitarian Law' (2003) 85 *International Review of the Red Cross* 529–553 at 534.

[64] Fourth Geneva Convention, Art 33; Additional Protocol I, Art 51(2); Additional Protocol I, Art 4(2)(d), 13(2).

IHL treaty law prohibiting 'terrorism', 'acts or threat of violence the primary purpose of which is to spread terror among the civilian population', or the deliberate targeting of civilians from which these concepts derive; and the non-binding Basic Principles and Guidelines. The deliberate targeting of civilians in international or non-international armed conflict qualifies as a 'serious violation of IHL' and the threshold of a 'crime in international law' required by the Basic Principles and Guidelines.[65] Where this targeting of civilians amounts to 'terrorism' in IHL's specific sense of the term, victims of that 'terrorism' have a right to a remedy and reparations.

The Report of the UN Fact-Finding Mission on Operation Cast Lead made two **5.19** skilful points on victims' right to a remedy and reparation for serious violations of IHL.[66] Having concluded that at least one fléchette missile attack on civilians by the Israeli Defence Forces was intended to 'spread terror among the civilian population',[67] and that there was 'significant evidence to suggest that one of the primary purposes of' Hamas' rocket and mortar shells was to 'spread terror' among the Israeli population,[68] the Report first ensured that public hearings were held in Gaza and Geneva for victims from the Gaza Strip and Israel respectively,[69] and second recommended that the General Assembly establish an escrow fund to provide reparation for the Palestinian victims of the conflict,[70] in addition to the potential for reparations in Israeli domestic law.[71] Reparations can be provided for Israeli victims through Israel's Compensation for Victims of Terrorism Law 1970,[72] which includes a comprehensive strategy for rehabilitation, burial costs, and educational costs for victims of terrorism and their families.[73]

The Philippines Comprehensive Agreement on Respect for Human Rights and **5.20** International Humanitarian Law 1998 (Comprehensive Agreement) binds the government and the National Democratic Front of the Philippines to provide reparations for victims of violations committed by either side in this non-international armed conflict.[74] While the Comprehensive Agreement does not refer to IHL's prohibition of 'terrorism' or 'spread[ing] terror among the civilian

---

[65] Basic Principles and Guidelines, Principle 4; see para 5.41.
[66] Report of the United Nations Fact-Finding Mission on the Gaza Conflict, UN Doc A/HRC/12/48, 15 September 2009.
[67] Ibid, para 880.
[68] Ibid, para 108, see also para 1722.
[69] Ibid, para 141.
[70] Ibid, paras 1768, 1757.
[71] Ibid, paras1666, 1667, 1757.
[72] Compensation for Victims of Terrorism Law 1970.
[73] Permanent Mission of Israel to the UN, Statement by Ambassador Daniel Carmon to the 63rd session of the General Assembly, 9 September 2008.
[74] Comprehensive Agreement on Respect for Human Rights and International Humanitarian Law between the Government of the Philippines and the National Democratic Front of the Philippines, 16 March 1998, see especially Part III, Art 3.

population', Article 2(b) of Part II 'affirm[s] and appl[ies]' the principle of distinction between combatants and civilians and civilians' immunity from attack.[75]

5.21 In contrast, Colombia has a mixed record on reparations for victims. The Justice and Peace Law, promulgated in 2005, allowed demobilized paramilitary members to avoid extradition to the US and lengthy prison terms for drug trafficking or attacks on civilians, in return for confessions as to their involvement in paramilitary activity.[76] The Justice and Peace Law has been criticized by NGOs, *inter alia* for limiting access to reparations.[77] The Office for the High Commissioner for Human Rights (OHCHR) has noted that insufficient resources have been allocated to reparations under the Trust Fund for victims established under Law 975 and Decree 1290 (2008) on the administrative reparations programme.[78] During the first cycle of the UN Human Rights Council Universal Periodic Review mechanism, France noted deficiencies in the law's provisions for reparations. It stated that:

> It noted also that the Justice and Peace Law made possible the demobilization of about 31,000 paramilitaries and a considerable reduction in violence, but was concerned at the low rate of criminal prosecutions and that the rights of victims to justice, truth and reparations was not sufficiently integrated.[79]

The OHCHR noted the multiple cease-fire violations by paramilitaries, despite the law; and Human Rights Watch reported that the demobilization process hampered investigation of alleged IHL violations, rendering reparations impossible.[80] In June 2009, Colombia's Congress failed to pass a Victims' Bill, leading the OHCHR to conclude that Colombia has still to implement the right to reparation for victims of paramilitary groups and victims of state violence.[81]

Reparations for victims of violations of IHRL committed by states in their counter-terrorism operations

5.22 A Higher Council for Reparations to Victims of the Former Regime in Iraq began work in 2004, to provide compensation to victims of Saddam Hussein's regime in Iraq.[82] This was bolstered by the promulgation of two laws in 2005 to provide

---

[75] Ibid, Part II, Art 2(b).

[76] Ley de Justicia y Paz (Justice and Peace Law), Law 975 of 2005.

[77] International Center for Transitional Justice (ICTJ), Amicus brief on Law 975 submitted to the Constitutional Court of Colombia, 17 January 2006.

[78] Report of the United Nations High Commissioner for Human Rights on the situation of human rights in Colombia, A.HRC/13/72, 4 March 2010, para 84.

[79] Human Rights Council, 'Report of the Working Group on the Universal Periodic Review: Colombia', A/HRC/10/82, 9 January 2009, para 27.

[80] Human Rights Watch, 'Smoke and Mirrors: Colombia's Demobilisation of Paramilitary Groups', 31 July 2005, V. The Government's Record to Date.

[81] Report of the United Nations High Commissioner for Human Rights on the situation of human rights in Colombia, A.HRC/13/72, 4 March 2010, para 85.

[82] ICTJ, 'Iraq'.

reparations to former political prisoners and the families of those killed by the Saddam Hussein regime.[83] An additional Accountability and Justice Law, promulgated in January 2008, also provides for reparations for victims of Saddam Hussein's regime.[84] However, there has been no system for reparations for victims of IHL violations in the international and then non-international armed conflict in Iraq since 2003. This is a significant omission: although there is no treaty-based duty to provide individual remedies or reparations for violations of IHL in the Four Geneva Conventions or their Additional Protocols, the Basic Principles and Guidelines considered in paragraphs 5.38–5.53 below do provide for reparations for victims of serious violations of IHL.

In other conflicts which include counter-terrorism operations, victims' right to a **5.23** remedy and reparation for serious violations of IHL has been honoured far more in the breach than the observance. Victims have not received reparation for violations of IHL committed in Afghanistan, despite recommendations to this effect from NGOs,[85] a recent civil action in Germany,[86] and the establishment of a Trust Fund by UN Security Council Resolution 1386 (2001).[87]

Sri Lanka established a Commission of Inquiry shortly following the killings of **5.24** French aid workers in 2006 in the non-international armed conflict between the Sri Lankan armed forces and the LTTE.[88] Despite the efforts of the OHCHR to increase witness protection and ensure even-handedness in the Commission of Inquiry, and to urge the Sri Lankan government to establish an independent international investigation into violations of IHL, civilian victims of the conflict remain without redress. A special session of the UN Human Rights Council on human rights in Sri Lanka failed to call for an investigation into alleged violations of international law or to refer to the post-conflict internment of Tamils,[89] and instead welcomed the Sri Lankan government's record on human rights.[90] Human Rights Watch has indicated a lack of independence and impartiality in the existing domestic inquiries into the conflict in Sri Lanka.[91]

---

[83] Ibid.

[84] Accountability and Justice Law, Art 3, cited in ICTJ, 'Briefing Paper: Iraq's New "Accountability and Justice" Law', 22 January 2008, p 8.

[85] Amnesty International, 'Afghanistan: NATO Must Ensure Justice for Victims of Torture and Civilian Deaths', 27 November 2006.

[86] Deutsche Welle, 'Relatives of Kunduz Airstrike Victims Seek Reparation', 21 November 2009.

[87] UN Security Council Resolution 1386 (2001), 20 December 2001, operative para 8.

[88] See paras 2.108–2.113.

[89] Human Rights Watch, 'Sri Lanka: UN Rights Council Fails Victims', 27 May 2009.

[90] UN Human Rights Council, 11th special session, The Human Rights Situation In Sri Lanka, Resolution S-11/1, 27 May 2009.

[91] Human Rights Watch, 'Sri Lanka: Domestic Inquiry into Abuses a Smokescreen', 27 October 2009.

The right to an effective remedy, to investigation, and compensation for violations of IHRL

The right to an effective remedy for violations of IHRL

5.25   In contrast to the ambiguities in IHL as to whether individual victims have a right to compensation, victims have a right to an effective remedy for violations of the International Covenant on Civil and Political Rights (ICCPR),[92] the International Convention for the Elimination of All Forms of Racial Discrimination (ICERD),[93] the Convention against Torture,[94] and a range of regional treaties.[95] This right is embedded in the structure of international human rights treaties and in the courts and treaty bodies which supervise their enforcement.[96] The Inter-American system has the best developed jurisprudence in this area. The Inter-American Commission of Human Rights has emphasized that protecting victims and implementing victims' right to reparation is central to the 'objective of international human rights law',[97] while the Inter-American Court of Human Rights (IACtHR) has found that the right to remedy 'is one of the fundamental pillars of the rule of law in a democratic society'.[98] The IACtHR held that 'States must prevent, investigate and punish any violation of [the ACHR] and . . . if possible to restore the right violated and provide compensation as warranted for damages resulting from the violation'.[99] As the jurisprudence has developed, the range of reparations granted has expanded, to include pecuniary compensation, medical rehabilitation services, and educational costs.[100] This requires enforceable domestic remedies, implemented by the states parties to IHRL treaties, and not simply the international and regional scrutiny of regional human rights courts and the UN human rights system, although these regional human rights courts may be empowered to award 'just satisfaction' to the victims of violations.[101] Remedies must not be illusory:[102] they must be capable of addressing the violation of the particular right which has been infringed.[103]

---

[92] ICCPR, Art 2(3).

[93] ICERD, Art 6.

[94] Convention against Torture, Art 14.

[95] ECHR, Art 15; ACHR, Art 25.

[96] Optional Protocol to the International Covenant on Civil and Political Rights (OP-ICCPR); European Convention for the Protection of Human Rights and Fundamental Freedoms (ECHR), Arts 13, 34; American Convention on Human Rights, Art 63.

[97] *Juan Carlos Abella v Argentina*, Report No 55/97, Case 11.137, 18 November 1997, para 198.

[98] Inter-American Court of Human Rights, *Blake v Guatemala (Reparations)*, 22 January 1999, Series A) No 48, para 63.

[99] Inter-American Court of Human Rights, *Velásquez Rodriguez v Honduras* [1989] 28 ILM 291, para 166; see also para 3.36.

[100] Inter-American Court of Human Rights, *Barrios Altos v Peru,* Judgment of 30 November 2001, Series C, No 87.

[101] ECHR, Art 50.

[102] Human Rights Committee, General Comment No 29, States of Emergency (Article 4), CCPR/C/21/Rev.1/Add.11, 31 August 2001, para 14.

[103] *Aksoy v Turkey* (1996) 23 EHRR 553.

In addition to the right to an effective remedy for all violations of IHRL, states are **5.26**
obliged to investigate cases of arbitrary deprivation of life,[104] torture,[105] and enforced
disappearance;[106] to provide an enforceable right to fair and adequate compensation for victims of torture,[107] arbitrary detention,[108] and miscarriages of justice;[109]
while, if and when the Enforced Disappearances Convention enters into force, the
victims of enforced disappearance will be entitled to 'reparation and prompt, fair
and adequate compensation',[110] and the right to truth.[111] In the Inter-American
system, reparation for enforced disappearance may include the exhumation of a
victim's remains, and their return to the victim's family.[112]

General Comment No 31 of the Human Rights Committee emphasizes that the **5.27**
'failure to bring to justice' perpetrators of torture, arbitrary killings, and enforced
disappearance 'could in and of itself give rise to a separate breach' of the ICCPR,
which gives rise to the right to an effective remedy.[113] There is an overlap between
states' obligation to investigate and prosecute serious violations of IHRL and a
victim's right to an effective remedy for violations of IHRL. In *Selmouni v France*,
the European Court of Human Rights held that an effective remedy for violations
of Article 3 (the prohibition on torture and inhuman or degrading treatment or
punishment) required a thorough, effective investigation which could lead to the
identification and punishment of the perpetrators.[114]

In *Juan Carlos Abella v Argentina*,[115] the IACtHR identified the provision of repar- **5.28**
ation as one of the central purposes of IHRL. The UN Human Rights Committee's
General Comment No 31 shows that the grant of effective remedies is a requirement of Article 2(3) of the ICCPR: there is no reference to a state's discretion not
to investigate alleged violations of the ICCPR, or to fail to grant reparation in any

---

[104] European Court of Human Rights, *Mahmut Kaya v Turkey* (28 March 2000); *Ergi v Turkey*
(2001) 23 EHRR 388; *Finucane v United Kingdom* (2003) 37 EHRR 29; Inter-American Court of
Human Rights, *Velásquez Rodríguez v Honduras* [1989] 28 ILM 291; *Bámaca Velásquez v Guatemala*,
25 November 2000; *Barrios Altos v Peru*, 14 March 2001; *Goiburú et al v Paraguay*, 22 September
2006; *Almonacid-Arellano et al v Chile*, 26 September 2006.
[105] Convention against Torture, Art 12.
[106] See paras 3.87, 3.90–3.101.
[107] Convention against Torture, Art 14.
[108] ICCPR, Art 9(5); ECHR, Art 5(4).
[109] ICCPR, Art 14(6).
[110] International Convention for the Protection of All Persons from Enforced Disappearance (not
yet in force), Art 24(1).
[111] Ibid, Art 24(2).
[112] Inter-American Court of Human Rights, *Bámaca Velásquez v Guatemala*, Judgment,
Reparations, 22 February 2002.
[113] Human Rights Committee General Comment No 31, The Nature of the General Legal
Obligation Imposed on State Parties, CCPR/C/21/Rev.1/Add.13, 26 May 2004, para 18.
[114] *Selmouni v France* (1999) 29 EHRR 403, para 79.
[115] *Juan Carlos Abella v Argentina*, Report No 55/97, Case 11.137, 18 November 1997, para 198.

of the forms considered in the General Comment.[116] However, for the European Court of Human Rights, monetary compensation is a discretionary remedy: 'just satisfaction' under Article 41 of the ECHR may be provided 'if necessary'. The finding of a violation may be deemed to be sufficient 'just satisfaction' for a victim of a violation under IHRL so that there was no financial remedy for the family members of the IRA members killed on Gibraltar Rock, despite the Court finding a violation of Article 2 ECHR.[117] The Court did not 'consider it appropriate' to award monetary damages, 'having regard to the fact that the three terrorist suspects who were killed had been intending to plant a bomb in Gibraltar'.[118] This contrasts with the Court's approach in *A and Others v United Kingdom*, where non-nationals detained under the Anti-Terrorism, Crime and Security Act 2001 received limited monetary compensation of €4,000 each for violations of Article 5(1) ECHR.[119] Although there is a role for regional and national courts to decide whether financial compensation is appropriate in the individual case, states should respect and ensure victims' right to a remedy and reparation—whether they are victims of terrorist attacks or victims of violations of international law in counter-terrorism operations.

Remedies for victims of terrorist attacks

5.29 IHRL does confer an obligation on a state which is responsible for terrorist attacks to provide effective remedies in its domestic law for victims of that violation of the right to life.[120] Similar obligations exist where paramilitaries affiliated to a state arbitrarily deprive citizens of their lives, abduct them, or take hostages.[121]

5.30 As the IHRL chapter makes clear, non-state terrorist groups are not bound *de jure* by IHRL.[122] Instead, states have a due diligence obligation to prevent, investigate, and prosecute violations of the right to life by non-state actors, which includes non-state terrorist groups.[123] However, an effective remedy for violation of that due diligence obligation would be provided by the state if a court found a violation of the relevant rights: not by individuals convicted of terrorist attacks. A victim seeking damages from a convicted terrorist would have to pursue an action in private

---

[116] Human Rights Committee, General Comment No 31, CCPR/C/21/Rev.1/Add.13, 26 May 2004.

[117] *McCann v United Kingdom* (1995) 21 EHRR 97.

[118] Ibid, para 219.

[119] *A and Others v United Kingdom*, Grand Chamber of the European Court of Human Rights, Application No 3455/05, Judgment of 19 February 2009 (not yet reported), para 252.

[120] Also see the analysis of state terrorism and state sponsorship of terrorism in paras 1.13–1.15 and 6.07–6.09.

[121] Report of the UN Special Rapporteur on Extralegal, Summary and Arbitrary Executions to the 61st session of the UN Commission on Human Rights, E/CN.4/2005/7, para 69; Report of the UN Special Rapporteur on Extralegal, Summary and Arbitrary Executions to the 60th session of the UN Commission on Human Rights, E/CN.4/2004/7, cited in para 3.109.

[122] See para 3.109.

[123] Inter-American Court of Human Rights, *Velásquez Rodriguez v Honduras* [1989] 28 ILM 291. See also paras 3.01-3.02, 3.14, 3.16.

law: it would not be the domestic implementation of the right to an effective remedy under IHRL.

The victims of terrorism and their families do have a right to remedy and reparation **5.31** under the Basic Principles and Guidelines, where the terrorist acts in question qualify as gross violations of IHL or serious violations of IHRL. The role of public inquiries, of compensation, rehabilitation, satisfaction, and guarantees of non-repetition for victims of terrorism will be considered in paragraphs 5.42–5.48 below.

Remedies for victims when states' counter-terrorism policies or operations violate IHRL

Chapters 3 and 4 discussed the settlement of monetary compensation for the **5.32** family of Baha Mousa, who suffered torture and died in UK custody in Iraq;[124] and the case of Jean Charles de Menezes, killed in error as a suspected suicide bomber by armed police in London in July 2005.[125] These payments of compensation represent inadequate processes of investigation and prosecution in each case. In Baha Mousa's case, Corporal Donald Payne was convicted of inhumane treatment, while no defendants were prosecuted for arbitrary deprivation of life; and in the de Menezes case, the Metropolitan Police were convicted only of offences under health and safety legislation. In neither case was criminal responsibility established for the arbitrary deprivation of life. These cases illustrate the overlap between duties of accountability (the obligation to investigate and prosecute violations) and victims' right to a remedy and reparation. In both cases, the family members' right to compensation was nominally respected, but without the concomitant right to truth and right to justice. In other words, money was paid, but the full context shows an inadequate grasp of the right to an effective remedy in IHRL. Victims' right to remedy and reparation is not dependent upon the violator's conviction in a criminal trial, but monetary compensation does not remove the obligation to conduct an effective investigation and, where evidence exists, to prosecute. As Redress noted in an *amicus curiae* brief prior to Maher Arar's unsuccessful appeal to the US 2nd Circuit Court of Appeals, victims' right to an effective remedy 'is necessary . . . to ensure' that IHRL (in Arar's case the principle of *non-refoulement*) is 'practical and effective', and to avoid impunity for violations of this right.[126]

The extensive reliance of some states on a state secrets doctrine presents grave con- **5.33** cern for victims' rights to a remedy and reparation, although judges do have an important role in adjudicating between a state's interest to maintain its national security and individual rights in litigation. As Chapter 6 argues, while there may be legitimate reasons for evidence relating to matters of national security to be heard

---

[124] See paras 3.49–3.50, 3.33, 3.44, and 4.36.
[125] See paras 3.33 and 3.44.
[126] *Arar v Ashcroft*, Redress Trust *amicus curiae* brief, supra, p 1.

in camera, judges should not accept uncritically mere assertions on the part of the executive or intelligence agencies that particular evidence is too sensitive to be examined. Such assertions should be backed by strong evidence which again can be heard *in camera*. Moreover, a state secrets privilege should not be asserted to prevent the consideration by a court of evidence relating to violations of IHL or IHRL, or otherwise to forestall the investigation, prosecution, or civil suits relating to such violations.[127]

- Until the publication of seven formerly redacted paragraphs in February 2010, the prolonged litigation in the case of Binyam Mohamed is one such example of lengthy and wide-ranging reliance on a state secrets doctrine.[128]
- In Italy's successful prosecution of 22 CIA operatives and one military officer in Abu Omar's case, state secrets were invoked to prevent the examination of evidence and, as noted in Chapters 3 and 4, the US refused to extradite the individual suspects, who were later convicted *in absentia*.[129] According to reports from Human Rights Watch, Italian Prosecutor Amando Spataro planned to appeal against US cases which invoked the state secrets doctrine.[130]
- In June 2010, the Supreme Court denied Maher Arar's petition for *certiorari* following the dismissal of his civil suit by the Court of Appeals for the 2nd Circuit in November 2009.[131] The Supreme Court did not provide reasons for dismissing the petition for *certiorari*. However, the majority of the Court of Appeals ruled that Mr Arar did not have standing to obtain relief relating to torture allegedly committed outside the US. There were also pressures relating to national security. The majority reasoned that 'special factors', including foreign policy and national security, precluded a Bivens suit (a private cause of action to enforce constitutional rights); and that Congress should specifically authorize such a cause of action if there was a risk that the case would impact on foreign policy or national security.[132]
- In contrast, in September 2008, and without the government invoking a state secrets doctrine, Sweden granted Ahmed Agiza compensation for his unlawful transfer to torture in violation of Article 3 of the Convention against Torture.[133]

---

[127] See paras 6.02, and 7.21.
[128] *R (Binyam Mohamed) v Secretary of State for Foreign and Commonwealth Affairs* [2010] EWCA Civ 158; see paras 3.66, 4.46.
[129] See paras 3.68 and 4.32–4.33.
[130] Human Rights Watch, 'Italy/US: Italian Court Rebukes CIA Rendition Practice', 4 November 2009.
[131] *Arar v Ashcroft, Former Attorney-General*, 09-923, US Supreme Court Order List 560 US, 14 June 2010; David Cole, 'Getting Away With Torture' NYRB, 16 December 2009.
[132] *Arar v Ashcroft et al*, US 2nd Court of Appeals, 06-4216-cv, 2 November 2009; see para 3.65.
[133] The compensation payment was made in September 2008: International Commission of Jurists submission on the Universal Periodic Review of Sweden, Human Rights Council, 8th session of the Working Group on Universal Periodic Review, 3–14 May 2010, November 2009, p 2.

Victims of arbitrary detention, miscarriages of justice, and enforced disappearance **5.34** committed during counter-terrorism operations also have rights under IHRL to compensation. The IHRL chapter notes the failures of the Russian Federation to implement the judgments of the European Court of Human Rights relating to unlawful killings and enforced disappearances in Chechnya and Ingushetia.[134] All victims of violations of IHRL have a right to an effective remedy, whether or not this takes the form of monetary compensation. Where states fail to implement judgments or rely unjustifiably on state secrets doctrines, this violates the right to an effective remedy for violations of IHRL.

Reparations in international criminal law

The right to reparation before the International Criminal Court

Prior to the Rome Statute of the International Criminal Court (ICC), there was no **5.35** treaty to provide for victims' right to reparation for international crimes,[135] nor for victims' participation in the international criminal process.[136] Both the International Criminal Tribunal for Rwanda (ICTR) and the International Criminal Tribunal for the former Yugoslavia (ICTY) had Victim and Witness Units to protect the safety of victims and witnesses, but they did not provide for victims' right to a remedy and reparations. Victims may obtain reparation, in the form of restitution, compensation, or rehabilitation, for any of the crimes within the jurisdiction of the ICC: genocide, war crimes, or crimes against humanity. Chapter 4 has sketched the possible prosecution of terrorist attacks before the ICC if they amount to genocide, war crimes, or crimes against humanity; and of war crimes and crimes against humanity committed in counter-terrorism operations. This chapter will simply note that the Rome Statute provides for victims' participation and reparations to victims, financed in the first instance by fines and forfeiture of the proceeds of crime of those convicted,[137] or by a Victims' Trust Fund.[138]

The ICC has not yet rendered its first judgment in any case, and there is no juris- **5.36** prudence to assess on victims' right to a remedy and reparation in relation to terrorism or counter-terrorism. Although the Office of the Prosecutor of the ICC has conducted preliminary inquiries relating to war crimes which are alleged to have been committed in Afghanistan,[139] and although there is a possibility of

---

[134] See paras 3.93–3.95.
[135] Rome Statute, Art 75.
[136] Ibid, Art 68.
[137] Ibid, Art 77.
[138] Ibid, Art 79.
[139] ICC Office of the Prosecutor (OTP) Weekly Briefing, 6–12 April 2010, II.1, Afghanistan; Luis Moreno-Ocampo, Prosecutor of the ICC, Keynote Address at the Council on Foreign Relations, 4 February 2010, p 8.

Security Council referral of war crimes and crimes against humanity committed in Operation Cast Lead following the report of the UN Fact-Finding Mission on that conflict, it is impossible to predict at this stage whether these cases will pass the jurisdictional and evidential hurdles to prosecution, and whether victims will be given reparations for international crimes committed in these conflicts.

The right to reparation before hybrid tribunals

5.37 The Statute of the Special Tribunal for Lebanon (STL) provides for victims to participate in the proceedings,[140] and allows the STL to identify 'victims who have suffered harm as a result of the commission of crimes by an accused convicted by the Tribunal'.[141] 'Based on the decision of the Special Tribunal and pursuant to the relevant national legislation', these victims can then seek compensation by 'bring[ing] an action in a national court or other competent body to obtain compensation'.[142] Victims can only receive compensation under these strict conditions, and a decision of the Special Tribunal under Article 25(1) is final,[143] with no possibility of appeal. This is far from an implementation of the five types of reparation outlined in the Basic Principles and Guidelines, as the following paragraphs will explain. The STL will not therefore offer thoroughgoing reparations to victims of terrorism. This restrictive approach is regrettable.

The Basic Principles and Guidelines on the Right to a Remedy and Reparation

Non-binding yet enforceable?

5.38 The Basic Principles and Guidelines on the Right to a Remedy and Reparation for Victims of Gross Violations of International Humanitarian Law and Serious Violations of International Human Rights Law (the Basic Principles and Guidelines) were adopted in Resolution 60/147 of the UN General Assembly in 2005.[144] The Resolution calls on states to disseminate and to promote respect for the Basic Principles among executive, legislative, and judicial branches of government, military and security forces, law enforcement officials, human rights defenders, the media, and the general public.[145] Restitution, compensation, rehabilitation, satisfaction, or guarantees of non-repetition should be the subject of enforceable

---

[140] Statute of the Special Tribunal for Lebanon, Security Council Resolution 1757 (2007), Art 17.
[141] Ibid, Art 25(1).
[142] Ibid, Art 25(3).
[143] Ibid, Art 25(4).
[144] UN General Assembly Resolution 60/147 of 16 December 2005.
[145] Ibid, operative para 2

judgments, and granted 'proportional[ly] to the gravity of the violation and the circumstances of each case'.[146]

While General Assembly Resolutions do not create binding international law on a par with treaties and customary international law, they can reflect existing custom, authoritative interpretations of international law, and general principles of law.[147] The Basic Principles and Guidelines derive from and catalogue victims' rights to a remedy and reparation in existing international law. The Preamble to the Basic Principles and Guidelines references these existing obligations in international and regional human rights treaties, IHL relating to international armed conflicts, and the Rome Statute of the ICC. These binding treaties oblige states to make enforceable victims' right to a remedy and reparation. To this extent, the Basic Principles and Guidelines codify existing international law and are binding on states.   **5.39**

However, the Basic Principles and Guidelines contain elements of progressive development of international treaty law. The typology of restitution, compensation, rehabilitation, satisfaction, and guarantees of non-repetition (defined in Principles 18–23) goes further than that in Article 78 of the Rome Statute of the ICC, which only permits the first three types of reparation to victims. This five-part structure of reparations has been adopted in the new Convention on Enforced Disappearances, which awaits two more ratifications before it can enter into force.   **5.40**

The requirement of severity

The obligations in the Basic Principles and Guidelines restate existing IHRL, IHL (relating to international armed conflict), and provisions of the Rome Statute for the ICC. There is a strong overlap between states' duty to investigate and prosecute international crimes as defined in the Rome Statute and the victims' right to a remedy in the Basic Principles of Guidelines; and between the international crimes in the Rome Statute and the concepts of 'gross' and 'serious' violations of international law.[148] These adjectives refer to the severity of violations rather than their prevalence: a single instance of torture triggers an enforceable right to compensation under Article 14 of the Convention against Torture, and the victims' right to a remedy and reparation under the Basic Principles and Guidelines.[149]   **5.41**

---

[146] Basic Principles and Guidelines, Principles 18–23.

[147] Peter Malunczuk and Michael Barton Akehurst, *Akehurst's Modern Introduction to International Law* (7th edn, Routledge, 1997), p 397.

[148] Final Report submitted by Mr Theo van Boven, Special Rapporteur, Study concerning the right to restitution, compensation and rehabilitation for victims of gross violations of human rights and fundamental freedoms, E/CN.4/Sub.2/1993/8, 2 July 1993, para 8.

[149] Redress Trust, 'Implementing Victims' Rights: A Handbook on the Basic Principles and Guidelines on the Right to a Remedy and Reparation', March 2006, p 12.

However, Principle 26 of the Basic Principles and Guidelines emphasizes that the document is without prejudice to the duty to provide an effective remedy for victims of all violations of IHRL and IHL.[150]

Using the basic principles and guidelines to provide remedies for victims of terrorism

5.42 Applying the Basic Principles and Guidelines to victims of terrorism presents an initial hurdle: the Basic Principles and Guidelines apply only to gross violations of IHL and serious violations of IHRL. In order for the Basic Principles and Guidelines to apply to a terrorist attack, that attack must reach the threshold of '[a] crime . . . under international law'.[151] Where terrorist attacks reach this threshold, states should investigate and prosecute suspected offenders, either under the terrorism conventions outlined in Chapter 1, or in international criminal law, if the attacks constitute war crimes or crimes against humanity (see Chapter 4). These crimes also trigger obligations of inter-state cooperation and mutual legal assistance in investigation and prosecution.[152] It is suggested that there are several means by which the Basic Principles and Guidelines might be said to apply to victims of terrorism:

- Where IHL applies (ie in international or non-international armed conflict, or during belligerent occupation), 'terrorism' or 'acts or threat of violence the primary purpose of which is to spread terror among a civilian population' in the IHL-specific sense may constitute a gross IHL violation under the Basic Principles and Guidelines, despite the lack of a defined crime of terrorism in international criminal law. Where a state armed force perpetrated 'terrorism' in an international or non-international armed conflict, it would have to provide reparation to victims. Where a non-state armed group perpetrated 'terrorism' in the IHL sense and where IHL applies, reparations may be provided following the conviction of members of that armed group for the crimes in question.
- Where IHL does not apply, state terrorism or state-sponsored terrorist attacks which result in violations of the right to life would oblige the state in question to provide reparation as part of the duty to provide effective remedies for violations of IHRL. The range of reparations available in the Basic Principles and Guidelines might instruct states as to how these remedies might be made more effective.
- In the rare cases where it might be proven that a state had failed to exercise its due diligence obligation to protect individuals from violations of the right to life by non-state terrorist groups, then the state would be obliged to provide an effective remedy under IHRL, and the Basic Principles and Guidelines might be instructive yet again.

---

[150] Basic Principles and Guidelines, Principle 26.
[151] Ibid, Principle 4.
[152] Ibid, Principle 4.

- Where a non-state group commits a terrorist attack in peacetime, this is not a violation per se of IHRL, as non-state actors cannot be bound as a matter of law by IHRL treaties. However, states may use the Basic Principles and Guidelines as a source to ground their domestic law in reparations.

The Basic Principles and Guidelines provide for states to exert universal jurisdiction, to extradite offenders;[153] for the non-applicability of statutes of limitation;[154] and for victims' access to judicial (rather than merely administrative) remedies.[155] They emphasize individual victims' right to reparation, and call on states to institute procedures by which groups of victims can present claims for reparations.[156] Reparations under international law should be separate from and without prejudice to national remedies.[157] **5.43**

As restitution aims to restore victims, as far as possible, to the situation they were in prior to the crime in question, it is impossible for those killed or maimed in terrorist attacks.[158] **5.44**

Compensation should be given in the alternative, as defined in Principle 20. Where possible, those convicted after a fair trial of involvement in terrorist attacks should be fined and their assets seized to finance victims' reparations: including but not limited to monetary compensation. In terrorist attacks which cause many casualties, assets-seizure from one or several convicted of terrorist crimes may be insufficient. The Basic Principles and Guidelines indicate that states should establish national reparations programmes to finance reparation to victims where those found liable for a violation are unable or unwilling to pay reparation.[159] The UK has proposed the establishment of a Victims of Overseas Terrorism Compensation Scheme, which is part of the Crime and Security Bill 2010.[160] States which cannot finance a national trust fund to compensate victims of terrorist attacks may benefit from a UN-administered international fund, which was first considered by a working group set up by UN Security Council Resolution 1566 (2004).[161] Compensation payments may also finance rehabilitation costs.[162] **5.45**

Rehabilitation, including medical, psycho-social, and legal support, and detailed in Principle 21, is highly relevant to victims of terrorism, particularly to those who are injured or escape with trauma. **5.46**

---

[153] Ibid, Principle 5.
[154] Ibid, Principle 6.
[155] Ibid, Principle 11.
[156] Ibid, Principle 13.
[157] Ibid, Principle 14.
[158] Ibid, Principle 19.
[159] Ibid, Principle 16.
[160] Ministry of Justice, 'New Support for Victims of Terrorism Overseas', 18 January 2010.
[161] UN Security Council Resolution 1566 (2004), para 8.
[162] Basic Principles and Guidelines, Principle 20(e).

5.47 Satisfaction may take many forms, as Principle 22 indicates. The 'cessation of continuing violations'[163] can be appropriate for victims of terrorist acts which are ongoing, such as the hostage-taking by members of the FARC considered in Chapter 2. Those injured or bereaved as a result of terrorist bombings may gain satisfaction from the 'verification of the facts and full and public disclosure of the truth'.[164] This right to truth element in satisfaction may be satisfied by a comprehensive, independent, and impartial public inquiry, where victims' participation is encouraged. Other relevant forms of satisfaction include 'judicial and administrative sanctions against persons liable' for the terrorist attacks,[165] and 'commemorations and tributes to the victims'.[166]

5.48 Guarantees of non-repetition, as defined in Principle 23, add detail to states' obligation to prevent gross violations of IHRL and serious violations of IHL. They are closely related to the prevention of violations by state actors, legislative reform, and conflict monitoring and resolution. Victims of terrorist attacks by non-state actors would be poorly served by all but the reparation to 'promot[e] mechanisms for preventing and monitoring social conflicts and their resolution'.[167] Victims of terrorist attacks by paramilitary groups affiliated to a state, or by state actors, may benefit from the guarantees of non-repetition which include the establishment of 'effective civilian control of military and security forces'.[168]

Using the basic principles and guidelines to provide remedies for victims of violations in counter-terrorism

5.49 Restitution may be appropriate for victims of counter-terrorism policies or operations which violate IHL or IHRL. For example, a victim of arbitrary detention or enforced disappearance who is still alive can receive restitution through his or her release. This underlines the importance of the right to habeas corpus for all detainees, including those held as terrorism suspects.

5.50 Compensation is also appropriate for victims of violations of IHL and IHRL committed in counter-terrorism operations: paid initially by those found liable for the violations, whether these are state officials or corporations complicit in counter-terrorism abuses.[169] In the alternative, or where those found liable are 'unable or unwilling' to pay reparation, compensation should be financed by national funds

---

[163] Ibid, Principle 22(a).

[164] Ibid, Principle 22(b).

[165] Ibid, Principle 22(f).

[166] Ibid, Principle 22(g).

[167] Ibid, Principle 23(g).

[168] Ibid, Principle 23(a).

[169] *Mohamed et al v Jeppesen Dataplan Inc*, US 9th Circuit Court of Appeals, *en banc* rehearing December 2009, No 08-15393; Civil suit against the private military and security company Blackwater/Xe was settled in January 2010, see BBC News, 'Blackwater Iraq Allegations Prompt US Review', 6 March 2010.

established by states. Where states cannot finance these national funds, as recommended by Principle 16 of the Basic Principles and Guidelines, a UN-administered fund may be appropriate. The UN Voluntary Fund for Victims of Torture is one such fund,[170] which should also be used to finance reparation for victims of torture committed in counter-terrorism operations. Compensation cannot take the place of the requirement to respect and ensure IHL and IHRL, however. The UN Special Rapporteur on extrajudicial, summary, and arbitrary executions noted very significant concerns in his mission to the US, as Chapter 2 notes.[171] However, he commended in part the US' compensation programmes for the families of civilians killed in Afghanistan and Iraq.[172] He also noted 'the unintentional exclusion of some victims' in the ad hoc processes for compensation payments,[173] and the 'acute' 'lack of systematic compensation for civilian casualties caused by private contractors'.[174]

National or UN-administered funds can be used to finance rehabilitation for **5.51** victims of violations of IHL and IHRL committed in counter-terrorism operations: the UN Voluntary Fund for Victims of Torture disburses grants to NGOs which give legal, medical, or psycho-social assistance. States should establish national funds for victims' reparations,[175] which could be supplemented by UN-administered escrow funds.

Satisfaction, including the 'cessation of continuing violations', '[v]erification of the **5.52** facts and full and public disclosure of the truth' relating to violations, a search for bodies or the whereabouts of victims of enforced disappearance, public apologies, and orders restoring the reputation, dignity, or rights of a victim (such as by stating publicly that a victim was arbitrarily or mistakenly detained or tried in the course of counter-terrorism) are all of relevance to the victims of violations of IHL and IHRL committed by states in counter-terrorism. Public inquiries which might '[v]erify . . . the facts' and provide 'full and public disclosure of the truth' must not be unduly delayed. The report into the 14 killings by UK paratroopers in Northern Ireland on 30 January 1972 ('Bloody Sunday') is scheduled to be published on 15 June 2010, some six years after the Saville inquiry of 1998–2004.[176] Memorials to the victims of violations of IHL and IHRL would be another form of satisfaction, although the controversy of memorials to members of terrorist groups cannot be overstated. In Peru, a sculpture memorial to victims of terrorism which included deceased *Sendero Luminoso* militants was vandalized in protest at the inclusion of

---

[170] UN General Assembly Resolution 36/151 of 16 December 1981.
[171] UN Special Rapporteur on extrajudicial, arbitrary and summary executions, Mission to the USA, A/HRC/11/2/Add.5, 28 May 2009.
[172] Ibid, para 69.
[173] Ibid, para 69.
[174] Ibid, para 70.
[175] Basic Principles and Guidelines, Principle 16.
[176] BBC News, 'Bloody Sunday Report will be published on 15 June', 26 May 2010.

names of former militants.[177] The inclusion of their names had been required by a judgment of the Inter-American Court of Human Rights.[178] The '[i]nclusion of an accurate account' of violations in human rights training materials can also amount to satisfaction for victims.[179]

5.53 Guarantees of non-repetition delineate states' duties to prevent violations of IHL and IHRL.[180] Recommendations for civilian control of security and military forces, the independence of the judiciary, and training of law enforcement officials and armed forces personnel are listed in the IHRL chapter of this volume, but should also be considered as a form of reparation for victims of violations of international law committed by states in their counter-terrorism operations. Reparations have both a preventive and a retrospective dimension. In its Views in the *non-refoulement* case of *Mansour Ahani v Canada*, the Human Rights Committee combined reparations and prevention.[181] Having found violations of Articles 9, 4, and 13 of the ICCPR, in conjunction with Article 7, it called on Canada 'to take such steps as may be appropriate to ensure that [Mansour Ahani] is not, in the future, subjected to torture as a result of . . . his presence in, and removal from, the State party'.[182] Guarantees of non-repetition relate to ongoing duties to prevent violations of IHL and IHRL, as Chapter 6 explores, and to states' treaty-based obligation to prevent and repress terrorism, as outlined in Chapter 1.

Conclusion

5.54 Although the Basic Principles and Guidelines are non-binding, they reflect existing binding IHRL and international criminal law which requires effective remedies for victims, and participation rights and reparations respectively. International law has moved from a focus on inter-state reparations to the beginnings of a victim-centred perspective, in IHRL treaties and case law, the Rome Statute of the International Criminal Court, and UN standards. Without implementation, however, this victim-centred perspective is wishful thinking only. This chapter has indicated that both the victims of terrorism and victims of violations of international law committed in counter-terrorism operations are unable to secure their rights to a remedy and reparation. The rights to truth, to justice, and to the five types of reparation outlined in the Basic Principles and Guidelines remain paper guarantees only,

---

[177] Inter-American Court of Human Rights, *Miguel Castro-Castro Prison v Peru*, 25 November 2006, Series C No 160, para 454.

[178] Ibid.

[179] Basic Principles and Guidelines, Principle 22(h).

[180] Ibid, Principle 23.

[181] Human Rights Committee, *Mansour Ahani v Canada*, Communication No 1051/2002, CCPR/C/80/D/1051/2002, Views, 29 March 2004.

[182] Ibid, para 12.

with court enforcement hampered by state secrets doctrines and the refusal to extradite some suspects for trial overseas. Regional human rights courts have a well-developed jurisprudence on victims' remedies and reparation, which have not been sufficiently implemented at the national level.

States should respect and ensure the right to a remedy and reparation for victims of **5.55** terrorist attacks and victims of violations of IHL and IHRL committed in counter-terrorism operations. States should encourage victims' participation in criminal proceedings, civil suits, and public inquiries relating to terrorist attacks and violations of international law committed in counter-terrorist operations. States should make judicial remedies available to victims, and should legislate to implement in enforceable judgments the five types of reparation detailed in the Basic Principles and Guidelines.[183] There should be national compensation funds, supported by UN-administered escrow funds, for victims of terrorism, and another for victims of IHL and IHRL violations committed in the course of countering terrorism. In the latter case, states should enforce the rights of torture victims to fair and adequate compensation; provide information, compensation, and reparation for victims of enforced disappearances and their families; compensate victims of arbitrary, prolonged, secret, or incommunicado detention; and compensate those convicted of terrorist crimes following an unfair trial, where their conviction is subsequently overturned on appeal. These recommendations should be viewed alongside the analysis on accountability in Chapter 4, and Chapter 6, which considers measures to prevent terrorist attacks and violations of international law in counter-terrorism.

---

[183] Basic Principles and Guidelines, Principle 19 (restitution), Principle 20 (compensation), Principle 21 (rehabilitation), Principle 22 (satisfaction), and Principle 23 (guarantees of non-repetition).

6

REFORM: PREVENTING TERRORISM IN ACCORDANCE WITH INTERNATIONAL LAW

Introduction

This chapter lays the groundwork for the 'Conclusion and Recommendations' by **6.01** focusing on preventing terrorist attacks and violations of international law in states' counter-terrorism operations. The chapter's three main sections relate to the prevention of terrorist attacks in accordance with international law (drawing on the duties of states in the subject-specific treaties and UN Security Council Resolutions discussed in Chapter 1);[1] the prevention of violations of IHL in counter-terrorism operations (drawing on the analysis in Chapter 2);[2] and the prevention of violations of IHRL in counter-terrorism (which should be read alongside Chapter 3).[3]

There are four premises for this chapter's arguments: **6.02**

• First, states must place international law at the centre of their counter-terrorism efforts,[4] engaging fully with the ratification, implementation, and enforcement

---

[1] See paras 6.03–6.17.
[2] See paras 6.18–6.27.
[3] See paras 6.28–6.41.
[4] UN Security Council Resolution 1624 (2005), Preamble, para 2; UN Security Council Resolution 1373 (2001), para 3(f); UN Global Counter-Terrorism Strategy, annexed to General Assembly Resolution 60/288, 8 September 2006, para 3; UN General Assembly Resolution 60/158, 16 December 2005.

of IHL and IHRL treaties. States should ensure that their reports to the UN Counter-Terrorism Committee (CTC) take full account of their counter-terrorism policies' compliance with IHL and IHRL. In addition, the piecemeal, gradual inclusion of human rights monitoring at the UN CTC should be expanded.[5] States should remove, or other states parties to treaties should object to, any reservations which are incompatible with a treaty's object and purpose.[6] States should submit reports to UN treaty bodies; allow visits or extend an open invitation to the special procedures of the UN Human Rights Council; and implement in full not only treaty obligations but also the judgments or views of regional courts and UN treaty bodies where the latter have found violations of IHRL by that state.

- Second, states should train their armed forces personnel, law enforcement officials, and intelligence officials in applicable IHL and IHRL, as a means of preventing violations of IHL and IHRL. Continuing education in applicable IHL and IHRL should be a condition of permanent employment in these fields. Continued training in IHL and IHRL is necessary but clearly not sufficient for the prevention of arbitrary killings, torture and cruel, inhuman, or degrading treatment or punishment, enforced disappearances, and arbitrary, secret, or incommunicado detention.

- Third, in addition to complying with the monitoring mechanisms which exist at the international and regional levels, states should monitor their own enforcement of IHL and IHRL by ensuring compatibility between their treaty obligations and conditions in practice. There should be civilian oversight of intelligence services; an independent and expert body to monitor places of detention; and independent and impartial national human rights institutions. These bodies can conduct systematic oversight to prevent complicity in torture, enforced disappearances, and secret or incommunicado detention, and should initiate investigations when these violations are alleged to have occurred. These investigations should supplement and not replace criminal investigations and prosecutions to establish individual criminal responsibility, and civil suits by victims seeking a remedy and reparation. In addition, there should be legislative reform where necessary to ensure that domestic criminal definitions of terrorist offences are not so expansive that they criminalize the peaceful exercise of the freedoms of conscience and religion, expression, assembly, or association.

- Fourth, the prevention of future violations may be encouraged by a full implementation of states' obligations to investigate and prosecute violations of IHL and IHRL; and by states' obligations to ensure a remedy and reparation both

---

[5] UN Security Council Resolution 1535 (2004), establishing a Counter-Terrorism Committee Executive Directorate (CTED), with a human rights expert, and a mandate to liaise with the Office of the High Commissioner for Human Rights (OHCHR); UN Security Council Resolution 1805 (2008), establishing a working group to consider human rights issues raised by UN Security Council Resolutions 1373 (2001) and 1625 (2004) within the CTED.

[6] Vienna Convention on the Law of Treaties 1969, Art 19.

for victims of terrorist attacks and for victims of violations of international law committed in counter-terrorism operations. This fourth set of obligations links to the arguments in Chapters 4 and 5 above and requires reform of the state secrets privileges which are operational in multiple jurisdictions. Judges should examine classified information *in camera* and should not accept uncritically mere assertions on the part of the executive or intelligence agencies that particular evidence is too sensitive to be examined. Such assertions should be backed by strong evidence which again can be heard *in camera*. As discussed earlier in Chapters 4 and 5,[7] a state secrets privilege should not be asserted to prevent the consideration by a court of evidence relating to violations of IHL or IHRL, or otherwise to forestall the investigation, prosecution, and civil suits relating to such violations.

Preventing terrorist attacks

Preventing terrorist attacks in accordance with international law

As Chapter 1 has explained, the UN Global Counter-Terrorism Strategy ('the **6.03** Strategy') and a number of UN Security Council and General Assembly Resolutions have emphasized that states' obligations to prevent and repress terrorism must be implemented with full respect for international law, including IHRL, IHL, and international refugee law (IRL).[8] Chapter 1 includes a brief note on IRL's provisions on exclusion and *refoulement* in the counter-terrorism context.[9] The subject-specific Conventions briefly outlined in Chapter 1 require states to prevent and repress aircraft hijackings,[10] hostage-taking by terrorist groups,[11] attacks against the safety of sea vessels,[12] and the proliferation of nuclear weapons to terrorist groups.[13] States must prosecute or extradite terrorism suspects,[14] denying them

---

[7] See paras 4.26, 4.29, 4.42–4.47, 5.05, 5.33–5.34, 5.54.

[8] UN Global Counter-Terrorism Strategy, annexed to General Assembly Resolution 60/288, 8 September 2006, para 3; UN General Assembly Resolution 60/158, 16 December 2005; UN Security Council Resolution 1624 (2005), preambular para 2.

[9] Refugee Convention 1951, Arts 1(F) and 33(9).

[10] Convention on Offences and Certain Other Acts Committed on Board Aircraft 1963; Convention for the Suppression of Unlawful Seizure of Aircraft 1970; Convention for the Suppression of Unlawful Acts against the Safety of Civil Aviation 1971, and its Protocol 1988.

[11] International Convention against the Taking of Hostages 1979.

[12] Convention for the Suppression of Unlawful Acts against the Safety of Maritime Navigation 1988, and its Protocol 2005.

[13] Convention on the Physical Protection of Nuclear Material 1980, as amended 2005; International Convention for the Suppression of Acts of Nuclear Terrorism 2005.

[14] Convention for the Suppression of Unlawful Seizure of Aircraft 1970, Art 7; Convention for the Suppression of Unlawful Acts against the Safety of Civil Aviation 1971, Art 7; Convention on the Prevention and Punishment of Crimes against Internationally Protected Persons 1973, Art 3(2); International Convention against the Taking of Hostages 1979, Art 5(2); International Convention for the Suppression of Terrorist Bombings 1997, Art 7(2); International Convention for the Suppression of the Financing of Terrorism 1997, Art 7(4); International Convention for the Suppression of Acts of Nuclear Terrorism 2005, Art 9(4).

safe haven,[15] and exercising jurisdiction on the basis of territory, nationality, or passive personality.[16] Under treaty law and UN Security Council Resolution 1267 (as subsequently amended), states must cooperate to prevent the financing of terrorism.[17] When states implement these subject-specific treaties proscribing terrorist acts,[18] or act pursuant to General Assembly and Security Council Resolutions aimed at combating terrorism, they must act in accordance with their obligations under IHL, IHRL, and IRL.[19] As discussed earlier, compliance with IHL, IHRL, and IRL in states' action to combat terrorism is not a mere political nicety: it is obligatory and embedded in the framework of intergovernmental efforts to combat terrorism.

6.04 However, states' implementation of IHL, IHRL, and IRL in counter-terrorism requires more than a simple acknowledgement in intergovernmental documents. States should be required to monitor their compliance with existing international law as part of the interaction between states and the UN CTC. States should ensure that their reports to the CTC take full account of their counter-terrorism policies' compliance with IHL, IHRL, and IRL; and the piecemeal, gradual inclusion of human rights monitoring at the UN CTC should be expanded.[20] States should remove any reservations and understandings which are incompatible with a treaty's object and purpose, and should submit reports to UN treaty bodies; allow visits or extend an open invitation to the special procedures of the UN Human Rights Council; and implement in full not only treaty obligations but also the judgments or views of regional courts and UN treaty bodies where the latter have found violations of IHRL by that state.

Preventing the proliferation of weapons to terrorist groups, whether state or non-state

6.05 The UN Global Counter-Terrorism Strategy emphasizes inter-state, regional, and international cooperation in preventing the proliferation of 'small arms and light weapons, conventional ammunition and explosives, and nuclear, chemical, biological or radiological weapons and materials'.[21] The Strategy emphasizes the importance

---

[15] UN Security Council Resolution 1373, 28 September 2001, para 2(c).

[16] Convention on Offences and Certain Other Acts Committed on Board Aircraft 1963; International Convention for the Suppression of Terrorist Bombings 1997, Art 6(1) and (2).

[17] International Convention for the Suppression of the Financing of Terrorism 1999; UN Security Council Resolution 1267 (1999).

[18] See paras 1.01, 1.17–1.22.

[19] UN Global Counter-Terrorism Strategy, para 2(a)–(c).

[20] UN Security Council Resolution 1373 (2001); UN Security Council Resolution 1535 (2004), establishing a Counter-Terrorism Committee Executive Directorate (CTED), with a human rights expert, and a mandate to liaise with the Office of the High Commissioner for Human Rights (OHCHR); UN Security Council Resolution 1805 (2008), establishing a working group to consider human rights issues raised by UN Security Council Resolutions 1373 (2001) and 1625 (2004) within the CTED.

[21] Ibid, para 13.

of inter-state cooperation and assistance as regards the illicit trade and smuggling in these weapons,[22] and calls on the International Atomic Energy Agency (IAEA) and the Organisation for the Prohibition of Chemical Weapons to build states' capacities to prevent terrorist groups from having access to nuclear and chemical weapons.[23] Preventing the proliferation of weapons and explosives to terrorist groups, whether state or non-state, is an important mechanism for the prevention of terrorist attacks. It can be carried out without risking violations of IHL, IHRL, or IRL, and can be bolstered by investigation, prosecution, extradition, and mutual legal assistance as appropriate for crimes connected to the trade or smuggling of these weapons.

Broad strategies for prevention: promoting dialogue, good governance, and the rule of law

Scholars have documented the correlation between failed states, internal unrest, or poor governance on the one hand and the growth of militant terrorist cells on the other.[24] Intergovernmental organizations have pointed to the importance of governance and rule of law programmes as one means among many to prevent further recruitment of terrorists.[25] The UN Global Counter-Terrorism Strategy asserts that conflict prevention and resolution, peace building, inter-state, inter-religious, and inter-community dialogue, and development and social inclusion programmes are integral to the prevention of terrorism.[26] The Strategy urges an increase in UN programmes to support the rule of law, human rights, and good governance.[27] There is no detail as to how these programmes might be conceived or implemented effectively to prevent terrorist attacks, nor references to research proving a link between these factors and the spread of terrorism. A lack of such references does not suggest that these programmes fail to prevent terrorism, but does indicate the need for careful research into the effectiveness of good governance and rule of law programmes in preventing the recruitment of terrorists and terrorist attacks.

6.06

---

[22] Ibid, para 5.

[23] Ibid, III, Measures to build States' capacity to prevent and combat terrorism and to strengthen the role of the United Nations system in this regard, para 9.

[24] Robert I Rotberg, 'Failed States in a World of Terror' (2002) 81 *Foreign Affairs* 127; Chester A Crocker, 'Engaging Failed States' (2003) 82 *Foreign Affairs* 32; Mai Yamani, 'Yemeni Detainees and Jihadis: Guantanamo Repatriation and Saudi Arabia', Chatham House, 16 April 2009; Fawaz A Gerges, 'A Broken Middle East: A Wasted Decade of War on Terror', Inaugural Lecture, London School of Economics and Political Science, 10 February 2010.

[25] Council of the European Union, Declaration on Combating Terrorism; European Union at the UN, EC External Assistance under UN Security Council Resolution 1373, Summary, 25 February 2002; OSCE, 'The Role of Civil Society in Preventing Terrorism', Informal Working Level Meeting, 14–16 March 2007, para 21.

[26] UN Global Counter-Terrorism Strategy, I, Measures to address the conditions conducive to the spread of terrorism, paras 1–6.

[27] Ibid, para 7.

Preventing state terrorism and state-sponsored terrorism

6.07   Improving governance and rule of law in so-called 'failed' or failing states may help prevent state terrorism and state-sponsored terrorism,[28] as well as terrorist attacks by non-state actors. Preventing the proliferation of explosives, and conventional, nuclear, chemical, biological, and radiological weapons to states suspected of encouraging or financing terrorist attacks is another important strategy. The US Department of State tries to circumvent the activity of so-called 'State Sponsors of Terrorism' by prohibiting the conclusion of Department of Defense contracts with those states; lifting diplomatic immunity so that victims of terrorist attacks perpetrated by those states can seek redress and reparation; and imposing a number of economic sanctions, tax penalties, and a policy against World Bank loans to those countries, and to individuals seeking to enter into business transactions with the governments of 'State Sponsors of Terrorism'.[29] As noted in Chapter 1, the evidence for each state's involvement in terrorism needs to be established separately, and with attention to regional, institutional, and political interactions between armed groups and the states alleged to be involved in the sponsorship of terrorism.[30] Unsubstantiated assertions that these states are 'State Sponsors of Terrorism' may conceal political motives, and are insufficient.

6.08   Furthermore, there are IHRL implications: only if these policies do not affect the full implementation of economic, social, and cultural rights within the states concerned, can these targeted financial and tax penalties be recommended as a means of preventing state terrorism. However, these policies are applied currently only to four states: Cuba, Iran, Sudan, and Syria. These policies do not apply to other states which may have financed or encouraged terrorist groups, or permitted the trade in weapons to those terrorist groups. The imposition of sanctions to prevent the financing of terrorism should be even-handed and free of any political partiality.

6.09   The Israeli scholar Tal Becker has recommended a change to the traditional international law on the responsibility of states for internationally unlawful acts, so as to provide for state responsibility where factual causation, legal causation, and policy reasons indicate that a state has encouraged or acquiesced in the development of terrorist groups.[31] Under both the ILC Articles on State Responsibility,[32] and Tal Becker's recommended approach, a state which caused terrorist attacks through its

---

[28] Robert I Rotberg, 'Failed States in a World of Terror' (2002) 81 *Foreign Affairs* 127.

[29] US Department of State, Country Reports on Terrorism 2008, Chapter 3, 'State Sponsors of Terrorism'.

[30] Katerina Dalacoura, 'Middle East Studies and Terrorism Studies: Establishing Links via a Critical Approach', in Richard Jackson, Marie Breen Smyth, and Jeroen Gunning, *Critical Terrorism Studies: A New Research Agenda* (Routledge, 2009), pp 124–138, at p 130.

[31] Tal Becker, *Terrorism and the State: Rethinking the Rules of State Responsibility* (Hart Publishing, 2006).

[32] ILC Articles on the Responsibility of States for Internationally Unlawful Acts 2001, adopted by UN General Assembly Resolution 56/83, 12 December 2001.

own practice or that of its agents would be responsible for those attacks. Under Becker's reasoning, both factual causation and policy reasons are added to increase the scope of state responsibility. A state should be held responsible where it has failed to exercise due diligence to prevent terrorist attacks, according to Becker,[33] in reasoning that is compatible with the development of a due diligence principle to prevent arbitrary deprivation of life by non-state actors.[34] While the reliance on policy factors or an undefined 'fairness' as grounds for state responsibility may be troublesome in its lack of completeness, Tal Becker's analysis attempts to fill a gap where states permit, encourage, or fail to prevent terrorist attacks.

Preventing terrorism by non-state actors: de-radicalization and reintegration programmes in Yemen and Saudi Arabia

The Working Group on Radicalisation and Extremism that Lead to Terrorism of **6.10** the UN Counter-Terrorism Implementation Task Force (CTITF) collected information from 34 states on their programmes to prevent radicalization.[35] Among these states was Yemen, which includes de-radicalization programmes in its education policy,[36] and conducts re-education and reintegration programmes for repatriated suspected terrorists and those convicted of terrorist crimes.[37] Saudi Arabia uses a similar process, based on prevention (education and public outreach programmes), rehabilitation (individual counselling and mentoring of suspected terrorists by religious scholars and psychological professionals), and after-care (in Care Rehabilitation centres, followed by assistance in finding a job after-release).[38] In Saudi Arabia, those subjected to rehabilitation and after-care may be detained, with release contingent either on the organizers of the rehabilitation programme having determined that the individual suspected terrorist has revoked his or her terrorist ideology, or on those convicted and sentenced to prison terms having served their sentences.[39] Human Rights Watch has noted concerns at the prolonged pre-charge detention which has been involved in these schemes, and at the closed nature of the belated trials in Saudi Arabia, which began five years after the first detentions under that state's rehabilitation programme.[40] Defendants did not have

---

[33] Ibid, p 334.

[34] See paras 3.01, 3.14, 3.16.

[35] UN Counter-Terrorism Implementation Task Force, First Report of the Working Group on Radicalisation and Extremism that Lead to Terrorism, UN Counter-Terrorism Implementation Task Force: Inventory of State Programmes.

[36] Ibid, para 16.

[37] Mai Yamani, 'Yemeni Detainees and Jihadis: Guantanamo Repatriation and Saudi Arabia', Chatham House, 16 April 2009.

[38] Christopher Boucek, 'Saudi Arabia's "Soft" Counterterrorism Strategy: Prevention, Rehabilitation and Aftercare', Carnegie Papers No 97, September 2008.

[39] Ibid, p 11.

[40] Human Rights Watch, 'US/Yemen: Break Impasse on Yemeni Returns from Guantanamo', 28 March 2009; Human Rights Watch, 'Human Rights and Saudi Arabia's Counterterrorism Response: Religious Counseling, Indefinite Detention and Flawed Trials', 9 August 2009.

the right to challenge the lawfulness of their detention before a judge, and their right to have access to a lawyer of their choice and to prepare a defence was in doubt, with outside observers not permitted to attend trials.[41] An IHRL approach to preventing terrorism would require that re-education policies which involve prolonged detention be applied only to those convicted of terrorist offences after a fair trial.

Sanctions on individuals: travel bans and assets-freezing

6.11 Preventing the financing of terrorism and the travel of those involved in terrorist groups, may serve to prevent terrorist attacks. Where states have not yet ratified the provisions of the Terrorism Financing Convention, they should be urged to do so; but urgent reform is required of the intergovernmental mechanisms for terrorist 'listing' and assets-freezing. Preventing the financing of terrorism should be considered alongside measures to prevent the sales or smuggling of weapons to terrorist groups. However, when these measures are applied to individuals who have not been convicted of terrorist crimes, without a fair hearing or possibility of appeal on the merits, they violate IHRL.

6.12 Individuals and groups listed as terrorist by the UN and regional intergovernmental organizations have faced travel bans and the freezing of assets since UN Security Council Resolution 1267 in 1999, which was passed following the bombings of US Embassies in Kenya and Tanzania, and which established the UN Sanctions Committee (the Sanctions Committee). The processes mandated by this and subsequent Resolutions do not permit a formal appeal on the merits; the Sanctions Committee remains a political, not a judicial, body; and there is no duty to give reasons for a 'listing' decision. Chapter 3 considers these flaws in the light of case law and views before the Court of First Instance and the European Court of Justice, and the Human Rights Committee, which monitors states' implementation of the ICCPR.[42]

6.13 There have been gradual reforms in the UN system for terrorist listing and assets-freezing, but these institutional changes remain insufficient to address concerns under IHRL. Since 2006, there has been a delisting system before the Sanctions Committee, and 'limited release' of the reasons for listing made to the persons affected. Further amendments were made in UN Security Council Resolution 1822 in 2008. Most recently, UN Security Council Resolution 1904 of 17 December 2009 amends the sanctions regime pursuant to UN Security Council Resolution 1267. Resolution 1904 establishes an Office of the Ombudsperson to be appointed by the Secretary-General in consultation with the Sanctions Committee. An Ombudsperson is not a court, and cannot offer merits-based review, even if he or she is appointed on the basis of merit and impartiality as

---

[41] Human Rights Watch, 'Human Rights and Saudi Arabia's Counterterrorism Response', supra.
[42] See paras 3.149–3.151.

foreseen by Resolution 1904. These reforms must accelerate, as the current, insufficient administrative review does not respect the right to a fair hearing in IHRL.

Additional measures of prevention: security checks, surveillance, and law enforcement

This final category of preventive measures constitutes the last in time prior to a possible terrorist attack. They consist of security checks for explosives at airports and other sites of mass transit, surveillance of potential terrorists prior to making an arrest, and the arrest and questioning of terrorism suspects. These policies require careful attention to the right to privacy, and to the risk of unlawful discrimination through ethnic, racial, national, or religious 'profiling' of terrorism suspects.[43] **6.14**

Following a failed attempt to bomb a passenger aircraft near Detroit in December **6.15** 2009, policy-makers debated the introduction of full-body scanners at airports to identify injected or ingested explosives. These scanners present a tension between the right to privacy and the prevention of terrorist attacks. Whether the scanners constitute a disproportionate interference with the right to privacy has yet to be determined by a court. However, the UN Special Rapporteur on the promotion and protection of human rights while countering terrorism, Martin Scheinin, observed that 'human rights standards have been tested, stretched and breached' through a range of surveillance and search mechanisms. He argued that all these measures, including advanced body scanners, 'racial or ethnic profiling', and the 'creation of privacy-intrusive databases' should be subjected to a proper human rights assessment.[44] The question of whether or not such scanners might serve as a deterrent to terrorists requires careful research. The results of that research can help inform policy choices on the necessity and proportionality of these measures and the extent of their intrusion into IHRL, but cannot replace that inquiry into the necessity and proportionality tests in IHRL.

In a report released in December 2009, Martin Scheinin urged greater awareness of **6.16** the need to 'counterbalance' counter-terrorism 'with greater awareness of the necessary safeguards for the protection of individuals' dignity'.[45] He noted the plethora of coordinated policies for surveillance of communication by law enforcement officials and intelligence agencies, including cross-border communications supervised without judicial warrant.[46] Secret surveillance, the retention of data, and ethnic or

---

[43] See paras 3.181–3.182.

[44] UN Special Rapporteur on the promotion and protection of human rights while countering terrorism, 'Counter-terrorism: Intrusive Measures in Fight Against Terrorism Should be Opposed, Says UN Expert', Press Release, 19 January 2010.

[45] Report of the UN Special Rapporteur on the promotion and protection of human rights while countering terrorism to the 13th session of the Human Rights Council, A/HRC/13/37, 28 December 2009, para 72.

[46] Ibid, paras 21–22.

religious profiling also present concerns in terms of the right to a fair trial, and miscarriages of justice may result.[47]

6.17   While surveillance and security checks have an important role in preventing terrorist attacks, and contributing evidence to investigations and prosecutions, they risk violations of the right to privacy and unlawful discrimination.[48] Surveillance may require some secrecy in order not to 'tip-off' suspected terrorists that they may be subject to investigation, but the frequency of surveillance and extent of security checks should be the subject of a full audit of compliance with IHRL. This audit can take place through legislative oversight of the intelligence services, through reference to surveillance schemes in a state's reports to the UN Counter-Terrorism Committee, to UN treaty bodies, to the UN Human Rights Council universal periodic review mechanism and special procedures, and to regional human rights mechanisms. This echoes the first premise of this chapter's arguments, on states' full implementation of international law as they prevent and repress terrorism.

Preventing violations of IHL in counter-terrorism operations

Ratification of Additional Protocols to the Four Geneva Conventions of 1949 and of treaties on the means and methods of warfare; removal of reservations incompatible with the object and purpose of treaties

Ratification

6.18   The Four Geneva Conventions of 1949 are universally ratified, with 194 states parties.[49] Additional Protocols I and II of 1977, applicable in international armed conflicts and non-international armed conflicts respectively, have 169 and 165 states parties.[50] A brief glance at the list of states parties to Additional Protocol I reveals that of the states considered in the IHL case studies in Chapter 2, Israel, Somalia, and the US are all absent. Of the states involved in non-international armed conflicts considered in Chapter 2, Somalia, Sri Lanka, Iraq, Israel, and the US have not ratified Additional Protocol II.[51]

6.19   States parties to the Four Geneva Conventions which have not ratified either Additional Protocol I or II should be urged to do so. A number of provisions in the Additional Protocols are binding on all states as customary IHL, with the best

---

[47] Ibid, para 38.
[48] See paras 3.157 and 3.181–3.182.
[49] See para 2.14.
[50] The ICRC regularly updates its database of treaties with lists of signatories, states parties, and any reservations, at <http://www.icrc.org/ihl.nsf/INTRO?OpenView>.
[51] See paras 2.08, 2.27, 2.35, 2.83, 2.87–2.89, 2.94, 2.96, 2.105–2.107, 2.108–2.113.

example being Article 75 of Additional Protocol I.[52] Ratification of these documents is to be strongly encouraged for two reasons:

- first, where treaties are ratified, the binding law is accessible to armed forces personnel, rather than being deduced from customary IHL. The content of treaty texts should be integrated into their training programmes; and
- second, states can be held accountable by the ICRC's confidential outreach and promotion of IHL;[53] by international fact-finding mechanisms set up by treaty,[54] or by intergovernmental organizations. States parties can hold other states accountable for grave breaches and violations of IHL which are short of grave breaches.[55]

Ratification rates are far lower for treaties on the means and methods of warfare **6.20** than for the Four Geneva Conventions and their Additional Protocols.[56] While it is now in force, the Convention on Cluster Munitions currently has only 30 states parties. The Convention on Prohibitions or Restrictions on Certain Conventional Weapons which may be deemed to be Excessively Injurious or to Have Indiscriminate Effects 1980 (CCW Convention) has only 72 states parties, and none of its Protocols on specific types of such weapons has more than 110 states parties. As Chapter 2's discussion of white phosphorus munitions makes clear, the low rate of ratification of Protocol III to the CCW Convention, the Protocol on Prohibitions or Restrictions on the Use of Incendiary Weapons, is highly problematic. The lack of an explicit treaty prohibition on the use of white phosphorus munitions (Protocol III covers white phosphorus munitions implicitly only) should be reconsidered, and states parties to the CCW Convention should be encouraged to amend Protocol III to ensure that its text explicitly refers to white phosphorus munitions.

Reservations

In 2009, the US ratified Protocol III to the CCW Convention, noting upon ratifica- **6.21** tion that the US 'reserves the right to use incendiary weapons against military objectives located in concentrations of civilians where it is judged that such use would cause fewer casualties and/or less collateral damage than alternative weapons'.[57] The prohibition 'in all circumstances' to target individual civilians or civilian objects with incendiary weapons is one of the objects and purposes of

---

[52] Jean Marie Henckaerts and Louise Doswald-Beck, *Customary International Humanitarian Law, Volume 1: Rules* (International Committee of the Red Cross (ICRC) and Cambridge University Press, 2005), Rules 87–88.

[53] ICRC, 'Promoting International Humanitarian Law: Extract from ICRC Annual Report 2008', 27 May 2009.

[54] Additional Protocol I, Art 90. (The International Humanitarian Fact-Finding Commission requires the consent of the parties subject to investigation. It remains unused.)

[55] Fourth Geneva Convention, Art 149, Additional Protocol I, Art 85

[56] See para 2.18.

[57] USA, Reservation text, 21 January 2009.

Protocol III,[58] and it reflects the customary IHL principle of distinction between combatants and civilians, which binds the US regardless of its reservation text. Moreover, Protocol III sets strict controls on the use of incendiary weapons on military targets which are 'located within a concentration of civilians'.[59] If the US' reservation is contrary to the object and purpose of Protocol III, it should be withdrawn, and other states parties to Protocol III of the CCW Convention should be encouraged formally to object to it, as provided by Article 19(c) of the Vienna Convention on the Law of Treaties (VCLT) 1969. Although the US has signed but not ratified the VCLT, Article 19 may be considered binding as customary international law.[60] Moreover, the phrasing of the US' reservation suggests that, despite the US' considerable military arsenal, the only 'alternative weapons' available to military planners would be more harmful to civilians than incendiary weapons prohibited by Protocol III. Given that those weapons are 'primarily designed to set fire to objects or to cause burn injury to persons through the action of flame, heat or combination thereof, produced by a chemical reaction of a substance delivered on the target', it is difficult to conceive of a weapon which would be more harmful.

6.22 The UK's reservation text to the CCW Convention is problematic as it relates to armed conflicts fought with a counter-terrorist aim. As for the UK's reservation to Additional Protocol I to the Four Geneva Conventions,[61] the UK defines 'armed conflict' so as to exclude 'a situation of a kind which is constituted by the commission of ordinary crimes, including acts of terrorism, whether concerted or in isolation'.[62] While IHL cannot apply to terrorist acts committed in peacetime, the existence of acts of terrorism during an international or a non-international armed conflict does not make IHL inapplicable. Where IHL applies, states must respect and ensure the Four Geneva Conventions 'in all circumstances', as provided by Common Article 1.

Training armed forces personnel and private military and security companies in IHL

6.23 States engaged in armed conflicts with a counter-terrorist aim must 'respect and ensure respect' for the Four Geneva Conventions at all times:[63] the aim of counter-terrorism does not decrease the force of this obligation. The Rules of Engagement and the training for armed forces personnel must be comprehensive and clear, with ongoing explanations of the principle of distinction between combatants and civilians, the prohibition on indiscriminate attacks, and the requirement to take

---

[58] CCW Convention, Protocol III, Art 2(1).
[59] CCW Convention, Protocol III, Art 2(3).
[60] Frederic L Kirgis, 'Reservations to Treaties and United States Practice', *ASIL Insights*, May 2003.
[61] Additional Protocol I, UK Reservation/Declaration Text, para (d).
[62] CCW Convention, Protocol III, UK Reservation/Declaration Text, para (a)(i).
[63] Four Geneva Conventions of 1949, Common Article 1.

precautions in attack; as well as prohibitions on certain weapons which are deemed to cause indiscriminate or excessive suffering—whether to civilians or combatants. There should be additional, specific training in IHL for armed forces personnel with responsibility for targeting decisions and the capture and treatment of prisoners of war and civilian internees.

There is a strong case for continued and career-long education and training in IHL **6.24** for all armed forces personnel, including reservists, and for the members of private military and security companies who accompany the armed forces. Continuing education in IHL should be a condition of deployment and ongoing employment in the armed forces, and state armed forces should insist on giving training in IHL to any private military and security personnel who carry out functions aligned to those of the armed forces. Where private military and security companies act as agents of state armed forces, and where they act unlawfully, violating IHL, the state for which they act as an agent can be responsible under the international law of state responsibility for those violations of IHL.[64] This consequence for states should encourage them to include the employees of private military and security companies in IHL training courses, as a condition for the approval of contracts between state armed forces and the private companies involved.[65]

Repression of grave breaches; the duty to 'respect and ensure respect' for IHL 'in all circumstances'

States parties to the Geneva Conventions must prevent and repress grave breaches **6.25** of those provisions, which include wilful killing, including the deliberate targeting of civilians or other persons who are *hors de combat*, torture and inhuman treatment, unlawful deportation and transfer, and hostage-taking.[66] States must proscribe these grave breaches in their criminal legislation, search for those suspected to have committed grave breaches, and prosecute them fairly or extradite them.[67] States must cooperate to prevent and repress grave breaches of the Geneva Conventions. This includes a duty to prosecute or extradite suspected offenders, but the broader duty to 'respect and ensure respect' for the Geneva Conventions 'in all circumstances' requires that states must condemn violations of IHL (including grave breaches) whatever the circumstances, regardless of whether an armed conflict is waged with a counter-terrorist aim. 'Terrorism' and 'acts or threat of violence the primary purpose of which is to spread terror among the civilian

---

[64] ILC Articles on the Responsibility of States for Internationally Unlawful Acts 2001, adopted by UN General Assembly Resolution 56/83, 12 December 2001.

[65] See paras 2.82 and 2.86.

[66] First Geneva Convention, Art 50; Second Geneva Convention, Art 51; Third Geneva Convention, Art 130; Fourth Geneva Convention, Art 147; Additional Protocol I, Arts 11, 85(3)–(4); see para 2.13.

[67] First Geneva Convention, Art 49; Second Geneva Convention, Art 50; Third Geneva Convention, Art 129; Fourth Geneva Convention, Art 146; Additional Protocol I, Art 85.

population' are also unequivocally prohibited in IHL, in both international and non-international armed conflicts, as a corollary of the principle of distinction between combatants and civilians, and related to the prohibition on collective punishment in Article 33 of the Fourth Geneva Convention.[68]

6.26 States can initiate an 'enquiry' under Article 149 of the Fourth Geneva Convention into any breach of IHL, whether or not it amounts to a grave breach. The specific IHL notions of 'terrorism' and 'spread[ing] terror among a civilian population' should be the subject of such enquiries when they are suspected to have occurred, and that enquiry should include findings of fact as to the 'primary purpose' of the acts or threats of violence in question.[69] Prolonged post-conflict detention, or the mass internment of civilians, can and should be the subject of such enquiries; as should attempts to create a third category of 'unlawful combatants' who are left unprotected by either the Third or Fourth Geneva Convention regimes.[70]

6.27 While Chapter 2 has pointed to the limitations of Common Article 3 to the Four Geneva Conventions and Additional Protocol II fully to regulate the protection of civilians in non-international armed conflict,[71] and especially to regulate detention in non-international armed conflict,[72] this branch of IHL is no less binding on states in their counter-terrorism operations. Moreover, the development of customary IHL and of the case law of international criminal tribunals suggests a gradual convergence of the IHL applicable to international and non-international armed conflicts,[73] so that the lacunae in the IHL of non-international armed conflict may become less significant. Violations of IHL in non-international armed conflict should be the subject of international condemnation, and war crimes and crimes against humanity committed in non-international armed conflict should be investigated and prosecuted.[74]

Preventing violations of IHRL in counter-terrorism operations

Ratification of treaties implementation of obligations full engagement with treaty bodies and regional human rights courts

6.28 States should be encouraged to ratify all universal human rights treaties, including the Convention on Enforced Disappearances, which at the time of writing requires

---

[68] Fourth Geneva Convention, Art 33; Additional Protocol I, Art 51(2); Additional Protocol II, Arts 4(2)(d) and 13(2).

[69] See para 2.24.

[70] See paras 2.34–2.35.

[71] See paras 2.08, 2.69, 2.82, 2.86, 2.111.

[72] See paras 2.38, 2.76–2.77, 2.78, 2.112.

[73] Henckaerts & Doswald-Beck, supra; *Prosecutor v Tadić*, Appeals Chamber Judgment, 15 July 1999.

[74] Rome Statute of the International Criminal Court, Arts 7 and 8; see para 4.02.

only two more ratifications to enter into force.[75] Also relevant are Optional Protocols to universal human rights treaties, which provide *inter alia* for the abolition of the death penalty,[76] the right of individual petition to the UN Human Rights Committee,[77] prohibitions on the recruitment and use of child soldiers,[78] and a mechanism to monitor all places of detention in order to prevent torture and cruel, inhuman, or degrading treatment or punishment.[79]

Although derogation provisions are rarely invoked, states derogating from IHRL **6.29** treaties in time of war or public emergency should ensure that any derogating action is 'strictly limited to the exigencies of the situation'.[80] The proclamation of a state of emergency is insufficient for formal derogation, and the long-term states of emergency in Egypt[81] and Sri Lanka,[82] to name just two states, neither justify nor excuse human rights violations committed in the name of counter-terrorism. States should ensure that limitations to certain rights in the name of national security, public order, or public safety do not have a disproportionate impact on IHRL.[83] States should be attentive to the risk of violations of economic, social, and cultural rights and of unlawful discrimination on the grounds of race, religion, national or social origin, gender, or other status as a result of their counter-terrorism policies, and should refrain from implementing counter-terrorism policies which unlawfully discriminate or which violate economic, social, and cultural rights.[84]

A full engagement in the intergovernmental monitoring and enforcement of **6.30** IHRL includes the acceptance of a right of individual petition to regional human rights bodies and UN treaty bodies; should extend an open invitation to the special procedures of the UN Human Rights Council; and certainly includes the implementation of judgments and views of regional human rights courts and UN treaty

---

[75] Updates to the list of status of the Convention after May 2010 may be found at <http://treaties.un.org/Pages/ViewDetails.aspx?src=TREATY&mtdsg_no=IV-16&chapter=4&lang=en> (last accessed 20 May 2010).

[76] Second Optional Protocol to the ICCPR, aiming at the abolition of the death penalty.

[77] Optional Protocol to the ICCPR.

[78] Optional Protocol to the Convention on the Rights of the Child, on the involvement of children in armed conflicts.

[79] Optional Protocol to the Convention against Torture and Other Cruel, Inhuman or Degrading Treatment or Punishment.

[80] See para 3.17.

[81] Concluding Observations of the Human Rights Committee: Egypt, CCPR/CO/76/EGY, 28 November 2002, para 6; Human Rights Watch, 'Egypt: Cosmetic Changes Can't Justify Keeping Emergency Law', 12 May 2010.

[82] Report of the Special Rapporteur on torture and other cruel, inhuman or degrading treatment or punishment, Manfred Nowak, Mission to Sri Lanka, Human Rights Council, 7th session, A/HRC/7/3/Add.8, 26 February 2008; Human Rights Committee, *Jegatheeswara Sarma v Sri Lanka*, Communication No 950/2000, 31 July 2003; International Bar Association, 'Justice in Retreat: A Report on the Independence of the Legal Profession and the Rule of Law in Sri Lanka' (2009).

[83] See paras 3.22–3.24 and 3.156–3.169.

[84] See paras 3.170–3.179 and 3.180–3.184.

bodies where the latter have found a state in violation of IHRL.[85] States should report promptly and comprehensively to UN treaty bodies, and should ensure the implementation of judgments.

Prevention of arbitrary deprivation of life in counter-terrorism operations

6.31 The prevention of extrajudicial executions and other arbitrary deprivation of life requires thorough training of law enforcement officials in IHRL and standards including the Code of Conduct for Law Enforcement Officials and the Body of Principles on the Use of Force and Firearms by Law Enforcement Officials.[86] The right to life is non-derogable, and the continued retention of the death penalty by a minority of states, including for terrorist crimes, remains a concern. States are obliged to investigate deaths in custody,[87] and if such investigations yield evidence of unlawful killings, those suspected of involvement should be prosecuted in fair trials.

6.32 'Targeted killings' of terrorism suspects outside armed conflict are extrajudicial executions, prohibited by IHRL.[88] Whereas in IHL, the killing of combatants is permitted, as is the targeting of civilians who take a direct part in hostilities for the time that they do so,[89] IHRL imposes a law enforcement model, in which the use of lethal force should be a measure of absolute last resort.[90] IHRL standards provide that law enforcement officials can use force 'only when strictly necessary and to the extent required for the performance of their duty'.[91] Law enforcement officials can use firearms only 'in self-defence or in defence of others against the imminent threat of death or serious injury', to prevent a 'particularly serious crime involving grave threat to life', or to effect an arrest of someone who is resisting arrest and presents 'such a danger'.[92] There are strict proportionality requirements,[93] and the 'intentional lethal use of firearms' is only permissible 'when strictly unavoidable in order to protect life'.[94]

6.33 Case law has determined that counter-terrorism operations must be planned and controlled so as to respect the right to life, not only of terrorism suspects, but also

---

[85] Committee of Ministers of the Council of Europe, 'Actions of the Security Forces in the Chechen Republic of the Russian Federation: General Measures to Comply with the Judgments of the European Court of Human Rights', CM/Inf/DH(2008)33, 11 September 2008.

[86] See paras 3.28–3.35.

[87] See paras 3.47–3.50, 4.02.

[88] See paras 2.04, 2.48, 2.116, 3.40–3.45,

[89] Additional Protocol I, Art 51(3); ICRC, *Interpretive Guidance on the Notion of Direct Participation in Hostilities in International Humanitarian Law* (2009).

[90] See paras 3.30–3.35.

[91] UN Code of Conduct for Law Enforcement Officials, Art 3.

[92] Basic Principles on the Use of Force and Firearms by Law Enforcement Officials, Principle 9.

[93] Ibid.

[94] Ibid.

of bystanders who may be killed as a result.[95] Any use of lethal force which results in death must be the subject of a prompt, independent, and impartial investigation, with prosecution following if a violation is suspected, and full reparation being paid to the victim's relatives.[96]

Prevention of torture, enforced disappearances, and secret or incommunicado detention

The prohibition of torture and of cruel, inhuman, or degrading treatment or pun- **6.34** ishment is absolute and non-derogable. The prohibition of torture is also a peremptory or *jus cogens* norm. It can never be justified, nor rendered inapplicable by national security or counter-terrorism considerations. It results in a number of corollary obligations, including the inadmissibility of evidence obtained by torture,[97] and an obligation not to transfer individuals to another state where they would face a real risk of torture.[98] Enforced disappearances are also unequivocally prohibited by IHRL, as a *jus cogens* obligation. Secret and incommunicado deten-tion are equally prohibited by IHRL.[99] These three violations can overlap, so that victims of secret and incommunicado detention or enforced disappearance may also be victims of torture and cruel, inhuman, or degrading treatment or punish-ment. There are four priority recommendations to prevent these linked violations:

First, torture and enforced disappearances should be criminal offences in national **6.35** law, with the definitions from IHRL implemented in full in national legislation. Chapter 4 considers the implementation of this national criminal legislation in the form of investigation and prosecution of these crimes.

Second, where torture, enforced disappearances, and secret or incommunicado **6.36** detention has been committed by intelligence agencies, these bodies should be monitored by teams of independent experts, who are civilians and unaffiliated to the executive, legislature, or intelligence services. These independent experts should report regularly to either to a human rights ombudsperson, to legislative commit-tees for intelligence oversight, to judges and prosecutors, if necessary raising concerns on classified matters *in camera*. Mere legislative oversight may be insuffi-cient, as party political pressures may militate against the full implementation of IHRL.[100]

---

95 *Ergi v Turkey* (2001) 23 EHRR 388; *McCann v United Kingdom* (1995) 21 EHRR 97.
96 See paras 3.26–3.27, 3.29–3.35, 5.01, 5.32.
97 Convention against Torture, Art 15.
98 Convention against Torture, Art 3.
99 See paras 3.105 and 3.124–3.128.
100 US Congress, Enemy Belligerent Interrogation, Detention and Prosecution Act of 2010 which was introduced to the Congress on 4 March 2010 and at the time of writing had been referred to Committee.

6.37 Third, independent experts should monitor all places of detention, ensuring that there are no 'ghost detainees' or terrorism suspects whose fate or whereabouts is/are unknown. The monitoring by national experts should be accompanied by visits from the ICRC or the United Nations High Commissioner for Refugees (UNHCR) as appropriate, and by Special Procedures of the UN Human Rights Council, the Committee for the Prevention of Torture, established by the Optional Protocol to the Convention against Torture, and their regional equivalents. This will assist with the implementation of the prohibition on secret and incommunicado detention, and may serve as a national implementation of the obligation to prevent torture and enforced disappearances. States should maintain registries of all detainees to prevent enforced disappearances,[101] and secret or incommunicado detention, and to act as a safeguard against torture. As the Inter-American Convention on the Forced Disappearances of Persons maintains, such registries should be made available to 'relatives, judges, attorneys, any other person having a legitimate interest, and other authorities'.[102]

6.38 Fourth, the absolute prohibition on *refoulement* under Article 3 of the Convention against Torture requires states to refrain from transferring terrorism suspects to a state where there is a real risk that they will be subjected to torture. In *Saadi v Italy*, the European Court of Human Rights confirmed that there is no national security exemption to this principle.[103] Terrorism suspects must not be 'outsourced' for coercive interrogation, or deported to their state of nationality if there is a real risk that they will suffer torture in custody. When the Convention on Enforced Disappearances enters into force, a similar *non-refoulement* obligation will apply to prohibit the transfer of individuals to states where they face a risk of enforced disappearances.

Prevention of arbitrary detention and prolonged detention without charge or trial

6.39 Administrative detention is permitted by IHRL in some circumstances,[104] for example to bring a criminal suspect to a competent legal authority,[105] to detain someone for non-compliance with a court order,[106] to prevent unauthorized entry to a country or to provide for extradition or deportation,[107] and to pursue a number of health or welfare goals.[108] The UN Human Rights Committee allows for preventive or administrative detention 'for reasons of public security',[109] subject to certain

---

[101] Inter-American Convention on Forced Disappearances of Persons, Art XI.
[102] Ibid.
[103] European Court of Human Rights, *Saadi v Italy* (2008) 24 BHRC 123.
[104] ECHR, Art 5(1)(b)–(f); Human Rights Committee, General Comment No 8, Right to liberty and security of persons (Article 9), 16th session, 1982, 30 June 1982, para 4.
[105] ECHR, Art 5(1)(c).
[106] Ibid, Art 5(1)(b).
[107] Ibid, Art 5(1)(f).
[108] Ibid, Art 5(1)(d)–(e).
[109] Human Rights Committee, General Comment No 8, supra, para 4.

procedural requirements. However, the paradigmatically lawful deprivation of liberty occurs after conviction following a fair trial in a competent, independent, and impartial court.[110] Prolonged detention without charge or trial can be arbitrary detention, and a violation of the right to liberty and security of the person. The Human Rights Committee in its General Comment No 8 sets out several limitations on administrative detention, where it is 'used . . . for reasons of public security', including that it be 'based on grounds and procedures established by law', that reasons be given, that detainees have 'court control of the detention' or the right to challenge the lawfulness of detention, and 'compensation in the case of a breach'.[111] The following principles should guide states' response:

- 'court control' of administrative detention should become progressively stricter with time;
- individual cases of counter-terrorist administrative detention should be treated on their own merits; and
- the executive should be required to give consistently stronger evidence for an extended period of administrative detention.

A denial of the right to challenge the lawfulness of detention before a judge who is **6.40** empowered to order release is also a violation of the right to liberty and security of the person. According to the Inter-American Court on Human Rights, this right is non-derogable in emergency situations,[112] so counter-terrorism cannot be cited as a justification for a refusal to grant habeas corpus or amparo.[113] The US Supreme Court has acknowledged that Guantánamo Bay detainees have a right to habeas corpus.[114] Paragraphs 3.103–3.133 examine the prevalence of violations of the right to liberty and security of the person in many states' counter-terrorism practices. This chapter makes two recommendations, the implementation of which is imperative for ending arbitrary detention in counter-terrorism:

- First, all detainees, regardless of their identity and the political sensitivity of terrorism detention, must be afforded the right promptly to challenge the lawfulness of their detention before a judge, who is empowered to order their release if the detention is found to be unlawful. If a person has been administratively detained, there must be periodic judicial review of the lawfulness of that administrative detention in the individual case.
- Second, just as secret and incommunicado detention are both prohibited by IHRL, prolonged detention without charge or trial should also be prohibited in national law. Wide variations in state practice on this point are unwelcome, with

---

[110] ECHR, Art 5(1)(a).
[111] Human Rights Committee, General Comment No 8, supra, para 4.
[112] Inter-American Court of Human Rights, *Habeas Corpus in Emergency Situations,* Advisory Opinion OC-8 187, 30 January 1987, Series A No 8.
[113] See paras 3.105, 3.119 et seq.
[114] US Supreme Court *Boumediene v Bush*, 128 S Ct 2229, 2262, 171 L.Ed. 2d 41 (2008).

some states permitting or proposing indefinite pre-charge detention, citing the exceptional nature of the terrorist threat, secret evidence, unspecified 'dangerousness' of specific detainees, or the impossibility of prosecution where the only evidence against a detainee was obtained through torture.[115] A notional limit of 72 hours before a detainee is brought before a judge, and before charge, would be a strong curb on growing state practice to use administrative detention as a national security measure instead of investigating and prosecuting all terrorism suspects in fair trials.

Ensuring the rule of law in terrorism legislation and fair trials for terrorism suspects

6.41 Paragraphs 3.134–3.155 examine overly broad definitions of terrorist crimes in national legislation; violations of the right to fair trial in military commissions and courts in the US and the Middle East; and denials of the right to a fair hearing prior to the imposition of control orders, compulsory residence orders, terrorist 'listing', and assets-freezing orders. This section of the current chapter makes recommendations relating to each of these sets of violations:

- States should amend or repeal legislation which defines 'terrorism' or terrorist crimes too broadly, or which permit broad and overlapping emergency powers which fall foul of the principle of legality.[116]
- To implement the right to a fair trial in criminal cases before a competent, independent, and impartial tribunal established by law, states should prosecute criminal defendants in terrorism cases in municipal criminal courts. Military courts and military commissions are insufficiently independent from the executive. The reforms on the admissibility of hearsay evidence and evidence obtained by torture in US military commissions do not remove this concern.[117] There should be a strong presumption in favour of holding terrorism trials in public, where defendants have prompt access to a lawyer, a full opportunity to prepare a defence, and knowledge of the charges against them.
- Individuals subjected to control orders and compulsory residence orders must have access to an independent and impartial court to challenge the imposition of these quasi-criminal measures. Control orders and compulsory residence orders should be imposed only following conviction in a fair trial for terrorism offences.

---

[115] Guantánamo Review Task Force Final Report, 22 January 2010 released; President Barack Obama, 'Protecting Our Security and Our Values', Speech at the National Archives Museum, 21 May 2009; American Society of International Law Annual Meeting 2009, 'Closing Guantanamo', Panel Discussion March 2009; Human Rights Watch, 'Counterterrorism and Human Rights: A Report Card on President Obama's First Year', January 2010, p 4.

[116] See paras 3.137–3.141.

[117] Military Commissions Act of 2009; Human Rights Watch, 'Counterterrorism and Human Rights: A Report Card on President Obama's First Year', 14 January 2010, p 5.

- To implement the right to a fair hearing in civil matters, persons subjected to terrorist 'listing', travel bans, and assets-freezing should have the right to an adversarial process before a civil court or tribunal, which is obliged to give reasons for its decision, and provide the possibility for appeal on the merits. The recent introduction of an Ombudsperson to review the imposition of assets-freezing orders under UN Security Council Resolution 1904 goes some way towards providing independence of review, but is administrative rather than judicial, providing those subjected to assets-freezing orders with insufficient opportunity to challenge the order. The recommendation of the Financial Action Task Force (FATF) on the introduction of an adversarial process to challenge terrorist 'listing' and assets-freezing should be preferred over these administrative measures, and over the restrictive duty to give reasons which was imposed by the European Court of Justice in the *Kadi* case.[118]

Conclusion

This chapter has demonstrated states' duties to put international law at the centre of their counter-terrorism efforts: to implement the subject-specific treaties and UN Security Council Resolutions to combat terrorism while acting in accordance with international law. Sanctions, surveillance, and rehabilitative approaches to preventing terrorism must all comply with IHRL. The listing of 'state sponsors of terrorism' requires solid corroborative evidence to establish that the states in question do indeed support terrorist groups, and an audit of the implications for economic, social, and cultural rights of any sweeping sanctions. Where states have not yet ratified the Additional Protocols to the Four Geneva Conventions and treaties on the means and methods of warfare, they should be encouraged to do so. All armed forces personnel and employees of private military and security companies should receive continuing education in IHL, as a means of preventing violations of IHL in all armed conflicts, including those fought with a counter-terrorist aim. States should engage fully with the ratification and implementation of IHRL, with a particular focus on the prevention of arbitrary killings, torture, enforced disappearances, and secret or incommunicado detention. Careful attention should be paid to the lawfulness of derogations and limitations to IHRL treaties. A full list of recommendations of the IBA Task Force on Terrorism can be found in the following chapter.

6.42

---

[118] Financial Action Task Force (FATF-GAFI), International Best Practices: the Freezing of Terrorism Assets, July 2009; *Kadi and Al Barakaat International Foundation v Council of the European Union and Commission of the European Communities*, Joined Cases C-402/05P and C-415/05P, 3 September 2008; see paras 1.22, 3.150–3.151.

7

CONCLUSION AND
RECOMMENDATIONS

Conclusion

States' obligations to prevent and repress terrorism derive from 15 subject-specific **7.01** multilateral treaties and protocols, supported by regional conventions and UN Security Council resolutions. Although there is no single internationally accepted definition of terrorism, states must criminalize terrorist crimes, as defined by those treaties and Security Council resolutions, and prosecute or extradite those suspected of being responsible. All actions taken in counter-terrorism must comply with existing international law: in particular IHL, IHRL, and IRL.

IHL applies to regulate counter-terrorism operations which take place in interna- **7.02** tional armed conflict, belligerent occupation, and non-international armed conflict. It should not be assumed that terrorist attacks trigger the applicability of IHL, nor that states' obligations to counter terrorism are necessarily a 'war'. IHL has its own context-specific meaning of the term 'terrorism' and 'acts or threat of violence the primary purpose of which is to spread terror among a civilian population'. This relates to the principle of distinction between combatants and civilians in IHL, and to civilians' immunity from attack. Neither the political aims of an armed group nor the imperative to counter terrorism can justify violations of IHL. States must criminalize grave breaches of the IHL of international armed conflict, prosecuting or extraditing those suspected of being responsible. Other violations of IHL can be the subject of 'enquiries' and states must cooperate to bring them to an end. Chapter 2 showed that violations of IHL are not restricted to the US-led 'war on terror': the chapter explained the applicability and scope of IHL in counter-terrorism operations, and studied a variety of controversies and case studies.

7.03   IHRL regulates state actions in counter-terrorism in peace and war. Although some rights can be the subject of derogation, or temporary suspension in time of war or public emergency threatening the life of the nation, derogation procedures are rarely used. Chapter 3 revealed documented instances of violations of IHRL, including of non-derogable rights (those which cannot be the subject of temporary suspension) in all regions of the world. Different states have resorted to prolonged, secret, incommunicado, or arbitrary detention of terrorism suspects; and torture and enforced disappearances have increased in frequency. Under the Bush Administration, Department of Justice legal advisers attempted to redefine torture to negate severe mental suffering and to include physical suffering which was equivalent to organ failure or death. The 'Torture Memos' raise issues of professional responsibility and of complicity in torture, far more than the 'poor judgment' which was the conclusion reached by an internal Department of Justice inquiry. The term 'extraordinary rendition' is shorthand for a composite set of human rights violations in the counter-terrorism context: which can include in any individual case abduction, unlawful transfer, *refoulement* to torture in another state, secret detention, incommunicado detention, and enforced disappearances. Chapter 3 considered instances of enforced disappearances in the Horn of Africa, China, the Russian Federation, Sri Lanka, and Turkey; and historic and contemporary examples of torture and ill-treatment of terrorism detainees in Argentina, Algeria, China, Israel, Jordan, Pakistan, the Russian Federation, Sri Lanka, and Uzbekistan. The prevalence and severity of human rights violations in the counter-terrorism context requires systematic accountability mechanisms, remedies for victims, and pervasive reform.

7.04   Chapters 4–6 addressed these issues in turn. Chapter 4 considered the restricted scope for prosecuting terrorism in international criminal law, despite the few precedents for prosecution of 'terrorism' in IHL's context-specific sense. The obligation to prosecute terrorist attacks falls on states and their domestic criminal law, and trials must comply with IHRL on fair trials. Grave breaches of IHL in counter-terrorism operations must be criminalized, and suspected offenders prosecuted or extradited. Under IHRL, torture, extrajudicial executions, and enforced disappearances should all be the subject of criminal inquiries, and the aim should be to establish individual criminal responsibility for these serious violations. Yet accountability for violations of international law in the course of countering terrorism is gradual and piecemeal. There have been intergovernmental and national inquiries, findings against states by regional courts, UN treaty bodies, and special procedures. Despite a small number of court-martial convictions for unlawful killings and prisoner abuse in the UK and US, there has been only one *in absentia* conviction (of 22 CIA operatives and one military officer) of crimes relating to 'extraordinary rendition'. States have relied on comprehensive state secrets doctrines in an attempt to prevent the revelation of evidence of torture and ill-treatment. Slowly, these accountability mechanisms are increasing, especially in Europe; but the obligation to investigate and prosecute serious violations of international law is far from fulfilled.

International law has long established a duty to provide inter-state reparation for **7.05** violations of international law. Individual victims have a right to an effective remedy for violations of IHRL, and to fair compensation for violations of the right to life, torture, and arbitrary detention. The non-binding UN Basic Principles and Guidelines on the Right to a Remedy and Reparation for Victims of Gross Violations of IHL and Serious Violations of IHRL set out a five-part structure of reparations for victims, comprising restitution, compensation, rehabilitation, satisfaction, and guarantees of non-repetition. Chapter 5 examined the political complexities around making these remedies available both to victims or terrorism and to victims of IHL and IHRL violations committed in the course of countering terrorism, and concluded that states should employ an even-handed approach, implementing to a far greater extent than they have to date the international law and standards on victims' rights.

Chapter 6 addressed much-needed reform in states' counter-terrorism policies, **7.06** considering sanctions, weapons controls, re-education programmes, and security checks in terms of their compliance with existing international law; and recommending treaty ratification, full implementation of IHL and IHRL, training of armed forces, private military and security companies, and law enforcement officials, and careful scrutiny and oversight of intelligence agencies in order to prevent a myriad of violations of IHL and IHRL in the course of countering terrorism. Chapter 6's reasoning provides the foundation for many of the recommendations which follow. All of these recommendations are directed to states and relate to the obligation to prevent and repress terrorism in full compliance with existing international law.

Recommendations of the IBA Task Force on Terrorism

Preventing terrorist attacks

States must: **7.07**

- prevent and repress terrorist acts, prosecute or extradite terrorism suspects, and subject them to fair trials before independent and impartial civilian courts;
- prevent and repress aircraft hijackings, hostage-taking by terrorist groups, and attacks against the safety of sea vessels;
- cooperate to prevent the proliferation of weapons and explosives to terrorist groups, whether state or non-state;
- fund or assist rule of law, human rights, and good governance programmes which are designed to prevent extremism and recruitment to terrorist groups, especially in failed states;
- address state terrorism and state sponsorship of terrorism through even-handed financial sanctions and good governance programmes, without political partiality, and in full compliance with economic, social, and cultural rights.

The obligation to prevent and repress terrorism in accordance with international law

7.08 States must:

- implement counter-terrorism laws, policies, and operations in full compliance with international legal obligations under IHL, IHRL, and IRL;
- ensure that state reports to the UN Counter-Terrorism Committee (CTC) take full account of their counter-terrorism policies' compliance with IHL, IHRL, and IRL;
- implement the following specific recommendations, aimed at preventing violations of IHL and IHRL in the course of countering terrorism.

Preventing violations of IHL in counter-terrorism operations

Ratification and implementation of IHL treaties

7.09 States must:

- ratify, and urge other states to ratify, the Additional Protocols to the Four Geneva Conventions of 12 August 1949, the Cluster Munitions Convention, and the Convention on Certain Convention Weapons (CCW Convention) and its Protocols, especially Protocol III;
- respect and ensure respect for IHL at all times: this obligation does not lapse in conflicts fought with a counter-terrorist aim;
- monitor regularly armed forces' compliance with IHL treaty law and customary IHL, and initiate enquiries into all apparent violations of IHL, swiftly bringing them to an end;
- participate in standard-setting exercises aimed at increasing the protection of civilians and other non-combatants in armed conflict. In particular, states should consider amending Protocol III to the CCW Convention to include an explicit prohibition on the use of white phosphorus munitions;
- liaise with the ICRC and ensure ICRC access to those detained in counter-terrorism operations;
- facilitate the implementation of IHL by armed groups, by conducting state-funded outreach and by supporting the ICRC's work training armed groups.

Training

7.10 States must:

- train armed forces personnel, intelligence officials, and members of private military and security companies in IHL. In particular states should:
  - make continuing education an precondition of continued service in the armed forces;

- make ongoing training in IHL of private military and security companies (PMSCs) personnel a condition of contracts between the armed forces and individual companies, and insist that PMSCs are not involved in targeting decisions;
- give additional IHL training to members of armed forces with responsibility for targeting decisions, and for the capture and treatment of detainees;
- ensure that Rules of Engagement (ROE) clearly reflect the principles of distinction and proportionality, the prohibition on indiscriminate attacks, and IHL treaties on the means and methods of warfare.

Enforcement

States must: **7.11**

- criminalize and investigate grave breaches of the Geneva Conventions and their Additional Protocols, prosecuting or extraditing suspected offenders;
- initiate enquiries into all apparent violations of IHL, whether or not they are grave breaches, and whether they are committed in international armed conflict, belligerent occupation, or non-international armed conflict. In particular, states should:
  - investigate the primary purpose of acts or threat of violence which are alleged to have spread terror among a civilian population;
  - investigate prolonged post-conflict detention of prisoners of war, and the mass internment of civilians or other combatants;
  - investigate the detention of 'unlawful combatants' or any other category of persons whom the detaining power alleges are outside the protection of the Third or Fourth Geneva Conventions.

Preventing violations of IHRL in counter-terrorism

Ratification and implementation of IHRL treaties

States must: **7.12**

- ratify, or urge other states to ratify, all universal human rights treaties, including the Convention on Enforced Disappearances and the Optional Protocol to the Convention against Torture;
- ensure that any derogation to specific IHRL treaty articles is 'strictly limited to the exigencies of the situation' and that any limitation to IHRL rights is both necessary and proportionate to the aim pursued;
- submit reports to UN treaty bodies; allow visits or extend an open invitation to the special procedures of the UN Human Rights Council;
- implement in full not only treaty obligations but also the judgments or views of regional courts and UN treaty bodies where the latter have found violations of IHRL by that state;

- accept the right of individual petition to UN treaty bodies and regional human rights courts;
- make police and judicial cooperation in criminal cases contingent upon full respect for IHRL, including respect for the prohibition of torture, and the right to a fair trial.

Training

7.13 States must:

- train law enforcement officials, armed forces, and intelligence personnel in IHRL and standards. In particular, states should:
  - make continuing education in IHRL a condition of permanent employment in law enforcement, the armed forces, and intelligence agencies.

Preventing violations of the right to life

7.14 States must:

- criminalize, investigate, and prosecute those suspected of committing extrajudicial executions in counter-terrorism, including so-called 'targeted killings' outside armed conflict. In particular, states should:
  - legislate to incorporate the Basic Principles on the Use of Force and Firearms by Law Enforcement Officials into domestic law, and to provide sanctions for the unauthorized use of force and firearms;
  - plan and control counter-terrorism operations which use force, so as to respect the right to life, not only of terrorism suspects, but also of bystanders who may be killed as a result;
- repeal legislation which provides for capital punishment for terrorist offences, and move towards the abolition of the death penalty for all offences;
- investigate all deaths in custody, and prosecute anyone suspected of causing the death of a detainee.

Preventing torture and ill-treatment

7.15 States must:

- develop formal mechanisms for monitoring and oversight of intelligence and security services. In particular, states should:
  - ensure that independent experts, who are unaffiliated to the executive, legislature, or intelligence services, regularly report either to a human rights ombudsperson, to legislative committees for intelligence oversight, or to judges and prosecutors, if necessary raising concerns on classified information *in camera;*
- establish an independent and expert body with a mandate to monitor places of detention, and to initiate investigations where human rights violations are alleged to have occurred;

- prevent complicity in torture by ensuring that law enforcement officials, armed forces, and intelligence personnel perceive and act upon a duty to intervene to prevent torture in interrogations held outside a state's boundaries;
- prohibit all transfers of terrorism suspects where there are substantial grounds for believing that they may face torture or other ill-treatment in the receiving state:
  - terrorism suspects must not be 'outsourced' for coercive interrogation, or deported to their state of nationality if there is a real risk that they will suffer torture in custody;
- prohibit the use of evidence obtained by torture in court proceedings, and by intelligence agencies.

Preventing enforced disappearances

States must: **7.16**

- extend a standing invitation to the ICRC, the Committee for the Prevention of Torture, and UN Special Procedures to visit all places of detention, to ensure that there are no 'ghost detainees' or terrorism suspects whose fate or whereabouts is unknown;
- prohibit unauthorized places of detention, and maintain meticulous registers of detainees, permitting detainees access to relatives, judges, lawyers, and any other person with a legitimate interest.

Preventing arbitrary detention

States must: **7.17**

- prohibit secret detention and incommunicado detention;
- afford all detainees the right promptly to challenge the lawfulness of their detention before a judge, who is empowered to order their release if the detention is found to be unlawful;
- respect in full detainees' right to trial within a reasonable time or release;
- prohibit prolonged detention without charge or trial in national law, imposing a notional upper limit of 72 hours in both criminal and administrative detention before a detainee is charged or released. In particular, states should:
  - permit periodic judicial review of the lawfulness of administrative detention in each individual case;
  - provide for court control of administrative detention to become progressively stricter with time;
  - treat individual cases of counter-terrorist administrative detention on their own merits; and
  - require the executive to give consistently stronger evidence for an extended period of administrative detention;
- ensure that terrorist re-education programmes which involve prolonged detention apply only to those convicted of terrorist crimes after a fair trial.

Fair trials and the rule of law

7.18 States must:

- implement in full the right to a fair and public hearing by a competent, independent, and impartial tribunal established by law. In particular, states should:
  - try terrorism suspects before municipal criminal courts, and not by military courts or military commissions;
  - allow terrorism suspects prompt access to a lawyer of their choice who can access all evidence against them to assist in their defence;
- amend or repeal legislation which defines 'terrorism' or terrorist crimes too broadly, or which permit broad and overlapping emergency powers which fall foul of the principle of legality, or which criminalize the peaceful exercise of the freedoms of expression, assembly, or association;
- ensure that individuals subjected to control orders and compulsory residence orders must have access to an independent and impartial court to challenge the imposition of these quasi-criminal measures. Control orders and compulsory residence orders should be imposed only following conviction in a fair trial for terrorism offences;
- rapidly reform UN and EU terrorist 'listing' and assets-freezing procedures to ensure merits-based review of 'listing' decisions by an independent and impartial court.

Compliance with IHRL in security measures

7.19 States must:

- conduct a full audit of security measures in terms of their compliance with IHRL, considering the right to privacy and the scope for unlawful discrimination in security checks, surveillance, and profiling of terrorism suspects;
- examine the likely impact of counter-terrorism policies on economic, social, and cultural rights, and on a risk of unlawful discrimination; and refrain from implementing any policies which would violate these rights or discriminate unlawfully on prohibited grounds.

Ensuring accountability for terrorist attacks

7.20 States must:

- prosecute terrorist attacks under domestic criminal law;
- prosecute terrorist attacks pursuant to ICL where the crimes in question qualify as war crimes or crimes against humanity;
- where a state or its agents have caused terrorist attacks, publicly acknowledge state responsibility for those attacks, prosecute those responsible, and provide reparations for victims.

Ensuring accountability for violations of IHL and IHRL committed in counter-terrorism

States must: 7.21

- ensure that any use of lethal force which results in death must be the subject of a prompt, independent, and impartial investigation, with prosecution following if a violation is suspected, and full reparation being paid to the victim's relatives;
- investigate all deaths in civilian or military custody, and prosecute anyone suspected of torture or ill-treatment which is thought to have led to a detainee's death;
- investigate and prosecute all allegations of torture, and ensure fair and adequate compensation for victims;
- conduct prompt and effective investigations of any case of alleged enforced disappearance, and prosecute those suspected of being responsible;
- prosecute all public officials, without reliance on official immunity, amnesties, or statutes of limitation, where there is a prima facie case that they are responsible for grave breaches of IHL or serious violations of IHRL committed in counter-terrorism operations;
- acknowledge state responsibility for internationally unlawful acts where a state has committed, aided, or abetted violations of international law in the course of counter-terrorism operations, or where the acts of militias or private military and security companies can be attributed to a state;
- refrain from asserting a state secrets privilege to prevent the consideration by a court of evidence relating to violations of IHL or IHRL, or otherwise to forestall the investigation, prosecution, and civil suits relating to such violations. In particular:
  - in the exceptional instances where a state secrets privilege must be asserted, states should produce strong evidence of the threat to national security in each individual case.

Implementing victims' rights to a remedy and reparation

Victims of terrorism

States must: 7.22

- make judicial remedies available to the victims of terrorism;
- encourage the participation of victims in criminal proceedings, civil suits, public inquiries, and truth commissions relating to terrorist violence;
- establish public inquiries to support victims' right to truth where there is evidence of state sponsorship of terrorism, or evidence that a terrorist attack might have been prevented but for failures of state funding or expertise;
- support the establishment of national trust funds, supported by a UN-administered escrow fund to finance compensation for victims of terrorism;

- legislate to implement by enforceable judgments the full range of reparations which should be available to victims of terrorism: restitution (where possible), compensation, rehabilitation, satisfaction, and guarantees of non-repetition.

Victims of IHL and IHRL violations in counter-terrorism

7.23 States must:

- make judicial remedies available to victims of IHL and IHRL violations in counter-terrorism;
- encourage victims' participation in criminal proceedings, civil suits, and public inquiries relating to violations of international law committed in counter-terrorist operations;
- respect and ensure the right to an effective remedy for violations of IHRL committed in the course of states' counter-terrorism policies. In particular, states should:
  - enforce the right of victims of torture to fair and adequate compensation, including where appropriate, access by the victims to the UN Voluntary Fund for Victims of Torture;
  - provide information, compensation, and reparation for victims of enforced disappearances and their families;
  - compensate victims of arbitrary, prolonged, secret, or incommunicado detention;
  - compensate those convicted of terrorist crimes following an unfair trial, where their conviction is subsequently overturned on appeal;
- facilitate public access to freedom of information procedures to ensure the publication of documents relating to counter-terrorism policies where there is evidence that they have violated international law;
- support the establishment of national trust funds, supported by a UN-administered escrow fund to finance compensation for victims of violations of IHL and IHRL in counter-terrorism operations;
- legislate to implement by enforceable judgments the full range of reparations which should be available to victims of gross violations of IHL or serious violations of IHRL: restitution (where possible), compensation, rehabilitation, satisfaction, and guarantees of non-repetition.

BIBLIOGRAPHY

Agence France Presse, 'US Defends Use of White Phosphorus Against Iraq Insurgents', 16 November 2005

Akehurst, M B and Malunczuk, P, *Akehurst's Modern Introduction to International Law* (7th edn, Routledge, 1997)

American Civil Liberties Union, 'Documents Obtained by ACLU Provide Further Evidence that Abuse of Iraqi Detainees was Systematic', 19 November 2008

American Civil Liberties Union, 'DOD Refuses to Turn Over List of Bagram Detainee Information', 13 August 2009

American Civil Liberties Union, 'Unredacted Church Report Documents' (Previously Classified), 11 February 2009

Amnesty International, 'Afghanistan: NATO Must Ensure Justice for Victims of Torture and Civilian Deaths', 27 November 2006

Amnesty International, 'Algeria: Unrestrained Powers: Torture by Algeria's Military Security', 9 July 2006

Amnesty International, 'Countering Terrorism with Repression', August 2009

Amnesty International, 'Enforced Disappearance: Stephen Sunthararaj', 14 May 2009

Amnesty International, 'Human Rights Activist Natalia Estemirova Murdered in Russia', 16 July 2009

Amnesty International, 'Lithuania Admits Existence Of Secret Prison', 22 December 2009

Amnesty International, 'Rule Without Law: Human Rights Violations in the North Caucasus', 30 June 2009

Amnesty International, 'Rwanda Abolishes Death Penalty', 2 August 2007

Amnesty International, 'Turkey: Justice Delayed and Denied: The Persistence of Protracted and Unfair Trials for Those Charged under Anti-Terrorism Legislation', 5 September 2006

Amnesty International, 'Unjust and Unfair: The Death Penalty in Iraq', 20 April 2007

Amnesty International USA, 'Israel/Lebanon: Israel and Hizbollah Must Spare Civilians: Obligations under International Humanitarian Law', 15 July 2006

Associated Press, 'Two Gunmen Kill Judge In Spain's Basque Country: ETA Separatists Suspected', 11 July 2001

Association for the Prevention of Torture, 'Incommunicado, Unacknowledged and Secret Detention under International Law', 2 March 2006

Barrett, J, 'Chechnya's Last Hope: Enforced Disappearances and the European Court of Human Rights' (2009) *Harvard Human Rights Journal* (Harvard University Law School)

Bassiouni, M C (ed), *International Criminal Law* (Martinus Nijhoff, 2008)

Bassiouni, M C, 'International Recognition of Victims' Rights' (2006) *Human Rights Law Review* (Oxford University Press)

BBC News, 'Afghans "Abused at Secret Prison" at Bagram Air Base', 15 April 2010

BBC News, 'Baha Mousa Inquiry: Chief Officer "Punched Detainee"', 19 January 2010

BBC News, 'Bomb Hits Philippine Church-goers', 5 July 2009

BBC News, 'Obama Admits Delay on Guantanamo', 18 November 2009

BBC News, 'Red Cross Confirms Second Jail at Bagram', 11 May 2010

BBC News, 'Shift Needed in Afghan combat', 25 June 2009

BBC News, 'Two Former Blackwater Guards Charged with Afghan Murder', 7 January 2010

BBC News, 'US Reprimands Six Over Deadly Air Strike in Afghanistan', 29 May 2010

Becker, T, *Terrorism and the State: Rethinking the Rules of State Responsibility* (Hart Publishing, 2006)

Beckett, J, 'Interim Legality: A Mistaken Assumption? An Analysis of Depleted Uranium Munitions under Contemporary International Humanitarian Law' (2004) 3 *Chinese Journal of International Law* (Oxford University Press)

Ben-Naftali, O and Shany, Y, 'Living in Denial: The Application of Human Rights in the Occupied Territories' (2004) *Israel Law Review* (Israel Law Review Association)

Biersteker, T J, Spiro, P J, Sriram, C L, and Raffo, V (eds), *International Law and International Relations: Bridging Theory and Practice* (Routledge, 2007)

Boucek, C, 'Saudi Arabia's "Soft" Counterterrorism Strategy: Prevention, Rehabilitation and Aftercare' (2008) *Carnegie Papers No 97*

Burke, J, *Al-Qaeda: The True Story of Radical Islam* (Penguin Books, 2004)

Burke, J, 'Sri Lanka's Tamils Freed—But Future Bleak for Those Who Backed Tigers', *Guardian*, 5 April 2010

Burnham, G, Lafta, R, Doocy, S, and Roberts, L, 'Mortality After the 2003 Invasion in Iraq: a Cross-Sectional Cluster Sample Survey' (2006) *The Lancet* (Elsevier)

Butt, S, 'Indonesian Terrorism Law and Criminal Process', *Sydney Law School Legal Studies Research Paper* (University of Sydney, 2009)

Cerone, J, 'Re-examining International Responsibility: "Complicity" in the Context of Human Rights Violations' (2008) *ILSA Journal of International and Comparative Law*

Cerone, J, 'Status of Detainees in International Armed Conflict, and their Protection in the Course of Criminal Proceedings' (2002) *ASIL Insight*

CNN, 'Accused New York Plotter Faces New York Trial', 13 November 2009

CNN, 'Newsweek Retracts Quran Story', 17 May 2005

CNN, 'Spanish Judge Orders Guantánamo Probe', 29 April 2009

Cole, D, 'Getting Away with Torture', *New York Review of Books*, 16 December 2009

Conetta, C, 'Operation Enduring Freedom: Why a Higher Rate of Civilian Bombing Casualties?', *Project on Defense Alternatives Briefing Report*, No 13, 18 January 2002

Crawford, E, 'Unequal Before the Law: the Case for the Elimination of the Distinction Between International and Non-International Armed Conflict' (2007) *Leiden Journal of International Law* (Cambridge University Press)

Crocker, C A, 'Engaging Failed States' (2003) *Foreign Affairs*

Denbeaux, M and Denbeaux, J W, 'Report: June 10th Suicides at Guantanamo: Government Words and Deeds Compared', 21 August 2006

Deutsche Welle, 'Relatives of Kunduz Airstrike Victims Seek Reparation', 21 November 2009

Dörmann, K and Colassis, L, 'International Humanitarian Law in the Iraq Conflict' (2004) *German Yearbook of International Law* (Duncker & Humblot)

Economist, The, 'The Kurds: Turkey Invades Northern Iraq', 1 March 2008

European Center for Constitutional and Human Rights (ed), *CIA Extraordinary Rendition Flights, Torture and Accountability: A European Approach* (ECCHR, 2008)

Fédération Internationale des Droits de l'Homme, 'Egypt: Counter-terrorism Against the Background of an Endless State of Emergency', January 2010

Fédération Internationale des Droits de l'Homme, Observatory for the Protection of Human Rights Defenders Annual Report 2009

Fernández-Sánchez, P A (ed), *International Legal Dimension of Terrorism* (Brill, 2009)

Foot, R, *Human Rights and Counter-Terrorism in America's Asia Policy* (International Institute for Strategic Studies, 2004)

Gillard, E-C, 'Reparations for Violations of International Humanitarian Law' (2003) *International Review of the Red Cross* (International Committee of the Red Cross)

Gillard, E-C, 'The Complementary Nature of Human Rights Law, International Humanitarian Law and Refugee Law, in *Terrorism and International Law: Challenges and Responses* (International Institute for Humanitarian Law et al, 2002)

Ginbar, Y, *Why Not Torture Terrorists? Moral, Practical and Legal Aspects of the 'Ticking Bomb' Justification for Torture* (Oxford University Press, 2008)

Guardian, 'Britain "Complicit in Mistreatment and Possible Torture", says UN', 27 January 2010

Guardian, 'Timeline: Baha Mousa Case', 13 July 2009

Guardian, 'US Army Rejects Court Martial of Abu Ghraib Commander', 11 January 2008

Harris, D J, *Cases and Materials on International Law* (Sweet and Maxwell, 2004)

Heintz, H, 'On the Relationship between Human Rights Law Protection and International Humanitarian Law' (2004) *International Review of the Red Cross* (International Committee of the Red Cross)

Henckaerts, J-M and Doswald-Beck, L, *Customary International Humanitarian Law, Volume 1: Rules* (International Committee of the Red Cross and Cambridge University Press, 2005)

Horton, S, 'The Guantánamo "Suicides": A Camp Delta Sergeant Blows the Whistle', *Harper's Magazine*, 18 January 2010

Huffington Post, 'Blackwater Settles Series of Lawsuits', 7 January 2010

Human Rights First, 'Command's Responsibility: Detainee Deaths in US Custody in Iraq and Afghanistan', February 2006

Human Rights First, *Pursuit of Justice: Prosecuting Terrorism Cases in the Federal Courts*, May 2008

Human Rights Watch, 'Canada/Afghanistan: Investigate Canadian Responsibility for Detainee Abuse', 27 November 2009

Human Rights Watch, 'Civilians Under Assault: Hezbollah's Rocket Attacks on Israel: Legal Standards'

Human Rights Watch, 'Counterterrorism and Human Rights: A Report Card on President Obama's First Year', 14 January 2010

Human Rights Watch, 'Cruel Britannia: British Complicity in the Torture and Ill-Treatment of Terror Suspects in Pakistan', 24 November 2009

Human Rights Watch, 'Egypt: Cosmetic Changes Can't Justify Keeping Emergency Law', 12 May 2010

Human Rights Watch, 'Egypt: Transfer Zeitoun Trial to Criminal Court', 14 February 2010

Human Rights Watch, 'Enduring Freedom: Abuses by US Forces in Afghanistan', 7 March 2004

Human Rights Watch, 'France: Headscarf Ban Violates Religious Freedom', 27 February 2004

Human Rights Watch, 'Human Rights and Saudi Arabia's Counterterrorism Response: Religious Counseling, Indefinite Detention and Flawed Trials', 9 August 2009

Human Rights Watch, 'In the Name of Prevention: Insufficient Safeguards in National Security Removals' VII, 5 June 2007

Human Rights Watch, 'Italy/US: Italian Court Rebukes CIA Rendition Practice', 4 November 2009

Human Rights Watch, 'Memory Loss and Torture', 25 May 2010

Human Rights Watch, 'Off Target: The Conduct of the War and Civilian Casualties in Iraq', December 2003

Human Rights Watch, 'Precisely Wrong: Gaza Civilians Killed by Israeli Drone-Launched Missiles', 30 June 2009

Human Rights Watch, 'Rain of Fire: Israel's Unlawful Use of White Phosphorus in Gaza', 25 March 2009

Human Rights Watch, 'Russia: Complying with European Court Key to Halting Abuse', 27 September 2009

Human Rights Watch, 'Smoke and Mirrors: Colombia's Demobilisation of Paramilitary Groups', 31 July 2005

Human Rights Watch, 'Sri Lanka: UN Rights Council Fails Victims', 27 May 2009

Human Rights Watch, 'Still at Risk: Diplomatic Assurances No Safeguard against Torture', 14 April 2005

Human Rights Watch, 'Syria: Dissolve the State Security Court', 24 May 2009

Human Rights Watch, 'The Road to Abu Ghraib', 8 June 2004

Human Rights Watch, 'Troops in Contact', 8 September 2008

Human Rights Watch, 'Turkey: Headscarf Ban Stifles Academic Freedom', 28 June 2004

Human Rights Watch, 'Update on European Court of Human Rights Judgments against Russia regarding Cases from Chechnya', 20 March 2009

Human Rights Watch, 'US: Lawyers' Misconduct Shows Need for Torture Inquiry', 19 February 2010

Human Rights Watch, 'US: Release the Full Report into Guantanamo Deaths', 7 December 2009

Human Rights Watch, 'US: Revisions Can't Fix Military Commissions', 8 July 2009

Human Rights Watch, 'US/Yemen: Break Impasse on Yemeni Returns from Guantanamo', 28 March 2009

Human Rights Watch, '"We Are Afraid to Even Look for Them": Enforced Disappearances in the Wake of Xinjiang's Protests', October 2009

Human Rights Watch, 'What Your Children Do Will Touch Upon You', 2 July 2009

Human Rights Watch, '"Why Am I Still Here?" The 2007 Horn of Africa Renditions and the Fate of Those Still Missing', October 2008

Hurwitz, D R, Satterthwaite, M L, and Ford, D B (eds), *Human Rights Advocacy Stories* (Foundation Press, 2009)

International Bar Association, *A Long March to Justice: A Report on Judicial Independence and Integrity in Pakistan* (IBA, 2009)

International Bar Association, *Justice in Retreat: A Report on the Independence of the Legal Profession and the Rule of Law in Sri Lanka* (IBA, 2009)

International Bar Association, *The Struggle to Maintain an Independent Judiciary: A Report on the Attempt to Remove the Chief Justice of Pakistan* (IBA, 2007)

International Center for Transitional Justice, 'Universal Jurisdiction: the "War on Terror"', 17 April 2009

International Committee of the Red Cross, 'Afghanistan Accedes to Additional Protocols I and II in Historic Step to Limit Wartime Suffering', 24 June 2009

International Committee of the Red Cross, 'Interpretive Guidance on the Notion of Direct Participation in Hostilities under International Humanitarian Law', 26 February 2009

International Committee of the Red Cross, 'Iraq Post 28 June 2004: Protecting Persons Deprived of Freedom Remains a Priority', 5 August 2004

International Committee of the Red Cross, 'Persons Detained by the US in Relation to Armed Conflict and the Fight Against Terrorism—The Role of the ICRC', 26 October 2009

International Committee of the Red Cross, 'Sri Lanka: Situation of Civilians Nothing Short of Catastrophic', 21 April 2009

International Committee of the Red Cross, 'Switzerland: freed ICRC Staff Member Eugenio Vagni Arrives in Geneva', 16 July 2009

International Security Assistance Force Afghanistan, 'US Releases Uruzgan Investigation Findings', 28 May 2010

IRIN Asia, 'Afghanistan: UNAMA Raps New Report By Rights Watchdog', 22 January 2009

Jackson, R, Smyth, M B, and Gunning, J, *Critical Terrorism Studies: A New Research Agenda* (Routledge, 2009)

Jane's Defence Business News, 'Yemen Drone Strike: Just the Start?', 8 November 2002

Jividen, D D, '*Jus in bello* in the 21st Century', *Yearbook of International Humanitarian Law* (Cambridge University Press, 2004)

JURIST—Paper Chase, 'House Committee Votes Not to Fund US Facility for Guantanamo Transfers', 22 May 2010

JURIST—Paper Chase, 'Italy Agrees to Take Two More Guantánamo Bay Detainees', 26 May 2010

Kaleck, W and Schüller, A, 'Litigating Extraordinary Renditions', *INTERIGHTS Bulletin* (Interights, 2010)

Kretzmer, D, 'Targeted Killings of Suspected Terrorists: Extra-Judicial Executions or Legitimate Means of Defence?' (2005) *European Journal of International Law* (Oxford University Press)

Lift weblog, 'Spanish Prosecutors Seek the Arrest of 13 CIA Agents', 13 May 2010

Lubell, N, 'Parallel Application of International Humanitarian Law and International Human Rights Law: An Examination of the Debate' (2007) *Israel Law Review* (Israel Law Review Association)

de Maio, J (interview with), *Pakistan: Protection of Civilians a Priority as Violence Grows* (International Committee of the Red Cross, 2009)

Mayer, J, *The Dark Side: The Inside Story of How the War on Terror Turned into a War on American Ideals* (Doubleday, 2009)

Mayer, J, 'The Predator War: What Are the Risks of the CIA's Covert Drone Program?' (2009) *The New Yorker*

Melzer, N, *Targeted Killing in International Law* (Oxford University Press, 2008)

Messineo, F, '"Extraordinary Renditions" and State Obligations to Criminalize and Prosecute Torture in the Light of the Abu Omar Case in Italy' (2009) *Journal of International Criminal Justice* (Oxford University Press)

Milanovic, M, 'Lessons for Human Rights and Humanitarian Law in the War on Terror: Comparing *Hamdan* and the Israeli *Targeted Killings* Case' (2007) *International Review of the Red Cross* (International Committee of the Red Cross)

del Moral, I, 'The Swan Song of Universal Jurisdiction in Spain' (2009) *International Criminal Law Review* (Martinus Nijhoff)

Murphy, S, 'The International Legality of US Military Cross-Border Operations from Afghanistan into Pakistan', *International Law Studies* (US Naval War College, 2009)

Nesi, G (ed), *International Cooperation in Counter-Terrorism* (Martinus Nijhoff, 2006)

New Scientist, 'Depleted Uranium Casts Shadow over Peace in Iraq', 15 April 2003

New York Times, 'Egypt's Emergency Law is Extended for Two Years', 11 May 2010
New York Times, 'More Airstrikes as Hezbollah Rockets Hit Deeper', 15 July 2006
New York Times, 'Russia Ends Operations in Chechnya', 16 April 2009
O'Connell, M E, 'Defining Armed Conflict' (2009) *Journal of Conflict & Security Law* (Oxford University Press)
O'Connell, M E, 'Unlawful Killing with Combat Drones: A Case Study of Pakistan, 2004–2009', *Notre Dame Law School Legal Studies Research Paper Series* (Notre Dame Law School, 2009)
Pejic, J, 'Procedural Principles and Safeguards for Internment/Administrative Detention in Armed Conflict and Other Situations of Violence' (2005) *International Review of the Red Cross* (International Committee of the Red Cross)
Pictet, J (ed), *Commentary to the Articles of the Four Geneva Conventions* (International Committee of the Red Cross, 1952)
Proulx, V, 'Rethinking the Jurisdiction of the International Criminal Court in the Post-September 11th Era: Should Acts of Terrorism Qualify as Crimes against Humanity' (2004) *American University International Law Review* (American University)
Radio Free Asia, 'China: Standoff over Death in Custody', 19 September 2009
Redress, 'Court Martial Acquittals in Baha Mousa Case: The Full Truth of What Happened Remains Unknown', Statement, 14 March 2007
Redress, 'Implementing Victims' Rights: A Handbook on the Basic Principles and Guidelines on the Right to a Remedy and Reparation' (Redress, 2006)
Reuters, 'Not Guilty Plea Entered for Nigerian Bomb Suspect', 8 January 2010
Reuters AlertNet, 'Iraq Death Toll', 12 October 2006
Reuters AlertNet, 'US General Vows to Curb Afghan Civilian Casualties', 3 June 2009
Roberts, L, Lafta, R, Garfield, R, Khudhairi, J, and Burnham, G, 'Mortality Before and After the Invasion in Iraq: Cluster Sample Survey' (2004) *The Lancet* (Elsevier)
Roehrig, T, 'North Korea and the US State Sponsors of Terrorism List', *Pacific Focus* (Inha University, 2009)
Rona, G, 'International Law under Fire: Interesting Times for International Humanitarian Law: Challenges from the "War on Terror"' (2009) *Fletcher Forum of World Affairs* (Fletcher School of Law and Diplomacy)
Rotberg, R, 'Failed States in a World of Terror' (2002) *Foreign Affairs* (Council on Foreign Relations)
Sambei, A, Du Plessis, A, and Polaine, M, *Counter-Terrorism Law and Practice: An International Handbook* (Oxford University Press, 2009)
Sassòli, M, 'Terrorism and War' (2006) *Journal of International Criminal Justice* (Oxford University Press)
Sassòli, M and Olson, L, 'The Relationship between International Humanitarian and Human Rights Law Where It Matters: Admissible Killing and Internment of Fighters in Non-International Armed Conflicts' (2008) *International Review of the Red Cross* (International Committee of the Red Cross)
Saul, B, *Defining Terrorism in International Law* (Oxford University Press, 2006)
Saul, B, 'Speaking of Terror: Criminalising Incitement to Violence', *Sydney Law School Legal Studies Research Paper* (University of Sydney, 2005)
Schmitt, M, 'The Interpretive Guidance on the Notion of Direct Participation in Hostilities: A Critical Analysis' (2010) *Harvard National Security Journal* (Harvard University Law School)
Scholars at Risk Network publication, Azzaman.com, '340 Academics and 2,334 Women Killed in 3 Years, Human Rights Ministry says', 1 July 2008

Somer, J, 'Acts of Non-State Armed Groups and the Law Governing Armed Conflict, *ASIL Insight*, Vol 10, Issue 21, 24 August 2006

Spiegel Online International, 'Abu Omar Case: Italian Court Delivers Damning Verdict on CIA Renditions', 4 November 2009

Steel, J, 'Forgotten Victims', *Guardian*, 20 May 2002

Stewart, J, 'Towards A Single Definition of Armed Conflict in International Humanitarian Law: A Critique of Internationalized Armed Conflict' (2003) *International Review of the Red Cross* (International Committee of the Red Cross)

Tomuschat, C, 'Human Rights and International Humanitarian Law' (2010) *European Journal of International Law* (Oxford University Press)

Tomuschat, C, *Human Rights: Between Idealism and Realism* (Oxford University Press, 2008)

UK Ministry of Justice, 'New Support for Victims of Terrorism Overseas', 18 January 2010

UN News, 'Reports from Somalia Suggest Possible War Crimes, Says UN Human Rights Chief', 10 July 2009

US Department of Justice, 'Departments of Justice and Defense Announce Forum Decisions for Ten Guantanamo Bay Detainees', 13 November 2009

Vité, S, 'Typology of Armed Conflicts in International Humanitarian Law: Legal Concepts and Actual Situations' (2009) *International Review of the Red Cross* (International Committee of the Red Cross)

Washington Post, '"Global War on Terror" is Given New Name', 25 March 2009

Washington Post, 'Justice Task Force Recommends About 50 Guantánamo Bay Detainees to be Held Indefinitely', 22 January 2010

Washington Post, 'Pentagon Details Abuse of Koran', 4 June 2005

Washington Post, 'Study Claims Iraq's "Excess" Death Toll Has Reached 655,000', 11 October 2006

Weissbrodt, D and Nesbitt, N H 'The Role of the United States Supreme Court in Interpreting and Developing Humanitarian Law', Minnesota Law Review (forthcoming); *Minnesota Legal Studies Research Paper No. 10-31* (available on SSRN, draft dated 25 May 2010)

Wilmshurst, E and Breau, S (eds), *Perspectives on the ICRC Study on Customary International Humanitarian Law* (Cambridge University Press, 2005)

Xinhua News Agency, 'Police Prevent Terrorist Attacks in Xinjiang', 3 August 2009

Yamani, M, 'Yemeni Detainees and Jihadis: Guantanamo Repatriation and Saudi Arabia', 16 April 2009 (Chatham House)

INDEX

References are to chapter and paragraph number, eg 4.45, or to preliminary pages in italics, eg ix
Footnotes are denoted by n, eg 3.04n

Abbreviations

IHL   international humanitarian law
IHRL   international human rights law

Aamer, Shaker 4.45
accountability for violations of international law in
    counter-terrorism 4.02–4.04, 4.25–4.27,
    4.51–4.52, 7.04
  civil suits
    Canada: complicity in torture 4.41
    state secrets 4.42–4.47
  criminal investigations and prosecutions
    court-martial hearings 4.35–4.36
    delayed prosecution of anonymous intelligence
      officer 4.38
    failed prosecution of Blackwater/Xe 4.40
    incomplete prosecutions 4.37
    investigation into US Department of Justice
      'Torture Memos' 4.39
    prosecutions before domestic criminal courts
      Germany and Spain: Khaled El-Masri 4.34
      Italy: Abu Omar 4.26, 4.32–4.33
  IBA Task Force recommendations 7.21
  intergovernmental organizations 4.28–4.31
  national inquiries into CIA secret detention 4.48–4.49
ad hoc criminal tribunals 4.15–4.18
  see also ICTR; ICTY; Special Court for Sierra
    Leone; Special Tribunal for Lebanon
Afghanistan 2.34, 2.36, 2.37
  Bagram Air Base 2.77, 3.61, 3.113, 3.123, 3.126
  belligerent occupation 2.76–2.77
  classification of the conflict post-2001 2.68–2.70
  cluster munitions 2.58
  continued detention 2.76–2.77, 3.113
    habeas corpus for detainees at Bagram Air
      Base 3.123
  grave breaches of IHL 2.71–2.72
  indiscriminate use of weapons 2.65
  international armed conflict 2.68–2.70
  non-international armed conflict 2.83–2.84
  targeted killings 2.46, 2.49, 2.50
  torture 3.61
  transfer of detainees 3.79

Agiza, Ahmed 3.64, 4.30, 4.44, 5.02, 5.33
aircraft hijackings 1.18, 2.23
airport security 6.14–6.15
Al Megrahi, Abdelbaset Ali Mohamed 4.17
Al-Qaeda 1.21, 2.34, 2.83
Al-Zari, Mohamed 3.78
Algeria: torture 3.61
Al-Shabaab 2.105–2.107
Alzery, Mohamed 4.31
Amnesty International 2.29, 2.61*n*, 2.64, 2.84*n*,
    2.96, 2.99, 2.100*n*, 2.107*n*, 3.04*n*, 3.06*n*,
    3.08*n*, 3.40, 3.46*n*, 3.52*n*, 3.53*n*, 3.61*n*, 3.63*n*,
    3.80*n*, 3.84*n*, 3.89*n*, 3.90*n*, 3.99*n*, 3.111*n*,
    3.125*n*, 3.129*n*, 3.137*n*, 3.140, 3.146*n*,
    3.147*n*, 3.183*n*, 3.185*n*, 4.16, 4.24*n*, 4.33*n*,
    4.43*n*, 4.48*n*, 5.04*n*, 5.23*n*
anti-personnel mines 2.18
Arar, Maher 3.65, 3.78, 5.05, 5.32, 5.33
arbitrary deprivation of life 3.28
  case law 3.31–3.33
  death penalty 3.51–3.53
  deaths in custody
    Baha Mousa (UK custody in Iraq) 3.49–3.50
    China, Russian Federation, US 3.46
    duty to investigate 3.47–3.48
  extrajudicial executions of terrorism suspects
    cross-border strikes and drone attacks 3.40–3.41
    Israel: Supreme Court of Israel
      jurisprudence 2.53
    Pakistan 3.43
    UK: Jean Charles de Menezes 3.33, 3.44–3.45
    US: 'kill-capture-detain' orders 3.42
  IHRL right to life during armed
    conflict 3.36–3.39
  non-binding standards 3.34–3.35
  preventive mechanisms 6.31–6.33, 7.14
  treaty law 3.29–3.30
  use of force and firearms by law enforcement
    officials 3.31–3.33, 3.43, 3.45